Children of Incarcerated Parents: From Understanding to Impact

Series Editor

Judy Krysik
Center for Child Well-Being
Arizona State University
Phoenix, AZ, USA

This book series is based on the National Children of Incarcerated Parents Conference, hosted by Arizona State University's Center for Child Well-Being. Attended by over 500 researchers and professionals, the multidisciplinary conference addresses critical issues related to parental incarceration, organized around four main tracks:

- Understanding the impact of parental incarceration on the child and family
- Evidence of program and policy effectiveness
- Training and support for professionals who work with children of the incarcerated
- Coordinating systems for positive impact

Imprisonment is a salient aspect in the lives of many American families, especially among African Americans and Latinos. An estimated 2 million U.S. children are currently experiencing parental incarceration—a number greater than those diagnosed with autism or juvenile diabetes. Yet, this issue remains largely invisible. The conference and book series bring together professionals in diverse areas such as social work, criminal justice, education, behavioral health, and child welfare. The series aims to promote a greater understanding of the challenges facing children of incarcerated parents and the impact of programs and policies, creating unique opportunities to coordinate work being done across social services sectors and promote more comprehensive, effective, and sustained approaches.

More information about this series at http://www.springer.com/series/16063

Judy Krysik • Nancy Rodriguez
Editors

Children of Incarcerated Parents

Integrating Research into Best Practices and Policy

Springer

Editors
Judy Krysik
Center for Child Well-Being
Arizona State University
Phoenix, AZ, USA

Nancy Rodriguez
Department of Criminology
Law and Society
University of California, Irvine
Irvine, CA, USA

ISSN 2524-3349 ISSN 2524-3357 (electronic)
Children of Incarcerated Parents: From Understanding to Impact
ISBN 978-3-030-84712-8 ISBN 978-3-030-84713-5 (eBook)
https://doi.org/10.1007/978-3-030-84713-5

This Springer imprint is published by the registered company Springer Nature Switzerland AG
The registered company address is: Gewerbestrasse 11, 6330 Cham, Switzerland

This edited volume is dedicated to the countless children and families who, now or in the past, have faced the incarceration of a parent in jail, prison, or detention center, their voice largely silent and experience hidden.

Preface

Keywords Parental incarceration, Incarcerated mothers, Incarcerated fathers, Families

Due in large part to the historic rise in imprisonment over the past four decades, reducing mass incarceration and its collateral consequences have become key elements of criminal justice reform. A recent national survey shows that one in two adults has had a family member in jail or prison (Elderbroom, Bennett, Gong, Rose, & Towns, 2018). To be clear, the impact of incarceration on children and families is devastating. Studies have found parental incarceration is associated with an array of harmful social, health, and financial outcomes (Kirk & Wakefield, 2018). Incarceration impacts parent-child relationships, contact with children, and custodial outcomes (Arditti, 2003; Christian, 2005; Comfort, 2003; Johnson & Waldfogel, 2002; Genty, 1991; Genty, 1998; Halperin & Harris, 2004). In response to these adverse outcomes, including the emotional toll and related pain for parents, children, and caregivers (Arditti, Smock, & Parkman, 2005; Johnson & Easterling, 2012; Nesmith & Ruhland, 2008), an increasing number of programs and policies have been designed to reduce the harms associated with parental incarceration.

In 2014, we joined those efforts and held a summit at Arizona State University on children of incarcerated parents. We invited 60 professionals across Arizona systems, including the adult and juvenile justice systems, child welfare, education, service providers, and policymakers to share knowledge and commit to doing what we could to serve children of incarcerated parents. There were many things we learned from the summit, including an overall lack of awareness about the number of children impacted and how many became child welfare involved due to the incarceration of one or both parents, or due to the circumstances that led to the incarceration, such as family violence, trafficking, and substance abuse. Financial hardship, childhood trauma, stigma, and elderly grandparents as caregivers to four, five, six, or more children were common realities among these families. We learned that systems were struggling and often not coordinating or engaged with one another in serving incarcerated persons and their loved ones. The summit confirmed the importance of having discussions, planning, and sharing resources across sectors.

Today, in the midst of COVID-19 and a pursuit for racial justice, there are numerous efforts dedicated to reducing the number of people held in state prisons and jails, decreasing sentence lengths and time served, and to offer community-based supervision and non-custodial sanctions. Yet, despite such reforms, we know that the effects of incarceration disproportionately impact people of color and the poor. This is not to say that the effects of incarceration are uniform. In fact, research has established the variability in the effects of parental incarceration (Geller et al., 2011; Haskins 2014; Kirk & Wakefield, 2018; Murray, Loeber, & Pardini, 2012; Turanovic, Rodriguez, & Pratt, 2009; Wildeman & Turney 2014). In light of continued disparate impacts of mass incarceration, the varied effects of parental incarceration, and the growing segment of women in prisons, we felt it necessary to highlight and support the various systems that interface with children and families impacted by mass incarceration.

Within this context, we asked ourselves what we could do to most comprehensively and effectively serve children and families impacted by the justice system and incarceration. We knew that our efforts had to begin with creating a national forum to gather, share best practices, and engage in action planning. The product was the creation and launch of the first National Children of Incarcerated Parents Conference in April 2018. Our goal with the national conference was to bring together people across different disciplines to address the needs of children and families. We learned that for change to occur, it was necessary to reach across the silos, recognize our similar intentions to support children and families, and work together, not always agreeing, but learning from one another. Our discussions would center on research approaches and gaps, multiple perspective, and the importance of accountability. It is these dynamic discussions, many which took place during our conference, that represent the collection of essays in this volume.

We rely on Bronfenbrenner's (1979) ecological theory as an organizing framework for the volume, given the multidimensional knowledge presented by the authors. The book is divided into four corresponding parts that include the micro, meso, exo, and macro systems. The authors include a broad sector of experts from government agencies, academia, advocates, corrections officials, and individuals with lived experience. The chapters are diverse in theoretical and methodological approaches. We are grateful for their wisdom, dedication, and guidance on this important topic and indebted to them for their willingness to be part of this volume.

Part 1 of the volume addresses the micro system, which centers on the child and personal relationships with family members, and the circumstances of the home and its impact at varying stages of child development. In Chapter 1, Rosalyn D. Lee, Denise V. D'Angelo, and Kim Burley from the Centers for Disease Control and Prevention address how expectant and new mothers exposed to incarceration can benefit from engaging in home visitation programs. The authors provide valuable insight into how such programs may impact child (e.g., low birth weight, preterm birth) and mothers' outcomes (e.g., smoking, alcohol use, breastfeeding, hypertension, and depression). In Chapter 2, Elizabeth I. Johnson and Joyce A. Arditti provide a rich review of research on the impact of parental incarceration on adolescents, summarizing the major developmental changes during this period and guidelines for developmentally informed research and practice with adolescents. Particular attention is paid to elements that may heighten or mitigate risk during adolescence, as well as factors that help promote positive youth development. By focusing on family and school-based sources of resiliency, Jennifer E. Copp, Peggy C. Giordano, Monica A. Longmore, and Wendy D. Manning complete the coverage of the micro system. The authors rely on longitudinal data and in-depth qualitative interviews with a subset of transition-age young adults who experienced parental incarceration and illustrate the important intersection between parental incarceration, educational attainment, relationship commitment, and emotional well-being.

Part II highlights the meso system or the interaction of different micro systems, such as the interaction between home and school, peer group and family, and between family and community. We begin this part with Jennifer Wyatt Bourgeois, Jasmine Drake, and Howard Henderson's discussion on the various ways in which the incarceration of parents and family members impacts minority families living in disadvantaged neighborhoods. Considering the different cultural and situational dimensions faced by families impacted by incarceration, the authors propose an interdisciplinary, culturally responsive, and localized approach for parental incarceration research and policy. In Chapter 5, William J. Sabol, Samuel L. Myers, Jr., and MariTere Molinet examine the patterns of racially disparate child welfare processes related to imprisonment. The authors describe the trends in imprisonment and children's entry to the foster care system and discuss the various ways in which foster care and incarceration may be related. They offer key insight into child welfare decision making and the role of federal child welfare policies in disparate child welfare processes and outcomes. In the following chapter, Tanya Krupat and Whitney Q. Hollins discuss the importance of humane language and terminology in supporting and serving children impacted by parental incarceration. They argue humanizing language can create safe spaces for children and families, and reduce stigma and the negative effects of separation. Such language can also help to humanize the way in which systems interact with children, family members, and parents who are incarcerated.

Part III of the volume contains essays on the exo system, which pertains to the linkages that may exist between two or more settings that do not directly include the child, but may still impact him/her/they. In Chapter 7, Margaret L. Kerr, Pajarita Charles, Michael Massoglia, Sarah Jensen, Jennifer Wirth, Kerrie Fanning, Karen Holden, and Julie Poehlmann-Tynan describe an attachment-based visit-coaching model to support the child/parent relationship through technology-assisted visits. They present findings on the impact of the model to support the promise of this approach in a jail setting. In the subsequent chapter, J. Mark Eddy, Jean M. Kjellstrand, Pajarita Charles, and Kim Gonzalez-Quiles provide a summary of research on reentry programs relevant to incarcerated parents. Focusing on parents and their reentry process, the authors discuss key dimensions of reentry programs that specifically target children and families. They share important recommendations for future program content, program development, and evaluation research. In Chapter 9, Jean M. Kjellstrand, J. Mark Eddy, Gabriella Damewood, Kimberley Gonzalez-Quiles, and Jean Schumer discuss the importance of gender-sensitive reentry programs for parents. The authors highlight the distinct roles and life circumstances of incarcerated mothers and fathers and the implications for correctional systems, families, and communities, at large.

Part IV includes chapters that illustrate the macro system, comprised of societal values and cultural norms, as well as political and economic systems. In the first chapter of this part, Isabel Coronado provides examples of how policy making can be used as a tool to address the hardships children, families, and cultural communities face due to mass incarceration. In Chapter 11, Alexandria S. Pech and Kevin L. Henry Jr. draw from critical race theory (CRT) to examine the experiences of parental incarceration for youth of color. The authors highlight parental incarceration across multiple intersectional identities (i.e., Black, Latinx, Native, and Asian youth), discuss how parental incarceration can compound oppression for youth of color, and convey the implications for adolescent development. The next chapter, authored by Judy Krysik and Natalia Vasiliou, examines how gendered perceptions and treatment disadvantage mothers in the corrections and how such treatment is perpetuated in policy. In Chapter 13, Pajarita Charles, Amy Blank Wilson, Jean Kjellstrand, Aaron Gottlieb, and Branden McLeod discuss the heterogeneity in experiences of incarcerated parents and their children, and offer a review of the protective and risk factors associated with variations in the experiences and outcomes for children. The authors outline how the Smart Decarceration initiative can develop research, policies, partnerships, and interventions designed to foster resiliency and improve outcomes for families that experience incarceration. In the epilogue, Reginald Wilkinson, former director of the Ohio Department of Rehabilitation and Correction, offers insight into what we need to know to better serve children of incarcerated parents and their caretakers. He presents examples on how to build partnerships and infrastructure across disciplines and systems to advance science and provide guidance for practitioners who work in this space.

Children of Incarcerated Parents: Integrating Research into Best Practices and Policy is a collection of diverse perspectives and inquiries on children of incarcerated parents and effective or promising policy responses. In light of the current fight towards racial justice, the volume illustrates one model for addressing complex problems and raising issues around the treatment of people of color. We believe all perspectives and knowledge presented here are critical in advancing research and developing evidence-based responses. We believe the volume is important for academic communities across different disciplines, as well as professionals working in advocacy, child welfare, corrections, behavioral health and human services, and of course, the men, women, and children who have experienced having a loved one incarcerated. In the end, our hope is to reduce the criminal justice footprint, find alternative systems of care and support for children and families, and strengthen those systems in this important effort. We encourage future assessments such as ours and the incorporation of other systems (e.g., education, immigration) that impact the well-being of children in the USA. Of crucial need is an assessment of how pandemic-related considerations have affected children and families with incarcerated loved ones. This includes, for example, ceasing in-person visits, and the release of some parents with little to no preparation or support, whereas others who remain in correctional facilities face increased health risk and stress. As more interventions are developed and adapted, evidence supporting their implementation and effectiveness will help move the field forward from awareness to action.

Phoenix, AZ, USA Judy Krysik
Irvine, CA, USA Nancy Rodriguez

References

Arditti, J. A. (2003). Locked doors and glass walls: Family visiting at a local jail. *Journal of Loss &Trauma*, *8*(2), 115–138.
Arditti, J. A., Smock, S. A., & Parkman, T. S. (2005). "It's been hard to be a father": A qualitative exploration of incarcerated fatherhood. *Fathering: A Journal of Theory, Research & Practice about Men as Fathers*, *3*, 267–288.
Bronfenbrenner, U. (1979). *The ecology of human development*. Harvard.
Christian, J. (2005). Riding the bus: Barriers to prison visitation and family management strategies. *Journal of Contemporary Criminal Justice*, *21*(1), 31–48.
Comfort, M. L. (2003). In the tube at San Quentin: The "secondary prisonization" of women visiting inmates. *Journal of Contemporary Ethnography*, *32*(1), 77–107.
Elderbroom, B., Bennett, L., Gong, S., Rose, F., & Z. Towns. (2018). *Every Second: The Impact of the Incarceration Crisis on America's Families*. FWD.us.
Genty, P. M. (1991). Procedural due process rights of incarcerated parents in termination of parental rights proceedings: A fifty state analysis. *J. Fam. L.*, *30*, 757–767.
Genty, P.M. (1998). Permanency planning in the context of parental incarceration: Legal issues and recommendations. *Child Welfare, 77*, 543–559.
Geller, A., Garfinkel, I., & Western, B. (2011). Paternal incarceration and support for children in fragile families. *Demography*, *48*(1), 25–47.
Halperin, R., & Harris, J. L. (2004). Parental rights of incarcerated mothers with children in foster care: A policy vacuum. *Feminist Studies, 30*, 339–352.
Haskins, A. R. (2014). Unintended consequences: Effects of paternal incarceration on child school readiness and later special education placement. *Sociological Science*, *1*, 141–157.
Johnson, E. I., & Easterling, B. (2012). Understanding unique effects of parental incarceration on children: Challenges, progress, and recommendations. *Journal of Marriage and Family*, *74*(2), 342–356.
Johnson, E., & Waldfogel, J. (2002). Parental incarceration: Recent trends and implications for child welfare. *Social Service Review*, *76*(3), 460–479.
Kirk, D. S., & Wakefield, S. (2018). Collateral consequences of punishment: a critical review and path forward. *Annual Review of Criminology*, *1*, 171–194.
Murray, J., Loeber, R., & Pardini, D. (2012). Parental involvement in the criminal justice system and the development of youth theft, marijuana use, depression, and poor academic performance. *Criminology*, *50*(1), 255–302.
Nesmith, A., & Ruhland, E. (2008). Children of incarcerated parents: Challenges and resiliency, in their own words. *Children and Youth Services Review*, *30*(10), 1119–1130.
Turanovic, J., Rodriguez, N., & Pratt, T. (2012). The collateral consequences of incarceration revisited: A qualitative analysis of the effects on caregivers of children of incarcerated parents. *Criminology*, *50*(4), 913–959.
Wildeman, C., & Turney, K. (2014). Positive, negative, or null? The effects of maternal incarceration on children's behavioral problems. *Demography*, *51*(3), 1041–1068.

Contents

About the Authors

Joyce A. Arditti, Ph.D., is a Professor of Human Development and Family Science at Virginia Tech. She received her doctorate in Family Studies from the University of North Carolina, Greensboro. Her research interests include family disruption, parent-child relationships in vulnerable families, and public policy. Her scholarship is recognized nationally and abroad and she has published numerous empirical and review articles in therapy, human services, family studies, and criminal justice journals. She is the author of the book *Parental incarceration and the family: Psychological and social effects of imprisonment on children, parents, and care-givers* published by New York University Press, for which she was the 2014 recipient of the Academy of Criminal Justice Sciences (ACJS) Outstanding Book Award, an honor awarded to a member of ACJS who has authored a book representing extraordinary contribution in the field of criminal justice. Additionally, in August of 2016, Joyce was awarded the Alumni Award for Research Excellence by Virginia Tech for her significant research achievement in the area of parental incarceration. Joyce is also the editor of the recently released textbook: *Family Problems: Stress, Risk, & Resilience* published by John Wiley & Sons. Joyce served as the Editor in Chief of *Family Relations: The Interdisciplinary Journal of Applied Family Studies* from 2004 to 2009. She is a fellow of the National Council on Family Relations (NCFR) and served as the Research and Policy Brief Editor for NCFR (2015–16). She serves on various editorial boards and is actively involved in research projects dealing with families involved in the criminal justice system.

Kim Burley is a statistician in the Division of Reproductive Health at the Centers Disease and Prevention, National Center for Chronic Disease Prevention and Health Promotion. Mr. Burley has a B.S. degree in Statistics from the University of Tennessee and is a candidate for an M.S. degree in Applied Statistics. Mr. Burley provides SAS programming and statistical analysis support for the Perinatal Infant Health Team, Pregnancy Risk Assessment Monitoring System (PRAMS) Teams, and the Teen Pregnancy Team over the course of 13 years. Also, Mr. Burley has co-authored over 13 peer-review journals.

Pajarita Charles, Ph.D., M.S.W., M.P.A., is an assistant professor at the University of Wisconsin-Madison Sandra Rosenbaum School of Social Work. She received her doctorate in social work from the University of North Carolina at Chapel Hill. Her work focuses on the development, implementation, and testing of family-focused preventive interventions to promote positive psychosocial and behavioral health outcomes among families affected by the criminal justice system. She has particular interest in promoting the well-being of fathers with a history of incarceration and justice-system involvement. Dr. Charles' efforts include fostering research, practice, and public sector partnerships to build capacity for social justice and criminal justice reform. Her research, which uses both quantitative and qualitative methods, is published in social work, family studies, and criminal justice journals. She is a co-leader of the national Promote Smart Decarceration Grand Challenge for the American Academy of Social Work and Social Welfare. She also frequently collaborates with local and state organizations to provide expertise and guidance on issues pertinent to families impacted by the criminal justice system.

Jennifer E. Copp is an assistant professor in the College of Criminology and Criminal Justice at Florida State University. Her research examines the influence of intimate and familial relationships on developmental outcomes across a variety of domains, including crime and other problem behaviors. Her recent work considers how incarceration, and other forms of system contact, influence future behavior, family life, and child well-being.

Isabel Coronado is a policy entrepreneur at Next100 and a citizen of the Mvskoke (Creek) Nation. Her clan is the Wind Clan, and her tribal town affiliation is Thlopthlocco Tribal Town. At Next100, Isabel is focused on creating policy aimed at reducing the generational cycle of incarceration in Native communities. Her vision for the future is to see Indian Country prosper for years to come. Isabel has witnessed the effects of mass incarceration on Indigenous people throughout her life, and they inspired her to help create the American Indian Criminal Justice Navigation Council (AICJNC), a nonprofit in Oklahoma aimed at reducing recidivism among tribal members and helping reduce the trauma family members endure as a result. At AICJNC, Isabel served as deputy director. Isabel was selected by the Center for Native American Youth at the Aspen Institute as a 2018 Champions for Change recipient, and by Mvskoke Women's Leadership as the 2019 College Student of the Year. She is also a member of Alpha Pi Omega. Isabel received her B.S. in 2017 from Northeastern State University and her master's degree in public health with an emphasis on rural and underserved populations from Oklahoma State University in 2019.

Gabriella Damewood completed her B.A. at St. John's University. Upon graduation, she was hired as a Junior Research Scientist at NYU's Family Translational Research Group, where she acted as a program coordinator for several federally funded studies from the National Institutes of Health, the Department of Defense, and National Institute of Justice. Currently, she is a first-year doctoral student in clinical psychology at St. John's University. Her main research interests are understanding mechanisms of coercion and aggression in couples and families, promoting family well-being and preventing family violence.

Denise V. D'Angelo is an epidemiologist in the Division of Reproductive Health at the Centers for Disease Control and Prevention, National Center for Chronic Disease Prevention and Health Promotion. Ms. D'Angelo has a graduate degree in public health and supports maternal and infant health surveillance activities at the state and national level, including protocol development, questionnaire design, and study implementation for the Pregnancy Risk Assessment Monitoring System (PRAMS). Ms. D'Angelo also works to publish and disseminate findings from PRAMS on topics including health insurance coverage, pregnancy intention, substance use during pregnancy, postpartum depression, and health disparities.

Jasmine Drake is an associate professor and laboratory coordinator of the Forensic Science Learning Laboratory in the Barbara Jordan- Mickey Leland School of Public Affairs Administration of Justice Department at Texas Southern University (TSU) in Houston. Dr. Drake has over 10 years of forensic science practitioner experience. Currently, she is a Governor-appointed member of the Texas Forensic Science Commission. She is also a Faculty Research Fellow at the TSU Center for Justice Research, where she studies how racial disparities in drug policies impact vulnerable populations.

J. Mark Eddy, Ph.D., is a professor in the Department of Educational Psychology and the Department of Kinesiology and Health Education within the College of Education at the University of Texas at Austin. As a prevention scientist, he develops and rigorously tests prevention and intervention programs intended to benefit children and families, and particularly those who are living in stressful circumstances. His recent work centers on the conduct of randomized controlled trials of multimodal interventions in partnership with school systems, the juvenile justice system, the adult corrections system, the child welfare system, and the military, as well as with nonprofits that work with these and related systems. His research has focused on communities in the USA. and in Central America. Dr. Eddy is a licensed psychologist.

Kerrie Fanning is a Ph.D. student in Human Development and Family Studies in the School of Human Ecology at the University of Wisconsin – Madison. Her research focuses on the impacts of trauma and toxic stress on young children and their families through a resilience lens. Her work currently focuses on the impacts of family homelessness on families with infants and toddlers, exploring the protective nature of family relationships, caregiver-child interactions, child-caregiver attachment relationships, and perception of and engagement with community-based programs in this high-risk context. Kerrie utilizes a variety of methods in her work, including observations, micro-coding of behaviors, self-report measures, standardized assessments, and in-depth semi-structured and unstructured interviews.

Peggy C. Giordano is a distinguished research professor of sociology at Bowling Green State University. Her research centers on basic social network processes, and the ways in which close relationships influence delinquency and criminal behavior over the life course. She is especially interested in family dynamics associated with the intergenerational transmission of crime and other problem outcomes, as well as the impact of extra-familial influences such as peers and romantic partners.

Kimberley Gonzalez-Quiles, M.A., is a research scientist committed to investigating interpersonal violence, maltreatment, and social justice among vulnerable populations in criminal justice, healthcare, and government settings. For 5 years, she has managed and evaluated government-funded programs targeting service members and military mental health providers, individuals and families involved in the criminal justice system, and at-risk youth. Her current work focuses on: 1) gender and racial disparities during all phases of criminal proceedings, 2) interventions for children of incarcerated parents, and 3) gender-responsive approaches to reentry programs. While serving as a Junior Research Scientist at NYU, she worked with the U.S. Army Family Advocacy Program on a project aimed at improving their substantiation models for various forms of maltreatment. Through her work in all areas relating to criminal justice and evidence-based research, she hopes to bring families and communities together for positive futures.

Aaron Gottlieb, Ph.D., is an assistant professor at the Jane Addams College of Social Work, University of Illinois at Chicago (UIC). His research examines the causes and consequences of criminal justice involvement, as well as policy approaches to reducing incarceration and racial disparities in incarceration. In addition to being published in a wide range of academic journals, Aaron's research has been cited in a number of media outlets, including the New York Times and the Atlantic. In the community, Aaron is active in working towards police accountability through community oversight. He was recently appointed to Chicago's Police Use of Force Work Group, a working group that is tasked with producing recommendations about how to improve the Chicago Police Department's use of force policies.

Howard Henderson is the Director of the Center for Justice Research and a professor in the Barbara Jordan – Mickey Leland School of Public Affairs at Texas Southern University. Beyond directing a team of researchers utilizing a culturally responsive, evidence-informed approach to decarceration, Howard serves as a member of the national scientific advisory committee for the Institute of Justice Research and Development and the Vera Institute's Rural Jails Research and Policy Network. He received his Ph.D. in Criminal Justice from Sam Houston State University in 2006.

Karen Holden is Emerita Professor, Consumer Science, School of Human Ecology and the Robert M. La Follette School of Public Affairs, both at the University of Wisconsin-Madison. She received her Ph.D. in Economics from the University of

Pennsylvania, with a concentration in Demography. The primary areas of her academic research and teaching are household financial well-being, the role of individual decisions and public policy in shaping outcomes, and the evaluation of programs intended to address financial vulnerabilities. In her research, she sought to provide better data and analysis of the sources of economic vulnerability, including the social and institutional context in which decisions were made. She was Co-principal Investigator of the Social Security Administration grant that established the Center on Financial Literacy Research at the University of Wisconsin, which focuses on vulnerable populations. She advised Sesame Street Workshop on a program (and DVD) teaching children about saving: "For Me, for You, for Later: First Steps to Spending, Sharing, and Saving" which was accompanied by kits for parents and caregivers and an activity book for children, on which she also advised. She has co-authored one of the few articles on how young children develop concepts important to sound personal financial management.

Whitney Q. Hollins, Ph.D., is a researcher, educator, advocate, author, and daughter of a formerly incarcerated father. Her dissertation focused on children who have justice involved parents with an emphasis on lived experience as expertise. She is also the author of a children's book, *Anna's Test* (2019), a story of resilience featuring a girl whose father is incarcerated.

Sarah Jensen, is a dual J.D./Ph.D. student in Sociology at the University of Wisconsin-Madison. Her research focuses on the collateral consequences of the criminal justice system on children and families. Her current work uses interview data to examine how incarcerated parents teach their children about the criminal justice system. Prior to starting her graduate studies, Sarah conducted a mixed-methods program evaluation on a juvenile mental health court.

Elizabeth I. Johnson, Ph.D., is an associate professor in the Department of Child and Family Studies at the University of Tennessee, Knoxville and Co-Director of the Well-Being in Adolescents and Emerging Adults lab. She received a joint Ph.D. in Developmental Psychology and Social Work from the University of Michigan, Ann Arbor. Reflecting this interdisciplinary training, her research is broadly focused on how individuals grow and change in contexts of accumulated adversity. She is particularly interested in adolescents with incarcerated parents, and her research uses both quantitative and qualitative methodologies to identify patterns of risk and resilience in this population. She has published extensively on parental incarceration in leading developmental, family studies, and criminal justice journals and is currently a member of the editorial board for *Journal of Marriage and Family*. Johnson also collaborates with local community-based agencies to conduct research and to provide guidance to mentors and caregivers of youth with incarcerated parents.

Margaret L. Kerr, Ph.D., is an Assistant Professor in Human Development & Family Studies at the University of Wisconsin-Madison School of Human Ecology and a State Specialist in Vulnerable and Underserved Children with the Division of Extension. She is also an affiliate of the Institute for Research in Poverty and Center for Child & Family Well-Being. She received her doctorate in Positive Developmental Psychology from Claremont Graduate University. Her work focuses on examining parents' emotional experiences, with a particular focus on the factors that influence how adults perceive and experience parenting, including attachment, relationship quality, and socioeconomic status. She also works on brief interventions, such as relational savoring, that support parents' well-being by helping them to identify and relish moments of positive connection with their children. In her outreach work through Extension, she develops and implements parent-focused programming, including a parenting podcasts for fathers who are incarcerated. Her research has been published in family studies and developmental psychology journals.

Jean M. Kjellstrand, Ph.D., M.S.W., is an assistant professor in the Department of Counseling Psychology and Human Services within the College of Education at the University of Oregon. Her research interests focus on positive youth development and interventions to prevent problematic behavior among children in vulnerable situations. Dr. Kjellstrand's most recent research examines 1) the impact of parental incarceration on children and the specific mechanisms through which risk is transmitted, and 2) interventions to support incarcerated parents and their children both during the parents' incarceration and after release. Her work is informed by her previous career as a social worker where she developed and coordinated a variety of individual, group, and community interventions for children and families in high-risk circumstances.

Tanya Krupat, LMSW, M.P.H., is currently the Director of the Osborne Center for Justice Across Generations. She has worked with and on behalf of children with incarcerated parents for the past 20 years.

Judy Krysik, Ph.D., is an associate professor in the School of Social Work at Arizona State University and Director of the ASU Center for Child Well-Being, host of the National Children of Incarcerated Parents Conference. Her research interests include the prevention of child maltreatment among infants and toddlers, the efficacy of specialized court programs directed at young children removed for reasons of neglect and child maltreatment, and the promotion of evidence-based practices and programs for parents. She has developed child safety prevention programming that is utilized in schools and preschools across the nation.

Kevin Lawrence Henry Jr. is an Assistant Professor of Educational Leadership and Policy Analysis in the School of Education and currently holds an Anna Julia Cooper Fellowship at the University of Wisconsin-Madison. Henry's interdisciplinary research and teaching primarily focuses on the political economy of education, racial capitalism and neoliberal restructuring, charter schools and school choice policy, leadership for equity and educational justice, carceral logics and education, and the politics of education. Henry's work is grounded in and shaped by culturally relevant and transformative justice approaches to education, critical theories of race, gender, sexuality, and class, and Black Studies. He has served on the editorial boards of *Educational Studies*, *American Educational Research Journal*, and currently serves on the *Journal of Research on Leadership Education*. Henry also is a fellow at the Transformative Justice in Education Center at the University of California-Davis.

Rosalyn D. Lee is a scientist in the Division of Violence Prevention (DVP) at the Centers for Disease Control and Prevention, National Center for Injury Control and Prevention. Dr. Lee holds graduate degrees in public health and public policy. Dr. Lee supports sexual and intimate partner violence research and evaluation activities within DVP. Her research interests are centered at the intersection of the fields of public health and criminal justice with a particular focus on health and social inequities. She has published on the health impacts of parental incarceration, adverse childhood experiences, child maltreatment, intimate partner violence, and youth violence. She also currently co-chairs the DVP Race and Violence Workgroup which engages in initiatives to enhance the division's approach to addressing the role of social determinants, including racism, in the production of racial/ethnic inequities in risk for violence.

Monica A. Longmore is a Professor of Sociology at Bowling Green State University. Her interests include parenting and family dynamics, social psychological processes, and ways in which these family circumstances and subjective understandings affect adolescent and young adult behavior and well-being. Her research also focuses on precursors and consequences of intimate partner violence.

Wendy D. Manning is a Distinguished Research Professor of Sociology at Bowling Green State University, director of the Center for Family and Demographic Research, and co-director of the National Center for Family and Marriage Research. Her research focuses on relationships that exist outside the boundaries of marriage, including cohabitation, and effects of varied family forms on relationship dynamics, stability, and parenting practices.

Michael Massoglia, Ph.D., is Romnes Professor of Sociology at the University of Wisconsin-Madison. He received his doctorate in Sociology from the University of Minnesota. His work focuses on the social consequences of the expansion of the correctional system, the relationship between state controls and demographic change in the United States, and patterns of criminal behavior over the life course. He has published widely in a range of academic journals across sociology, criminology, and public health. His recent work focuses on how the expansion of the penal system has re-shaped American life. Mike is co-author of the forthcoming book "*Public Health in an Era of Mass Incarceration*" (Oxford University Press 2021) and his work has been supported by the National Science Foundation, the National

Institutes of Health and Child Development and the Bureau of Labor Statistics. Mike serves on the editorial board of multiple academic publications, and actively collaborates with community-based advocacy groups.

Branden McLeod, Ph.D., M.S.W., is an assistant professor at Jane Addams College of Social Work, University of Illinois Chicago. Branden teaches social welfare policy, policy analysis, and research methods. Branden's research examines how social policies and systems shape Black men's well-being and their relationships with their families, with particular focus on how these systems shape their roles as fathers. Given the ubiquitous nature of the criminal justice system in communities of color, much of his research unpacks how this system potentially attenuates fathers' role and explores factors that mitigate, sustain, and strengthen paternal involvement, as well as personal and familial well-being.

MariTere Molinet is a Ph.D. student at Georgia State University whose interests focus on crime from a social psychology perspective. Her research includes gender differences, technology and crime, and white-collar crime. Before pursuing an academic career, MariTere was a former international media executive for over 15 years.

Samuel L. Myers Jr. is the director and professor at Roy Wilkins Center for Human Relations and Social Justice at the Hubert H. Humphrey School of Public Affairs, University of Minnesota. He is an often-cited Massachusetts Institute of Technology-trained economist who has published extensively on applied microeconomic and policy issues in leading economics and interdisciplinary journals and in books and monographs. He is a pioneer in the use of applied econometric techniques to examine racial disparities in crime, to detect illegal discrimination in home mortgage lending and consumer credit markets, to assess the impacts of welfare on family stability to evaluate the effectiveness of government transfers in reducing poverty, and to detect disparities and discrimination in government contracting. He is an expert on conducting disparity studies for state and local governments and analyzes race-neutral public procurement and contracting policies. He has served as an expert witness in the ground-breaking federal cases of GEOD vs New Jersey Transit (3rd Circuit Court of Appeals) and Geyer vs. MnDOT (8th Circuit Court of Appeals). Myers is an elected Fellow of the National Academy of Public Administration; a past president of the Association for Public Policy Analysis and Management (APPAM); the former chair of the National Science Foundation's Committee on Equal Opportunity in Science and Engineering (CEOSE); and a former president of the National Economic Association (NEA).

Hyo-Mi Pak completed her B.A. at California State University at Long Beach. Upon graduation, she worked for 10 years as an elementary school public school teacher. Currently, she is a graduate student in School Psychology at the University of Texas at Austin.

Alexandria S. Pech, M.S., is a doctoral student in the Norton School of Family and Consumer Sciences at the University of Arizona. Her doctoral research is accountable to children, youth, and families impacted by parental and familial incarceration. Specifically, Alexandria's dissertation centers adolescent Girls of Color experiencing familial incarceration by using counterstories to understand how they form their identity at the intersection of race, class, and gender. Alexandria is also a ReFraming Justice Leader with American Friends Service Committee AZ and an Actionist leader with We Got Us Now.

Julie Poehlmann-Tynan, Ph.D., is the Dorothy A. O'Brien Professor of Human Ecology at the University of Wisconsin-Madison. She is a Professor in Human Development and Family Studies and an affiliate of the Institute for Research on Poverty and the Center for Healthy Minds. She is also a licensed psychologist in Wisconsin. The goal of her research is to facilitate social justice for young children and their families and to understand and promote resilience processes while decreasing risk and trauma exposure. Her research has been funded by the National Institutes of Health, the Institute for Clinical and Translational Research, the Department of Justice, the Department of Health and Human Services, and the Mind and Life Institute. Dr. Poehlmann-Tynan served as an advisor to Sesame Street to help develop and evaluate their Emmy-nominated initiative for young children with incarcerated parents called Little Children, Big Challenges: Incarceration and is currently working with the national organization ZERO TO THREE on materials for infants and toddlers separated from a parent. She has more than 100 publications and is the editor of three monographs, a book, and a handbook focusing on children with incarcerated parents, which is in its second edition. Her blog can be found at www.kidswithincarceratedparents.com.

Andrea Reino is a recent graduate of Princeton University with a bachelor's degree in public and international affairs and a minor in Spanish. Her research interests include prison reform, policy, and the incarcerated. She recently completed a comparative analysis of the humaneness of the American and Norwegian prison systems on the basis of prison culture, solitary confinement, and prison architecture.

Claudia Reino is a graduate student in the Department of Educational Psychology at The University of Texas at Austin. Her research interests focus on the incarcerated, as well as other underserved populations, such as Latinx immigrants in the United States. Her most recent work has examined bilingual language development and critical language periods, sexual harassment and exploitation in the workplace, parental and family adjustment to pediatric cancer, and psychopathology among medical professionals.

Nancy Rodriguez, Ph.D., is a professor in the Department of Criminology, Law and Society at the University of California, Irvine. In 2014, Dr. Rodriguez was appointed by President Barack Obama as Director of the National Institute of Justice, which is the scientific research arm of the U.S. Department of Justice. Prior to that, Dr. Rodriquez was a professor in Arizona State University's School of Criminology and Criminal Justice. Her research interests include inequality and the collateral consequences of mass incarceration, and she has collaborated with law enforcement, courts, and correctional agencies to better understand and improve conditions for those incarcerated and their families.

William J. Sabol, Professor in the Department Criminal Justice & Criminology at Georgia State University, teaches and conducts research on corrections, sentencing policy, and crime statistics. During the past 30 years, he has held positions in government, private sector research institutions, and universities, including serving as the Director of the Bureau of Justice Statistics. He earned his Ph.D. from the University of Pittsburgh and was a Fulbright Scholar at Cambridge University's Institute of Criminology.

Jean Schumer, LCSW, Ph.D., is an instructor at Linn-Benton Community College, a licensed clinical social worker in private practice, and registered Inside-Out Prison Exchange Program Instructor. Her early career experiences in child welfare, foster care and child psychiatric hospitals informed her interest in child abuse and violence prevention. Her practice is informed by research on evidence-based interventions that have been designed to strengthen and support families.

Natalia Vasiliou, M.S.W., is a research specialist at Arizona State University's Center for Child Well-Being. Natalia has over 10 years of experience working with marginalized communities in rural areas. She received her B.A. in Psychology and Gender Studies from Arizona State University in 2018, and her Master of Social Work degree with a concentration in policy, administration, and community practice from Arizona State University in 2020.

Melissa Villodas is a Ph.D. student in the School of Social Work at the University of North Carolina – Chapel Hill. Her research interests are on the impact of neighborhood structures and characteristics on the mental health of youth living in socioeconomically disadvantaged communities. Melissa works as a research assistant with Dr. Amy Blank Wilson on a novel NIMH-funded R34 project evaluating an intervention for justice involved individuals with serious mental illness and on a demonstration project developing a Tiny Homes Village for individuals living with mental illness. Before arriving at UNC-CH, Melissa worked as a clinical therapist for a treatment family foster care program in NYC and as the project director for the Youth and Young Adult Mental Health Research Group at New York University.

Reginald A. Wilkinson has nearly 50 years of experience in leadership, higher education, and criminal justice work. He retired in 2006 after 33 years managing corrections operations in Ohio including serving over 15 years as director of the Department of Rehabilitation and Correction. He is a past president of both the American Correctional Association and the Correctional Leaders Association. He is a founding member and former vice chair of the International Corrections and

Prisons Association. As well, Dr. Wilkinson has served on the National Institute of Corrections Advisory Board for over 20 years including serving as its chairperson. He earned B.A. and M.A. degrees from The Ohio State University and an Ed.D. from the University of Cincinnati. In addition to leading two non-profit higher education groups, he was appointed by Governor Mike DeWine to the Board of Trustees of his alma mater, Ohio State. Moreover, he is currently president of Connecting the Dots, LLC.

Amy Blank Wilson, Ph.D., M.S.W., is an associate professor and the Prudence F. and Peter J. Meehan Early Career Distinguished Scholar at the School of Social Work at the University of North Carolina at Chapel Hill. Amy is a social worker and mental health services researcher with expertise in both quantitative and qualitative research methods. She is an expert in the development and testing of interventions for people with serious mental illness involved in the criminal justice system. Her research includes over a dozen studies focused on different aspects of people with mental illnesses' involvement in the criminal justice system, including substance use, service accessibility, criminogenic risk factors, jail and prison reentry, community participation, prison mental health services and gender responsive interventions for people with serious mental illness in the justice system. Her 20 years' experience working and conducting research in the criminal justice settings has led her to expand her research and scholarship on the criminal justice system to include projects focused on solitary confinement, incarcerated pregnant women, and autistic individuals who come into contact with the justice system.

Jennifer Wirth received her master's degree in Human Ecology from the University of Wisconsin-Madison with a focus on Human Development and Family Studies. Her thesis work involved examining the lived experiences of parents with a history of multiple incarcerations. She received her dual bachelor's degree from Seattle University in Economics and French Language.

Jennifer Wyatt Bourgeois is a doctoral student in the Department of the Administration of Justice in the Barbara Jordan – Mickey Leland School of Public Affairs and graduate research fellow in the Center for Justice Research at Texas Southern University. Her research interests include risk and resilient factors associated with children and youth impacted by familial and/or parental incarceration, the intersection of race, gender, and class disparities in the criminal justice system, criminal justice program evaluation, and the intersection of criminal justice and forensic science. Jennifer holds a B.S. in Forensic Science from Baylor University, and an M.S. in Criminal Justice from Sam Houston State University.

Part I
The Micro System

Women and Infants Affected by Incarceration: The Potential Value of Home Visiting Program Engagement

Rosalyn D. Lee, Denise V. D'Angelo, and Kim Burley

Abstract Having a parent with an incarceration history is an adverse childhood experience (ACE; i.e., potentially traumatic events and aspects of a child's environment that undermines a sense of safety, stability, and bonding). Research indicates that children exposed to parental incarceration are exposed to more overall ACEs than children not exposed to this situation. Because the risk of negative outcomes increases with the number of ACEs to which one is exposed, children exposed to parental incarceration face greater health and social risks. Given this, consideration of interventions that focus on mitigating and/or preventing risks as early as the prenatal and immediate post-partum periods is needed. Enhancing efforts to engage women affected by incarceration in home visitation programs is one opportunity for intervention. Women with incarceration histories face barriers to program participation that may be unique as compared to other home visitation program participants. Studies indicate that home visitation programs, particularly those designed for families that exhibit one or more risk factors for child abuse and neglect, were more impactful than those designed to generally provide support to families. Thus, extending outreach of home visitation programs designed for families facing high levels of risk, to populations impacted by incarceration, may be of value. Efforts are needed to increase engagement of this sub-group of women and children in home visitation programs and to evaluate whether home visitation improves outcomes for them. Additional studies may further understanding of reasons why women affected by incarceration do and do not utilize such services and may help inform how programs, as well as recruitment and retention strategies, might be tailored to best address the needs of this sub-group.

R. D. Lee (✉)
Division of Violence Prevention, National Center for Injury Prevention and Control, Centers for Disease Control and Prevention, Atlanta, GA, USA
e-mail: rdl3@cdc.gov

D. V. D'Angelo · K. Burley
Division of Reproductive Health, National Center for Chronic Disease Prevention and Health Promotion, Center for Disease Control and Prevention, Atlanta, GA, USA

J. Krysik, N. Rodriguez (eds.), *Children of Incarcerated Parents*, Children of Incarcerated Parents: From Understanding to Impact,
https://doi.org/10.1007/978-3-030-84713-5_1

Keywords Parental incarceration · Pregnancy · Early childhood · Maternal health · Home visitation programs

Introduction

The rate of persons in the U.S. over age 18 under correctional supervision (i.e., held in prisons or jails or serving probation or parole) has been decreasing in recent years (i.e., from 3210 to 2640 per 100,000 between 2007 and 2016; Kaeble & Cowhig, 2018); but it remains the highest in the world (Walmsley, 2018). It is generally recognized that the overall exponential growth in persons under correctional supervision since the 1970s has not been due to increases in criminality or violent behavior but, instead, largely driven by changes to drug policies and law enforcement practices (National Resource Center on Justice Involved Women, 2016). Further, these changes have inequitably impacted racial/ethnic minorities (Cole, 2011) and increased the risk of children of color growing up with a parent that has been incarcerated (Wildeman, 2009). Consequently, programs that address the needs of parents and children impacted by incarceration are needed.

Growing up with a household member who has an incarceration history is considered an adverse childhood experience (ACE). Research has found that across the life course, ACEs, potentially traumatic events, and aspects of the child's environment that undermine sense of safety, stability, and bonding (e.g., child abuse and neglect, witnessing intimate partner violence, growing up in a household with substance use disorders, mental health problems, and instability due to parental separation or household member incarceration) have negative impacts on health (i.e., risk behaviors, physical and mental health outcomes) and well-being (i.e., levels of educational attainment and other factors that influence life potential; Felitti et al., 1998; CDC, 2019a). ACEs may facilitate chronic, severe, or prolonged exposure to stress which, in the absence of protective factors, may disrupt brain circuitry and metabolic systems during sensitive developmental periods. Such disruptions may result in anatomic changes and/or physiologic dysregulations that subsequently influence development of learning and behavior impairments and chronic stress-related physical and mental illnesses (Shonkoff & Garner, 2012). ACEs are generally strongly inter-related; however, their exposure is more common among children exposed to parental incarceration than children not exposed to parental incarceration. Children whose parents have experienced incarceration are exposed to nearly five times as many ACEs as children not exposed to parental incarceration (Turney, 2018).

The higher burden of ACEs among children impacted by parental incarceration is particularly concerning given studies that have found that risk of negative outcomes increases with the number of ACEs to which one is exposed (Felitti et al., 1998; Dube et al., 2003; Gilbert et al., 2015; Lee & Chen, 2017; Merrick et al.,

2019). This dose-response relationship has been found to be consistent, strong, and graded across a number of health outcomes and population cohorts (Dube et al., 2003). Over the past 20 years, in response to the exponential growth of incarceration in the U.S., an emergent body of literature has focused specifically on the impacts of parental incarceration on child health. This literature has concentrated on the period of childhood through young adulthood (Lee et al., 2013; Roettger & Boardman, 2012; Wildeman et al., 2018) and furthers understanding of the relationship between a parent's incarceration and negative impacts on children's health risk behaviors (Nebbitt et al., 2017), as well as mental health, infectious disease, and chronic disease outcomes (Lee et al., 2013; Roettger & Boardman, 2012; Wildeman et al., 2018). Studies have also investigated whether parental incarceration is associated with increased risk of violence (Turney, 2014; Muftic & Smith, 2018); but many of these studies rely solely on child welfare-based samples (Austin, 2016).

Fewer studies have examined incarceration-related risks immediately before, during, and after pregnancy. Findings of extant research focused on this early period appears to be mixed with some studies indicating associations between maternal incarceration and poor birth outcomes (Testa & Jackson, 2020; McMillan Dowell et al., 2019; Howard et al., 2009; Bell et al., 2004). Though additional studies could clarify links between incarceration and birth outcomes, the health risk profile of women with incarceration histories and evidence from existing research on children whose parents have been incarcerated suggests early interventions are warranted (Lee et al., 2013; Dallaire et al., 2018; Wildeman et al., 2018). Such interventions may prevent or buffer the impact of risks associated with incarceration exposure, including ACEs, such as maternal mental health problems and substance use disorders, factors which also may increase the risk of another ACE – child abuse and neglect.

CDC identified several strategies for the prevention of ACEs before they occur and the mitigation of risks associated with existing ACEs (CDC, 2019a). One of these strategies is to ensure a strong start for children. An approach that aligns with this strategy and can be implemented before, during, and immediately after pregnancy is early childhood home visitation. Early childhood home visitation has been found to be especially effective for women and children who are at increased risk for poor maternal and child health, child development, parenting practices, and child abuse and neglect outcomes (Sama-Miller et al., 2019). Furthermore, programs tailored to the needs of particularly vulnerable sub-groups have been found effective. For example, a review study by Casillas et al. (2016) found that early childhood home visiting programs aimed at families that exhibit one or more risk factors for child abuse and neglect (e.g., maternal mental health and substance use disorders) were more impactful than those designed to generally provide support to families. Though incarceration widely impacts family systems and home visitation programs may involve fathers and other family members, this chapter will discuss the potential for home visitation to address many of the factors that place women and infants affected by incarceration at increased risk for poor health and well-being.

Female Involvement in U.S. Correctional Systems

Though males greatly outnumber females (e.g., comprising about 85% of the total) with respect to correctional supervision, the female population is generally growing, while the male population is declining or growing at a slower rate. Between 2000 and 2010, with the exception of parole, the total rate of increase in correctional supervision among females exceeded that of males for the overall population (17.2% vs 8.1%), as well as for probation (16.5% vs. 2.6%), jail (30.1% vs. 19.3%), and prison (21.1% vs. 15.4%) (Glaze & Kaeble, 2014). Between 2010 and 2013, while the overall correctional population declined, female populations either declined at a slower rate than the male populations (e.g., probation, parole, and prison populations) or increased (e.g., jail). By 2016, the most recent year for which there is data on community supervision, slightly more than 1 million women were under community supervision, including just over 900,000 on probation (25% of all probationers) and slightly more than 100,000 on parole (13% of all of all paroles) (Kaeble, 2018). With respect to incarceration, slightly more than 200,000 women were held in correctional facilities at the year-end of 2017 (the most recent year for incarceration data). Nearly half of these women were detained in jails (Bronson & Carson, 2019; Zeng, 2019) for short durations (i.e., less than a year). Further, between 2005 and 2017, the female jail population grew 12%, while the male jail population decreased by 10% (Zeng, 2019). These trends indicate that the growth in women's involvement with incarceration has disproportionately been located in local jails. However, data limitations preclude gender-specific analyses that might identify factors that underlie the increases (Kajstura, 2019).

Incarceration, Women's Health, and the Perinatal Period

Though additional research is needed to better understand factors driving increasing rates of female involvement with U.S. correctional systems, existing information suggests these women are in need of programs and services. Most women who come into contact with the correctional system are of childbearing age, and they live with their children before incarceration more frequently than males (Glaze & Maruschak, 2008). Additionally, women with incarceration histories tend to experience high rates of disadvantage and health problems (Browne et al., 1999; Hammett & Drachman-Jones, 2006; Lee & Wildeman, 2013). Studies indicate women who are incarcerated have high rates of substance dependence, sexually transmitted infections, and other health problems (Hammett & Drachman-Jones, 2006). These women also are more likely to have experienced ACEs during their childhood and other forms of interpersonal violence as adults (Browne et al., 1999). These risks may affect maternal well-being, and they represent ACEs (e.g., maternal mental health and substance use disorders, witnessing intimate partner violence) which may have short- and long-term impact on infant health and well-being.

Birth Outcomes

Although estimates among jail populations are unknown (Bronson & Sufrin, 2019), the Department of Justice indicated in 2004 that 3–4% of women who entered prisons were pregnant (Maruschak, 2004). These prison-based estimates, which have not been updated since 2004, are further limited because they do not consider women who become pregnant while incarcerated (Bronson & Sufrin, 2019). This lack of data represents a significant data gap. Though more needs to be done to estimate the overall number of pregnant women affected by incarceration, it is of value to give consideration to potential proximal consequences of incarceration on infant health. One potential consequence is negative birth outcome, as risks for preterm birth (i.e., less than 37 weeks gestation) and low birth weight (LBW; i.e., less than 2500 grams) increase with unfavorable socioeconomic conditions, maternal medical risks, and poor access to healthcare (Valero de Bernabe et al., 2004) – all factors that women with incarceration histories are more likely to experience (Browne et al., 1999; Hammett & Drachman-Jones, 2006; Lee & Wildeman, 2013). These birth outcomes can have significant life course impacts. Pre-term birth (PTB) and LBW are associated with an increased risk of infant mortality (see McMillan Dowell et al., 2019). Furthermore, children born prematurely may have more problems with motor/neurologic functions, visuomotor integrative skills, IQ, academic achievement, language, executive function, and attention-deficit hyperactivity disorder/behavioral issues than their normal birth weight counterparts (Aylward, 2014). The limited research that examines the relationship between maternal incarceration and birth outcomes is mixed with some studies indicating that incarceration improves outcomes, while others suggest it is linked to poorer outcomes (Testa & Jackson, 2020; Dallaire et al., 2018; McMillan Dowell et al., 2019; Howard et al., 2009, ; Bell et al., 2004). Though more research is warranted, given the health risk profiles of women with incarceration histories and consequences of poor birth outcomes, it appears programs that engage women with incarceration histories during the perinatal period may be of value.

Mental Health

Maternal mental health, particularly depression and other mental health conditions, can also influence maternal health promotive behaviors, parenting behaviors, and child well-being (Wouk et al., 2016; Stein et al., 1991; Kingston et al., 2012). This is of concern because with respect to perinatal mental health, research indicates notable disparities between women with and without incarceration histories. For example, about one in nine American women experience symptoms of postpartum depression (PPD) (Ko et al., 2017). However, in a scoping review of studies on maternal health outcomes that included women incarcerated at any point during the perinatal period, Paynter et al. (2019) examined four studies

(Fogel, 1993; Fogel & Belyea, 2001; Hutchinson et al., 2008; Williams & Schulte-Day, 2006) that looked at depression and/or anxiety. The studies had relatively small sample sizes; but three of the four studies found moderate to high levels of depressive symptomology above a level indicative of clinical depression (e.g., two studies >70% of participants) among incarcerated women. Though the extant research suggests disparities in perinatal mental health by incarceration history, additional studies with larger sample sizes are needed to confirm and extend these findings.

Maternal PPD has also been shown to affect child health and well-being, including increasing risk of communication and language problems, cognitive functioning, and emotional and behavioral problems (Kaplan et al., 2014; Murray, 1992; Stein et al., 1991; Surkan et al., 2014). Providing services and supports to prevent or mitigate PPD may also help prevent or mitigate poor PPD-related child outcomes such as increased anxiety, attachment disorders, and depression (Earls, 2010), as well as sleeping and eating difficulties, temper tantrums, and separation problems (Murray, 1992). PPD also appears to interfere with parenting quality, which can impact the level of safety in the child's environment. For example, PPD has been associated with lower likelihood of implementing injury prevention measures, and in the extreme it may increase likelihood of a parent committing fatal harm to themselves and their child (e.g., suicide and infanticide; Barr & Beck, 2008; Lindahl et al., 2005).

Breastfeeding

Breastfeeding can have many positive health effects including reduced risk for some short- and long-term health conditions for both infants and mothers (e.g., ear, respiratory, and gastrointestinal infections in infants and type 2 diabetes, hypertension, reproductive cancers in mothers; Feltner et al., 2018; Ip et al., 2007) and can increase levels of maternal-infant interaction (Earls, 2010). Recent research indicates that women with jail contact compared to their counterparts are already less likely to breastfeed: 64.4% and 79.1, respectively, where $p<0.0001$ and the relative risk (RR)=0.86 (Dumont et al., 2014). Furthermore, disparities in breastfeeding exist among racial/ethnic minority sub-groups disproportionately impacted by incarceration, 69.4% of African American infants initiated to breastfeeding compared to 85.9% of white infants (Beauregard et al., 2019). In addition, women who have been exposed to ACEs, such as child abuse and neglect, may have more challenges forming high-quality bonds with their children (Rikhye et al., 2008). Thus, programs that can encourage breastfeeding and bonding may be especially important for women with incarceration histories since they are more likely to have experienced violence in childhood and adulthood (Browne et al., 1999). Taken together, women with incarceration histories have poor health profiles and may be at increased risk for poor birth outcomes and PPD and may be less likely to engage in health behaviors that have positive impacts for themselves and their infants. When combined with other risks they face (e.g., substance use disorders), increased attention to engaging them in programs as early as the perinatal period may be of value for them and their children.

Home Visiting

Increasing safety, stability, and degree of nurturing in relationships and environments may counter high levels of stress and adversity (CDC, n.d.-a, n.d.-b) in the lives of children whose parents have histories of incarceration. For example, research demonstrates that responsive, contingent, nurturing relationships function as a buffer to high cumulative or toxic psychosocial stress, preventing the rise of cortisol and other hormonal mediators which can damage brain architecture (See Lowell et al., 2011). Programs that can intervene to prevent poor birth outcomes, help promote maternal mental health and substance abuse treatment, and support the development of strong parent-child bonds (i.e., responsive and nurturing behaviors) during the perinatal period may hold significant preventive potential for women and children affected by incarceration. An approach that attempts to address many of these protective factors and has become increasingly accepted as effective is early childhood home visiting (Olds et al., 1986a, b; Council on Child and Adolescent Health, 1998; Sama-Miller et al., 2019). Such programs may help buffer against high levels of intersecting disadvantages that can influence poor maternal and child outcomes across the life course.

The broad and varied array of programs under the umbrella of early childhood home visiting include programs designed to be universal as well as those designed to target high-risk, often low-income and first-time mothers. Programs are often designed to improve maternal and child health, child development, parenting practices, family economic sufficiency, child abuse and neglect, juvenile delinquency, family violence, and crime (Sama-Miller et al., 2019). In addition to working directly with women and children, many programs aim to connect families with services and supports that are tailored to their specific needs (Lowell et al., 2011). Support and referrals provided by early childhood home visiting are intended to improve parental mental health by lowering stress, anxiety, and depression and improving confidence and motivation (Sandstrom, 2019). Many programs help ensure that parents have support to care for their children by screening caregivers for postpartum depression, substance abuse, and family violence and connecting them to relevant resources (HRSA, Maternal & Child Health, n.d.-a). Numerous program models exist – some requiring enrollment prenatally and others enrolling children in infancy or later in early childhood; but programs generally include four components – screening, case management, family support or counseling, and caregiver skills training. A meta-analysis that focused on the components of home visiting programs, however, revealed no consistent pattern of effective home visiting components across outcome domains (e.g., maternal outcomes, child outcomes, etc.) of interest (Filene et al., 2013).

Maternal Outcomes

Though some evaluations have found unfavorable or ambiguous impacts, studies have also found that home visiting programs can prevent poor birth outcomes (Brooten et al., 2001; Chapman et al., 1990; Harrison et al., 2001; Norbeck et al., 1996; Olds et al. 1986b), address maternal mental health (Porter et al., 2015), and support parent-child bonding and child development outcomes (Ammerman, 2016; Avellar et al., 2016) – all of which appear to be significant needs of women and infants affected by incarceration. Specifically, programs have resulted in maternal reports of lower levels of PPD symptoms (Armstrong et al., 1999; Gelfand et al., 1996;); increased parent responsivity, sensitivity, and parent-child bonds (Flemington & Fraser, 2016; Goldfeld et al., 2019; Guthrie et al., 2009; Kemp et al., 2011; Oxford et al., 2016; Sadler et al., 2013; Spieker et al., 2012); as well as an increased use of health promotive practices (Kitzman et al., 1997; Lowell et al., 2011; Shah & Austin, 2014).

Child Outcomes

With respect to child outcomes, several studies have demonstrated that early childhood home visiting programs can lower risk of child abuse and neglect victimization, which has significant implications for later delinquency and substance use (Gomby et al., 1999; Love et al., 2005; Lowell et al., 2011; Sweet & Applebaum, 2004). Research has shown links between early childhood home visiting programs and the reductions in healthcare visits for acute conditions and/or problems. This is attributed to reductions in both intentional (child abuse and neglect) and unintentional injuries in children. Specifically, studies indicate associations between early childhood home visiting and reduced number of family doctor visits (Fergusson et al., 2005; Kilburn & Cannon, 2017), emergency department visits (Kilburn & Cannon, 2017; Olds et al., 1986a), hospitalizations (Koniak-Griffin et al., 2000, 2002), and overnight stays in hospitals (Dodge et al., 2013). In addition to showing protective effects against injury and child abuse, there is also evidence that these types of programs positively affect young children's cognitive and language development, as well as child problem behaviors (Stein et al., 1991). Taken together, these benefits may greatly contribute to preventing or reducing both child and parent adversity associated with exposure to incarceration.

Other Considerations

It is important to recognize that individual home visiting models are designed to address different sets of outcomes. Additionally, only certain models have been found to meet the U.S. Department of Health and Human Services (HHS) criteria for being an evidence-based early childhood home visiting model. In the most recent Home Visiting Evidence of Effectiveness (HomVee) review, 21 of 50 (42%) home visiting models were identified as meeting the HHS criteria for being an evidence-based model (Sama-Miller et al., 2019). An earlier HomVee review also indicated that the most common favorable effects of effective models were child development and healthcare usage outcomes (Avellar & Supplee, 2013).

Data from the Pregnancy Risk Assessment Monitoring System (PRAMS), which currently covers about 83% of all U.S. births, can be used to describe experiences, maternal behaviors, and experiences that occur before, during, and shortly after pregnancy from women who deliver live-born infants in select U.S. states, cities, and territories (Shulman et al., 2018). The 2012–2015 PRAMS data from 37 sites indicate that 28.6% of women with jail contact (defined as those who reported that she and/or her partner went to jail in the 12 months before her most recent live birth) received early childhood home visiting services during or after pregnancy compared to 16.8% of women without incarceration exposure (see Table 1). When comparing women with and without jail contact who received early childhood home visiting services, it was observed that higher proportions of women with jail contact were younger, less educated, unmarried, publicly insured, and participants in the Special Supplemental Program for Women and Infants (WIC). The higher proportion of women with jail contact receiving early childhood home visiting services presents a unique opportunity for interventions from these programs to prevent and mitigate effects of ACEs in the lives of mothers and infants, impacts of incarceration, as well as mental health, substance abuse problems, and other risks that are highly correlated with incarceration. However, a large proportion of women in the sub-group with jail contact reported they did not receive early childhood home visiting services (71.4%), which indicates there is a potential for targeted service provision given the potential benefit to this special population. When considering this gap, it will be important not only to engage these women in evidence-based early home visiting programs but also to connect them with programs that show favorable effects for the outcomes with which they need assistance.

Families Affected by Incarceration as a Target Sub-group for Home Visitation

Considering women with jail contact as an at-risk sub-group to receive early childhood home visiting services represents a valuable opportunity for an intervention. This is particularly the case given Casillas et al. (2016) found that early childhood home visiting programs aimed at families that exhibit one or more risk factors for child abuse and neglect (e.g., household mental health and substance use problems) were more impactful than those designed to generally provide support to families. Participants in federally funded early childhood home visiting programs tend to live below poverty (71% with household incomes at or below 100% poverty), have low

Table 1 Characteristics of women with and without jail contact by home visitation status, Pregnancy Risk Assessment Monitoring System (PRAMS), 2012–2015

Characteristics	Total population*	Prevalence any home visit† % (95% CI)	No jail contact Total*	No jail contact Any home visit† % (95% CI)	Jail contact Total*	Jail contact Any home visit† % (95% CI)	p value
Total	148792	17.3 (17.0–17.6)	139940	16.8 (16.5–17.1)	6389	28.6 (26.7–30.6)	
Age (years)							0.000*
<20	10065	31.2 (29.6–32.8)	8914	30.6 (28.9–32.3)	898	37.5 (31.9–43.5)	
20–24	31882	20.2 (19.5–21.0)	28959	19.7 (19.0–20.5)	2268	27.2 (24.2–30.5)	
25–34	83273	15.4 (15.0–15.8)	79293	15.0 (14.7–15.4)	2745	27.3 (24.5–30.2)	
=35	23568	15.2 (14.5–15.9)	22770	15.0 (14.3–15.7)	478	26.6 (20.2–34.1)	
Race/ethnicity							0.000*
White, non-Hispanic	75845	14.4 (14.0–14.7)	72620	13.9 (13.6–14.3)	2523	27.7 (25.0–30.5)	
Black, non-Hispanic	24322	25.7 (24.8–26.6)	21729	25.3 (24.3–26.2)	1902	31.1 (27.5–34.9)	
American Indian/ Alaska native, non-Hispanic	4507	19.6 (17.7–21.7)	3913	19.2 (17.2–21.4)	485	23.5 (17.8–30.2)	
Other, non-Hispanic	18501	18.1 (17.2–19.1)	17572	17.7 (16.8–18.7)	541	28.8 (21.9–36.7)	
Hispanic	24902	20.5 (19.7–21.3)	23433	20.2 (19.4–21.1)	908	29.1 (24.2–34.6)	
Education							0.000*
< High school	21324	26.1 (25.2–27.1)	19104	25.5 (24.4–26.5)	1558	37.7 (33.3–42.4)	
High school	36871	19.4 (18.8–20.1)	33797	18.9 (18.3–19.6)	2331	26.6 (23.6–29.9)	

(continued)

Table 1 (continued)

Characteristics	Total population*	Prevalence any home visit† % (95% CI)	No jail contact Total*	No jail contact Any home visit† % (95% CI)	Jail contact Total*	Jail contact Any home visit† % (95% CI)	p value
> High school	88705	14.4 (14.1–14.8)	85290	14.1 (13.8–14.5)	2407	25.5 (22.8–28.5)	
Marital status							0.000*
Married	87689	13.4 (13.1–13.8)	85318	13.3 (13.0–13.6)	1344	21.0 (17.7–24.7)	
Other	60534	23.5 (22.9–24.1)	54093	22.9 (22.3–23.5)	5024	30.7 (28.5–33.0)	
Health insurance for prenatal care							0.000*
Private	76566	12.0 (11.7–12.3)	74663	11.9 (11.6–12.2)	1208	18.7 (15.5–22.5)	
Medicaid	58818	24.1 (23.6–24.7)	53245	23.6 (23.0–24.2)	4533	31.4 (29.1–33.9)	
Other	5478	21.7 (20.0–23.6)	5071	21.1 (19.3–23.0)	281	37.7 (27.5–49.0)	
None	4344	22.8 (20.8–24.9)	4074	22.4 (20.4–24.5)	175	27.5 (17.6–40.2)	
WIC recipient during pregnancy							0.000*
No	77696	12.1 (11.7–12.4)	75651	12.0 (11.6–12.3)	1503	18.6 (15.7–21.9)	
Yes	68950	24.1 (23.6–24.6)	63265	23.5 (23.0–24.1)	4826	31.6 (29.3–34.0)	

Note: Jail contact is defined as those who reported that she and/or her partner went to jail in the 12 months before her most recent live birth

*Unweighted sample size. †Weighted percent and confidence interval. CI, confidence interval. The *p* value is significant (*) when $p < 0.05$

The sum of the population for jail contact and non-jail contact women does not equal to the total count for each characteristic level due to missing values

Data is from 37 sites: Alabama, Alaska, Arkansas, Colorado, Connecticut, Delaware, Georgia, Hawaii, Illinois, Iowa, Louisiana, Maine, Maryland, Massachusetts, Michigan, Minnesota, Missouri, Nebraska, New Hampshire, New Jersey, New Mexico, New York State, New York City, Ohio, Oklahoma, Oregon, Pennsylvania, Rhode Island, Tennessee, Texas, Utah, Vermont, Virginia, Washington, West Virginia, Wisconsin, and Wyoming levels of education (65% with high school education or less), rely heavily on public health insurance programs (76% Medicaid or CHIP), and experience high levels of violence and substance abuse (19% history of child abuse and 13% current substance abuse) (HRSA, Maternal & Child Health, n.d.-a, n.d.-b). What is not known is the rate at which participants are also impacted by a history of incarceration. Given that women affected by incarceration frequently experience significant levels of health, social, and economic disadvantage (Subramanian et al., 2015) and their children experience significantly more ACEs than other children (Turney, 2018), prioritizing recruitment of these women with incarceration histories into home visitation programs may assure such programs reach populations that may benefit the most from them. It is important for implementers of programs to be aware of barriers to access and utilization that may be unique for these women, as well as consider strategies for expanding and tailoring outreach to assure this population has the opportunity to participate in such programs.

Unique Engagement Challenges

Women affected by incarceration fall into numerous sub-categories. Some may have recently been released from correctional systems, while others may have past incarceration histories, may be in a supervised status, or may have been diverted from corrections into a special program. Though all of these sub-groups of women and their children are affected by the criminal justice system and may benefit from engaging in home visitation programs, the discussion herein will largely focus on experiences of women with recent jail contact.

Incarceration is de-stabilizing; even a short period of detention can have severe impacts on residential stability and employment (Subramanian et al., 2015), as individuals who cannot meet bail may lose jobs and be evicted from residences. A study by Kulkarni et al. (2010) examined access to healthcare among former prisoners and found that persons with an incarceration history were similar to their peers who did not have an incarceration history (i.e., with regard to predisposing, enabling, and need factors), but their access to medical care was worse, likely due to financial barriers . In addition, individuals with incarceration histories often face formal and informal sanctions that consequently result in them being restricted from gaining access to needed services and supports. For example, some states suspend public benefits while women are in custody (Bell et al., 2004; Kaiser Family Foundation, 2020) and prohibit those with felony convictions from accessing benefits (Wang et al., 2013). Implications of such policies may include interruptions to needed health and social services as women navigate complex systems to re-establish benefits such as Medicaid, or find alternative resources, before obtaining care. Having to navigate around such sanctions can increase the complexity of increasing engagement among those at risk of poor outcomes. Research, however, indicates that access and utilization of healthcare services among the formerly incarcerated are facilitated when indirect and non-monetary resources (e.g., corrections-based discharge planning and social support) are made available (Lee et al., 2006; Wang et al., 2008).

Discharge planning appears to be a key point of intervention for pregnant women leaving jail, yet it often is a significant unmet need as local correctional systems are often under-staffed and not funded to provide such services. According to a qualitative study, jail staff do not believe there are sufficient resources, housing, or programming for women who are leaving jail (Belknap et al., 2016). Belknap et al. (2016) suggest that to most effectively work with incarcerated women, jail staff trainings will need to be updated to include content on trauma-informed care, mental illness, and gender-responsive programming. Given what is known about the impact of ACEs, it would also be helpful for jail staff to be trained on ACEs and how they can impact the lives of women and children. This may help guide development of policy and practices that address women's needs during the time they are detained and when they are preparing for discharge from jail detention.

Changes in local correctional systems that would bring about improvements to discharge planning may begin with the aforementioned staff trainings but may also require development of partnerships between local public health authorities, professional associations, and local jails. Such partnerships may ultimately facilitate home visitation program recruitment of detainees released from jail during the course of their pregnancies.

An example of a professional association that supports development of partnerships in this area is the Association of Women's Health, Obstetric, and Neonatal Nurses (AWHONN). AWHONN supports comprehensive, high-quality, perinatal care for women who are incarcerated during pregnancy and the postpartum period. While they recognize a role for nurses in the care of these women, they suggest changes are needed at a system level. Specifically, they have proposed that the correctional infrastructure support maternal-infant contact by establishing prison nurseries and family visiting spaces, providing support for breastfeeding regardless of whether the dyad will remain together post hospital discharge, and sentencing women to facilities in proximity to their family (AWHONN, 2018). Though many of their recommendations apply to prison settings where women typically serve longer sentences, they may also be relevant to jail settings. Applying these practices in jail settings may help build capacity for re-entry planning for women discharged from jails during pregnancy. This in turn may facilitate their enrollment in early childhood home visiting programs.

As noted earlier, given the diversity of statuses among women affected by incarceration, there will be multiple entry points to home visitation program participation. Multiple strategies may be needed to identify and secure commitments to participation. Other approaches may involve development of partnerships between providers and community-based organizations that already serve populations with high concentrations of individuals impacted by incarceration. For example, AWHONN suggests nurses can collaborate with other healthcare providers to develop action plans that may help women affected by incarceration with breastfeeding (Shlafer et al., 2018), child care, and housing (Guthrie, 2011).

Conclusion

Having a parent with an incarceration history is an adverse childhood experience. Research indicates that children exposed to parental incarceration are exposed to more overall ACEs than children not exposed to this situation. Because the risk of negative outcomes increases with the number of ACEs one is exposed to, children exposed to parental incarceration face greater health and social risks. Effective programs, policies, and practices that focus on mitigating and/or preventing risks as early as the perinatal period can improve the well-being of children. CDC has identified several strategies for the prevention of ACEs before they occur and the mitigation of risks associated with existing ACEs (CDC, 2019a). One of these strategies is to ensure a strong start for children. An approach that aligns with this strategy that can be implemented before, during, and immediately after pregnancy is early childhood home visitation. Enhancing efforts to engage women affected by incarceration in home visitation programs is one opportunity for intervention. Women with incarceration histories face barriers that may be unique as compared to other home visitation program participants. Compared to their peers, they may require additional support in order to achieve stable housing, as well as access to health insurance and health care. A review study by Casillas et al. (2016) found that programs aimed at families that exhibit one or more risk factors for child abuse and neglect were more impactful than those designed to generally provide support to families. Therefore, extending outreach to a sub-group known to experience increased risk of mental health challenges and substance use disorders may be of value. Analysis of 2012–2015 data from the PRAMS surveillance system indicates that a higher proportion of women with jail contact, compared to those without such contact, reported utilizing home visitation services. Of the jail contact group, about 70% had not utilized these services (Table 1). This suggests there may be a significant number of women and children that could benefit from these services who are currently not being engaged. Efforts are needed to increase engagement with these women and children. Additional studies may assist us in understanding the reasons women affected by incarceration who are eligible for home visiting services in their jurisdiction do and do not utilize such services and whether the services improve their outcomes. Findings of such studies may help inform how programs, as well as recruitment and retention strategies, might be tailored to best address the needs of this sub-group. Establishing partnerships between correctional systems, community-based organizations that serve women affected by incarceration, and early childhood home visiting programs may be a critical next step toward preventing or buffering ACEs in the lives of these women and children in ways that can impact lifelong health and well-being (CDC, 2019b).

Financial Disclosures This research did not receive any specific grant funding from agencies in the public, commercial, or not-for-profit sectors.

Conflicts of Interest The authors have no conflicts of interest to report.

Disclaimer The findings and conclusions in this report are those of the authors and do not necessarily represent the official position of the Centers for Disease Control and Prevention (CDC).

References

Ammerman, R. T. (2016). Commentary: Toward the next generation of home visiting programs – New developments and promising directions. *Current Problems in Pediatric and Adolescent Health Care, 46(4)*, 126–129.

Armstrong, K. L., Fraser, J. A., Dadds, M. R., & Morris, J. (1999). A randomized, controlled trial of nurse home visiting to vulnerable families with newborns. *Journal of Pediatrics and Child Health, 35*, 237–244.

Association of Women's Health, Obstestric, and Neonatal Nurses. (2018). AWHONN Position Statement: Nursing care of incarcerated women during pregnancy and postpartum period. *Journal of Gynecological and Neonatal Nursing, 47*(2), 236–238.

Austin, A. (2016). Is prior parental criminal justice involvement associated with child maltreatment? A systematic review. *Child and Youth Services Review, 68*, 146–153.

Avellar, S. A., & Supplee, L. H. (2013). Effectiveness of home visiting in improving child health and reducing child maltreatment. *Pediatrics, 132*, S90–S99.

Avellar, S., Paulsell, D., Sama-Miller, E., Del Grosso, P., Akers, L., & Klienman, R. (2016). *Home visiting evidence of effectiveness review: Executive summary*. Office of Planning, Research and evaluation, Administration for Children and Families, U.S. Department of Health and Human Services.

Aylward, G. P. (2014). Neurodevelopmental outcomes of infants born prematurely. *Journal of Developmental and Behavioral Pediatrics, 35(6)*, 394–407.

Barr, J. A., & Beck, C. T. (2008). Infanticide secrets: qualitative study on postpartum depression. *Canadian Family Physician, 54(12)*, 1716.e5–1717.e5.

Beauregard, J. L., Hamner, H. C., Chen, J., Avila-Rodriguez, W., Elam-Evans, L. D., & Perrine, C. G. (2019). Racial disparities in breastfeeding initiation and duration among U.S. infants born in 2015. *Morbidity and Mortality Weekly Report, 68*(34), 745–748.

Belknap, J., Lynch, S., & DeHart, D. (2016). Jail staff members' views on jailed women's mental health, trauma, offending, rehabilitation, and reentry. *The Prison Journal, 96(1)*, 79–101.

Bell, J. F., Zimmerman, F. J., Huebner, C. E., Cawthon, M. L., Ward, D. H., & Schroeder, C. A. (2004). Perinatal health service use by women released from jail. *Journal of Health Care for the Poor and Underserved, 15(3)*, 426–438.

Bronson, J., & Carson, E. A. (2019). *Prisoners in 2017*. Bureau of Justice Statistics. April: NCJ 252156. https://www.bjs.gov/content/pub/pdf/p17.pdf. Accessed 2 Oct 2019

Bronson, J., & Sufrin, C. (2019). Pregnant women in prison and jail don't count: Data gaps on maternal health and incarceration. *Public Health Reports, 134(Supplement 1)*, 57S–62S.

Brooten, D., Youngblut, J. M., Brown, L., Finkler, S. A., Neff, D. F., & Madigan, E. (2001). A randomized trial of nurse specialist home care for women with high-risk pregnancies: outcomes and costs. *American Journal of Managed Care, 7*(8), 793–803.

Browne, A., Miller, B., & Maguin, E. (1999). Prevalence and severity of lifetime physical and sexual victimization among incarcerated women. *International Journal of Law Psychiatry, 22(3-4)*, 301–322.

Casillas, K. L., Fauchier, A., Derkash, B. T., & Garrido, E. F. (2016). Implementation of evidence-based home visiting programs aimed at reducing child maltreatment: A meta-analytic review. *Child Abuse & Neglect, 53*, 64–80.

CDC. (2019a). *Preventing adverse childhood experiences: Leveraging the best available evidence*. National Center for Injury Prevention and Control, Centers for Disease Control and Prevention. https://www.cdc.gov/violenceprevention/pdf/preventingACES-508.pdf. Accessed 12 Dec 2019
CDC. (2019b). *Preventing early trauma to improve adult health*. CDC Vital Signs. www.cdc.gov/vitalsigns/aces. Accessed 12 Dec 2019
CDC. (n.d.-a). *Children benefit when parents have safe, stable, nurturing, relationships*. https://www.cdc.gov/violenceprevention/pdf/SSNRs-for-Parents.pdf. Accessed 18 June 2019.
CDC. (n.d.-b). *Essentials for childhood: Creating safe, stable, nurturing relationships for all children*. https://www.cdc.gov/violenceprevention/pdf/essentials-for-childhood-framework508.pdf. Accessed 18 June 2019.
Chapman, J., Siegal, E., & Cross, A. (1990). Home visitors and child health: Analysis of selected programs. *Pediatrics, 85*, 1059–1068.
Cole, D. (2011). Turning the corner on mass incarceration. *Ohio State Journal of Criminal Law, 9*, 27–51.
Council on Child and Adolescent Health. (1998). The role of home-visitation programs in improving health outcomes for children and families. *Pediatrics, 101(3)*, 486.
Dallaire, D. H., Woodards, A., & Kelsey, C. (2018). Impact of parental incarceration on neonatal outcomes and newborn home environments: a case-control study. *Public Health, 165*, 82–87.
Dodge, K. A., Goodman, W. B., Murphy, R. A., O'Donnell, K., & Sato, J. (2013). Randomized controlled trial of universal postnatal nurse home visiting: Impact on emergency care. *Pediatrics, 132(Supplement 2)*, S140–S146.
Dube, S. R., Felitti, V. J., Dong, M., Giles, W. H., Dong, M., & Anda, R. F. (2003). The impact of adverse childhood experiences on health problems: evidence from four birth cohorts dating back to 1900. *Preventive Medicine, 37*, 268–277.
Dumont, D. M., Wildeman, C., Lee, H., Gjelsvik, A., Valera, P. A., & Clarke, J. G. (2014). Incarceration, maternal hardship, and perinatal health behaviors. *Maternal and Child Health Journal, 18*(*9*), 2179–2187.
Earls, M. (2010). Clinical report – Incorporating recognition and management of perinatal and postpartum depression into pediatric practice. American Academy of Pediatrics. *Pediatrics, 126*(*5*), 1032–1039.
Felitti, V. J., Anda, R. F., Nordenberg, D., Williamson, D. F., Spitz, A. M., Edwards, V., … Marks, J. S. (1998). Relationship of childhood abuse and household dysfunction to many of the leading causes of death in adults: The adverse childhood experiences (ACE) study. *American Journal of Preventive Medicine, 14*(*4*), 245–258.
Feltner, C., Weber, R., Stuebe, A., Grodensky, C., Orr, C., & Viswanathan, M. (2018). *Breastfeeding programs and policies, breastfeeding uptake, and maternal health outcomes in developed countries* (Comparative effectiveness review no. 210). US Department of Health and Human Services, Agency for Healthcare Research and Quality. https://www.ncbi.nlm.nih.gov/books/NBK525106. Accessed 20 July 2019
Fergusson, D. M., Grant, H., Horwood, L. J., & Ridder, E. M. (2005). Randomized trial of the early start program of home visitation. *Pediatrics, 116(6)*, e803.
Filene, J. H., Kaminski, J. W., Valle, L., & Cachat, P. (2013). Components associated with home visiting program outcomes: A meta-analysis. *Pediatrics, 132*(02), S100–S109.
Flemington, T., & Fraser, J. A. (2016). Maternal involvement in a nurse home visiting programme to prevent child maltreatment. *Journal of Children's Services, 11*(*2*), 124–140.
Fogel, C. I. (1993). Pregnant inmates risk factors and pregnancy outcomes. *Journal of Obstetric, Gynecologic & Neonatal Nursing, 22(1)*, 33–39.
Fogel, C. I., & Belyea, M. (2001). Psychosocial risk factors in pregnant inmates: A challenge for nursing. *The Journal of Maternal/Child Nursing, 26(1)*, 10–16.
Gelfand, D. M., Teti, D. M., Seiner, S. A., & Jameson, B. (1996). Helping mothers fight depression: Evaluation of a home based intervention program for depressed mothers and their infants. *Journal of Clinical Child Psychology, 25*, 406–422.

Gilbert, L. K., Breiding, M. J., Merrick, M. T., Parks, S. E., Thompson, W. W., Dhingra, S. S., & Ford, D. C. (2015). Childhood adversity and adult chronic disease: An update from ten states and the District of Columbia, 2010. *American Journal of Preventive Medicine, 48*(3), 345–349.

Glaze, L. E., & Kaeble, D. (2014). *Correctional populations in the United States, 2013* (Publication NCJ 248479). Bureau of Justice Statistics, Office of Justice Programs. https://bjs.gov/content/pub/pdf/cpus13.pdf. Accessed 2 Oct 2019

Glaze, L. E., & Maruschak, L. M. (2008, August). *Parents in prison and their minor children* (Revised March 2010). Publication NCJ 1222984. Bureau of Justice Statistics, Office of Justice Programs. https://www.bjs.gov/content/pub/pdf/pptmc.pdf. Accessed 2 Oct 2019.

Goldfeld, S., Price, A., Smith, C., Bruce, T., Bryson, H., Mensah, F., Orsini, F., Gold, L., Hiscock, H., Bishop, L., Smith, A., Perlen, S., & Kemp, L. (2019). Nurse Home visiting for families experiencing adversity: A randomized trial. *Pediatrics, 143(1)*, e20181206.

Gomby, D. S., Culross, P. L., & Behrman, R. E. (1999). Home visiting: Recent program evaluations: Analysis and recommendations. *The Future of Children, 9*, 4–26.

Guthrie, B. (2011). Toward a gender-responsive restorative correctional health care model. *Journal of Obstetric, Gynecologic, and Neonatal Nursing, 40(4)*, 497–506.

Guthrie, K. F., Gaziano, C., & Gaziano, E. P. (2009). Toward better beginnings: Enhancing healthy child development and parent-child development and parent-child relationships in a high risk population. *Home Health Care Management and Practice, 21(2)*, 99–108.

Hammett, T. M., & Drachman-Jones, A. (2006). HIV/AIDS, sexually transmitted diseases, and incarceration among women: national and southern perspectives. *Sexually Transmitted Diseases, 33(7 Suppl)*, S17–S22.

Harrison, M. J., Kushner, K. E., Benzies, K., Kimak, C., Jacobs, P., & Mitchell, B. F. (2001). In-home nursing care for women with high-risk pregnancies: outcomes and cost. *Obstetrics and Gynecology, 97(6)*, 982–987.

Howard, D. L., Strobino, D., Sherman, S. G., & Crum, R. (2009). Timing of incarceration during pregnancy and birth outcomes: Exploring racial differences. *Maternal and Child Health Journal, 13*, 457–466.

Howard, D. L., Strobino, D., Sherman, S. G., & Crum, R. (2011). Maternal incarceration during pregnancy and infant birthweight. *Maternal and Child Health Journal, 15*, 478–486.

HRSA, Maternal and Child Health. (n.d.-a). https://mchb.hrsa.gov/maternal-child-health-initiatives/home-visiting-overview. Accessed 18 June 2019.

HRSA. (n.d.-b). *The Maternal, Infant, and Early Childhood Home Visiting Program: Program Overview.* https://mchb.hrsa.gov/sites/default/files/mchb/MaternalChildHealthInitiatives/HomeVisiting/pdf/2018-MIECHV-program-overview.pdf. Accessed 18 June 2019.

Hutchinson, K. C., Moore, G. A., Propper, C. B., & Mariaskin, A. (2008). Incarcerated women's psychological functioning during pregnancy. *Psychology of Women Quarterly, 32(4)*, 440–453.

Ip, S., Chung, M., Raman, G., Chew, P., Magula, N., DeVine, D., Trikalinos, T., & Lau, J. (2007). Breastfeeding and maternal and infant health outcomes in developed countries. In *Evidence reports technology assessments (Report No: 07-E007, April)*. Agency for Healthcare Research and Quality.

Kaeble, D. (2018). *Probation and parole in the United States, 2016*. Bureau of Justice Statistics. April, NCJ 251148. https://www.bjs.gov/content/pub/pdf/ppus16.pdf. Accessed 20 Dec 2019

Kaeble, D., & Cowhig, M. (2018). *Correctional Populations in the United States, 2016*. Bureau of Justice Statistics. April, NCJ 251211. https://www.ncjrs.gov/App/Publications/abstract.aspx?ID=273391. Accessed 2 Oct 2019

Kaiser Family Foundation. (2020). *States reporting corrections-related medicaid enrollment policies in place for prisons or Jails*. https://www.kff.org/medicaid/state-indicator/states-reporting-corrections-related-medicaid-enrollment-policies-in-place-for-prisons-or-jails/?currentTimeframe=0&sortModel=%7B%22colId%22:%22Location%22,%22sort%22:%22asc%22%7D. Accessed 13 May 2020.

Kajstura, A. (2019). *Women's mass incarceration: The whole pie 2019*. Prison Policy Initiative. https://www.prisonpolicy.org/reports/pie2019women.html. Accessed 20 Dec 2019

Kaplan, P. S., Danko, C. M., Everhart, K. D., Diaz, A., Asherin, R. M., Vogeli, J. M., & Fekri, S. M. (2014). Maternal depression and expressive communication in one-year-old infants. *Infant Behavior and Development, 37*, 98–405.

Kemp, L., Harris, E., McMahon, C., Matthey, S., Impani, G. V., Anderson, T., Schmied, V., Aslam, H., & Zapart, S. (2011). Child and family outcomes of a long-term nurse home visitation programme: A randomized controlled trial. *Archives of Disease in Childhood, 96(6)*, 533–540.

Kilburn, M. R., & Cannon, J. S. (2017). Home visiting and use of infant health care: A randomized clinical trial. *Pediatrics, 139(1)*, e20161274.

Kingston, D., Tough, S., & Whitfield, H. (2012). Prenatal and postpartum maternal psychological distress and infant development: A systematic review. *Child Psychiatry & Human Development, 43*, 683–714.

Kitzman, H., Olds, D. L., Henderson, C. R., Hanks, C., Cole, R., Tatlebaum, R., McConnochie, K. M., Sidora, K., Luckey, D. W., Shaver, D., Englehardt, K., James, D., & Barnard, K. (1997). Effect of prenatal and infancy home visitation by nurses on pregnancy outcomes, childhood injuries, and repeated childbearing: A randomized controlled trial. *Journal of the American Medical Association, 278*, 644–652.

Ko, J. Y., Rockhill, K. M., Tong, V. T., Morrow, B., & Farr, S. L. (2017). Trends in postpartum depressive symptoms—27 States, 2004, 2008, and 2012. *Morbidity Mortality Weekly Report, 66*, 153–158.

Koniak-Griffin, D., Anderson, N. L., Verzemnieks, I., & Brecht, M. L. (2000). A public health nursing early intervention program for adolescent mothers: outcomes from pregnancy through 6 weeks postpartum. *Nursing Research, 49(3)*, 130–138.

Koniak-Griffin, D., Anderson, N. L., Brecht, M. L., Verzemnieks, I., Lesser, J., & Kim, S. (2002). Public health nursing care for adolescent mothers: Impact on infant health and selected maternal outcomes at 1 year postbirth. *Journal of Adolescent Health, 30(1)*, 44–54.

Kulkarni, S. P., Baldwin, S., Lightstone, A. S., Gelberg, L., & Diamant, A. L. (2010). Is incarceration a contributor to health disparities? Access to care of formerly incarcerated adults. *Journal of Community Health, 35*, 268–274.

Lee, R. D., & Chen, J. (2017). Adverse childhood experiences, mental health, and excessive alcohol use: Examination of race/ethnicity and sex differences. *Child Abuse & Neglect, 69*, 40–48.

Lee, H., & Wildeman, C. (2013). Things fall apart: Health consequences of mass imprisonment for African American women. *Review of Black Political Economy, 40(1)*, 1–14.

Lee, J., Vlahov, D., & Freudenberg, N. (2006). Primary care and health insurance among women released from New York City jails. *Journal of Health Care for the Poor and Underserved, 17(1)*, 200–217.

Lee, R. D., Fang, X., & Luo, F. (2013). The impact of parental incarceration on the physical and mental health of young adults. *Pediatrics., 131(4)*, e1188–e1195.

Lee, R. D., D'Angelo, D. V., Dieke, A., & Burley, K. (2019, April). *Recent incarceration among parents of newborn infants: Maternal and child health outcomes*. Children of Incarcerated Parents National Conference. Phoenix, Arizona.

Lindahl, V., Pearson, J. L., & Colpe, L. (2005). Prevalence of suicidality during pregnancy and the postpartum. *Archives of Women's Mental Health, 8(2)*, 77–87.

Love, J. M., Kisker, E. E., Ross, C., Raikes, H., Constantine, J., Boller, K., … Vogel, C. (2005). The effectiveness of Early Head Start for 3 year old children and their parents: Lessons for policy and programs. *Developmental Psychology, 41*, 885–901.

Lowell, D. I., Carter, A. S., Godoy, L., Paulicin, B., & Briggs-Gowan, M. J. (2011). A randomized controlled trial of child FIRST: A comprehensive home-based intervention translating research into early childhood practice. *Child Development, 28(1)*, 193–208.

Maruschak, L. M. (2004). *Medical Problems of Jail Inmates*. Bureau of Justice Statistics. https://www.bjs.gov/content/pub/pdf/mpp.pdf. Accessed 20 Dec 2019

McMillan Dowell, C., Mejia, G. C., Preen, D. B., & Segal, L. (2019). Low birth weight and maternal incarceration in pregnancy: A longitudinal linked data study of Western Australian infants. *SSM-Population Health, 7*, 100324.

Merrick, M. T., Ford, D. C., Ports, K. A., Guinn, A. S., Chen, J., Klevens, J., Metzler, M., Jones, C. M., Simon, T. R., Daniel, V. M., Ottley, P., & Mercy, J. A. (2019). Vital Signs: Estimated Proportion of Adult Health Problems Attributable to Adverse Childhood Experiences and Implications for Prevention—25 States, 2015–2017. *Morbidity and Mortality Weekly Report, 68(44)*, 999–1005.
Muftic, L. R., & Smith, M. (2018). Sex, parental incarceration, and violence perpetration among a sample of young adults. *Journal of Interpersonal Violence, 33*(2), 316–338.
Murray, L. (1992). The impact of postnatal depression on infant development. *Journal of Child Psychology and Psychiatry, 33*(3), 543–561.
National Resource Center on Justice Involved Women. (2016). *Fact sheet on justice involved women in 2016*. Retrieved from www.cjinvolvedwomen.org/wp-content/uploads/2016/06/Fact-Sheet.pdf. Accessed 2 Oct 2019.
Nebbitt, V. E., Voisin, D. R., & Tirmazi, M. T. (2017). Early Onset of Sexual Intercourse and Parental Incarceration among African American Youth Living in Urban Public Housing. *Journal of Urban Health, 94*, 125–135.
Norbeck, J. S., DeJoseph, J. F., & Smith, R. T. (1996). A randomized trial of an empirically-driven social support intervention to prevent low birthweight among African-American women. *Social Science and Medicine, 43*(6), 947–954.
Olds, D. L., Henderson, C. R., Jr., Chamberlin, R., & Tatelbaum, R. (1986a). Preventing child abuse and neglect: A randomized trial of nurse home visitation. *Pediatrics, 78*(1), 65–78.
Olds, D. L., Henderson, C. R., Jr., Tatelbaum, R., & Chamberlin, R. (1986b). Improving the delivery of prenatal care and outcomes of pregnancy: A randomized trial of nurse home visitation. *Pediatrics, 77*(1), 16–28.
Oxford, M. L., Spieker, S. J., Lohr, M. J., & Fleming, C. B. (2016). Promoting first relationships: Randomized trial of a 10-week home visiting program with families referred to child protective services. *Child Maltreatment, 21*, 267–277.
Paynter, M. J., Drake, E. K., Cassidy, C., & Snelgrove-Clarke, E. (2019). Maternal health outcomes for incarcerated women: A scoping review. *Journal of Clinical Nursing, 28*, 2046–2060.
Porter, L. S., Porter, B. O., McCoy, V., Bango-Sanchez, V., Kissel, B., Williams, M., & Nunnewar, S. (2015). Blended infant massage-parenting enhancement program on recovering substance-abusing mothers' parenting stress, self-esteem, depression, maternal attachment, and mother-infant interaction. *Asian Nursing Research, 9*(4), 318–327.
Rikhye, K., Tyrka, A. R., Kelly, M. M., Gagne, G. G., Jr., Mello, A. F., Mello, M. F., … Carpenter, L. L. (2008). Interplay between childhood maltreatment, parental bonding, and gender effects: Impact on quality of life. *Child Abuse & Neglect, 32*(1), 19–34.
Roettger, M. E., & Boardman, J. D. (2012). Parental incarceration and gender-based risks for increased body mass index: Evidence from the National Longitudinal Study of Adolescent Health in the United States. *American Journal of Epidemiology, 175*(7), 636–644.
Sadler, L. S., Slade, A., Close, N., Webb, D. L., Simpson, T., Fennie, K., & Mayes, L. (2013). Minding the baby: Enhancing reflectiveness to improve early health and relationship outcomes in an interdisciplinary home-visiting program. *Infant Mental Health Journal, 34*(5), 391–405.
Sama-Miller, E., Akers, L., Mraz-Esposito, A., Coughlin, R., & Zukiewicz, M. (2019). *Home visiting evidence of effectiveness review: Executive Summary*. https:// www.mathematica.org/our-publications-and-findings/publications/september-2019-home-visiting-evidence-of-effectiveness-review-executive-summary. Accessed 20 Dec 2019.
Sandstrom, H. (2019). *Early Childhood home visiting programs and health*. Health Affairs Health Policy Brief, April. https://www.healthaffairs.org/do/10.1377/hpb20190321.382895/full/. Accessed 18 June 2019
Shah, M. K., & Austin, K. R. (2014). Do home visiting services received during pregnancy improve birth outcomes? Findings from Virginia PRAMS 2007–2008. *Public Health Nursing, 31*(5), 405–413.
Shlafer, R. J., Davis, L., Hindt, L. A., Goshin, L. S., & Gerrity, E. (2018). Intention and initiation of breastfeeding among women who are incarcerated. *Nursing for Women's Health, 22*(1), 64–78.

Shonkoff, J. P., & Garner, A. S. (2012). The committee on psychosocial aspects of child and family health, committee on early childhood, adoption and dependent care, and section on developmental and behavioral pediatrics. The lifelong effects of early childhood adversity and toxic stress. *Pediatrics., 129(1)*, e232–e246.

Shulman, H. B., D'Angelo, D. V., Harrison, L., Smith, R. A., & Warner, L. (2018). The pregnancy risk assessment monitoring system (PRAMS): Overview of design and methodology. *American Journal of Public Health, 108(10)*, 1305–1313.

Spieker, S. J., Oxford, M. L., Kelly, J. F., Nelson, E. M., & Fleming, C. B. (2012). Promoting first relationships: Randomized trial of a relationship-based intervention for toddlers in child welfare. *Child Maltreatment, 17*, 271–286.

Stein, A., Gath, D. H., Bucher, J., Bond, A., Day, A., & Cooper, P. J. (1991). The relationship between postnatal depression and mother-child interaction. *British Journal of Psychiatry, 158*, 46–52.

Subramanian, R., Delaney, R., Roberts, S., Fishman, N., & McGarry, P. (2015). *Incarceration's front door: The misuse of Jail in America*. Vera Institute of Justice. https://www.vera.org/publications/incarcerations-front-door-the-misuse-of-jails-in-america. Accessed 2 Oct 2019

Surkan, P. J., Ettinger, A. K., Hock, R. S., Ahmed, S., Strobino, D. M., & Minkovitz, C. S. (2014). Early maternal depressive symptoms and child growth trajectories: a longitudinal analysis of a nationally representative US birth cohort. *BMC Pediatrics, 14*, 185.

Sweet, M. A., & Applebaum, M. I. (2004). Is home visiting an effective strategy? A meta-analytic review of home visiting programs for families with young children. *Child Development, 75*, 1435–1456.

Turney, K. (2014). The consequences of paternal incarceration for maternal neglect and harsh parenting. *Social Forces, 92*(4), 1607–1636.

Turney, K. (2018). Adverse childhood experiences among children of incarcerated parents. *Children and Youth Services Review, 89*, 218–225.

Valero de Bernabe, J., Soriano, T., Albaladejo, R., Juarranz, M., Calle, M. E., Martinez, D., & Dominguez-Rojas, V. (2004). Risk factors for low birth weight: A review. *European Journal of Obstetrics & Gynecology and Reproductive Biology, 116*, 3–15.

Walmsley, R. (2018). *World prison population list* (12th ed.). Institute for Criminal Policy Research (ICPR), University of London. www.prisonstudies.org/sites/default/files/resources/downloads/wppl_12.pdf. Accessed 2 Oct 2019

Wang, E. A., White, M. C., Jamison, R., Goldenson, J., Estes, M., & Tulsky, J. P. (2008). Discharge planning and continuity of health care: Findings from the San Francisco county jail. *American Journal of Public Health, 98(12)*, 2182–2184.

Wang, E. A., Zhu, G. A., Evans, L., Carroll-Scott, A., Desai, R., & Fiellin, L. E. (2013). A pilot study examining food insecurity and HIV risk behaviors among individuals recently released from prison. *AIDS Education and Prevention, 25*(2), 112–123.

Wildeman, C. (2009). Parental imprisonment, the prison boom, and the concentration of childhood disadvantage. *Demography, 46*(2), 265–280.

Wildeman, C., Goldman, A. W., & Turney, K. (2018). Parental incarceration and child health in the United States. *Epidemiologic Reviews, 40*, 146–156.

Williams, L., & Schulte-Day, S. (2006). Pregnant in prison-the incarcerated woman's experience: A preliminary descriptive study. *Journal of Correctional Health Care, 12*(2), 78–88.

Wouk, K., Stuebe, A. M., & Meltzer-Brody, S. (2016). Postpartum mental health and breastfeeding practices: An analysis using the 2010–2011 Pregnancy Risk Assessment Monitoring System. *Maternal and Child Health Journal, 21(3)*, 636–647.

Zeng, Z. (2019). *Jail inmates in 2017*. Bureau of Justice Statistics. April, NCJ 251774. https://www.bjs.gov/content/pub/pdf/ji17.pdf. Accessed 2 Oct 2019

Testa, A. & Jackson, D.B. (2020). Incarceration exposure during pregnancy and infant health: Moderation by public assistance. The Journal of Pediatrics, 226, 251-257.

Testa, A. & Jackson, D.B. (2020). Incarceration exposure during pregnancy and infant health: Moderation by public assistance. The Journal of Pediatrics, 226, 251-257.

Adolescents with Incarcerated Parents: Toward Developmentally Informed Research and Practice

Elizabeth I. Johnson and Joyce A. Arditti

Abstract A substantial portion of the millions of American children who have experienced parental incarceration are adolescents. Research on the intergenerational consequences of parental incarceration has largely focused, however, on either pre-adolescent samples or aggregated across childhood and adolescence or adolescence and young adulthood. The result is that we know comparatively little about how parental incarceration affects well-being during this unique, critical juncture of the lifespan. Normative developmental changes in physical, cognitive, and psychosocial development can influence how adolescents think about, cope with, and respond to the experience of parental incarceration. These changes also have implications for the kinds of research questions we ask and how we develop and implement intervention programs. This chapter provides an overview of the major biological, cognitive, and psychosocial transitions that occur during adolescence and reviews existing studies on adolescents with incarcerated parents. We also provide recommendations for developmentally informed research and practice with this population.

Keywords Parental incarceration · Parents in prison · Adolescent development · Developmentally informed practice

More than five million American youth are estimated to have experienced the incarceration of a residential parent (Murphey & Cooper, 2015), a substantial portion of whom are adolescents. Analysis of data from national inmate surveys suggest that between 42.5% and 50.4% percent of minor children reported by individuals in state and federal correctional facilities are between the ages of 10 and 17 (Glaze &

E. I. Johnson (✉)
Department of Child and Family Studies, University of Tennessee, Knoxville, TN, USA
e-mail: ejohns53@utk.edu

J. A. Arditti
Department of Human Development and Family Science, Virginia Polytechnic Institute and State University, Blacksburg, VA, USA

J. Krysik, N. Rodriguez (eds.), *Children of Incarcerated Parents*, Children of Incarcerated Parents: From Understanding to Impact,
https://doi.org/10.1007/978-3-030-84713-5_2

Maruschak, 2008; Mumola, 2000). Data from the National Survey of Children's Health, a representative sample of children under the age of 18 in the United States, further suggest that 8% of all US children between the ages of 12 and 17 have lived with a parent who has been to jail or prison (Murphey & Cooper, 2015). The majority of youth experience their fathers' incarceration; however the incidence of maternal imprisonment has increased at a dramatic pace with growing numbers of youth experiencing maternal and dual (i.e., maternal and paternal) incarceration by young adulthood (Wildeman & Turney, 2014). Even these conservative estimates, which either don't reflect children with parents incarcerated in local jails or nonresident parents' contact with the criminal justice system, suggest the wide scope of parental incarceration and underscore the importance of developmentally informed research and practice with adolescents.

Although a substantial portion of the millions of American children who experience parental incarceration are adolescents, research on the intergenerational consequences of parental incarceration has largely focused on either pre-adolescent samples or aggregated across childhood and adolescence or adolescence and young adulthood. The result is that we know comparatively little about the experiences of children with incarcerated parents during adolescence, a critical juncture in the lifespan that is characterized by biological, cognitive, and psychosocial transitions. These changes present unique opportunities for the expression of both risk and resilience and have important implications for how we study and work with adolescents and their families. In this chapter, we provide a brief overview of the fundamental changes that occur during adolescence and review existing work on parental incarceration and adolescent well-being. We also offer recommendations for developmentally informed research and practice with adolescents.

A Primer on Adolescent Development

Adolescence is a critical transitional period in the lifespan that is characterized by major physical, cognitive, and psychosocial changes. Although adolescence is often synonymous with "the teen years" in popular discourse, developmental scientists conceptualize it more broadly as encompassing the time between puberty and assuming adult roles and responsibilities (Dahl et al., 2018; Steinberg, 2014). The chronological boundaries of adolescence have shifted across historical time, with contemporary researchers largely embracing the view that adolescence roughly corresponds to the second decade of life.

The changes of the second decade begin with biological, neurological, and physical processes that set the stage for cognitive and psychosocial transitions (Dahl et al., 2018). Becoming capable of reproduction is one of the biological hallmarks of adolescence, but sexual maturation is just one component of a much larger set of physical changes that occur. The hormonal changes of puberty that begin in the neuroendocrine system stimulate the development of primary and secondary sex characteristics as well as changes in height, muscle mass, body fat, and sleep patterns. These physical developments can have important implications for how adolescents think and feel about themselves, especially when they occur early or late relative to peers. Puberty typically begins around age 10 for girls and age 12 for boys (Dahl et al., 2018), but there is important variability in the onset of puberty, and research suggests that early maturation can be particularly consequential for girls' mental and physical health (Graber, 2013). Timing of pubertal maturation is influenced by a number of factors including exposure to adversities such as economic disadvantage, stress, and father absence (Deardorff et al., 2011), and there is also evidence that the effects of pubertal timing on adolescent well-being are amplified by family and neighborhood disadvantage (Ge et al., 2002). Pubertal development and timing are therefore essential considerations in studies of mental health and distress among adolescents who have experienced parental incarceration. Parallel literatures examining adolescent development and father absence further highlight the need to embed adolescent development in broader contexts of family and community life. For example, there is evidence that father absence during early childhood appeared to connect with the early timing of menarche for adolescent girls; however, this relationship was fully mediated by maternal depression and financial problems (Culpin et al., 2014). Such a finding raises interesting questions about the timing of parental incarceration and adolescent development as well as the role of family-level instabilities in mediating these effects.

Puberty-related hormones also contribute to changes in the brain during adolescence (Goddings et al., 2019). Although the brain reaches its full size by age 10, major changes in brain structure, function, and connectivity occur throughout adolescence (Dahl et al., 2018; Steinberg, 2014). Particular attention has been paid to the nature and consequences of changes in the prefrontal cortex, the region of the brain that is particularly important for sophisticated thinking abilities such as planning, weighing risks and rewards, and controlling impulses. Neural changes that occur in the prefrontal cortex during adolescence enhance how the brain processes and integrates information, and there is also evidence of gradual, increased connectivity in regions of the brain responsible for processing emotional and social stimuli. The brain is thought to be particularly "plastic" or sensitive to experience during adolescence, meaning that brain development not only shapes adolescents' experiences of rewards, relationships, and regulation but is also shaped by them (Steinberg, 2014). This also means that acute and chronic stressors related to parental incarceration such as economic and residential stability, changes in family relationships, and trauma related to witnessing a parent's arrest may alter brain structure and function in ways that could have significant consequences for well-being. Importantly, however, sensitivity to experience also applies to positive and enriching experiences, making adolescence an especially crucial time to implement interventions designed to promote developmental assets and healthy family relationships.

Changes in brain structure, function, and connectivity are accompanied by significant developments in cognitive, emotional, and self-regulatory abilities. These changes culminate in the ability to "adaptively pursue new goals and priorities that can be increasingly abstract and extend far into the future" (Dahl et al., 2018; p. 442). The emergence of more sophisticated ways of thinking such as the capacity to think abstractly and hypothetically also contributes to changes in how adolescents view themselves and their futures. Identity work has long been viewed as one of the main psychosocial tasks of adolescence (Erikson, 1968), and identity processes are closely tied to the social, cultural, and historical contexts in which young people develop (Baumeister & Muraven, 1996). The explicit and implicit messages that adolescents receive about their future possibilities often inform how they construct and work toward images of themselves in the future (Oyserman & Fryberg, 2006). Parental incarceration may shape these "possible selves" and strategies in ways that can influence academic and behavioral outcomes. Youth may view incarceration as a likely outcome or "feared possible self," especially if they live in households or neighborhoods with high concentrations of incarceration. In this vein, youth with incarcerated parents may come to endorse or internalize identities that are focused on antisocial behavior which, in turn, increases their risk for delinquent behavior (c.f., Finkeldey et al., 2020).

Changes in cognitive, emotional, and self-regulatory abilities may also change how adolescents relate to others. Relationships with parents and friends evolve in both quantitative and qualitative ways during adolescence, and adolescents' intimacy and affiliation needs are increasingly also met through romantic relationships. Adolescents begin to spend more time with friends and less time with family (Larson et al., 1996); start to value abstract concepts such as trust, closeness, and intimacy more in their friendships (Smetana & Villalobos, 2009); and increasingly look to friends rather than parents for social support (Furman & Buhrmester, 1992). These changes likely have important implications for youth disclosure decisions in the context of parental incarceration and may also influence who they look to for support surrounding parental incarceration.

Parents continue, however, to be critical influences in their children's lives throughout adolescence. Structural dimensions of parenting such as monitoring and supervision as well as more affective dimensions such as warmth, support, and responsiveness serve a number of protective functions for adolescents (Fergus & Zimmerman, 2005). Researchers have also increasingly embraced the notion that normative developmental changes in parent-child relationships can present both challenges and opportunities (Suleiman & Dahl, 2019). Challenges may potentially be magnified in the context of parental incarceration because of physical or psychological distance between adolescents and their parents, but this phase of the lifespan also provides new opportunities to repair and rebuild relationships that may have been damaged prior to or because of parental incarceration.

In sum, adolescent development is characterized by a variety of physical, cognitive, and psychosocial changes. These changes interact to transform adolescents' inner worlds and their relationships with others and have important implications for what, when, and how we study adolescent development in the context of parental incarceration. Although these changes were once thought to usher in a period of inevitable, universal turmoil, developmental scientists have long since rejected this "storm and stress" characterization (Arnett, 1999). Rather, contemporary scholars view adolescence as a period of transformation and opportunity that should also be reflected in research on adolescents with incarcerated parents.

Research on Adolescents with Incarcerated Parents

Although approximately half of children with incarcerated parents are adolescents, it is only recently that researchers have focused specifically on child well-being during adolescence (Shlafer & Poehlmann, 2010). Recent scholarship has identified a host of psychological, social, and economic harms to children that stem from parental incarceration and may proliferate into early adulthood (e.g., Foster & Hagan, 2015; Wakefield & Wildeman, 2014). The fact that harms connected to the experience of parental incarceration during childhood may be long-lasting has contributed to greater efforts on the part of social scientists to understand the implications of a parent's confinement for adolescent adjustment (Mears & Siennick, 2016). As we outline below, existing research related to the second decade of life has focused on links between parental incarceration during childhood and adolescent emotional and behavioral problems, school-related outcomes, and sexual and physical health. A handful of studies, mostly qualitative in nature, have also focused on coping and more positive indicators of well-being.

Internalizing and Externalizing Problems

The majority of research on adolescents with incarcerated parents has focused on internalizing and externalizing problems. Internalizing problems encompass inwardly directed manifestations of distress such as depression or withdrawal, whereas externalizing problems reflect outwardly directed manifestations of distress such as aggression, antisocial behavior , and substance use. Although some studies suggest that parental incarceration heightens risk for problems such as depression, anxiety, and self-injurious behaviors (Davis & Shlafer, 2017a; Swisher & Shaw-Smith, 2015), other studies suggest that differences between adolescents with histories of parental incarceration and those without are not statistically significant after controlling for other adversities (Boch et al., 2019; Murray et al., 2012; Thurman et al., 2018). A similar pattern has emerged for externalizing problems. Several studies provide evidence that incarceration heightens risk for behavior problems and serious delinquency (e.g., Murray et al., 2012; Ruhland et al., 2020; Swisher & Shaw-Smith, 2015) and that this association may increase over time (Kjellstrand & Eddy, 2011). Other studies suggest, however, that parental incarceration may be a marker of accumulated adversity but not a mechanism of risk (Boch et al., 2019; Chavira et al., 2018; Porter & King, 2015).

One explanation for these seemingly divergent findings is that between-group comparisons of youth with incarcerated parents and those without may mask important within-group variability. The effects of parental incarceration during adolescence may depend, for example, on the age at which parents were incarcerated, how long they were incarcerated, and whether incarceration was temporally proximal or distal to the outcomes being assessed. Indeed, Kjellstrand and colleagues (Kjellstrand et al., 2018; Kjellstrand et al., 2020) have found that adolescents with incarcerated parents are at varying degrees of risk for trajectories of internalizing and externalizing problems. Although some adolescents with incarcerated parents may exhibit levels of internalizing and externalizing problems that are cause for concern – either at particular points in time or across adolescence – the majority do not.

Studies on substance use and drug-related problems have generally been more consistent in showing an adverse impact of parental incarceration. Davis and Shlafer (2017b) found that adolescents with currently and formerly incarcerated parents were more likely to experiment with alcohol at an early age, binge drink, and meet criteria for substance abuse or dependence than youth without a history of parental incarceration, with effects being most pronounced for youth with currently incarcerated parents. Studies with older adolescents and emerging adults have also indicated that parental incarceration is associated with increased frequency of substance use and drug-related problems (Kopak & Smith-Ruiz, 2016; Mears & Siennick, 2016), as well as accelerated trajectories of use across the transition from adolescence to young adulthood (Roettger et al., 2010). Although studies have been consistent in showing that parental incarceration increases risk for substance use above and beyond sociodemographic adversities, we know little about the extent to which this reflects ongoing exposure to substance use norms and behaviors or whether it reflects unique risk associated, for example, with efforts to self-medicate negative emotions related to parental incarceration.

School-Based Outcomes

Attention to school-based outcomes is particularly important during adolescence given the vast amount of time that adolescents spend at school and the implications of educational outcomes during adolescence for adult economic and employment security. Two studies suggest that youth with incarcerated parents have more school-related problems than comparison youth including decreased educational engagement and connectedness, lower grades, and more exposure to disciplinary actions than comparison youth that could not be explained by differences in sociodemographic and school-level characteristics (Nichols et al., 2016; Shlafer et al., 2017). Other studies suggest, however, that between-group differences in attention problems and academic performance are not robust to the inclusion of controls for pre-incarceration performance and other adverse childhood experiences (Boch et al., 2019; Murray et al., 2012). In terms of social networks at school, results have been consistent in showing a pattern of social marginalization among youth with incarcerated parents. Specifically, youth with incarcerated parents have friendship networks that are characterized by more disadvantage, more delinquency, and less academic success than comparison youth (Bryan, 2017; Cochran et al., 2018). Finally, the most recent study on this subject suggests that parental incarceration adversely impacts behavioral and disciplinary outcomes in high school above and beyond the impact of other adversities but that effects on grades are largely due to selection (McCauley, 2020).

Sexual and Physical Health

Findings related to sexual and physical health have been consistent in suggesting that youth with incarcerated parents are at an elevated risk for problems in this domain relative to peers, even after adjusting for differences in sociodemographic characteristics. Several studies with different samples have suggested that maternal (Le et al., 2019) and paternal (Nebbitt et al., 2017; Turney & Goldberg, 2019) incarcerations are associated with an increased likelihood of early sexual debut, a finding that may reflect exposure to stress that hastens pubertal maturation and/or leads to sexual activity as a way of meeting needs for affiliation and intimacy. Khan et al. (2018) also found evidence of risk related to sexual health, observing that parental incarceration before age 8 was associated with STI/HIV risk in adolescence for Black youth as well as a modest association between parental incarceration and having multiple sexual partners during adolescence. Intriguingly, parental incarceration before the age of 8 had a stronger impact on these outcomes than incarceration that occurred between the ages of 8 and 17. Work by Hiolski et al. (2019) further indicated that patterns of physical activity, fruit and vegetable consumption, and sleep are also adversely affected by parental incarceration, even after controlling for economic hardship. Given that health risk behaviors are a major cause of morbidity among adolescents (Bennett & Bauman, 2000) and may forebode a variety of health problems later in life, these findings underscore continued investigation and attention to the mechanisms by which parental incarceration may translate into poorer profiles of physical health and well-being.

Coping and Positive Youth Development

Although the majority of research on adolescents with incarcerated parents has been problem-focused (Eddy & Reid, 2003; Shlafer et al., 2019), findings from qualitative and mixed-methods studies have suggested evidence of resilience and positive youth development. These studies suggest that youth often cope with the challenges of parental incarceration in positive, resourceful, and multifaceted ways (Berman & Steinhoff, 2012; Johnson & Easterling, 2015a; Nesmith & Ruhland, 2008). They also suggest that some youth, particularly older adolescents, manage the stress and negative affect associated with parental incarceration by attempting to exert control in their relationships with parents – and that this gives them a sense of strength and purpose (Johnson & Easterling, 2015a). Work by Johnson et al. (2018) further suggests that even youth who are exhibiting adjustment problems may also display competencies. This finding is broadly consistent with research on positive youth development (Lewin-Bizan et al., 2010) and underscores the importance of conceptualizations of adjustment that encompass both problems and competencies.

Summary

Most existing studies of adolescents have focused on between-group comparisons of youth with incarcerated parents and those without in terms of adverse outcomes. These studies have primarily focused on the effects of parental incarceration before the age of 10 on adolescent outcomes and have largely considered the impact of whether any parent (mother or father) was ever incarcerated during this time frame. Results of these studies have been mixed, with some suggesting that parental incarceration heightens risk for emotional, behavioral, academic, and health-related problems and other studies suggesting that the differences between groups reflect the impact of other adversities. Thus, whereas some studies suggest that parental incarceration may be a mechanism of risk for adolescent development, other studies raise the possibility that it may better be conceptualized as a marker of accumulated adversity or what Giordano and Copp (2015) have called "packages of risk." Most recently, an emerging body of work has moved away from focusing on between-group differences to identifying variability among youth (Johnson et al., 2018; Kjellstrand et al., 2018, 2020). In the section that follows, we offer recommendations for additional research on within-group variability that is more focused on positive youth development and sensitive to developmental processes.

Developmentally Informed Research with Adolescents

Contemporary adolescent research has been focused on identifying assets and positive youth development, capturing the diversity of adolescent experiences, and explaining how changes across domains of development interrelate and interact to shape the lives of young people (Lerner & Steinberg, 2009). Adopting these foci in the literature on adolescents with incarcerated parents has the potential to transform the way we conduct research and advance our understanding of ecological adversity and well-being during this critical phase of the lifespan. We therefore suggest that future research should focus on development in multiple domains and connections between these domains, recognize both challenges and assets, and seek to identify variability in adolescents' experiences. Specific recommendations are provided below.

Recommendation #1: Focus More on the Nature and Sources of Within-Group Variability

Although between-group comparisons have been a critically important first step in the research on adolescents with incarcerated parents, they often mask important within-group variability and detract from the equally important work of identifying the nature and sources of heterogeneity among adolescents with incarcerated parents. At the most basic level, this means recognizing that youth with incarcerated parents are a diverse population at varying degrees of risk for problematic outcomes. Moreover, parental incarceration is not equitably distributed, and racial disparities in prison populations extend to children and youth. Black youth are far more likely than White youth to experience the incarceration of a parent and of multiple family members (Wildeman, 2009; Wakefield & Wildeman, 2014). The harms that minority youth experience are speculated to stem in part from their inequitible exposure not only to parental and familial incarceration but also other adverse childhood experiences (such as poverty and neighborhood violence) (Murphey & Cooper, 2015). It is essential to acknowledge these racial disparities while also considering within-group variation and sources of resilience in the day-to-day lives of Black youth. For example, strong and close intergenerational relationships with Black youth and their caregivers promote outcomes such as school success and help youth overcome adversity (see Arditti et al., 2020, for a review). A within-group sensibility contributes to a deep consideration of how best to promote adolescent well-being and resilience and contextualizes the lives of youth by attending to their social location and sources of systematic inequality that precede and exacerbate the implications of parental incarceration. Conceptualizing incarceration as a process that unfolds over time rather than a discrete event may also be helpful in illuminating additional sources of variability among youth and helping to reconcile seemingly contradictory findings (e.g., there may be an initial increase in a depression or anxiety that levels off as adolescents and their families adjust and then may resurface during reentry).

Recommendation #2: Integrate Strengths-Based Perspectives

Research on adolescents with incarcerated parents has been, and continues to be, largely problem-focused (Eddy & Reid, 2003; Shlafer et al., 2019). Although it is essential to document the many ways in which mass incarceration harms adolescents and their families, it is also important to challenge deficit-focused perspectives and recognize youth strengths, competencies, and resilience. Although successful adaptation is often operationalized in terms of the absence of problems, resilience researchers have long emphasized the importance of studying the presence of competence in age-salient developmental tasks (Masten, 2014). The nature of competence changes across development and needs to be considered in relation to what a given society, culture, or setting values at a particular point in time for people of a given age group. Examples of competence during adolescence include establishing autonomy while remaining meaningfully connected to others, planning for the future, and completing schooling. Examining these and other adaptive outcomes will advance our ability to document the nature and predictors of resilience.

Recommendation #3: "Zero in" on Regulation and Relationships

The major changes in brain structure, function, and connectivity that occur during adolescence have significant implications for cognitive, emotional, and psychosocial development (Dahl et al., 2018; Steinberg, 2014). Given the sensitivity of the brain to experience during adolescence, investigating how, when, and why parental incarceration affects aspects of brain development and neurocognitive functioning is a critical direction for future research. Self-regulation and relationships are thought to be particularly important foci (Steinberg, 2014), yet these areas have been underexplored in research on adolescents with incarcerated parents. One particularly important direction for future research is to examine how stress, instability, and trauma around parental incarceration affect developing self-regulatory processes during adolescence. It is also essential to devote more attention to investigating the quality and protective potential of adolescents' relationships with parents, caregivers, and/or peers. Resilience scholars have long argued that healthy relationships are essential to resilience in the face of adversity (Luthar & Brown, 2007), yet we know surprisingly little about the nature and quality of adolescents' relationships before, during, and after parental incarceration. Identifying the circumstances under which relationships with peers and family members heighten or mitigate risk would provide important new information for the development of adolescent-focused intervention programs (e.g., when and how to intervene).

Recommendation #4: Investigate Developmentally Relevant Mediators and Moderators

Although attention to mediators and moderators has increased in the more general literature on children with incarcerated parents, few studies have investigated them in relation to adolescent well-being. The results of these studies suggest that youth gender and whether or not children lived with their incarcerated parent function as moderators (Swisher & Shaw-Smith, 2015; Turney & Goldberg, 2019) and also reveal that family instability following incarceration may increase risk for behavior problems which, in turn, leads to problems in other domains of functioning (Turney & Goldberg, 2019). The latter finding suggests that parental incarceration may exacerbate existing adversities and set into motion new chains of events or cascades of adversity that are important to map out in future research.

The conceptual models that have most recently emerged posit that parental incarceration has both direct and indirect effects on child outcomes and that family processes such as parenting and family stability as well as youth emotional experiences play key mediating roles (Arditti, 2016, 2018; Foster & Hagan, 2015). All of these mechanisms are plausible across infancy, childhood, and adolescence but may differ in nature and kind. For example, parental supervision and monitoring take on special significance during adolescence, and coping strategies may also fluctuate in both productive (e.g., more active and engaged coping) and unproductive (e.g., self-medication) ways. In addition, new mediators may emerge. Future expectations, for example, may be shaped by parental incarceration and also influence academic engagement and young adult outcomes. Neurocognitive processes such as executive function and emotional regulation are also sensitive to adversity during adolescence and may influence later behavioral and academic outcomes. Examples of developmentally relevant moderators that are important to investigate in future research include pubertal development and timing, peer and neighborhood contexts, coping strategies, race, ethnicity, gender, and age. An intersectional approach that acknowledges the social location of adolescents and their families would be particularly helpful in understanding how oppression and privilege shape developmental trajectories within the context of parental incarceration (Poehlmann-Tynan & Arditti, 2018).

Recommendation #5: Integrate Youth Voices and Perspectives

Qualitative studies that capture youth voices and experiences have provided more evidence of competence and adaptive coping than quantitative studies and warrant additional use in the literature on adolescents with incarcerated parents. Continuing to explore youth narratives and meaning-making not only will provide a more complete and nuanced picture of risk, competence, and resilience but may also translate into advantages for young people themselves. For example, youth-based participatory research methods may be especially valuable in that they can empower youth and harness their experiences to create change (e.g., Checkoway et al., 2003). Regardless of the specific type of qualitative method, bringing a "qualitative consciousness" into the study of adolescents' experiences related to parental imprisonment has great value given the often stigmatizing and prohibitive context of criminal justice involvement. Qualitative methods are particularly apt for studying vulnerable populations (such as justice-involved families; see, e.g., Arditti, 2015) and relevant for honoring the "voices" of adolescent research participants. Giving voice to adolescents confers greater control over their narrative – something that is consistent with the emerging autonomy that is characteristic of this developmental stage (Rich & Ginsburg, 1999). Qualitative methods aimed at eliciting thick description also provide youth with an opportunity to explore their emotions regarding their incarcerated parent, family and social changes, and feelings about their own behaviors, thereby benefitting young people themselves as well as researchers' understanding of youth meaning-making and adaptation to parental incarceration.

Developmentally Informed Practice with Adolescents

Mobilizing support for adolescents who experience parental incarceration via intervention programs is an important complement to legislative and policy changes designed to reduce incarceration and increase supports to families (Arditti & Johnson, 2020). Given the plasticity of the brain during adolescence, Steinberg (2014) argues that "we must be exceptionally thoughtful and careful about the experiences we give young people as they develop from childhood to adulthood" (p. 22). In particular, it is important that intervention programs are sensitive to changing developmental resources and needs, respectful of adolescents' desires for both autonomy and connection, and strategically focused not only on reducing risk but also increasing resilience and positive youth development. Conceptualizing adolescence as a time of opportunity and capitalizing on the resources youth can bring to the table are important dimensions as well.

Recommendation #1: Develop and Evaluate Programs That Are Specific to Adolescents

Most existing programs for youth with incarcerated parents are focused on children (Hoffman et al., 2010; Johnston, 2012; Shlafer & Poehlmann, 2010). Developing programs that specifically serve adolescents – both within and outside of correctional facilities – is critical for ensuring that their unique developmental needs are met and that they are positioned for positive transitions into adulthood. At the most basic level, this means recognizing the breadth and depth of changes that adolescents are undergoing. Adolescents' brains and bodies are developing, they are thinking about themselves and their worlds in new ways, and they are experiencing changes in relationships with parents, friends, and peers. They may also be more aware of the stigma around parental incarceration and have different needs regarding communication and control in their relationships with their parents (Johnson & Easterling, 2015a). Whereas parents and caregivers may play important gatekeeping roles during childhood, adolescents may want or need more of a say what their relationships with parents look like and when and how they have contact with them. Adolescents may also have more complicated, mixed feelings about parents being in jail and/or coming home than children (Johnson & Easterling, 2015b), in part because of cognitive developments that enable them to think in more complicated, contradictory ways and in part because they may have experienced disappointments or setbacks with parents before. Helping youth to navigate these increasingly complex feelings is vital, as is programming that educates caregivers about the changing developmental landscape and helps youth formulate and enact visions for their futures.

Another component of developmentally informed intervention is situating programs in the settings where adolescents typically spend their time. Shlafer et al.

(2017) suggest, for instance, that schools are particularly important settings for interventions such as peer support groups, tutoring, and mentoring. They also recommend that teachers and administrators are educated in issues surrounding parental incarceration and that they are informed about how to avoid perpetuating harmful assumptions and biased about families whose lives have affected by criminal justice programming. After-school programs and community-based settings such as Boys and Girls Clubs and YMCAs may also be ideal settings for programming, especially to the extent that youth are already spending time in these settings.

Recognizing that there is variability within adolescence in terms of normative developmental changes is also critical for conducting developmentally sensitive interventions. Ten-year-olds are different from 17-year-olds, for example, in a variety of ways. Seventeen-year-olds are likely spending less time with parents, moving more freely and independently in their neighborhoods, engaging in romantic relationships, and thinking about their futures in ways that 10-year-olds are not. Because so many physical, cognitive, and psychosocial changes occur during adolescence, scholars have suggested the value of conceptualizing adolescence as being comprised of a series of phases that roughly correspond to major educational transitions – early adolescence (~10–13), middle adolescence (~14–17), and late adolescence (~18–21) – and these age demarcations may also be useful in developing and targeting intervention programs.

Recommendation #2: Recognize that Adolescents Have Different Needs

A handful of recent studies indicate that there is important variability among adolescents with incarcerated parents and their families. One important implication of these findings is that youth may have varying degrees of need for services and benefit from different types of interventions. Johnson et al. (2018), for instance, observed that some youth were thriving, some were functioning well, some were both struggling and exhibiting competences, and some were exhibiting problems across multiple settings. Youth that are exhibiting difficulties across settings are likely most in need of services because they are already displaying problems, but also because their social ecologies are characterized by more contextual strains and fewer caregiver-level protective factors to offset that risk. Although the vulnerable group and their caregivers may need the most intensive level of services, the other groups may also benefit from supports to help maintain their positive trajectories as they encounter normative developmental challenges during adolescence. Additionally, some youth may need help coping with stigma or trauma around witnessing a parent's arrest, whereas others may require guidance with navigating relationships with parents or reentry. Still other youth may benefit from more universal approaches such as anti-poverty programs and assistance with basic needs (Giordano et al., 2019; Poehlmann-Tynan & Arditti, 2018) – either alone or in conjunction with more targeted interventions.

Recommendation #3: Adopt Positive Youth Development Perspectives and Approaches

In general, interventions with adolescents have focused on preventing or remediating problems rather than promoting positive growth and development (Steinberg, 2014). Given that resilience is not just about the absence of problems but also the presence of competence, it is crucial to implement programs that reflect a positive youth development (PYD) focus. This approach "emphasizes the manifest potentialities rather than the supposed incapacities of young people – including youth from the most disadvantaged backgrounds and those with the most troubled histories" and is focused on "understanding, educating, and engaging children in productive activities rather than correcting, curing, or treating them for maladaptive tendencies" (Damon, 2004; p. 15). PYD-based approaches often emphasize the development of the "5 Cs" – competence, confidence, connection, character, and caring (Lerner et al., 2005) – and have proven effective with multiply disadvantaged youth. Including youth voices and lived experiences in conversations around what they need would bolster PYD-based approaches. Just as youth voices have helped transform narratives around parental incarceration, the recognition and inclusion of their perspectives may appreciably enhance both the nature and impact of intervention programs.

References

Arditti, J. A. (2015). Situating vulnerability in research: Implications for researcher transformation and methodological innovation. *The Qualitative Report, 20*, 1568–1575.

Arditti, J. (2016). A family stress-proximal process model for understanding the effects of parental incarceration on children and their families. *Couple and Family Psychology: Research and Practice, 5*, 65–88.

Arditti, J. A. (2018). Parental incarceration and family inequality in the United States. In R. Condry & P. Schaarf-Smith (Eds.), *Prison, punishment and the family: Towards a new sociology of punishment* (pp. 41–57). Oxford University Press.

Arditti, J. A., Christian, J., & Thomas, S. (2020). Mass incarceration and Black families. In A. James (Ed.), *Black families: A systems approach* (pp. 97–112). Cognella.

Arnett, J. J. (1999). Adolescent storm and stress, reconsidered. *American Psychologist, 54, 317–326.*

Baumeister, R. F., & Muraven, M. (1996). Identity as adaption to social, cultural, and historical context. *Journal of Adolescence, 19*, 405–416.

Bennett, D., & Bauman, A. (2000). Adolescent mental health and risky sexual behavior. *British Medical Journal, 321*, 251–252.

Berman, A., & Steinhoff, R. (2012). Children's experiences of having a parent in prison: "We look at the moon and then we feel close to each other". *Analele Ştiinţifice ale Universităţii »Alexandru Ioan Cuza« din Iaşi. Sociologie şi Asistenţă Socială, 2*, 77–96.

Boch, S., Warren, B. J., & Ford, J. L. (2019). Attention, externalizing, and internalizing problems of youth exposed to parental incarceration. *Issues in Mental Health Nursing, 6*, 446–475.

Bryan, B. (2017). Paternal incarceration and adolescent social network disadvantage. *Demography, 54*, 1477–1501.

Chavira, D., Fowler, P. J., & Jason, L. A. (2018). Parenting and the association between maternal criminal justice involvement and adolescent delinquency. *Children and Youth Services Review, 87*, 114–122.

Checkoway, B., Dobbie, D., & Richards-Schuster, K. (2003). Involving young people in community evaluation research. *Community Youth Development Journal, 4*, 7–11.

Cochran, J., Siennick, S., & Mears, D. (2018). Social exclusion and parental incarceration impacts on adolescents' networks and school engagement. *Journal of Marriage and Family, 80*, 478–498.

Culpin, I., Heron, J., Araya, R., Melotti, R., Lewis, G., & Joinson, C. (2014). Father absence and timing of menarche in adolescent girls from a UK cohort: The mediating role of maternal depression and major financial problems. *Journal of Adolescence, 37*, 291–301.

Dahl, R. E., Allen, N. B., Wilbrecht, L., & Ballonoff Suleiman, A. (2018). Importance of investing in adolescence from a developmental science perspective. *Nature, 554*, 441–450.

Damon, W. (2004). What is positive youth development? *Annals of the American Academy of Political and Social Science, 591*, 13–24.

Davis, L., & Shlafer, R. J. (2017a). Mental health of adolescents with currently and formerly incarcerated parents. *Journal of Adolescence, 54*, 120–134.

Davis, L., & Shlafer, R. J. (2017b). Substance use among youth with currently and formerly incarcerated parents. *Smith College Studies in Social Work, 87*, 43–58.

Deardorff, J., Ekwaru, J. P., Kushi, L. H., Ellis, B. J., Greenspan, L. C., et al. (2011). Father absence, body mass index, and pubertal timing in girls: Differential effects by family income and ethnicity. *Journal of Adolescent Health, 48*, 441–447.

Eddy, J. M., & Reid, J. B. (2003). Adolescent children of incarcerated parents: A developmental perspective. In J. Travis & M. Waul (Eds.), *Prisoners once removed: The impact of incarceration and reentry on children, families, and communities* (pp. 233–258). Urban Institute Press.

Erikson, E. H. (1968). *Identity: Youth and crisis*. Norton.

Fergus, S., & Zimmerman, M. A. (2005). Adolescent resilience: A framework for understanding healthy development in the face of risk. *Annual Review of Public Health, 26*, 399–419.

Finkeldey, J. G., Longmore, M. A., Giordano, P. C., & Manning, W. D. (2020). Identifying as a troublemaker/partier: The influence of parental incarceration and emotional independence. *Journal of Child & Family Studies, 29*, 802–816.

Foster, H., & Hagan, J. (2015). Punishment regimes and the multilevel effects of parental incarceration: Intergenerational, intersectional, and interinstitutional models of social inequality and systemic exclusion. *Annual Review of Sociology, 41*, 135–158.

Furman, W., & Buhrmester, D. (1992). Age and sex differences in perceptions of networks of personal relationships. *Child Development, 63*, 103–115.

Ge, X., Brody, G. H., Conger, R. D., Simons, R. L., & Murry, V. M. (2002). Contextual amplification of pubertal transition effects on deviant peer affiliation and externalizing behavior among African American children. *Developmental Psychology, 38*(1), 42–54.

Giordano, P. C., & Copp, J. E. (2015). "Packages" of risk: Implications for determining the effect of maternal incarceration on child wellbeing. *Criminology & Public Policy, 14*, 157–168.

Giordano, P. C., Copp, J. E., Manning, W. D., & Longmore, M. A. (2019). Linking parental incarceration and family dynamics associated with intergenerational transmission: A life-course perspective. *Criminology*. E-pub ahead of print.

Glaze, L. E., & Maruschak, L. M. (2008). *Parents in prison and their minor children*. Bureau of Justice Statistics.

Goddings, A., Beltz, A., Peper, J. S., Crone, E. A., & Braams, B. (2019). Understanding the role of puberty in structural and functional development of the brain. *Journal of Research on Adolescence, 29*, 32–53.

Graber, J. A. (2013). Pubertal timing and the development of psychopathology in adolescence and beyond. *Hormones and Behavior, 64*, 262–269.

Hiolski, K., Eisenberg, M. E., & Shlafer, R. J. (2019). Youth self-reported health and their experience of parental incarceration. *Families, Systems, & Health, 37*, 38–45.

Hoffman, H. C., Byrd, A. L., & Kightlinger, A. M. (2010). Prison programs and services for incarcerated parents and their underage children: Results from a national survey of correctional facilities. *The Prison Journal, 90*, 397–416.

Johnson, E. I., & Easterling, B. (2015a). Coping with confinement: Adolescents' experiences with parental incarceration. *Journal of Adolescent Research, 30*, 244–267.

Johnson, E. I., & Easterling, B. (2015b). Navigating discrepancy: Youth perspectives on parental reentry from prison. *Journal of Offender Rehabilitation, 54*, 60–83.

Johnson, E. I., Arditti, J. A., & McGregor, C. (2018). Risk, protection, and adjustment among youth with incarcerated and non-resident parents: A mixed-methods study. *Journal of Child & Family Studies, 27*, 1914–1928.

Johnston, D. (2012). Services for children of incarcerated parents. *Family Court Review, 50*, 91–105.

Khan, M. R., Scheidell, J. D., Rosen, D. L., Geller, A., & Brotman, L. M. (2018). Early age at childhood parental incarceration and STI/HIV-related drug use and sex risk across the young adult lifecourse in the US: Heightened vulnerability of black and Hispanic youth. *Drug & Alcohol Dependence, 183*, 231–239.

Kjellstrand, J. M., & Eddy, J. M. (2011). Mediators of the effect of parental incarceration on adolescent externalizing behaviors. *Journal of Community Psychology, 39*, 551–565.

Kjellstrand, J., Yu, G., Eddy, M., & Martinez, C. R. (2018). Children with incarcerated parents: Developmental trajectories of externalizing problems across adolescence. *Criminal Justice & Behavior, 45*, 1742–1761.

Kjellstrand, J., Yu, G., Eddy, M., & Clark, M. (2020). Children with incarcerated parents and developmental trajectories of internalizing problems across adolescence. *American Journal of Criminal Justice, 45*, 48–69.

Kopak, A. M., & Smith-Ruiz, D. (2016). Criminal justice involvement, drug use, and depression among African American children of incarcerated parents. *Race and Justice, 6*, 89–116.

Larson, R. W., Richards, M. H., Moneta, G., Holmbeck, G., & Duckett, E. (1996). Changes in adolescents' daily interactions with their families from ages 10 to 18: Disengagement and transformation. *Developmental Psychology, 32*, 744–754.

Le, G. T., Deardorff, J., Lahiff, M., & Harley, K. G. (2019). Intergenerational associations between parental incarceration and children's sexual risk taking in young adulthood. *Journal of Adolescent Health, 64*, 398–404.

Lerner, R. M., & Steinberg, L. (2009). The scientific study of adolescent development: Historical and contemporary perspectives. In R. M. Lerner & L. Steinberg (Eds.), *Handbook of adolescent psychology: Individual bases of adolescent development* (pp. 3–14). Wiley.

Lerner, R. M., Almerigi, J. B., Theokas, C., & Lerner, J. V. (2005). Positive youth development: A view of the issues. *Journal of Early Adolescence, 25*, 10–16.

Lewin-Bizan, S., Doyle Lynche, A., Fay, K., Schmid, K., Lerner, J. V., & Lerner, R. M. (2010). Trajectories of positive and negative behaviors from early- to middle-adolescence. *Journal of Youth and Adolescence, 39*, 751–763.

Luthar, S. S., & Brown, P. J. (2007). Maximizing resilience through diverse levels of inquiry: Prevailing paradigms, possibilities and priorities for the future. *Developmental Psychopathology, 19*, 931–955.

Masten, A. S. (2014). *Ordinary magic: Resilience in development*. Guilford.

McCauley, E. (2020). Beyond the classroom: The intergenerational effect of incarceration on children's academic and nonacademic school-related outcomes in high school. *Socius*. E-pub ahead of print.

Mears, D. P., & Siennick, S. E. (2016). Young adult outcomes and the life-course penalties of parental incarceration. *Journal of Research in Crime and Delinquency, 53*, 3–35.

Mumola, C. J. (2000). *Incarcerated parents and their children*. Bureau of Justice Statistics.

Murphey, D., & Cooper, P. M. (2015). *Parents behind bars: What happens to their children?* Child Trends.

Murray, J., Loeber, R., & Pardini, D. (2012). Parental involvement in the criminal justice system and the development of youth theft, marijuana use, depression, and poor academic performance. *Criminology, 50*, 255–302.

Nebbitt, V. E., Voisin, D. R., & Tirmazi, M. T. (2017). Early onset of sexual intercourse and parental incarceration among African American youth living in urban public housing. *Journal of Urban Health, 94*, 125–135.

Nesmith, A., & Ruhland, E. (2008). Children of incarcerated parents: Challenges and resiliency, in their own words. *Children and Youth Services Review, 30*, 1119–1130.

Nichols, E. B., Loper, A. B., & Meyer, J. P. (2016). Promoting educational resiliency in youth with incarcerated parents: The impact of parental incarceration, school characteristics, and connectedness on school outcomes. *Journal of Youth & Adolescence, 45*, 1090–1109.

Oyserman, D., & Fryberg, S. A. (2006). The possible selves of diverse adolescents: Content and function across gender, race and national origin. In J. Kerpelman & C. Dunkel (Eds.), *Possible selves: Theory, research, and applications* (pp. 17–39). Nova.

Poehlmann-Tynan, J., & Arditti, J. A. (2018). Developmental and family perspectives on parental incarceration. In C. Wildeman, A. Haskins, & J. Poehlmann-Tynan (Eds.), *When parents are incarcerated: Interdisciplinary research and interventions to support children* (pp. 53–81). American Psychological Association.

Porter, L. C., & King, R. D. (2015). Absent fathers or absent variables? A new look at paternal incarceration and delinquency. *Journal of Research in Crime & Delinquency, 52*, 414–443.

Rich, M., & Ginsburg, K. (1999). The reason and rhyme of qualitative research: Why, when, and how to use qualitative methods in the study of adolescent health. *Journal of Adolescent Health, 25*, 371–378.

Roettger, M. E., Swisher, R. R., Kuhl, D. C., & Chavez, J. (2010). Paternal incarceration and trajectories of marijuana and other illegal drug use from adolescence into young adulthood: Evidence from longitudinal panels of males and females in the United States. *Addiction, 106*, 121–132.

Ruhland, E. L., Davis, L., Atella, J., & Shlafer, R. J. (2020). Externalizing behavior among youth with a current or formerly incarcerated parent. *International Journal of Offender Therapy and Comparative Criminology, 64*, 3–21.

Shlafer, R. J., & Poehlmann, J. (2010). Adolescence in the context of parental incarceration: Family, school, and community factors. In J. M. Eddy & J. Poehlmann (Eds.), *Children of incarcerated parents: A handbook for researchers and practitioners* (pp. 121–140). Urban Institute Press.

Shlafer, R. J., Reedy, T., & Davis, L. (2017). School-based outcomes among youth with incarcerated parents: Differences by school settings. *Journal of School Health, 87*, 687–695.

Shlafer, R. J., Davis, L., & Dallaire, D. H. (2019). Parental incarceration during middle childhood and adolescence. In J. M. Eddy & J. Poehlmann-Tynan (Eds.), *Handbook on children with incarcerated parents: Research, policy, and practice* (pp. 101–116). Springer.

Smetana, J. G., & Villalobos, M. (2009). Social cognitive development in adolescence. In R. M. Lerner & L. Steinberg (Eds.), *Handbook of adolescent psychology: Individual bases of adolescent development* (pp. 187–228). Wiley.

Steinberg, L. (2014). *Age of opportunity: Lessons from the new science of adolescence*. Houghton Mifflin Harcourt.

Suleiman, A. B., & Dahl, R. (2019). Parent–child relationships in the puberty years: Insights from developmental neuroscience. *Family Relations, 68*, 279–287.

Swisher, R. R., & Shaw-Smith, U. R. (2015). Paternal incarceration and adolescent well-being: Life course contingencies and other moderators. *Journal of Criminal Law & Criminology, 104*, 929–959.

Thurman, W., Johnson, K., Gonzalez, D. P., & Sales, A. (2018). Teacher support as a protective factor against sadness and hopelessness for adolescents experiencing parental incarceration: Findings from the 2015 Texas Alternative School Survey. *Children & Youth Services Review, 88*, 558–566.

Turney, K., & Goldberg, R. (2019). Paternal incarceration and early sexual onset among adolescents. *Population Research and Policy Review, 38*, 95–123.

Wakefield, S., & Wildeman, C. (2014). *Children of the prison boom: Mass incarceration and the future of American inequality*. Oxford University Press.

Wildeman, C. (2009). Parental imprisonment, the prison boom, and the concentration of childhood disadvantage. *Demography, 46*, 265–280.

Wildeman, C., & Turney, K. (2014). Positive, negative, or null? The effects of maternal incarceration on children's behavioral problems. *Demography, 51*, 1041–1068.

Family- and School-Based Sources of Resilience Among Children of Incarcerated Parents

Jennifer E. Copp, Peggy C. Giordano, Monica A. Longmore, and Wendy D. Manning

Abstract Recent empirical evidence has identified deleterious effects of parental incarceration across multiple domains, both among young children and across the transition to adulthood. It is also increasingly recognized that children experiencing parental incarceration confront numerous additional adversities, including a broad range of family risks. Disentangling the effect of parental incarceration from these other problematic parental behaviors and family dynamics has become a focus within the incarceration effects tradition. Yet the overwhelming focus on "risk" has detracted attention from the sources of resilience that may be present within these populations. Drawing on five waves of structured interview data from the Toledo Adolescent Relationships Study (TARS), and in-depth qualitative interviews with a subset of young adults who had experienced parental incarceration while growing up, we examined associations between parental incarceration and educational attainment, relationship commitment, and emotional well-being, adjusting for family- and school-based sources of resilience. We found that parental incarceration is associated with lower levels of educational attainment and relationship commitment and higher levels of depressive symptoms. However, indicators of school attach-

This research received support from the Eunice Kennedy Shriver National Institute of Child Health and Human Development (HD036223, HD044206, and HD66087); the National Institute of Justice, Office of Justice Programs, US Department of Justice (Award Nos. 2009-IJ-CX-0503 and 2010-MU-MU-0031), and in part by the Center for Family and Demographic Research, Bowling Green State University, which has core funding from the Eunice Kennedy Shriver National Institute of Child Health and Human Development (R24HD050959). The opinions, findings, and conclusions or recommendations expressed in this publication are those of the authors and do not necessarily reflect those of the Department of Justice or the official views of the National Institutes of Health.

J. E. Copp (✉)
College of Criminology and Criminal Justice, Florida State University, Tallahassee, FL, USA
e-mail: jcopp@fsu.edu

P. C. Giordano · M. A. Longmore · W. D. Manning
Department of Sociology, and Center for Family and Demographic Research, Bowling Green State University, Bowling Green, OH, USA

J. Krysik, N. Rodriguez (eds.), *Children of Incarcerated Parents*, Children of Incarcerated Parents: From Understanding to Impact,
https://doi.org/10.1007/978-3-030-84713-5_3

ment and family stability contributed to more positive outcomes along these dimensions, even among youth exposed to parental incarceration. Furthermore, school-based sources of resilience appeared to be particularly central to overcoming this particular form of risk (i.e., parental incarceration), as reflected in the greater impact of school attachment on educational outcomes of children with parental incarceration backgrounds. We discussed the implications of our findings for future research and programmatic efforts targeting children of incarcerated parents.

Keywords Parental incarceration · Resilience · Young adulthood · Mixed-methods

Introduction

There are currently more than two million individuals incarcerated in America's prisons and jails, the majority of whom are parents of minor children (Glaze & Maruschak, 2008). This corresponds to roughly 2.7 million children with a currently incarcerated parent or 1 in 28 (Pew Charitable Trusts, 2010). If we extend our focus beyond those with a currently incarcerated parent, approximately ten million children have experienced a parent's imprisonment at some point in their lives (The Annie E. Casey Foundation, 2016). In light of the unprecedented number of children exposed to parental incarceration, there has been increasing scholarly attention to its latent consequences. Recent empirical evidence has demonstrated harmful effects of parental incarceration on the next generation, both among young children and across the transition to adulthood (e.g., Foster & Hagan, 2015a; Haskins, 2016; Mears & Siennick, 2016; Murray et al., 2012; Turney & Lanuza, 2017; Turney & Wildeman, 2015). Given disparities in arrests and the use of incarceration on the basis of race/ethnicity and social class, scholars (Gaston, 2019; Wakefield & Wildeman, 2013; Wildeman, 2009) have argued that parental incarceration may contribute to widening inequalities among children.

Yet, at the same time, other scholars (Giordano & Copp, 2015; Giordano et al., 2019) have noted that children experiencing parental incarceration confront numerous additional adversities, including a broad range of family risks such as parents' substance use and mental health problems as well as economic strain and family instability. Exposure to such adversities may both precede and follow periods of arrest and confinement and often form a more ongoing presence in the lives of youths with direct implications for their own development and well-being. Indeed, a key challenge within the incarceration effects tradition has been to disentangle the effect of parental incarceration from these other problematic parental behaviors and family dynamics (Copp et al., 2018; Giordano et al., 2019; Johnson & Easterling, 2012).

The continued focus on this plethora of risks has had the effect of obscuring the sources of family and individual strengths or resilience that may be present within these populations. Recent research has revealed that children vary in their reactions to parental incarceration, such that some children are more likely to experience negative outcomes following a parent's confinement. Focusing on the parents' propensities for experiencing incarceration, findings from this work has suggested that the deleterious consequences of incarceration are concentrated among children whose parents are least likely to experience incarceration (Turney, 2017; Turney & Wildeman, 2015). Others similarly have focused on behaviors and characteristics of the parent(s), including parenting stress, emotional well-being, the extent and type of offending, and levels of paternal involvement to explain variability in the outcomes of children exposed to parental incarceration (e.g., Antle et al., 2020; Geller et al., 2012; Wildeman, 2010). Yet there remains a need to examine child-specific factors to further develop our understanding of the conditions under which children of incarcerated parents fare better (or worse).

The current study followed up on some recent empirical work that has highlighted heterogeneity in parental incarceration effects and earlier qualitative studies that have concluded that not all children of incarcerated parents experience deleterious consequences. We drew on structured data collected in connection with a study of a large heterogeneous sample of youths followed up five times from adolescence to young adulthood and in-depth qualitative interviews with a subset of these individuals who had experienced parental incarceration. We explored the role of school and family factors associated with more successful transitions among the subset of individuals whose lives have been touched by parental incarceration. We considered young adult educational attainment (high school completion), relationship commitment, and emotional well-being as three anchors of a more successful transition to adulthood. As the sample included individuals who have not experienced parental incarceration, our analyses explored the degree to which resilience factors may be specific to overcoming this form of risk or parallel resiliency processes as observed across the sample as a whole.

Background

Parental Incarceration and Child Well-Being

Prior research on parental incarceration and child well-being has identified deleterious consequences associated with a parent's confinement across a range of domains, including children's behavioral, psychological, and educational outcomes. These broad conclusions are based on the findings of research conducted over the past few decades and that span multiple disciplines and methodological approaches. Using survey data from the Fragile Families and Child Wellbeing Study (FFCWB), scholars (Geller et al., 2012; Wildeman, 2010) have identified a link between parental incarceration and youths' physical aggression. This aligns well with the findings of several mixed-methods and qualitative studies, which suggested that children with incarcerated parents exhibit more frequent externalizing behavioral problems, such as aggression, delinquency, and behavioral concerns in school (Braman, 2007; Siegel, 2011). Similar support has been provided for the association between parental incarceration and children's internalizing behaviors, particularly during middle childhood and beyond. Results from a systematic review of research on parental imprisonment found that children of incarcerated parents were roughly twice as likely as their peers to exhibit internalizing problems, including depressive symptoms and anxiety (Murray et al., 2009). A handful of more recent studies in the incarceration effects tradition has corroborated these earlier findings, suggesting that parental incarceration may lead to increases in mental health problems during the adolescent years (e.g., Aaron & Dallaire, 2010; Hagan & Foster, 2012; Haskins, 2015; Turney, 2017). These findings coalesce with earlier qualitative research on the impact of incarceration on families (Arditti et al., 2003; Braman, 2007), which found that children with parental incarceration backgrounds often reported feelings of depression and other symptoms of internalizing problems.

Scholars also have considered the effects of parental incarceration on children's educational outcomes in an attempt to identify potential ways in which a parent's confinement may lead to reductions in children's life chances. Although much of this work has focused on younger samples, with particular attention to outcomes including children's test scores, grade retention, and school placement (Haskins, 2016; Turney & Haskins, 2019), results of studies drawing on samples of older adolescents and young adults similarly have found that parental incarceration is associated with lower levels of educational attainment (Hagan & Foster, 2012). In line with this longer life-course lens on incarceration effects, researchers have argued that parental incarceration may have consequences for youths' successful transitions to adulthood even beyond the educational realm (e.g., Foster & Hagan, 2015b; Lee et al., 2013; Roettger et al., 2011; Turney & Lanuza, 2017). Yet few studies have focused on relational considerations despite the centrality of romantic relationships to successful adulthood transitions. In a couple of exceptions, using data from the National Longitudinal Study of Adolescent to Adult Health, researchers have examined transitions to marriage (Turney & Lanuza, 2017) and cohabitation (Mears & Siennick, 2016). Findings from this work have suggested that young adults with parental incarceration backgrounds were more likely to form cohabiting unions, but were no less likely to marry. Given the ubiquity of cohabiting unions, and the reality that the majority of young adults spend some time in a cohabiting union (Manning et al., 2019; Manning & Stykes, 2015), it is limiting to construe transitions to cohabitation as itself a harmful relationship development. Instead, research is needed that includes attention to a range of relationship perspectives and dynamics, particularly the overall level of commitment that characterizes these romantic ties. The level of commitment is particularly important, as prior research (e.g., Umberson et al., 2010; Waite & Gallagher, 2001) has shown that stable romantic relationships are associated with health and longevity, as well as reduced involvement in various forms of antisocial behavior.

Heterogeneous Effects of Parental Incarceration

Overall, the existing evidence has suggested that the children of incarcerated parents fare worse in multiple respects, as documented above. However, some studies have found evidence of a null effect (particularly those focused on maternal incarceration) (Wildeman & Turney, 2014), while others have argued that parental incarceration may actually benefit some children (e.g., Siegel, 2011; Turanovic et al., 2012). In an effort to reconcile these findings, scholars increasingly have focused on variability in parental incarceration effects, with several attempts to identify the conditions under which exposure to a parent's confinement confers risk. Variation in the effects of parental incarceration has been documented in a series of qualitative studies (e.g., Arditti, 2012; Giordano, 2010; Siegel, 2011) and has more recently made its way into quantitative research on incarceration effects.

In two related studies based on the FFCWB study, Turney (2017) and Turney and Wildeman (2015) examined heterogeneity in parental incarceration effects as a function of parents' likelihood of experiencing incarceration. Across these studies, the authors found that the effects of parental incarceration on child well-being, including externalizing behaviors, internalizing behaviors, and juvenile delinquency (maternal incarceration only), were concentrated among children who were least at risk of experiencing a parent's imprisonment. Consistent with this line of research, others have considered whether specific parental characteristics contribute to variation in children's behavioral problems. In an earlier investigation, Wildeman (2010) exploring the link between paternal incarceration and children's physical aggression found that the positive effect of paternal incarceration on boys' aggression varied according to the father's offense type and use of violence in the home. That is, paternal incarceration was a stronger predictor of boys' physical aggression when fathers were incarcerated for non-violent offenses and did not report using physical violence with the boys' mothers. More recent work in the incarceration effects tradition (e.g., Haskins et al., 2018; Turney & Haskins, 2019) has called for additional attention to "variability" to more clearly articulate the pathways through which parental incarceration transmits risk to the next generation.

Resilience Among Children of Incarcerated Parents

Findings based on the above studies of parental incarceration effects have revealed a pattern of heightened risk but also have highlighted that not all young people exposed to these stresses and disadvantages inevitably experience negative outcomes as they develop and begin to mature into adulthood. This suggests the importance of investigating child perspectives and experiences that presage more favorable trajectories (see, e.g., Nesmith & Ruhland, 2008; Nichols et al., 2016).

The more general research tradition focused on resilience cuts across numerous types of stresses and adversities the child may face, ranging from poverty to natural disasters to chronic illness. In a recent overview of resilience research, Luthar and Eisenberg (2017) focused heavily on the presence of family strengths that included "nurturing, loving" interactions with parents and the development of positive coping strategies on the part of both the parent and child. This central focus on positive parenting dynamics clearly is warranted and is recognized as a key healthy child development. However, where the referent is children who have experienced parental incarceration, prior qualitative and quantitative studies have indicated that the family system is tested severely by the parent's incarceration (Geller et al., 2009; Rodriguez, 2016; Turanovic et al., 2012), as well as the broader pattern of behavior that generally is linked to criminal justice contact (Giordano et al., 2019). Researchers (Bronson et al., 2017) also have shown either that a high percentage of offenders report using drugs at the time of arrest or that they have a history of substance abuse problems. This suggests not only that the child may have been exposed to some of the concomitants of a drug-involved lifestyle but that substance abuse may not model the positive coping strategies that are referenced in the resilience literature. Accordingly, "home-life" factors that may distinguish this population may relate more to basic issues such as maintaining a relatively stable living situation, in spite of the parent's difficulties. It is also important to include attention to the child's experiences outside the family that may be associated with more favorable adolescent and young adult outcomes.

The school is one such extra-familial domain that has clear potential, as engagement with and success in academia serve as a pipeline to later prosocial activities (college, full-time employment) and enhance the odds of affiliating with prosocial companions and later developing a stable, committed relationship with a romantic partner. Prior research has provided a basis for focusing on school factors. For example, early on Zingraff et al. (1994), in a larger study of child abuse victims, found that while child abuse was significantly associated with delinquency, school performance mediated these effects.

The Current Study

Using quantitative and qualitative data from the Toledo Adolescent Relationships Study (TARS), we examine the association between parental incarceration and three indicators of a successful adulthood transition: (1) educational attainment, (2) relationship commitment, and (3) depressive symptoms. After establishing linkages between exposure to a parent's imprisonment and these young adult outcomes, we consider whether indicators of family- (family support, stability of family circumstances) and school-based (school attachment, school performance) resilience processes contribute to more positive outcomes across these dimensions, controlling for youth's exposure to parental incarceration. Recognizing that resiliency processes may be especially key to overcoming the risks associated with parental incarceration, we examine whether the effects of the family- and school-based sources of resilience identified in this investigation operate similarly or differently for youth with and without a background of parental incarceration.

Data and Methods

This research drew on data from the Toledo Adolescent Relationships Study (TARS), which is based on a stratified random sample of 1321 adolescents and their parents/guardians. The sampling frame of the TARS study encompassed 62 schools across 7 school districts. The initial sample was drawn from the enrollment records of registered students in the 7th, 9th, and 11th grades in Lucas County, Ohio. School attendance, however, was not a requirement for inclusion in the study. The stratified, random sample was devised by the National Opinion Research Center and included over-samples of Black and Hispanic adolescents. The TARS data were collected in the years 2001, 2002, 2004, 2006, and 2011. The analyses relied primarily on structured interviews conducted in connection with the first and fifth wave of interviews (2001 and 2011), but a parent questionnaire administered at the first interview provided information about parental incarceration and family sociodemographic characteristics. The analytic sample included all those who participated in the wave 5 interview (n = 1021), with the following exceptions. Respondents who did not identify as non-Hispanic Black, non-Hispanic White, or Hispanic were excluded due to small cell sizes (n = 26). In addition, we excluded a single respondent who had incomplete information on the items used to assess depressive symptoms. The final analytic sample comprised 997 respondents, including 535 women and 462 men.[1] Analyses of relationship commitment were restricted to respondents reporting on a current or recent (within past 2 years) relationship and thus excluded an additional 77 respondents (n = 920, 502 women and 418 men).

At waves 1, 3, 4, and 5, we chose a subsample of respondents to participate in the in-depth qualitative component of the study (n = 93, n = 92, n = 97, n = 102). For the current analyses, we drew on qualitative interviews from wave 5 and targeted respondents with parental incarceration backgrounds (n = 43). Although we focused on the qualitative interviews at wave 5, as they align with our young adult outcomes and reflect on the full adolescent and young adult periods, we also examined the content of qualitative interviews that were conducted with respondents who had parental incarceration backgrounds at earlier waves (n = 22) (for more information on the qualitative interview selection and procedure, see Giordano et al., 2019).

---

[1] The TARS data contain little missing data. For example, after the sample restrictions were made, data on the dependent variables and sociodemographic characteristics was complete. Less than 2% of observations were missing information on the resilience processes included in this investigation. Mean imputation was used to account for these few missing values.

Measures

Dependent Variables Educational attainment referred to the highest level of education obtained by the respondent at the time of the wave 5 interview. We dichotomized responses to distinguish between respondents who reported completing high school and those who did not (1 = yes). Relationship commitment, assessed with a single item at wave 5, asked: "How often have you seriously considered ending your relationship with X?" Responses ranged from 1 "never" to 5 "very often." We measured *depressive symptoms* using a revised 6-item version of the Center for Epidemiological Studies Depressive Symptoms Scale (CES-D) (Radloff, 1977). We asked respondents how often each of the following was true during the past 7 days: "you felt that you could not shake off the blues," "you had trouble keeping your mind on what you were doing," "you felt lonely," "you felt sad," "you had trouble getting to sleep or staying asleep," and "you felt that everything was an effort." Responses ranged from 1 "never" to 8 "every day" ($\alpha = .85$).

Parental Incarceration During the parent questionnaire administered at the time of the wave 1 interview, parents received the following prompt: "Many children experience changes in their living situation. The following are examples of such changes. For each experience, please circle the number of times your child has had that experience." Included in this series was the following: "One of your child's parents was sent to prison." Responses ranged from 1 "never" to 5 "four or more times." *Parental incarceration*, based on a dichotomized version of this item, indicated whether the focal child had ever experienced a parent's imprisonment (1 = yes).

Resilience Processes We measured school attachment as the mean of two items from the wave 1 interview. We asked respondents about their level of agreement with the following: "I feel close to people at school," and "I feel like I am part of my school." Responses ranged from 1 "strongly disagree" to 5 "strongly agree." *School performance*, also assessed at the time of the wave 1 interview, was taken as the mean of the following two items: "good grades are important to me," and "I try hard in school." Responses ranged from 1 "strongly disagree" to 5 "strongly agree."

During the parent questionnaire administered at wave 1, we asked parents how often they do the following in the average month: (1) "praise your child," (2) "hug your child," (3) "have an enjoyable time with your child," (4) "spend time working on a project together with your child," (5) "spend time in leisure activities with your child away from home," and (6) "have private talks with your child." Responses ranged from 1 "never" to 5 "very often." *Parental support* was taken as the mean of these six items (alpha = .84).

We measured *stability of living circumstances* with a 10-item summed scale from the wave 1 parent questionnaire. It included parents' responses to the series of items referenced above assessing changes in children's living situation. In particular, we asked parents about the number of times that their child experienced the following: (1) "your child and other family members moved to a different house"; (2) "a relative (other than a parent or sibling), friend, or boy-/girlfriend moved into your child's home"; (3) "your child went to live with her/his other parent (if parents not living in the same household) or another relative"; (4) "your child was placed in a juvenile detention facility"; (5) "one of your child's siblings moved to his/her own home or went away to school"; (6) "one of your child's parents spent more than a week in a hospital or treatment facility"; (7) "child welfare officials took your child away from her/his parents"; (8) "your child moved in with a friend's (or boy-/girlfriend's) family"; (9) "your child ran away"; or (10) "your child moved into his or her own apartment." Responses ranged from 1 "never" to 5 "four or more times." We first dichotomized and then summed the responses, such that the final scale represented a count of the number of changes in living situation experienced by respondents ranging from 0 to 10.

We included controls for a range of sociodemographic characteristics including *gender*; *age*, measured in years using a continuous variable reported from respondent's age at wave 5; as well as three categorical variables to measure race/ethnicity including *non-Hispanic White* (contrast category), *non-Hispanic Black*, and *Hispanic*. Family structure (wave 1) is based on four dichotomous variables indicating whether the respondent lived with *two biological parents* (contrast category), a *single parent*, *step-parent*, or some "*other*" family configuration at the time of the first interview. We controlled for socioeconomic status using the highest level of education reported in the wave 1 parent questionnaire. Because the parental sample consisted primarily of women, we referred to this measure as "mother's education" and is represented by four dichotomous variables including *less than high school*, *high school* (contrast category), *some college*, and *college or more*.

Analytic Strategy

We estimated zero-order logistic and OLS regression models examining relationships between parental incarceration and young adults' reports of educational attainment, relationship commitment, and depressive symptoms. Next, we examined the influence of resilience processes on each of the young adult outcomes in nested models. Model 2 added the indicators of resilience processes (i.e., school attachment and performance, parental support, and stability of family circumstances) as a block. A final model included parental incarceration, resilience processes, and sociodemographic characteristics. In supplemental analyses, we considered whether the family- and school-based resilience processes operated similarly for youths with and without a background of parental incarceration.

Results

Quantitative Findings

Table 1 showed the means/percentages and standard deviations of all variables used in the analysis, as well as the range of each variable. Nearly one in ten respondents (9.83%) experienced parental incarceration prior to the first interview wave, based on self-reports. Average levels of school attachment and school performance were 3.76 and 4.17, respectively. Individuals with parental incarceration backgrounds, compared to their peers, scored significantly lower on school attachment ($p < .05$), but scores were similar on self-reported school performance. Additionally, average levels of parental support were 3.72, suggesting that parents, on average, engaged "often" with their children, and these scores were similar according to parental incarceration. Respondents reported experiencing high levels of stability of family circumstances, as the average score on this indicator was roughly 8 (reflecting "never" having experienced 8 of the 10 potential changes in living circumstances assessed). However, respondents with and without parental incarceration backgrounds significantly differed on this indicator, such that those exposed to parental incarceration experienced significantly more instability in their living/household circumstances than their peers without such experience. Refer to Table 1 for additional information on the remaining covariates, including comparisons by parental incarceration.

Zero-order models (Table 2) focused on the implications of parental incarceration for key young adult anchors of a more successful transition, including educational attainment, relationship commitment, and emotional well-being. At the zero order, parental incarceration was associated with lower odds of high school completion, lower levels of relationship commitment, and greater depressive symptoms. Additionally, school attachment and performance indicators were significantly associated with all three outcomes, such that those who were more attached to school and exhibited higher levels of school performance were more likely to graduate from high school, to report higher levels of relationship commitment, and to report fewer depressive symptoms at the time of the wave 5 interview. Family resilience was generally not associated with the outcomes; however, one exception was that family stability was associated with greater educational attainment.

Focusing first on the models predicting educational attainment, model 2 examined the influence of parental incarceration and the family- and school-based resilience processes on the odds of high school completion. Net of school attachment/performance, parental support and stability of family circumstances, and the association between parental incarceration remained significant, suggesting that respondents with a background of parental incarceration are less likely to graduate from high school. In addition, school attachment and stability of family circumstances were both positively associated with educational attainment, controlling for parental incarceration. A final model included the full roster of sociodemographic characteristics. After controlling for age, gender, race/ethnicity, mother's education, and

Table 1 Descriptive statistics for the full sample and by the experience of parental incarceration

	Full sample			PI (n = 98)		No PI (n = 899)
	Means/ percentages	SD	Range			
Dependent variables						
Educational attainment	91.78%			79.59%	***	93.10%
Relationship commitment	3.873	1.14	1–5	3.586	*	3.903
Depressive symptoms	2.419	1.35	1–8	2.810	**	2.376
Parental incarceration	9.83%			–		–
Resilience processes						
School attachment	3.762	0.78	1–5	3.571	*	3.783
School performance	4.171	0.69	1–5	4.056		4.183
Parental support	3.727	0.67	1–5	3.627		3.738
Stability of family circumstances	8.06	1.47	0–10	6.694	***	8.207
Sociodemographic characteristics						
Age	25.395	1.84	22 – 29	25.153		25.422
Gender						
Male (ref. category)				38.78%		47.16%
Female	53.66%			61.22%		52.84%
Race/ethnicity						
Non-Hispanic white (ref. category)				34.69%	***	70.08%
Non-Hispanic black	22.27%			44.90%	***	19.80%
Hispanic	11.13%			20.41%	**	10.12%
Mother's education						
Less than high school	10.73%			18.37%	*	9.90%
High school (ref. category)				26.53%		33.37%
Some college	33.70%			45.92%	**	32.37%
College or more	22.87%			9.18%	***	24.36%
Family structure						
Two biological parents (ref. category)				14.29%	***	57.73%
Single parent	21.36%			32.65%	**	20.13%
Step parent	13.24%			21.43%	*	12.35%
Other family	11.94%			31.63%	***	9.79%

Source: Toledo Adolescent Relationships Study (TARS)
*$p < .05$; **$p < .01$; ***$p < .001$

family structure, the effect of parental incarceration was no longer significant. However, two of the resilience processes were significantly associated with the odds of high school completion in this full model. In particular, school performance and stability of family circumstances were associated with greater odds of graduating high school, net of the other variables included in this investigation.

Table 2 Odds ratios and coefficients for the logistic and OLS regressions of resilience processes on young adult outcomes among youth exposed to parental incarceration during childhood

	Educational attainment			Relationship commitment			Depressive symptoms		
	Zero order	Model 2	Model 3	Zero order	Model 2	Model 3	Zero order	Model 2	Model 3
Parental incarceration	0.289***	0.424**	0.646	−0.317*	−0.263	−0.014	0.433**	0.392**	0.233
Resilience processes									
School attachment	1.414**	1.220*	1.125	0.201***	0.179***	0.119*	−0.242***	−0.201***	−0.173**
School performance	1.656***	1.411	1.641**	0.120*	0.061	0.127*	−0.197**	−0.135*	−0.177**
Parental support	1.397	1.220	1.321	−0.028	−0.060	−0.005	0.022	0.067	0.046
Stability of family circumstances	1.353***	1.224**	1.197*	0.037	0.009	−0.003	−0.031	0.007	0.024
Sociodemographic characteristics									
Age	1.132*		1.288***	0.043*		0.056**	−0.015		−0.027
Gender (male)									
Female	1.173		1.256	−0.031		−0.053	0.054		0.077
Race/ethnicity (non-Hispanic white)									
Non-Hispanic Black	0.356***		0.540*	−0.752***		−0.669***	0.430***		0.346**
Hispanic	0.308***		0.546	−0.220		−0.163	0.157		−0.007
Mother's education (high school)									
Less than high school	0.357***		0.408**	−0.179		−0.078	0.370*		0.282
Some college	1.117		1.189	−0.151		−0.119	0.104		0.072
College or more	7.323**		5.188**	0.154		0.008	−0.146		−0.053
Family structure (bio parents)									
Single parent	0.371**		0.629	−0.454***		−0.222*	0.119		−0.075

	Educational attainment			Relationship commitment			Depressive symptoms		
	Zero order	Model 2	Model 3	Zero order	Model 2	Model 3	Zero order	Model 2	Model 3
Step parent	0.472*		0.775	−0.270*		−0.136	0.383**		0.281*
Other family	0.208***		0.530	−0.266*		−0.017	0.347*		0.123
Intercept		0.152	0.000***		3.118***	1.836**		3.390***	3.908***
Model X^2		36.74***	91.93***						
R^2					0.03	0.10		0.03	0.06

Source: Toledo Adolescent Relationships Study (TARS)
*$p < .05$; **$p < .01$; ***$p < .001$

Although the findings from the zero-order models indicated a significant association between parental incarceration and relationship commitment, the effect of parental incarceration is no longer significant after controlling for resilience processes (relationship commitment, model 2). Furthermore, of the resilience processes, school attachment has a significant and positive effect on relationship commitment. This effect remained significant in a full model, net of sociodemographic characteristics. This finding is of particular note, as it indicates that the positive value of school attachment reaches beyond the narrow confines of educational attainment, as reflected in the previous models. Finally, controlling for other factors, the link between school performance and relationship commitment was significant and positive.

In a final set of models, we examined the effect of parental incarceration on depressive symptoms. Similar to the findings from the zero-order analyses described above, we identified a significant and positive association between parental incarceration and depressive symptoms, after accounting for resilience processes. The school-related resilience factors continued to exert a negative influence on depressive symptoms in model 2, net of parental incarceration. The negative influence of the school attachment and performance indicators persisted in a full model, controlling for the full range of study variables. However, including the sociodemographic characteristics attenuated the association between parental incarceration and depressive symptoms.

Taken together, these findings revealed significant associations between parental incarceration and the young adult outcomes considered in this investigation; however, these associations were attenuated following the inclusion of resilience processes and, to an even greater extent, sociodemographic indicators. The findings also revealed that resilience processes are associated with more positive outcomes across educational, relational, and emotional domains. In particular, the school-related factors, school attachment and school performance, contributed to greater odds of educational attainment (school performance), higher levels of relationship commitment, and fewer depressive symptoms, even net of parental incarceration and sociodemographic indicators.

To explore whether the family- and school-based resilience factors were unique to overcoming exposure to parental incarceration or conversely, whether they represent more general resiliency processes for youths from all backgrounds, we estimated a series of interactions in supplemental models. In general, the interaction effects of the different resilience factors on young adult outcomes were non-significant, suggesting that the observed linkages between school attachment, school performance, family stability, and the different markers of a successful transition were similar among youths with and without parental incarceration. However, there were two notable exceptions. In particular, we found that the effect of school attachment on educational attainment was stronger among youths with a parental incarceration background, while school performance was a stronger predictor of relationship commitment among those who had not experienced parental incarceration.

The former finding is of interest, as developing a positive connection to the school may be more important to children of incarcerated parents precisely because they lack the high levels of parental social capital and family resources that may otherwise propel youths moving forward. In effect, their success is more dependent on their own engagement relative to more advantaged peers. With respect to relationship commitment, the significant interaction described above likely reflected the reality that school performance is a more straightforward pathway to becoming involved in a committed, long-term relationship among more advantaged youths. In contrast, young people whose backgrounds included parental incarceration and its attendant adversities and who are, nevertheless, highly focused on their educational pursuits may not feel that they have as many relationship options during their young adult years. At the same time, these youths may also clearly recognize that their choices in terms of who they may eventually partner with are limited and may seldom include a wide array of people who are going to be a positive influence in their lives. Recognizing that dynamics such as intimate partner violence, infidelity, drug and alcohol abuse, and partner criminality are relatively common among young people who grow up in contexts of extreme disadvantage (Edin & Kefalas, 2011), the more high-achieving among those exposed to parental incarceration may not be able to translate their educational achievements into a more stable partnership.

Examples from the Qualitative Analyses

Analyses of in-depth interviews with a subset of the respondents who had experienced parental incarceration revealed numerous family stresses and disadvantages, including parental substance use problems, chronic economic disadvantages, and at times deviance across the wider network of family members. Discussions of these broader and at times all-encompassing problems added to the stresses that related directly to parental incarceration itself. Yet some respondents managed to navigate the transition to adulthood in spite of this virtual panoply of disadvantages. These teens developed a strong identity in contrast to that of their family members but backed this up with a commitment to academic achievement as a way to cement a different way of life:

> I don't want to be like this [her mom's life]. Period. It's like she smoked and sold drugs and… so's everybody in my family. It seems like it. So, if like that inspires me to just do what you gotta do no matter what. Don't drop [out]. I don't want to have no kids neither. I mean my brother's got five kids. No house, no car, no license, no life insurance, no medical insurance. I'm like no! I don't want to have to worry. I don't want to struggle. I just want to go about my daily life. Like ok my mom ain't got no car. She's like I don't know how I'm gonna get food today… [Cheryl]

Although Cheryl focused on the importance of staying in school, it is interesting to note that this respondent paired this determination with a commitment to avoid an early pregnancy as well (*I don't want to have no kids either…my brother's got five kids*). As the interview progressed, responses to questions about her relationship with her boyfriend revived the discussion of the importance of school as a pathway to a more favorable adult life. For example, Cheryl indicated that she frequently gave advice to her boyfriend of 5 years Kevin. Kevin's own family background was difficult (*she wasn't the best of moms to me, so he's just moving to different schools…*). Yet she described her admonitions about staying in school regardless of these difficulties:

> "You need not to become a statistic," meaning as in cuz he's done got in trouble with Juvey… You need to get a state id…so he got that and then I said "go to school." Go to school, get that diploma…no matter what you think gotta have that diploma. I'm telling him that and he's like ok…if you don't do that you'll be a statistic…I don't want you to become that. I know I don't want to become that.

This kind of encouragement is important for understanding the progress Kevin has made, but also for reinforcing themes that motivated her own choices and emphases (*I don't want you to become that. I know I don't want to become that).*

Although the young people who focused on academic success provided the most straightforward link to the findings based on the structured data as described above, those who had not done well often expressed regrets as they considered the "paths not taken." This provides a window on the continued difficulties experienced by young respondents who had not focused heavily on academic achievement:

> The smart 18-year-olds when I was in high school were planning their colleges and they're probably doing very well for themselves now. All the time I spent smoking pot and screwing around and skipping school, I really could have spent more time investing in what I really wanted to do with my life. The first day of first grade I got kicked out for playing with some kid and I kicked him in the mouth…knocked his tooth out on accident and ever since then I kept going to different schools, and different schools getting kicked out. [Brian]

Brian indicated that he is less involved in things that could get him in trouble with the law now, "even though I may not have a college degree or a high school diploma." Nevertheless, while this respondent expressed a general commitment to settling into a more prosocial way of life, some of the basic elements are not in place. For example, he lived for a time in an abandoned house, and during part of that time, his mother came to live with him, as she also did not have a place to live. His life was closely monitored because he was on probation, and "I didn't have that car running," which made securing a job that much more difficult. Neither Brian nor Cheryl could reliably count on high levels of family support, but within that framework Cheryl appears to be better positioned to develop a solid footing during her young adult years.

The in-depth interviews with young adults who experienced incarceration also highlight the interrelationships between life course outcomes and experiences we have considered as distinct variables in the analyses. For example, records indicate that Jessica's mother had been incarcerated during her teen years, and she lived with her grandmother most of the time. At age 28, she indicated to the interviewer that she had recently moved into her own small apartment but was having difficulty making ends meet (*God it has turned me into a worry-wart, nervous wreck…I worry about next month's bills*). In addition to these new concerns, Jessica expresses regret about the kinds of relationships she had formed during the previous years and expressed a desire for something more serious (*the security, that, you know, that's your man, only your man*). Instead, she reflected on previous boyfriends that have not positioned her well in terms of this type of commitment:

> Gosh, I look back now, and I'm like…what was a doing with him, and oh…why would I have sex with him? I think that they were young punks. They were your average, on the streets, trying to make a buck, in the bars, with the flashy cars and the rims, and the loud music. I was into that…that's what I was looking for. And now, it's like man, with that comes this, that, and the other. When they're out here selling drugs and stuff like that…Half the people that I did sleep with they were either in and out of jail, or on drugs, or sold drugs, or you know they had terrible family relationships and they already had a kid or their baby's mom…

Although the lack of a stable relationship and economic concerns may be a source of stress, Jessica's narrative also highlighted that the risk factors typically positioned as "early family experiences" do not necessarily fade into the background. In the excerpt below, Jessica makes clear that her mother's difficulties have extended into her young adult years, and these contributed as well to a lack of emotional well-being:

> I think that my mom is a little bit jealous of me. For the first time, the other day, she told me she was proud of me [Jessica recently found a job]. We were driving down the street, she had just got out of prison, so she was clear, she didn't have no drugs in her system, no alcohol, no nothing. And I looked over at her, and I was like staring at her, and I'm like who, me? You, you're proud of me? Wait, OK I just heard that…You know, I'm like…my mom doesn't tell me things like that…you know she will do drugs, or you know, she has no respect for herself, but she sets my standards higher…that's what you're supposed to be doing, but yet she don't do it. And it's just like, I'm getting to the point where, I love my mom…but just the drugs and the fast life and the men, beating her up.
>
> [Interviewer: Do you feel pulled into her drama?]
>
> Yes, I do…If she gets beat up by her boyfriend, the first person she's calling is me. Crying, he just beat me up, this that and the other, and that's my mother! I love her and I still care for her, so I'm gonna run to her, and try to comfort her. That's my mommy…you know what I mean? But I'm getting to the point, where I can't deal no more. It's starting to be a burden on me. I'm losing sleep over my mom.

Discussion

Research over the past few decades has focused considerable attention on the harms associated with children's exposure to parental incarceration. In comparison, relatively little work has considered the potential sources of resilience among this population. In light of recent research identifying heterogeneity in parental incarceration effects, a logical extension of the parental incarceration literature is to consider the specific factors and/or processes that contribute to more positive functioning among youths despite their backgrounds, which often include not only parental incarceration but other interrelated adversities and family-based risks.

In the current investigation, we have attempted to contribute to existing research on parental incarceration and resilience by narrowing in on a set of family- and school-based sources of resilience that may operate as conduits to improved functioning among youth as they make the transition to adulthood. Consistent with prior research, we found that respondents with a history of parental incarceration fare worse across the different outcomes included in this investigation. In particular, parental incarceration was associated with reduced odds of high school completion, lower levels of relationship commitment, and greater depressive symptoms at the zero order; however, these associations were attenuated following the inclusion of family background indicators. Furthermore, resilience processes were important contributors to young adult well-being. Of the different resilience factors, the school-based indicators appeared to be particularly salient, as better performance in school was associated with improved educational, relational, and mental health outcomes. Even controlling for school performance, school attachment contributed to greater relationship commitment and fewer depressive symptoms. Thus, relative to the family-based sources of resilience, school factors appeared to emerge as a sort of "universal leveler," improving the outcomes of children with and without parental incarceration backgrounds alike.

Although these school factors have been shown to improve life chances across a number of prior studies, results of interaction models described above suggest that school attachment may matter to an even greater extent among children of incarcerated parents. That is, attachment to school among youths exposed to parental incarceration was more strongly related to educational attainment. We argued that as compared to their more advantaged peers who may rely heavily on their parents to access social capital and other resources, young people with parental incarceration backgrounds must rely on their own engagement within the schools to achieve a level of academic success. We also found that school performance was a stronger predictor of relationship commitment among youths who had not experienced parental confinement. Whereas more advantaged youths may require greater levels of education to achieve relationships, educational attainment may be less of a prerequisite for those from more disadvantaged backgrounds.

That the indicator of parental support did not contribute to improved young adult well-being is particularly notable, as it contrasts with much of the emphasis within existing theorizing and programming in this area. Much of the literature on parental incarceration has centered on the centrality of attachment processes, and the argument that poor outcomes observed among children with incarcerated parents may be due to the lack of attachment (the idea of attenuated bonds) that occurs as a result of the incarceration experience. Yet these findings demonstrate that variability in the character of the parent-child relationship, conceptualized here as parental support, was not a strong predictor of the young adult outcomes. The existing literature has also focused heavily on the extreme contexts of disadvantage that often characterize the family and broader community contexts of children exposed to parental incarceration. It is well established that children of incarcerated parents are more disadvantaged than their peers. Yet the findings of the current investigation suggest that enhancing the stability of family circumstances within these families can lead to improved outcomes—particularly in the educational realm.

Despite the contributions of the current investigation, a handful of limitations are worth noting. First, the measures of academic performance were limited, as they were based on respondents' subjective accounts of their efforts in school and the importance of good grades. A comprehensive treatment of school-based sources of resilience would benefit from the inclusion of objective indicators of academic achievement. Second, while our intention was to explore family- and school-based resilience processes and their influence on adulthood transitions among youths with and without exposure to parental incarceration, we recognize that peer influence is also particularly salient during this period. Thus, research is needed that considers peer factors associated with a more successful transition among youths with a background that includes parental incarceration. In this investigation, we wanted to focus on these "basics" of adult development; however, a remaining question is how parental incarceration and these sources of resilience figure into young adult involvement in offending or alcohol/substance use—behaviors more reflective of direct transmission processes.

Family dynamics clearly are important to a comprehensive understanding of healthy youth development, and parents generally continue to play a key role in the successful adulthood transitions of their young adult children. Yet from a programmatic perspective, the findings of our investigation suggest that efforts focused on maintaining or enhancing parent-child bonds (e.g., visiting programs), while generally beneficial, may not fully address the complex needs of children exposed to parental incarceration. In particular, our results provide support for the need to encourage academic performance (and engagement), as these school-based factors not only are direct pipelines to academic success but also provide a connection to prosocial activities and contexts. Thus, beyond playing a shaping role in the educational paths of young people, the school can serve to channel individuals' affiliations, providing a peer context that often represents a contrast to the social ties of parents and other family members. Efforts to improve the outcomes of children with a history of parental incarceration may include certain school-wide initiatives to enhance the overall climate; however, more targeted interventions for at-risk youth will likely need to be implemented alongside broader school-level changes. These may include providing an adult advocate to help students address any barriers to academic success and encouraging classroom teachers to provide the necessary supports to enhance youths' educational outcomes (Dynarski et al., 2008; Ecker-Lyster & Niileksela, 2016).

Long-term, a multifaceted approach is needed that addresses factors linked directly or indirectly to the odds that parents will face criminal justice exposure. This will necessarily include the provision of high-quality drug treatment, development of more effective programs that focus on violence in the home, and increased reliance on non-judicial strategies for handling emotional distress/mental illness. In addition, housing insecurity is generally deleterious but has a particularly devastating impact on children's lives at school and opportunities to form positive relationships with peers. A consistent, stable family environment will provide the basis for more favorable choices during adolescence that then enhance the likelihood of achieving along conventional lines, specifically educational attainment.

References

Aaron, L., & Dallaire, D. H. (2010). Parental incarceration and multiple risk experiences: Effects on family dynamics and children's delinquency. *Journal of Youth and Adolescence, 39*(12), 1471–1484.

Antle, K., Gibson, C. L., & Krohn, M. D. (2020). The mediating role of family dynamics in the relationship between paternal incarceration and child behavior problems. *Journal of Crime and Justice, 43*, 1–20.

Arditti, J. A. (2012). *Parental incarceration and the family: Psychological and social effects of imprisonment on children, parents, and caregivers*. New York University Press.

Arditti, J. A., Lambert-Shute, J., & Joest, K. (2003). Saturday morning at the jail: Implications of incarceration for families and children. *Family Relations, 52*(3), 195–204.

Braman, D. (2007). *Doing time on the outside: Incarceration and family life in urban America*. University of Michigan Press.

Bronson, J., Stroop, J., Zimmer, S., & Berzofsky, M. (2017). *Drug use, dependence, and abuse among state prisoners and jail inmates, 2007–2009*. United States Department of Justice, Office of Juvenile Justice and Delinquency Prevention.

Copp, J. E., Giordano, P. C., Manning, W. D., & Longmore, M. A. (2018). Parental incarceration and child well-being: Conceptual and practical concerns regarding the use of propensity scores. *Socius, 4*, 1–12.

Dynarski, M., Clarke, L., Cobb, B., Finn, J., Rumberger, R., & Smink, J. (2008). *Dropout prevention: A practice guide (NCEE 2008-4025)*. National Center for Education Evaluation and Regional Assistance, Institute of Education Science, U.S. Department of Education.

Ecker-Lyster, M., & Niileksela, C. (2016). Keeping students on track to graduate: A synthesis of school dropout trends, prevention, and intervention initiatives. *The Journal of At-Risk Issues, 19*(2), 24–31.

Edin, K., & Kefalas, M. (2011). *Promises I can keep: Why poor women put motherhood before marriage*. University of California Press.

Foster, H., & Hagan, J. (2015a). Punishment regimes and the multilevel effects of parental incarceration: Intergenerational, intersectional, and interinstitutional models of social inequality and systemic exclusion. *Annual Review of Sociology, 41*, 135–158.

Foster, H., & Hagan, J. (2015b). Maternal and paternal imprisonment and children's social exclusion in young adulthood. *The Journal of Criminal Law and Criminology, 105*(2), 387–429.

Gaston, S. (2019). Producing racial disparities: A study of drug arrests across place and race. *Criminology, 57*(3), 424–451.

Geller, A., Garfinkel, I., Cooper, C. E., & Mincy, R. B. (2009). Parental incarceration and child well-being: Implications for urban families. *Social Science Quarterly, 90*(5), 1186–1202.

Geller, A., Cooper, C. E., Garfinkel, I., Schwartz-Soicher, O., & Mincy, R. B. (2012). Beyond absenteeism: Father incarceration and child development. *Demography, 49*(1), 49–76.

Giordano, P. C. (2010). *Legacies of crime: A follow-up of the children of highly delinquent girls and boys*. Cambridge University Press.

Giordano, P. C., & Copp, J. E. (2015). 'Packages' of Risk: Implications for Determining the Effect of Maternal Incarceration on Child Well-being. *Criminology & Public Policy, 14*(1), 157–168.

Giordano, P. C., Copp, J. E., Manning, W. D., & Longmore, M. A. (2019). Linking parental incarceration and family dynamics associated with intergenerational transmission: A life-course perspective. *Criminology, 57*(3), 395–423.

Glaze, L. E., & Maruschak, L. M. (2008). *Parents in prison and their minor children*. U.S. Department of Justice, Office of Justice Programs.
Hagan, J., & Foster, H. (2012). Intergenerational educational effects of mass imprisonment in America. *Sociology of Education, 85*(3), 259–286.
Haskins, A. R. (2015). Paternal incarceration and child-reported behavioral functioning at age 9. *Social Science Research, 52*, 18–33.
Haskins, A. R. (2016). Beyond boys' bad behavior: Paternal incarceration and cognitive development in middle childhood. *Social Forces, 95*(2), 861–892.
Haskins, A. R., Amorim, M., & Mingo, M. (2018). Parental incarceration and child outcomes: Those at risk, evidence of impacts, methodological insights, and areas of future work. *Sociology Compass, 12*(3), e12562.
Johnson, E. I., & Easterling, B. (2012). Understanding unique effects of parental incarceration on children: Challenges, progress, and recommendations. *Journal of Marriage and Family, 74*(2), 342–356.
Lee, R. D., Fang, X., & Luo, F. (2013). The impact of parental incarceration on the physical and mental health of young adults. *Pediatrics, 131*(4), e1188–e1195.
Luthar, S. S., & Eisenberg, N. (2017). Resilient adaptation among at-risk children: Harnessing science toward maximizing salutary environments. *Child Development, 88*(2), 337–349.
Manning, W. D., & Stykes, J. B. (2015). *Twenty-five years of change in cohabitation in the U.S., 1987–2013 (FP-13-12)*. National Center for Family & Marriage Research. Retrieved from https://www.bgsu.edu/content/dam/BGSU/college-of-arts-andsciences/NCFMR/documents/FP/FP-15-01-twenty-five-yrs-cohab-us.pdf
Manning, W. D., Joyner, K., Hemez, P., & Cupka, C. (2019). Measuring Cohabitation in National Surveys. *Demography, 56*, 1195–1218.
Mears, D. P., & Siennick, S. E. (2016). Young adult outcomes and the life-course penalties of parental incarceration. *Journal of Research in Crime and Delinquency, 53*(1), 3–35.
Murray, J., Farrington, D. P., Sekol, I., & Olsen, R. F. (2009). Effects of parental imprisonment on child antisocial behaviour and mental health: A systematic review. *Campbell Systematic Reviews, 5*(1), 1–105.
Murray, J., Farrington, D. P., & Sekol, I. (2012). Children's antisocial behavior, mental health, drug use, and educational performance after parental incarceration: A systematic review and meta-analysis. *Psychological Bulletin, 138*(2), 175–210.
Nesmith, A., & Ruhland, E. (2008). Children of incarcerated parents: Challenges and resiliency, in their own words. *Children and Youth Services Review, 30*(10), 1119–1130.
Nichols, E. B., Loper, A. B., & Meyer, J. P. (2016). Promoting educational resiliency in youth with incarcerated parents: The impact of parental incarceration, school characteristics, and connectedness on school outcomes. *Journal of Youth and Adolescence, 45*(6), 1090–1109.
Pew Charitable Trusts. (2010). *Collateral costs: Incarceration's effect on economic mobility*. The Pew Charitable Trusts.
Radloff, L. S. (1977). The CES-D scale: A self-report depression scale for research in the general population. *Applied Psychological Measurement, 1*, 385–401.
Rodriguez, N. (2016). Bridging the gap between research and practice: The role of science in addressing the effects of incarceration on family life. *The ANNALS of the American Academy of Political and Social Science, 665*(1), 231–240.
Roettger, M. E., Swisher, R. R., Kuhl, D. C., & Chavez, J. (2011). Paternal incarceration and trajectories of marijuana and other illegal drug use from adolescence into young adulthood: Evidence from longitudinal panels of males and females in the United States. *Addiction, 106*(1), 121–132.
Siegel, J. A. (2011). *Disrupted childhoods: Children of women in prison*. Rutgers University Press.
The Annie E. Casey Foundation. (2016). *A Shared Sentence: The devastating toll of parental incarceration on kids, families and communities*. The Annie E. Casey Foundation.

Turanovic, J. J., Rodriguez, N., & Pratt, T. C. (2012). The collateral consequences of incarceration revisited: A qualitative analysis of the effects on caregivers of children of incarcerated parents. *Criminology, 50*(4), 913–959.
Turney, K. (2017). The unequal consequences of mass incarceration for children. *Demography, 54*(1), 362–389.
Turney, K., & Haskins, A. R. (2019). Parental incarceration and children's well-being: Findings from the Fragile families and child well-being study. In J. M. Eddy & J. Poehlmann-Tynan (Eds.), *Handbook on children with incarcerated parents* (pp. 53–64). Springer.
Turney, K., & Lanuza, Y. R. (2017). Parental incarceration and the transition to adulthood. *Journal of Marriage and Family, 79*(5), 1314–1330.
Turney, K., & Wildeman, C. (2015). Detrimental for some? Heterogeneous effects of maternal incarceration on child well-being. *Criminology & Public Policy, 14*(1), 125–156.
Umberson, D., Crosnoe, R., & Reczek, C. (2010). Social relationships and health behavior across the life course. *Annual Review of Sociology, 36*, 139–157.
Waite, L. J., & Gallagher, M. (2001). *The case for marriage: Why married people are happier, healthier, and better off financially*. Random House Digital, Inc..
Wakefield, S., & Wildeman, C. (2013). *Children of the prison boom: Mass incarceration and the future of American inequality*. Oxford University Press.
Wildeman, C. (2009). Parental imprisonment, the prison boom, and the concentration of childhood disadvantage. *Demography, 46*(2), 265–280.
Wildeman, C. (2010). Paternal incarceration and children's physically aggressive behaviors: Evidence from the Fragile families and child wellbeing study. *Social Forces, 89*(1), 285–309.
Wildeman, C., & Turney, K. (2014). Positive, negative, or null? The effects of maternal incarceration on children's behavioral problems. *Demography, 51*(3), 1041–1068.
Zingraff, M. T., Leiter, J., Johnsen, M. C., & Myers, K. A. (1994). The mediating effect of good school performance on the maltreatment-delinquency relationship. *Journal of Research in Crime and Delinquency, 31*(1), 62–91.

Part II
The Meso System

The Forgotten: The Impact of Parental and Familial Incarceration on Fragile Communities

Jennifer Wyatt Bourgeois, Jasmine Drake, and Howard Henderson

Abstract Incarceration is no longer an uncommon experience in the United States for racial and ethnic minorities or for the poor. Close to half of US adults have been impacted by the incarceration of a family member, and as many as 10 million children have experienced the incarceration of a parent at some point in their lives. Children and families are the forgotten victims of incarceration and are confronted with many challenges due to the incarceration of their parent(s) or family member. The purpose of this chapter is to provide a review of the current research on parental, familial, and the lesser-known reality of sibling incarceration. Additionally, this chapter will discuss the historical context of family separation in the periods before and after slavery. Informed by this research, we suggest different approaches for examining the impacts of parental and familial incarceration in fragile communities in an effort to change the narrative from one of disadvantage to resiliency.

Keywords Parental incarceration · Familial incarceration · Fragile · Slavery · Family separation

Introduction

The incarceration of a parent has impacted more than five million children in the United States (Murphey & Cooper, 2015). The list of barriers in communities impacted by incarceration is lengthy (Bourgeois & Henderson, 2019; Clear, 2007; Western & Wildeman, 2009). Incarceration is shared between the person imprisoned and the family members left behind. The forgotten are the millions of children and family members on the other side of the correctional facility walls who endure

J. W. Bourgeois (✉) · J. Drake · H. Henderson
Texas Southern University, Houston, TX, USA
e-mail: jennifer.bourgeois@tsu.edu

J. Krysik, N. Rodriguez (eds.), *Children of Incarcerated Parents*, Children of Incarcerated Parents: From Understanding to Impact,
https://doi.org/10.1007/978-3-030-84713-5_4

the spillover consequences of incarceration (Correa et al., 2019; Elderbroom et al., 2018). Notably, parental incarceration affects children in fragile or disadvantaged communities at a disparate rate. Disadvantaged communities are areas in which residents are impacted by poverty, low educational attainment, homelessness, and limited financial resources (Center for Advancing Opportunity, 2019; Clear, 2007; Wilson, 2012). In the context of this chapter, our definition of fragile communities is consistent with the Center for Advancing Opportunity's definition: residents living in areas that have limited opportunities and many barriers that prevent social mobility. In more cases than not, these obstacles are due to involvement with the criminal justice system. Among the millions of children that have experienced parental incarceration, the number is the highest among Black children, children living in poverty, and children living in rural areas. At some point after birth, 1 in 14 children have resided with a parent who was incarcerated. In comparison, one in nine Black children experienced an incarcerated parent, which is almost double compared to White children (Murphey & Cooper, 2015). Research has shown that the incarceration of a parent negatively affects children's physical and mental health (Davis & Shlafer, 2017; Gaston, 2016; Murray et al., 2012; Turnanovic & Rodriguez, 2017; Tasca et al., 2014; Turney, 2014). Children exposed to parental incarceration also have a higher likelihood of future involvement in the criminal justice system (Burgess-Proctor et al., 2016; Kopak & Ruiz, 2016; Novero et al., 2011; Mears & Siennick, 2016; Roettger & Swisher, 2011; Will et al., 2014, 2016).

The trauma of losing a parent due to incarceration is often overlooked. Previous research has suggested that children who have experienced the incarceration of a parent are more likely to have experienced other adverse childhood experiences (Balistreri & Alvira-Hammond, 2016; Bethell et al., 2017). An adverse childhood experience (ACE) is a traumatic experience that impacts children under the age of 18, such as abuse or neglect (Felitti, 2009). Past research has linked adverse childhood experiences to negative outcomes such as chronic health conditions, mental health, risky behaviors, and infectious diseases. Children whose parents are incarcerated suffer from stigma, shame, and the attachment of negative labels (Phillips & Gates, 2011). Turney (2018) found that approximately 32.5% of children have been exposed to at least one adverse childhood experience (ACE). ACEs are separated into three categories: abuse (physical, emotional, or sexual), neglect (physical or emotional), and household dysfunction (mental illness, domestic violence, divorce, household incarceration, or substance abuse). Whether short term or long term, when a parent is removed from a household, the entire family feels the effect. Families are subjected to countless hardships such as instability in the home, financial burdens, and physical and mental health-related issues. These hardships add to already difficult situations in fragile communities.

The authors' lived experiences with parental and sibling incarceration prompted our interest in the collateral consequences of incarceration. Our unfortunate familiarity with having a parent or sibling involved with the criminal justice system led us to ponder the notion of resiliency, single-parent households, and the spillover effects of incarceration on children and families. Parental incarceration research focuses heavily on negative outcomes. Few studies have identified what separates resilient children and families from those that succumbed to the negative effects of incarceration. Current studies about parental and familial incarceration fail to address the topic comprehensively. Commonly used surveys such as the Fragile Families and Child Well-Being Study, National Longitudinal Study of Adolescent to Adult Health, Survey of Inmates in State and Federal Correctional Facilities, and National Survey of Children's Health survey were not specifically designed for parental incarceration research. Therefore, the aforementioned surveys, although they contain valuable information, fail to address the spillover effects of incarceration on children and families at length.

The purpose of this chapter is to review the current research about parental, familial, and sibling incarceration. The chapter will commence with a brief discussion about the historical context of separation of families and the prevalence of individuals impacted by incarceration. The second part of the chapter will focus on the specific impacts of parental, familial, and sibling incarceration. Behind the shadows of incarcerated individuals are the forgotten: millions of children, siblings, and families who have experienced the trauma of parental and family incarceration (The Annie Casey Foundation, 2016). This chapter aims to serve as a resource for researchers, practitioners, and policymakers by emphasizing the importance of interdisciplinary, culturally responsive, and localized approaches to parental incarceration research. Unfortunately, the normalcy of crime and systematic barriers in certain underserved communities has led to incarceration being relatively common. However, by using different research approaches, we can begin a new conversation about breaking the intergenerational cycle of incarceration in disadvantaged communities and redirect the discourse toward data-driven solutions targeted toward fostering resiliency for children, families, and communities impacted by incarceration. Our approach recognizes that if the resiliency of children and families is the focus of future research, there is an opportunity for communities to shift from fragility to stability.

Historical Perspective of Family Separation

The historical context of family separation has deep roots in slavery (Northup, 1968; Williams, 2012). Four hundred years ago, Africa was invaded. People were kidnapped, sold, and traded, and families were separated. Family separation during slavery is documented in letters, newspaper want ads, and slave narratives. The selling of family members was used by slave owners for reasons such as settling debt or as a form of punishment. Families lived in constant fear that their families would be separated. On a regular basis, slave auctions were points of separation between enslaved African children and parents and husbands and wives (Williams, 2012). This form of punishment was intentional and used as a way to continue to control and oppress individuals, while destroying the family structure. The largest slave sale that resulted in the tearing apart and separation of men, women, and children took place in Georgia in 1859. Referred to as "The Weeping Time," it was a dreadful form of punishment used to pay the debts of a plantation owner (Bailey, 2017; DeGraft-Hanson, 2010).

After emancipation, the newspaper was used as a means for families to try to locate one another. Researchers from Villanova University's Department of History located and compiled several old newspapers with Information Want Ads after the Civil War depicting families' attempts of reunification after slavery was abolished. There was a notable change in postwar criminal justice practices. Although the Thirteenth Amendment abolished slavery, forced labor remains a form of punishment. After emancipation, slavery was no longer the means for controlling marginalized groups; rather, mass incarceration became the New Jim Crow (Alexander, 2010). This new form of slavery equated punishment with breaking the law. If a person committed a crime, their punishment was in the form of servitude (DuBois, 2013). The same system that abolished slavery was altered to keep Blacks as indigent servants and as property owned by Whites. States used the backbones of Blacks and profited by their labor through the convict-lease system. The convict-lease system has several parallels with the present state of incarceration. Yet again, families were separated and relationships were disrupted.

Despite recent measures taken to right the wrongs of the era of mass incarceration, families across the nation are still feeling the impact of family separation as a result of the war on drugs and harsh on punishment laws from the 1980s and 1990s. Although millions of children have experienced the incarceration of a parent at some point in their lives, some children are more likely than others to face this type of separation from one or both of their parents. A child's race or ethnicity, socioeconomic status, and type of offense increase the likelihood of parental incarceration. Communities with high concentrated areas of poverty have exacerbated rates of parental incarceration (Wildeman et al., 2018). Following is a discussion about the frequency of parental, family, and sibling incarceration.

The Prevalence of Parental Incarceration

Estimating the number of children impacted by the incarceration of a parent is not an easy task. Point-in-time estimates range from as low as 2 million upwards to 10 million children that have been impacted by the incarceration of a parent at some point during their lives. Currently, there are approximately 2.3 million people in correctional facilities, with the figure rising to almost 6 million when probation and parole are included (Sawyer & Wagner, 2020). In 2021, the Bureau of Justice Statistics (BJS) published a report about parents in prison using information from the 2016 Survey of Prison Inmates. Approximately 684,5000 imprisoned people were recognized as parents in both state and federal prisons. Females made up the majority of state and federally imprisoned parents (58%) (Maruschak et al., 2021). In the previous BJS special report about parents and their minor children, the number of mothers incarcerated doubled between 1991 and 2007. Four out of 10 fathers were Black (46%). Nearly half of mothers incarcerated were White (48%), and

Black and Hispanic mothers represented 28% and 19%, respectively. During 1991–1997, the most rapid increase for individuals in prison with children was noted at 44% (Glaze & Maruschak, 2008).

The rate of fathers incarcerated between 1991 and 2007 saw an increase of 77%, while during the same time period, mothers saw an increase by 122% (Glaze & Maruschak, 2008). There has been a notable change in the incarceration of females from 2000 to 2009. This change is significant because research shows that the primary caregiver of children with an incarcerated parent is the mother. The highest incarceration rate of women in the world is in the United States. Although 4% of the women's population is in the United States, the United States represents over 30% of the female incarceration population in the world (Kajstura, 2018). The incarceration of women has increased at a pace twice that of men, and women in local jails are impacted at a disparate rate (Kajstura, 2017). The burden of rendering care to children if both parents are incarcerated rests on grandparents and the foster care system. In 2004, a reported 42% of mothers in state correctional facilities indicated that the grandmother was the caregiver of their children, while they were incarcerated (Glaze & Maruschak, 2008). Although the 2007 national estimates about parental incarceration determined by the Bureau of Justice Statistics Survey of Inmates in State and Federal Correctional Facilities (SISFCF) are helpful, it is now outdated. Similar to research about mothers incarcerated and its impact on children, there is also a dearth of information about the outcomes of having a person in the household incarcerated that is not the mother or father. Although there is a growing body of literature about the impacts of maternal incarceration, the results have been mixed (Burgess-Proctor et al., 2016; Dallaire, 2007; Foster & Hagan, 2015; Murray & Farrington, 2008; Tasca et al., 2011). Later in the chapter is a discussion about the effects of the broad topic of parental incarceration. However, following is a brief discussion about the commonness of family incarceration.

The Prevalence of Familial Incarceration

Nearly half (45%) of adults in the United States have been impacted by the incarceration of an immediate family member at some point in their lives, and for Blacks the percentage is higher at 63% (Elderbroom et al., 2018; Enns et al., 2019). More alarming, Black adults are twice as likely to have an immediate family member incarcerated when compared to their White counterparts. A Black adult who is incarcerated is three times as likely to serve longer than 1 year when compared to White incarcerated adults. Family incarceration can be separated into two categories, which include immediate and extended family members, that are made up of individuals such as siblings, spouses, or individuals a person is currently involved with or have children with (Enns et al., 2019). Although the survey was based on the effects of incarceration of a family member on adults and not children, the information is still of value.

The incarceration rate in the United States is higher than that of any other country in the world (Walmsley, 2018), and Blacks and individuals from lower socioeconomic classes have a greater likelihood of incarceration (Pettit & Western, 2004). Due to the risk and disparities of incarceration for certain communities, there has been a growing body of literature that extends the topic of parental incarceration into other areas such as familial incarceration (Brown et al., 2016; Lee et al., 2015). As a result of the phenomena referred to as the prison boom, incarceration has overwhelming adverse disproportionate effects on minority families (Bruns & Lee, 2019; Lee et al., 2015; Wakefield & Wildeman, 2013; Western & Wildeman, 2009). As punitive legislation was implemented that resulted in hefty incarceration sentences, caught in the middle of the criminal justice system were families who were left to deal with the collateral consequences of imprisonment. Western and Wildeman (2015) attribute mass incarceration to the increase in harsh sentencing policies and as a response to drug control policies' focus on punitive measures.

Literature on family incarceration, similar to parental incarceration, has used point-in-time estimates to determine an estimate as to how many individuals are impacted by incarceration. Despite a significant amount of research examining the relationship between parental incarceration and effects on children and young adults (Foster & Hagan, 2015; Murray et al., 2012), there is still little known about the effects of having a family member incarcerated (Brown et al., 2016, Lee et al., 2014; Roberts, 2003; Wildeman et al., 2012; Nichols & Loper, 2012). Failure to consider other types of relationships besides parental does not provide an accurate portrayal of the prevalence of the impacts of incarceration.

Prior research about parental incarceration has focused heavily on the child's well-being, such as the effect incarceration will have on their education, housing, mental health, and behavioral problems. Few studies have taken into consideration the impact incarceration has on the entire household, such as the parent or caregiver(s) left behind (Western & Wildeman, 2009). It is necessary to understand the impact that incarceration has on all members of a household. Enns et al. (2019) examined not only the prevalence of family incarceration but also the frequency of another member within the family unit, siblings.

The Prevalence of Sibling Incarceration

To date, there is not an estimate of the number of children who have experienced the incarceration of a sibling. Information about siblings and their involvement with the criminal justice system are not common questions listed on surveys used in parental incarceration research. The majority of research that examines the impact of incarceration on children focuses on the incarceration of a mother or father. Overlooked within a family unit are the impacts of incarceration beyond parent-child relationships. The incarceration of a sibling and its effect are an understudied area. Similar to when a parent is incarcerated, sibling incarceration causes disruption in a family's household. A review of literature shows that there are few studies that have examined the prevalence and impacts of sibling incarceration (Heaton, 2014; Enns et al., 2019; Norris et al., 2018) or exposure to sibling delinquency (Aaron & Dallaire, 2010). A recent study found that for adults, sibling incarceration was the most common type of family incarceration. Twenty-seven percent of adults have been impacted by a sibling being incarcerated , and 48% of Black persons have experienced sibling incarceration (Enns et al., 2019). The majority of parental incarceration studies use survey data and typically only examine the prevalence and effects on the parent-child relationships. However, the first quasi-experimental study about parental incarceration not only utilized administrative data but also included sibling relationships into its analysis (Norris et al., 2018). Contrary to what has been researched about parental incarceration, a new study has challenged current findings and has shifted the direction of the conversation about parental and family incarceration. Results from the study found a decrease in the likelihood of incarceration of children who have experienced parental incarceration by 4.9 percentage points, and a decline of 7.2 percentage points for the likelihood of incarceration for individuals that experienced the incarceration of a sibling (Norris et al., 2018). Although this study adds to the body of literature and provides information about the lesser known benefits of incarceration in certain situations, additional research is needed about family and sibling incarceration.

Impacts of Parental Incarceration

The era of mass incarceration ultimately led to an increase in the number of individuals removed from society which affected children, families, and the communities. Previous research has shown the numerous effects of parental incarceration such as stigmatization (Phillips & Gates, 2011), child welfare (Shaw et al., 2015), mental health, drug use, educational performance health issues, and behavioral problems (Murray et al., 2012), and homelessness (Wildeman, 2014).

A review of household, school-related, and the economic effects of parental incarceration is discussed in the following section.

Household Impacts

When a person is incarcerated or involved in the criminal justice system, the entire household feels the burden. Household impacts can be in the form of socioeconomic disadvantages and disruption in the family that can cause instability (Geller, 2013; Geller et al., 2009). Literature about incarceration shows that the families left behind face several challenges such as disruption in the relationship between the parent and child, financial troubles, stigma, visitation barriers, and others in the household taking on the role as caregivers (Murray & Murray, 2010). Prior studies have shown that poverty is associated with parental incarceration, which can make an already challenging situation more difficult (Western & Wildeman, 2009). It is not uncommon for households that have been exposed to incarceration to experience hardships that contribute to poverty such as poor living conditions (Arditti, 2012), low household income (Kjellstrand & Eddy, 2011; Western & Wildeman, 2009), greater likelihood of receiving public assistance (Sugie, 2012), and overall lost wages and lack of upward mobility (The Pew Charitable Trusts, 2010). Prior to incarceration or arrest, over 50% of both mothers and fathers indicated that they were the main source of financial support for their children, and 75% of the parents were employed (Glaze & Maruschak, 2008). Additionally, when a father is incarcerated, the family's household income is lowered during and after their release (Johnson, 2009). Parents that are transferred to correctional facilities that are not near their families cause disruptions in relationships. If a family does not have the resources to travel to visit a loved one, it can lead to further instabilities within the household (Western & Pettit, 2010). When a parent is incarcerated, the other parent or grandparents become the primary caregiver at 84% and 15%, respectively. When the other parent or grandparents cannot take on the responsibility of caring for a child while a parent is incarcerated, another relative (6%) or foster care (3%) carries on the role as a caregiver (Glaze & Maruschak, 2008). The effects of incarceration spill over not only into families but also into the social institution of schools. The next section examines the influence incarceration has on school-related outcomes.

School-Based Impacts

Children who t have experienced parental incarceration have an increased likelihood of being removed from the classroom (Johnson, 2009). Research examining the impact of parental incarceration on school-based outcomes has typically centered on disciplinary and academic performance concerns. As a result, the body of literature that examines the impact of parental incarceration and school-based outcomes such as academic and behavior problems has grown (Cho, 2009a, b, 2010; Murphey & Cooper, 2015; Nichols et al., 2016; Shlafer et al., 2017; Turney & Haskins, 2015). Previous research has shown that parental incarceration impacts school-based outcomes such as poor academic performance (Dalaire & Aaron, 2010; Foster & Hagan, 2009) and a greater likelihood of dropping out (Cho, 2010). Children with incarcerated parents have been linked to having lower IQs, test scores, and GPAs (Foster & Hagan, 2009; Hagan & Foster, 2012; Murray & Farrington, 2005). While examining school-related outcomes, a few studies have found a relationship between parental incarceration and an increased likelihood of being suspended from school (Hanlon et al., 2005) and truancy (Murray & Farrington, 2008; Trice & Brewster, 2004). What may commence as short-term negative impacts has the potential to spill over into adulthood issues, such as future lower educational attainment (Miller & Barnes, 2015).

Although research is increasing in examining the relationship between parental incarceration and school-based outcomes, it is still unknown the number of children in school that have or currently are experiencing household incarceration. Due to stigma, families may not feel comfortable informing schools that a child has a parent that is incarcerated. However, schools cannot provide the necessary resources if they are unaware that a student is impacted by the incarceration of a parent. Therefore, there is a need for schools to work with other agencies to foster a safe and supportive environment. In addition to serving as a resource to students by listening to their concerns about school, school counselors or psychologists are also worried about students' overall well-beings. Therefore, school counselors should be trained in dealing with parental and familial incarceration, and school districts should have social workers as well. School counselors are typically focused on providing individual assistance to students, whereas social workers have the capability of providing resources and services that could be of benefit to not only the child but their entire household. Further research in this area is needed in order to create solutions to address early-onset issues in the school system that may be a result of parental or familial incarceration as a means to foster resiliency by breaking the school to prison pipeline.

Health Impacts

Prior studies have determined a relationship between parental incarceration and various health-related outcomes. The two main health-related areas that have been researched in regard to parental incarceration are mental and physical health outcomes. The incarceration of a parent is a traumatic experience, and children can exhibit symptoms that are associated with posttraumatic stress disorder such as depression, disruption in sleep patterns, problems with concentration, and social withdrawal (Jose-Kampfner, 1995). Parental incarceration has also been linked to depression, anxiety in children (Murray & Farrington, 2008; Foster & Hagan, 2013), and a range of physical health concerns such as asthma, migraines, and high cholesterol (Lee et al., 2013). If a child is present during the arrest of a parent, the traumatic experience and PTSD symptoms are exacerbated.

Long-Term Impacts

A significant amount of literature about parental incarceration typically focuses on economic, educational, and mental and physical health outcomes of children under the age of 18 (Murray et al., 2012). An understudied area of parental incarceration is its effects across the life course. As a child ages, the adversities of parental incarceration can potentially follow them into adolescence and adulthood. Murray and Farrington's (2005, 2008) results found that heightened depression, anxiety, and antisocial behavior were exhibited in adult men who experienced parental incarceration as a child. A growing concern is identifying the likelihood of being arrested and/or incarcerated as an adult as a result of experiencing the incarceration of a parent. Novero et al.'s (2011) study concluded that there is a relationship between parental incarceration and second-generation incarcerated individuals' adjustment to prison. Prison adjustment was measured based on anger, perpetrated violence, and institutional misconduct. After controlling for adverse childhood experiences, second-generation incarcerated individuals displayed poorer levels of prison adjustment in comparison to first-generation offenders. Consistent with prior studies, Miller and Barnes (2015) found young adults that experienced paternal incarceration as a child were more unlikely not to graduate from high school or attend college and have a greater likelihood of poor physical and mental health.

Using Add Health longitudinal data, Gaston (2016) found a relationship between childhood exposure to parental incarceration and adult depressive symptoms in young adults. Mears and Siennick (2016) identified several harmful effects of parental incarceration arising during early young adulthood, including future criminal behavior, mental health, unlawful drug usage, education, wages, and close relationships. Findings indicated a strong relationship between parental incarceration and household illegal drug usage. Additionally, household socioeconomic status was a predictor of both parental incarceration and separation. Siennick (2016) examined the link between parental incarceration and material support of children transitioning to adulthood. Young adults who experienced parental incarceration were less likely to receive housing or financial support from their mother or father after their parents' period of incarceration. Muftic et al. (2016) evaluated the relationship between maternal incarceration and the likelihood of adult offspring involvement in the criminal justice system. Findings indicated age, sex, race, and education have a significant relationship in the likelihood of adult arrest. Additionally, adult conviction and incarceration resulted in the same outcomes. A gendered pathways study by Burgess-Proctor et al. (2016) found that same-sex parental incarceration is a strong predictor for adult arrest and conviction. However, maternal incarceration had a stronger correlation when predicting adult incarceration for both daughters and mothers.

Parental incarceration and its negative impacts during childhood have been examined at lengths. Given that the exposure to parental incarceration can also result in adversities into adolescence and adulthood, there is a need to identify solutions to identify how to stop the cycle of intergenerational crime and disadvantage in families and communities. Therefore, the next section will discuss our recommendations for approaches toward building resiliency in children, families, and communities that have experienced incarceration.

Impacts of Familial and Sibling Incarceration

As previously mentioned, when a parent or main financial provider is incarcerated, the entire household feels the strain and burden. A recent report published by Fwd. us found that families being exposed to the incarceration of a family member is not an uncommon experience; however, Black families and individuals from lower socioeconomic class are more likely to experience the loss of a family member due to incarceration more frequently than Whites (Elderbroom et al., 2018). Approximately 64% of adults have experienced the incarceration of an immediate or extended family member. An overwhelming amount of parental incarceration research focuses on young children, with a growing body of literature examining long-term effects into adulthood. Few studies comprehensively examine the relationship between incarceration and effects on individuals that have experienced the imprisonment of a family member (Rodriguez, 2013). Incarcerated individuals have an increased likelihood of suffering from chronic medical conditions (Glaze & Maruschak, 2008; Wilper et al., 2009), and research has also shown that family members and partners of incarcerated individuals are also more likely to experience poor health-related issues (Murray & Farrington, 2005; Foster & Hagan, 2007). Using a mixed-methods approach encompassing interviews and linking several types of administrative data, DeHart and Shapiro (2016) examined the relationship between incarceration, health, and economic outcomes of family members. Individuals who had a family member incarcerated were more likely to have mental and physical health-related diagnoses. Similar findings about the relationship between family incarceration and psychological distress were found in a study by Brown and his colleagues in 2016.

Similar to family incarceration research, little is known about the short-term and long-term effects of experiencing the incarceration of a sibling. Information about sibling incarceration is typically not available in existing data sets. Current research has just begun to expand parental incarceration conversations to other relationship categories by showing the prevalence of sibling incarceration (Enns et al., 2019; Heaton, 2014; Norris et al., 2018). To date, there has only been one study that has examined the causal effect of sibling incarceration and found a decrease in criminal justice-related activities (Norris et al., 2018). The relationship between sibling incarceration and future criminal justice involvement has not been thoroughly addressed in the literature. More studies are needed that examines the relationship between sibling incarceration and other outcomes such as health- and school-related factors.

Building Resiliency

Future contributions to the literature about parental incarceration should encompass an interdisciplinary and culturally responsive approach while also addressing the problem locally. There are several perspectives about parental incarceration, and therefore, research should involve the collaboration of researchers from different disciplines (Wildeman et al., 2017). Understanding the lived experiences of children, caregivers, and other family members impacted by incarceration is essential. It is imperative to understand the needs of families clearly, but also to understand the uniqueness of the population. In addition to an interdisciplinary approach, research needs to be culturally responsive. Often times, research involves studying vulnerable populations and their outcomes. However, missing from prior research designs are empirical culturally responsive approaches. Children of different races, ethnicity, and socioeconomic status are impacted by the incarceration of loved ones; however, each child is in need of different types of programs and resources. Utilizing various research methodologies that are culturally responsive provides an atmosphere where participants feel more comfortable sharing information (Berryman et al., 2013; Graham & Harris, 2013; Rodriguez et al., 2011).

The Need for Interdisciplinary Research

A topic typically researched through the lens of criminal justice has now branched into the interests of psychologists, medical doctors, social workers, and a wide range of other disciplines. Although parental incarceration research has seen an increase over the last several years in response to the mass incarceration era, lacking are a significant amount of interdisciplinary and collaborative research initiatives. Several disciplines have provided information and added to the body of literature about parental incarceration, but seldom has the research on the topic been truly interdisciplinary in nature. Researchers representing various disciplines study parental and family incarceration without the inclusion of other fields (Eddy & Poehlmann-Tynan, 2019). As a result of true collaborations from multiple entities, there are still several unanswered questions about parental incarceration (Wildeman et al., 2018). Although national, and now a growing body of state and local statistics, in conjunction with an increase in the literature about the negative effects of incarceration on parents, children, and the community, there are still several obstacles with research on this topic. Children of incarcerated parents are still a vulnerable population that is forgotten by policymakers. Simply stated, criminal justice and prison reform initiatives will not solely fix the problem related to the adverse effects of parental incarceration.

The Need for Program Evaluations

There are a number of programs nationally and locally that focus on providing services to children and families impacted by incarceration; however, a review of the literature revealed few evidence-based program evaluations that examined the outcomes for children and caregivers, nor a centralized list of programs and services available to children and families (Frye & Dawe, 2008; McClure et al., 2015; Menting et al., 2014; Miller et al., 2013). Program evaluations assess short- and long-term outcomes of individuals that participate in programs; simply stated, they determine if the program did what it was intended to do. The evaluation of current programs that aid children and families experiencing the impacts of incarceration can help identify what works and can help foster resilience. Typically, parental incarceration program evaluations consist of programs within state correctional facilities (Baradon et al., 2008; Carlson, 2001) and are focused on programs targeting mothers (Browne, 1989; Casey-Acevedo et al., 2005; Harm & Thompson, 1997). Although there is nothing wrong with the creation of mentorship and other programs targeting children who have experience with parental incarceration, developers and founders should first take a moment to think of measurable outcomes and pilot the program first. In order to acquire funding for programs to sustain its longevity, potential donors will be interested in whether or not the program is doing what it says it does effectively.

Localized Analysis

The majority of individuals incarcerated are at the state and local level. Notably, 3/4 of the persons in local jails have yet to be convicted of a crime (Sawyer & Wagner, 2019). Typically, incarceration is handled as a static silo event instead of as a process that has many moving parts. Although state and national research is necessary, in order to address the needs of children and families impacted by incarceration, we need to take a step back and examine the issue at the local level. Parental incarceration estimates at the national and state level fail to consider other forms of incarceration and criminal justice system involvement. Estimates that do not account for short-term imprisonment, such as jails, do not provide an accurate number of children and families impacted by incarceration. Overpopulated county jails and mass supervision add to the already complicated mass incarceration of prisons. Very few county and/or local jails have conducted studies to determine the estimation of parental incarceration and its impacts for short-term confinement. Each community is different, and therefore, the impact of incarceration affects populations differently. Black children, those living in poverty, parents with little education, and children living in rural communities are more likely to experience the incarceration of a parent. Children in various types of communities have different needs and different experiences regarding parental incarceration.

Although few in numbers, there has been an emergence of research relying less on national longitudinal studies and moving toward data collection at the local level. Although national data is helpful, examining this topic through a more localized perspective would produce more meaningful data. State institutions, local jails, and other entities such as child protective services, foster care, and reentry programs should record information pertaining to incarcerated individuals, their children, and families. Accurate and measurable data will assist in identifying the specific needs of children. The data can also identify who are the primary caregivers when incarceration is short term versus long term and if there are programs in place to assist with reunification of families after release. At the local level, the most important question is could the parents have been diverted to alternatives to incarceration if their offenses were considered low-level non-violent offenses? The following section and Box 1 highlights examples in which parental incarceration has been examined at the local level.

Example #1: Harris County (Houston, Texas)
Texas has more than 200,000 individuals incarcerated in jails and prisons, and approximately 477,000 children in Texas have experienced the incarceration of a parent at some point in their lives (The Annie Casey Foundation, 2016; Kaeble & Cowhig, 2018). Harris County is the third largest county in the United States, with approximately 4.6 million residents. Houston is the fourth largest city in the nation. In Harris County, approximately 92,000 children have experienced the incarceration of a parent annually via the Harris County Jail (Correa et al., 2019). First of its kind in Harris County, the study was able to provide an estimation as to how many children are impacted by the incarceration of a parent in the Harris County Jail. The study is an example of an interdisciplinary and public health approach to addressing the impact of parental incarceration at the local level. The purpose of the study was to conduct an assessment to identify the needs of children whose parents are incarcerated at the Harris County Jail, as well as fostering short- and long-term outcomes. Prior to this study, this type of information was not captured in Harris County, and therefore it was not possible to identify the depth of the problem of parental incarceration in the Houston area. In order to obtain this information, it was necessary for joint collaboration of multiple stakeholders to work together to gather this information. The Harris County Jail had a pivotal role in this study by including adding additional questions to their intake form to identify which inmates had children under the age of 18. The conclusions from the study were drawn from responses on the intake form and inmate and caregiver interviews.

Example #2: Minnesota
In 2017, a survey was administered in order to obtain a point-in-time estimate for the number of children impacted by the incarceration of a parent in Minnesota jails. The purpose of the study was to add to the body of literature about parental incarceration, but at the local level. By determining the scope of the problem in numbers, Minnesota was able to provide information to the jails in order to assist children and families impacted by having a parent or primary caregiver incarcerated.

Example #3: Alameda and San Francisco Counties (California)
In 2014, Alameda and San Francisco Counties surveyed over 2000 inmates in their local county jails in order to determine the number of children whose parents were incarcerated. The study was able to capture information pertaining to both the parent and child's demographics, caregiver information, the living situation of the child, the child's experience at the time of the parent's arrest, and whether or not there was changes in the child's residence, school, or family income. All of the

aforementioned information is of importance in order to identify the short-term impacts of having a parent incarcerated at the county jail which can lead to barriers regarding family reunification obstacles after the parent's release.

Box 1: Local Parental Incarceration Research Key Findings

Location	Key findings	Year
Harris County (Houston, Texas)	Inmates who reported being a parent or caregiver to at least one child under the age of 18 were overwhelmingly male (82%) and Black (53%). For male inmates, the mother (86%) is predominantly the primary caregiver; however, if the mother is incarcerated, the primary caregiver is either the father (39%) or a grandparent (31%). Among incarcerated parents, 61% were charged with felonies, and 37% were charged with misdemeanors. Assault (24%) and drug-related offenses (19%) were the two most common charges. 61% of inmates are the main financial providers for their households.	2018
Minnesota	Approximately 9898 children have a parent incarcerated in a county jail in Minnesota on any given day. About 69% (2 out of 3) of individuals incarcerated in Minnesota jails are parents to children under the age of 18. 53% of incarcerated parents are White; however, Blacks and other minority parents are disproportionately represented at about 21% for Blacks and approximately 16% for Hispanics/Latinos. The majority of the children (37%) were identified as being between the ages of 0 and 5.	2017
Alameda and San Francisco Counties (California)	An estimated 2891 children under the age of 25 have a parent or primary caregiver incarcerated in Alameda or San Francisco County Jail on a given day. Between Alameda and San Francisco Counties, approximately 69% of incarcerated individuals are parents or the primary caregivers to at least one child under the age of 25 and disproportionately Black (nearly 49%). Approximately 36% of inmates reported multiple cycles of incarceration since becoming a parent. Due to their parent's incarceration, 27% and 16% of children changed residences and schools at least once, respectively. Incarceration resulted in 63% of families losing income.	2014

Source: Correa, N., Bhalakia, A., Van Horne, B., Hayes, A., Cupit, T., Kwarteng-Amaning, V., Lopez, K., Keefe, R., & Greely, C. (2019). The Forgotten families*: A needs assessment of children with incarcerated parents in Harris County, Texas.* Texas Children's Hospital
Shlafer, R. & Saunders, J.B. (2017). Parents in Minnesota jails and their minor children. Minneapolis, MN: University of Minnesota
Kramer, K. and the Children of Incarcerated Parents Jail Survey Teams. (2016) *Descriptive Overview of Parents, Children and Incarceration in Alameda and San Francisco County Jails.* Alameda County Children of Incarcerated Parents Partnership & San Francisco Children of Incarcerated Parents Partnership. Zellerbach Family Foundation

Public Policy

In addition to raising awareness about the commonness of parental incarceration, public policy about the issue needs more attention. Children are forgotten by the system when a parent is sentenced to incarceration. Several states remain in the dark about the specific number of children that have a parent incarcerated. Many departments of corrections fail to do a good job of keeping track of how many of its inmates are parents or primary caregivers to minor children. However, hopefully this will change in the upcoming future. Recently, Texas, and other states, has new legislation that will help to identify the scope of the parental incarceration problem in numbers. Following is a discussion about policies that will impact children exposed to the incarceration of a parent or caregiver. Some of the policies are at the state level, and one is at the federal level. Nevertheless, they all have the potential to alleviate the burden of parental incarceration and begin the road to successful reentry and family reunification.

Federal Legislation

Although the majority of individuals incarcerated in the United States are at the state and local level, nearly 10% of individuals are housed in federal correctional facilities (Sawyer & Wagner, 2019). The last known point-in-time estimate for parental incarceration is from 2007. During that time, 123,800 parents were incarcerated which impacted 279,100 children (Glaze & Maruschak, 2008). The bipartisan House Bill (5682), commonly referred to as the First Step Act, signed into law at the end of 2018 changed the conversation about criminal justice reform. The Act will impact mandatory-minimum sentencing by giving judges more discretion. Individuals in correctional facilities will be allowed to earn good time credit which will ultimately decrease their sentence and increase training and work opportunities. Despite the First Step Act serving as a step in the right direction toward righting the wrongs of the inequities that resulted in mass incarceration, the law has its limitations. The new law is solely applicable to federal prisons; however, this bill is a step in the right direction and can serve as a model for future state legislation.

State Legislation

Gaining momentum during the 2019 Texas legislative session were bills that related to children impacted by the criminal justice system. Nearly 2 million individuals are in Texas state prisons and jails (Wagner & Rabuy, 2017). Each year in the Houston area, 1 out of 14 children has a parent in the Harris County jail (Correa et al., 2019). One of the bills that recently passed in Texas relates to the relationship between parental incarceration and school-based outcomes. Currently, the Texas Education Agency has 13 different types of criteria that identify a student as at risk such as being a pregnant or a parent, failing to advance to the next grade level, placement in an alternative education program, or homeless. The passing of Texas House Bill 2116/Senate Bill 1746 has added an additional at risk for dropping out indicator in order to identify children who are impacted by the incarceration of a parent. As a result of the bill passing, Texas will be able to track the number of students who are impacted by the incarceration of a parent in schools. Texas House Bill 659 was also passed during the 2019 legislative session and will require the Texas Department of Criminal Justice to obtain and keep a record about the parental status of individuals in Texas correctional facilities. After the information is compiled annually, it will be provided to the Texas Education Agency and Department of Family and Protective Services.

Alternatives to incarceration are an option to alleviate jail and prison overcrowding but also allow nonviolent, non-serious individuals to remain in the community while serving their sentence. If passed, Senate Bill 394 would create a pretrial diversion court in California with a focus on diverting primary caregivers into programs instead of incarceration. Similar to California's pretrial diversion opportunity for parents, Texas legislation has taken the necessary steps to consider children in sentencing matters. Sixty-four percent of women in the Texas Department of Criminal Justice are nonviolent offenders. Eighty-one percent of females in Texas correctional facilities are mothers (Linder, 2018). Consistent with past studies about parental incarceration in Texas, when a father is incarcerated, the mother is the primary caretaker, and if both the mother and father are involved in the criminal justice system, the grandmother often takes on the role as the caretaker (Correa et al., 2019). Therefore, the implementation of this Texas House Bill ensures that children whose parents are involved in the criminal justice system voices are heard and unnecessary disruption in families can be avoided if parents are provided with alternatives to incarceration.

Conclusion

The goals of this chapter were to provide a brief history about family separation before and after emancipation, the commonness and effects of parental and family incarceration, and provide recommendations for moving forward in this area of research. Overall a review of the research revealed several unknowns in the literature. Children of incarcerated parents are invisible in the criminal justice system. Labeled as at risk, children that have experienced parental incarceration leave many wondering if the apple falls far from the tree. This unique population is often missing from the conversation when a parent is involved in the criminal justice system. In comparison to White children, both Blacks and Hispanics are more likely to experience the incarceration of a parent at rates of eight and three times more likely, respectively (Glaze & Maruschak, 2008). Additionally, the unintended victims of incarceration are usually limited to children and families without the context of how incarceration has negative outcomes on communities as an entirety. Neighborhoods as a whole feel the impact of incarceration. Individuals released from correctional facilities have hopes to return back to not only their families, but they also quite frequently return back to the same communities and neighborhoods they lived prior to their imprisonment. In order to address the collateral consequences of incarceration, a new set of questions should be addressed, such as the following: (1) What are the characteristics of neighborhoods with high parental and familial incarceration rates? (2) How can research include solely parental incarceration into future studies, but also questions about familial and household incarceration? (3) Are there differences in individual versus community level impacts of parental and familial incarceration?

Existing longitudinal studies have been the primary means for examining parental incarceration; however, localized analyses are beneficial in order to examine the relationship of parental incarceration of short-term criminal justice system involvement such as probation and jail. The incarceration of a parent or primary caregiver impacts populations differently. Although estimations about the number of children exposed to parental incarceration have a wide range, the numbers still serve as a starting point for the continued conversation. Research at the local level will also provide opportunities for collaborative research initiatives among multiple social institutions such as schools, jails, juvenile correctional facilities, and social services. In addition to acquiring data from different sources, parental incarceration research needs to expand to include a broader definition such as family and household incarceration. The most recent literature about family incarceration has determined that sibling incarceration has a significant impact (Enns et al., 2019; Norris et al., 2018). Therefore, future research should continue to examine this understudied area of family and household incarceration.

By widening the scope of data collection and increasing the range of parental incarceration research to include other family members and characteristics of the neighborhood, additional questions about incarceration spillover effects can be examined. Questions remain such as whether or not a parent could have been diverted to alternatives to incarceration if their offenses were considered low level, non-violent, are there differences between the types of crimes that parents and non-parents commit, and what else is happening in a community that has high incarceration and parental incarceration rates? Most importantly, due to the new findings about the significant impact of sibling incarceration, this is an area in dire need of more research in order to understand the resiliency effect between offending and non-offending siblings. Incarceration is a shared sentence that has hefty negative consequences emotionally and financially on communities. Over 600,000 individuals are released from state and federal correctional confinement (Wagner & Rabuy, 2015), and many will face barriers during the family reunification process. Overall, our aim for this chapter was to provide researchers, policymakers, and the community stakeholders with a clearer understanding of the issues and solutions to the inevitable consequences of incarceration in order for communities to recover from adversities and to build resiliency.

References

Aaron, L., & Dallaire, D. H. (2010). Parental incarceration and multiple risk experiences: Effects on family dynamics and children's delinquency. *Journal of Youth and Adolescence, 39*(12), 1471–1484.

Alexander, M. (2010). *The new Jim Crow: Mass incarceration in the age of colorblindness*. The New York Press.

Arditti, J. A. (2012). Child trauma within the context of parental incarceration: A family process perspective. *Journal of Family Theory & Review, 4*(3), 181–219.

Bailey, A. C. (2017). *The weeping time: Memory and the largest slave auction in American history*. Cambridge University Press.

Baradon, T., Fonagy, P., Bland, K., Lenard, K., & Sleed, M. (2008). New beginnings-an experience-based program addressing the attachment relationship between mothers and their babies in prisons. *Journal of Child Psychotherapy, 34*, 240.

Berryman, M., SooHoo, S., & Nevin, A. (Eds.). (2013). *Culturally responsive methodologies*. Emerald Group Publishing.

Bourgeois, J., & Henderson, H. (2019). Thousands of fathers are imprisoned: How do we help their kids? *InsideSources*. Retrieved from https://www.insidesources.com/thousands-of-fathers-are-imprisoned-how-do-we-help-their-kids/

Brown, T. N., Bell, M. L., & Patterson, E. J. (2016). Imprisoned by empathy: Familial incarceration and psychological distress among African American men in the National Survey of American Life. *Journal of Health and Social Behavior, 57*(2), 240–256.

Browne, D. C. H. (1989). Incarcerated mothers and parenting. *Journal of Family Violence, 4*, 211–221.

Bruns, A., & Lee, H. (2019). Racial/ethnic disparities. In *Handbook on children with incarcerated parents* (pp. 37–52). Springer.

Burgess-Proctor, A., Huebner, B. M., & Durso, J. M. (2016). Comparing the effects of maternal and paternal incarceration on adult daughters' and sons' criminal justice system involvement. *Criminal Justice and Behavior, 43*(8), 1034–1055.

Carlson, J. R. (2001). Prison nursery 2000: A five-year review of the prison nursery at the Nebraska Correctional Center for Women. *Journal of Offender Rehabilitation, 33*, 75–98.

Casey-Acevedo, K., Bakken, T., & Karle, A. (2005). Children visiting mothers in prison: The effects on mothers' behavior and disciplinary adjustment. *Violence & Abuse Abstracts, 11*.

Center for Advancing Opportunity. (2019). *The state of opportunity in America: An understanding of barriers & identifying solutions*. Retrieved from http://www.advancingopportunity.org/wp-content/uploads/2018/08/The-State-of-Opportunity-in-America-Report-Center-for-Advancing-Opportunity.pdf

Cho, R. M. (2009a). Impact of maternal imprisonment on children's probability of grade retention. *Journal of Urban Economics, 65*(1), 11–23.

Cho, R. M. (2009b). The impact of maternal imprisonment on children's educational achievement results from children in Chicago Public Schools. *Journal of Human Resources, 44*(3), 772–797.

Cho, R. M. (2010). Maternal incarceration and children's adolescent outcomes: Timing and dosage. *Social Service Review, 84*(2), 257–282.

Clear, T. (2007). *Imprisoning communities: How mass incarceration makes disadvantaged neighborhoods worse* (3rd ed.). Oxford University Press.

Correa, N., Bhalakia, A., Van Horne, B., Hayes, A., Cupit, T., Kwarteng-Amaning, V., Lopez, K., Keefe, R., & Greely, C. (2019). *The forgotten families: A needs assessment on children with incarcerated parents in Harris County, Texas*. Texas Children's Hospital.

Dallaire, D. H. (2007). Incarcerated mothers and fathers: A comparison of risks for children and families. *Family Relations, 56*(5), 440–453.

DeGraft-Hanson, K. (2010). *Unearthing the weeping time: Savannah's ten broeck race course and 1859 slave sale*. Southern Spaces. Retrieved from http://www.southernspaces.org/contents/2010/degraft-hanson/la.htm

DeHart, D., & Shapiro, C. (2016). Integrated administrative data & criminal justice research. *American Journal of Criminal Research*. https://doi.org/10.1007/s12103-016-9355-5

DuBois, W. E. B. (2013). The spawn of slavery: The convict lease system in the south. In Gabbidon & Greene (Eds.), *Race, crime, and justice* (pp. 17–22). Routledge.

Eddy, J. M., & Poehlmann-Tynan, J. (2019). Interdisciplinary perspectives on research and intervention with children of incarcerated parents. In *Handbook on children with incarcerated parents* (pp. 3–10). Springer.

Elderbroom, B., Bennett, L., Gong, S., Rose, F., & Towns, Z. (2018). *Every second: The impact of the incarceration crisis on America's families*. Fwd.us.

Enns, P. K., Yi, Y., Comfort, M., Goldman, A. W., Lee, H., Muller, C., & Wildeman, C. (2019). What percentage of Americans have ever had a family member incarcerated? Evidence from the family history of incarceration survey (FamHIS). *Socius, 5*, 2378023119829332.

Foster, H., & Hagan, J. (2013). Maternal and paternal imprisonment in the stress process. *Social Science Research, 42*(3), 650–669.

Foster, H., & Hagan, J. (2015). Punishment regimes and the multilevel effects of parental incarceration: Intergenerational, intersectional, and interinstitutional models of social inequality and systemic exclusion. *Annual Review of Sociology, 41*, 135–158.

Frye, S., & Dawe, S. (2008). Interventions for women prisoners and their children in the post-release period. *Clinical Psychologist, 12*(3), 99–108.

Gaston, S. (2016). The long-term effects of parental incarceration: Does parental incarceration in childhood or adolescence predict depressive symptoms in adulthood? *Criminal Justice and Behavior, 43*(8), 1056–1075.

Geller, A. (2013). Paternal incarceration and father–child contact in fragile families. *Journal of Marriage and Family, 75*(5), 1288–1303.

Geller, A., Garfinkel, I., Cooper, C. E., & Mincy, R. B. (2009). Parental incarceration and child well-being: Implications for urban families. *Social Science Quarterly, 90*(5), 1186–1202.

Glaze, L. E., & Maruschak, L. M. (2008). P*arents in prison and their minor children (Report No. NCJ 222984)*. US Department of Justice, Bureau of Justice Statistics.

Graham, J. A., & Harris, Y. R. (2013). Children of color and parental incarceration: Implications for research, theory, and practice. *Journal of Multicultural Counseling and Development, 41*(2), 66–81.

Hagan, J., & Foster, H. (2012). Children of the American prison generation: Student and school spillover effects of incarcerating mothers. *Law and Society Review, 46*(1), 37–69.

Hanlon, T. E., Blatchley, R. J., Bennett-Sears, T., O'Grady, K. E., Rose, M., & Callaman, J. M. (2005). Vulnerability of children of incarcerated addict mothers: Implications for preventive intervention. *Children and Youth Services Review, 27*(1), 67–84.

Harm, N. J., & Thompson, P. (1997). Evaluating the effectiveness of parent education for incarcerated mothers. *Journal of Offender Rehabilitation, 24*, 135–152.

Heaton, K. (2014). *The sibling experience: Grief and coping with sibling incarceration*. Retrieved from Sophia, the St. Catherine University repository website: https://sophia.stkate.edu/msw_papers/327

Johnson, R. (2009). Ever-increasing levels of parental incarceration and the consequences for children. In *Do prisons make us safer* (pp. 177–206).

Kaeble, D., & Cowhig, M. (2018). *Correctional populations in the United States, 2016*. Bureau of Justice Statistics.

Kajstura, A. (2017). Women's mass incarceration: The whole pie 2017. *Mass Incarceration: The Whole Pie 2016| Prison Policy Initiative*.

Kajstura, A. (2018). States of women's incarceration: The global context 2018. *Prison Policy Initiative*.

Kramer, K. and the Children of Incarcerated Parents Jail Survey Teams. (2016). *Descriptive overview of parents, children and incarceration in Alameda and San Francisco County Jails*. Alameda County Children of Incarcerated Parents Partnership & San Francisco Children of Incarcerated Parents Partnership. Zellerbach Family Foundation.

Lee, R. D., Fang, X., & Luo, F. (2013). The impact of parental incarceration on the physical and mental health of young adults. *Pediatrics, 131*(4), e1188–e1195.

Lee, H., Porter, L. C., & Comfort, M. (2014). Consequences of family member incarceration: Impacts on civic participation and perceptions of the legitimacy and fairness of government. *The Annals of the American Academy of Political and Social Science, 651*(1), 44–73.

Lee, H., McCormick, T., Hicken, M. T., & Wildeman, C. (2015). Racial inequalities in connectedness to imprisoned individuals in the United States. *Du Bois Review: Social Science Research on Race, 12*(2), 269–282.

Linder, L. (2018). An unsupported population: The treatment of women in Texas' Criminal Justice System. *Report by the Texas Criminal Justice Coalition.*

McClure, H. H., Shortt, J. W., Eddy, J. M., Holmes, A., Van Uum, S., Russell, E., & Martinez, C. R. (2015). Associations among mother–child contact, parenting stress, and mother and child adjustment related to incarceration. In *Children's contact with incarcerated parents* (pp. 59–82). Springer.

Mears, D., & Siennick, S. E. (2016). Young adult outcomes and the life-course penalties of parental incarceration. *Journal of Research in Crime and Delinquency, 53*(1), 3–35.

Menting, A. T., de Castro, B. O., Wijngaards-de Meij, L. D., & Matthys, W. (2014). A trial of parent training for mothers being released from incarceration and their children. *Journal of Clinical Child & Adolescent Psychology, 43*(3), 381–396.

Miller, H. V., & Barnes, J. C. (2015). The association between parental incarceration and health, education, and economic outcomes in young adulthood. *American Journal of Criminal Justice, 40*(4), 765–784.

Miller, A. L., Perryman, J., Markovitz, L., Franzen, S., Cochran, S., & Brown, S. (2013). Strengthening incarcerated families: Evaluating a pilot program for children of incarcerated parents and their caregivers. *Family Relations, 62*(4), 584–596.

Muftic, L. R., Bouffard, L. A., & Armstrong, G. A. (2016). Impact of maternal incarceration on criminal justice involvement of adult offspring: A research note. *Journal of Research in Crime and Delinquency, 53*(1), 93–111.

Murphey, D., & Cooper, P. M. (2015). Parents behind bars: What happens to their children? *Child Trends.* Retrieved from https://www.childtrends.org/wp-content/uploads/2015/10/2015-42ParentsBehindBars.pdf

Murray, J., & Farrington, D. P. (2005). Parental imprisonment: Effects on boys' antisocial behaviour and delinquency through the life-course. *Journal of Child Psychology and Psychiatry, 46*(12), 1269–1278.

Murray, J., & Farrington, D. P. (2008). The effects of parental imprisonment on children. *Crime and Justice, 37*(1), 133–206.

Murray, J., & Murray, L. (2010). Parental incarceration, attachment and child psychopathology. *Attachment & Human Development, 12*(4), 289–309.

Murray, J., Farrington, D. P., & Sekol, I. (2012). Children's antisocial behavior, mental health, drug use, and educational performance after parental incarceration: A systematic review and meta-analysis. *American Psychological Association, 138*(2), 175–210.

Nichols, E. B., & Loper, A. B. (2012). Incarceration in the household: Academic outcomes of adolescents with an incarcerated household member. *Journal of Youth and Adolescence, 41*(11), 1455–1471.

Nichols, E. B., Loper, A. B., & Meyer, J. P. (2016). Promoting educational resiliency in youth with incarcerated parents: The impact of parental incarceration, school characteristics, and connectedness on school outcomes. *Journal of Youth and Adolescence, 45*(6), 1090–1109.

Norris, S., Pecenco, M., & Weaver, J. (2018). *The effects of parental and sibling incarceration: Evidence from Ohio.* Working paper.

Northup, S. (1968). *Twelve years a slave*. LSU Press.

Novero, C. M., Loper, A., & Warren, J. I. (2011). Second-generation prisoners: Adjustment patterns for inmates with a history of parental incarceration. *Criminal Justice and Behavior, 38*(8), 761–778.

Phillips, S., & Gates, T. (2011). A conceptual framework for understanding the stigmatization of children of incarcerated parents. *Journal of Child and Family Studies, 20*(3), 286–294.

Roberts, D. E. (2003). The social and moral cost of mass incarceration in African American communities. *The Stanford Law Review, 56*, 1271.

Rodriguez, N. (2013). Concentrated disadvantage and the incarceration of youth: Examining how context affects juvenile justice. *Journal of Research in Crime and Delinquency, 50*(2), 189–215.

Rodriguez, K. L., Schwartz, J. L., Lahman, M. K., & Geist, M. R. (2011). Culturally responsive focus groups: Reframing the research experience to focus on participants. *International Journal of Qualitative Methods, 10*(4), 400–417.

Sawyer, W., & Wagner, P. (2019). Mass incarceration: The whole pie 2018. *Prison Policy Initiative.*

Shlafer, R., & Saunders, J. B. (2017). *Parents in Minnesota jails and their minor children.* University of Minnesota.

Shlafer, R. J., Reedy, T., & Davis, L. (2017). School-based outcomes among youth with incarcerated parents: Differences by school setting. *Journal of School Health, 87*(9), 687–695.

Siennick, S. E. (2016). Parental incarceration and intergenerational transfers to young adults. *Journal of Family Issues, 37*(10), 1433–1457.

Sugie, N. F. (2012). Punishment and welfare: Paternal incarceration and families' receipt of public assistance. *Social Forces, 90*(4), 1403–1427.

Tasca, M., Rodriguez, N., & Zatz, M. S. (2011). Family and residential instability in the context of paternal and maternal incarceration. *Criminal Justice and Behavior, 38*(3), 231–247.

The Annie E. Casey Foundation. (2016). *Children of incarcerated parents, a shared sentence: The devastating toll of parental incarceration on kids, families and communities.* Baltimore. Retrieved from https://www.aecf.org/resources/a-shared-sentence/

The Pew Charitable Trusts. (2010). *Collateral costs: Incarceration's effect on economic mobility.* The Pew Charitable Trusts.

Trice, A. D., & Brewster, J. (2004). The effects of maternal incarceration on adolescent children. *Journal of Police and Criminal Psychology, 19*(1), 27–35.

Wagner, P., & Rabuy, B. (2015). Mass incarceration: The whole pie 2015. *Prison policy initiative.*

Wagner, P., & Rabuy, B. (2017). Mass incarceration: The whole pie 2016. *Prison policy initiative.*

Wakefield, S., & Wildeman, C. (2013). *Children of the prison boom: Mass incarceration and the future of American inequality.* Oxford University Press.

Western, B., & Pettit, B. (2010). Incarceration & social inequality. *Daedalus (Journal of the American Academy of Arts and Sciences), 139*(3), 8–19.

Western, B., & Wildeman, C. (2009). The Black family and mass incarceration. *The Annals of the American Academy of Political and Social Science, 621*, 221–242.

Wildeman, C. (2014). Parental incarceration, child homelessness, and the invisible consequences of mass imprisonment. *The Annals of the American Academy of Political and Social Science, 651*(1), 74–96.

Wildeman, C., Schnittker, J., & Turney, K. (2012). Despair by association? The mental health of mothers with children by recently incarcerated fathers. *American Sociological Review, 77*(2), 216–243.

Wildeman, C., Haskins, A. R., & Poehlmann-Tynan, J. (2018). Introduction: Invigorating research and practice on children of incarcerated parents. In C. Wildeman, A. R. Haskins, & J. Poehlmann-Tynan (Eds.), *APA Bronfenbrenner series on the ecology of human development. When parents are incarcerated: Interdisciplinary research and interventions to support children* (pp. 3–8). American Psychological Association.

Williams, H. A. (2012). *Help me to find my people: The African American search for family lost in slavery.* Univ of North Carolina Press.

Wilson, W. J. (2012). *The truly disadvantaged: The inner city, the underclass, and public policy* (2nd ed.). University of Chicago Press.

Davis, L., & Shlafer, R. J. (2017). Mental health of adolescents with currently and formerly incarcerated parents. Journal of adolescence, 54, 120–134.

Turanovic, J. J., & Rodriguez, N. (2017). Mental health service needs in the prison boom: the case of children of incarcerated mothers. Criminal justice policy review, 28(5), 415–436.

Tasca, M., Turanovic, J. J., White, C., & Rodriguez, N. (2014). Prisoners' assessments of mental health problems among their children. International Journal of Offender Therapy and Comparative Criminology, 58(2), 154–173.

Turney, K. (2014). The consequences of paternal incarceration for maternal neglect and harsh parenting. Social Forces, 92(4), 1607–1636.

Turney, K. (2018). Adverse childhood experiences among children of incarcerated parents. Children and Youth Services Review, 89, 218–225.

Kopak, A. M., & Smith-Ruiz, D. (2016). Criminal justice involvement, drug use, and depression among African American children of incarcerated parents. Raceand Justice, 6(2), 89–116.

Roettger, M. E., & Swisher, R. R. (2011). Associations of fathers' history of incarceration with sons' delinquency and arrest among Black, White, and Hispanic males in the united states. Criminology, 49(4), 1109–1147.

Felitti, V. J. (2009). Adverse childhood experiences and adult health. Academic Pediatrics, 9(3), 131.

Balistreri, K. S., & Alvira-Hammond, M. (2016). Adverse childhood experiences, family functioning and adolescent health and emotional well-being. Public Health, 132, 72–78.

Bethell, C., Gombojav, N., Solloway, M., & Wissow, L. (2016). Adverse childhood experiences, resilience and mindfulness-based approaches: common denominator issues for children with emotional, mental, or behavioral problems. Child and adolescent psychiatric clinics of North America, 25(2), 139.

Pettit, B., & Western, B. (2004). Mass imprisonment and the life course: Race and class inequality in US incarceration. American sociological review, 69(2), 151–169.

Shaw, T. V., Bright, C. L., & Sharpe, T. L. (2015). Child welfare outcomes for youth in care as a result of parental death or parental incarceration. Child abuse & neglect, 42, 112–120.

Kjellstrand, J. M., & Eddy, J. M. (2011). Parental incarceration during childhood, family context, and youth problem behavior across adolescence. Journal of offender rehabilitation, 50(1), 18–36.

Aaron, L., & Dallaire, D. H. (2010). Parental incarceration and multiple risk experiences: Effects on family dynamics and children's delinquency. Journal of youth and adolescence, 39(12), 1471–1484.

Foster, H., & Hagan, J. (2007). Incarceration and intergenerational social exclusion. Social Problems, 54(4), 399–433.

Foster, H., & Hagan, J. (2009). The mass incarceration of parents in America: Issues of race/ethnicity, collateral damage to children, and prisoner reentry. The ANNALS of the AmericanAcademy of Political and Social Science, 623(1), 179–194.

International Centre for Prison Studies. (2013). World prison population list. London: ICPS.

Turney, K., & Haskins, A. R. (2014). Falling behind? Children's early grade retention after paternal incarceration. Sociology of Education, 87(4), 241–258.

Kampfner, C. J. (1995). Post-traumatic stress reactions in children of imprisoned mothers. Children of incarcerated parents, 89–100.

Wilper, A. P., Woolhandler, S., Boyd, J. W., Lasser, K. E., McCormick, D., Bor, D. H., & Himmelstein, D. U. (2009). The health and health care of US prisoners: results of a nationwide survey. American journal of public health, 99(4), 666–672.

Maruschak, L. M., Bronson, J., & Alpher, M.A. (2021). Survey of Prison Inmates 2016: Parents in prison and their minor children (Report No. NCJ 252645). Washington, DC: US Department of Justice, Bureau of Justice Statistics.

Sawyer, W., & Wagner, P. (2020). Mass incarceration: The whole pie 2020. Prison Policy Initiative.

Norris, S., Pecenco, M., & Weaver, J. (2021). The effects of parental and sibling incarceration: Evidence from ohio. Available at SSRN 3590735.

Racial Differences in Female Imprisonment and Foster Care

William J. Sabol, Samuel L. Myers Jr., and MariTere Molinet

Abstract This chapter investigates the relationship between decline in racial disparities in foster care and female imprisonment. Growth in female imprisonment has been identified as a determinant of growth in foster care populations, but race-specific relationships between them have not been examined. Using a state-level panel of yearly data covering the period 2000 through 2016, we first describe trends in disparity in female imprisonment and foster care. We then estimate race-specific fixed-effects models of foster care entry rates and of foster care placement rates on female imprisonment rates. We include other theoretically relevant factors such as confirmed maltreatment rates, male imprisonment rate, measures of socio-economic status, state expenditures, and indicators of federal child welfare policy implemented through the Tittle IV-E waiver program. Our main findings are as follows: For black and Hispanic children, there were no significant effects of female imprisonment rates on entries or placements, but for white children, increases in white female imprisonment rates led to increases in white child foster care entry rates. For black children, black male imprisonment rates were positively correlated with black child foster care entry and placement rates. The elasticity of the black male imprisonment rate on foster care entries was about twice the magnitude of the white female imprisonment rate. Confirmed maltreatment rates were positively associated with foster care entry and placement rates for blacks, Hispanics, and whites. One speculation for the race differences in female imprisonment on foster care is the shift in the types of drugs subject to enforcement during this period, with the increase in white female involvement in and use of opioids causing conditions leading to the removal of children and the incarceration of women.

W. J. Sabol (✉)
Department Criminal Justice & Criminology, Georgia State University, Atlanta, GA, USA
e-mail: wsabol@gsu.edu

S. L. MyersJr.
Roy Wilkins Center for Human Relations and Social Justice at the Hubert H. Humphrey School of Public Affairs, University of Minnesota, Minneapolis, MN, USA

M. Molinet
Department Criminal Justice & Criminology, Georgia State University, Atlanta, GA, USA

J. Krysik, N. Rodriguez (eds.), *Children of Incarcerated Parents*, Children of Incarcerated Parents: From Understanding to Impact,
https://doi.org/10.1007/978-3-030-84713-5_5

Keywords Foster Care · Race · Incarceration · Criminal justice · Policy

Background and Motivation

Our motivations for this chapter are threefold. First is the observation that growth in female imprisonment during the 1980s and 1990s accounted for an estimated 31% of the growth in foster care caseloads over that period (Swann & Sylvester, 2006) and established a connection between the adult criminal justice and foster care systems that had not been formalized. A decade later Edwards (2016) confirmed that states with more punitive criminal justice practices had higher foster care placement rates. As a determinant of foster care placement, female imprisonment growth brought with it the attendant and generally negative consequences of foster care placement (Cutuli et al., 2016; Lawrence et al., 2006; Rubin et al., 2007; Lindquist & Santavirta, 2014; Yang et al., 2017) as well as affecting the maternal-child relationship (Phillips & Detlaff, 2009; Turney & Wildeman, 2013; Wildeman & Western, 2010).

Second, since 2000 there have been substantial declines in black child foster care and black female imprisonment rates. Specifically, between 2000 and 2016, both black child foster care placement rates and black female imprisonment rates halved (Myers Jr. et al., 2020). By comparison, while white child foster care rates increased slightly (about 8%), white female imprisonment rates increased by nearly 60%. Although the Swann and Sylvester work did not decompose effects by race, their work implies that decreases in black female imprisonment should explain decreases in black child foster care rates, and white female rates should account for growth in white child rates. Third, the magnitude of the racial differences in changes in female imprisonment rates and child foster care rates suggests that racially disparate processes may characterize the relationship between imprisonment and foster care.

Although the prior studies did not estimate the race-specific relationships between female imprisonment and foster care, we speculate that the growth in both that occurred during the 1990s was led primarily by increases of black women and children, respectively (e.g., Billingsley & Giovannoni, 1972; Hill, 2007; Myers & Sabol, 1987). It stands to reason, therefore, that a decline in black female imprisonment rates occurring during the 2000s would be associated with declines in black child foster care.

We examine this for foster care entry rates and foster care placement rates. We do not find support for this relationship. Rather, we find that *black male* imprisonment rates were positively related to black child foster care entry while black female imprisonment rates did not have an effect on black child entry rates. On the other hand, we find that white female (but not white male) imprisonment rates were positively associated with white child foster care entry rates. The same patterns held for foster care placement rates.

Our chapter is organized as follows: First, we describe the trends in imprisonment and foster care, documenting the changes in them that we summarized above.

Next, we discuss the ways in which foster care and incarceration may be related. This entails a discussion of child welfare decision-making and the role of federal child welfare policies. Following that, we present our hypotheses, describe our data, and present our findings, followed by a discussion of the findings and our conclusions.

For the purpose of this research, foster care entry rates and foster care placement rates are defined by the Adoption and Foster Care Analysis and Reporting System (AFCARS). Foster care entry rate is an estimated count of all children who entered foster care in a fiscal year. Foster care placement rate is an estimated count of all children who are physically placed in a foster care setting after being removed for their home. This includes placement with licensed family members or neighbors and temporary placements.

Decline in Black-White Foster Care Rates

Since 2000, black-white foster care placement rates (the number of children in foster care at a point in time per child population) have converged, as have the Hispanic-white rates.[1] By 2015 the white rate exceeded the Hispanic rate (Fig. 1). More specifically, the black rate fell from about 19 per 1000 black children in 2000 to half that rate in 2014 (or about 9.5 per 1000) before rising to 10 per 1000 in 2015 and 2016. The Hispanic child rate trended downward from 2000 to about 2012, falling from 6.2 to 4.5 before increasing to 4.8 by 2015. The white rate fell to its low point in 2012 to just above 4.1 per 1000, but since then it rose to 5 per 1000 in 2016.

Implicit in the rates is the decrease in racial and ethnic disparity in foster care placement rates (Fig. 2). The black-white racial disparity in foster care placement fell linearly from 4 to 1 in 2000 to 2 to 1 in 2016. Most of the decrease in the black-white disparity occurred between 2000 and 2010 when the disparity fell from 4 to 2.5. Since 2010, the rate of decrease in the black-white disparity slowed even as the white foster care rate increased slightly from 2012 to 2016. By comparison, the Hispanic-to-white disparity ratio fell throughout the 2000–2016 period from 1.5 to under 1. By 2015–2016, the Hispanic disparity ratio fell below 1, as white children had higher placement rates than Hispanic children.

On the foster care entry side, black child rates fell but not as rapidly as their foster care placement rates did (Fig. 3). The decline in black child foster care entry rates did not begin until about 2006, much later than the decline in their foster care placement rates. Between 2006 and 2012, the black child entry rate fell from 7.5 to 5.3, before increasing to 5.9 in 2015. Hispanic child foster care entry rates similarly did not fall until about 2006, and from 2008 to 2016, the rate has been fairly stable at about 3 per 1000. Finally, the white child entry rate peaked twice—in 2005 and

[1] Unless otherwise specified, all references to race groups refer to persons not of Hispanic origin. For example, "whites" means non-Hispanic whites. Hispanics may be of any race.

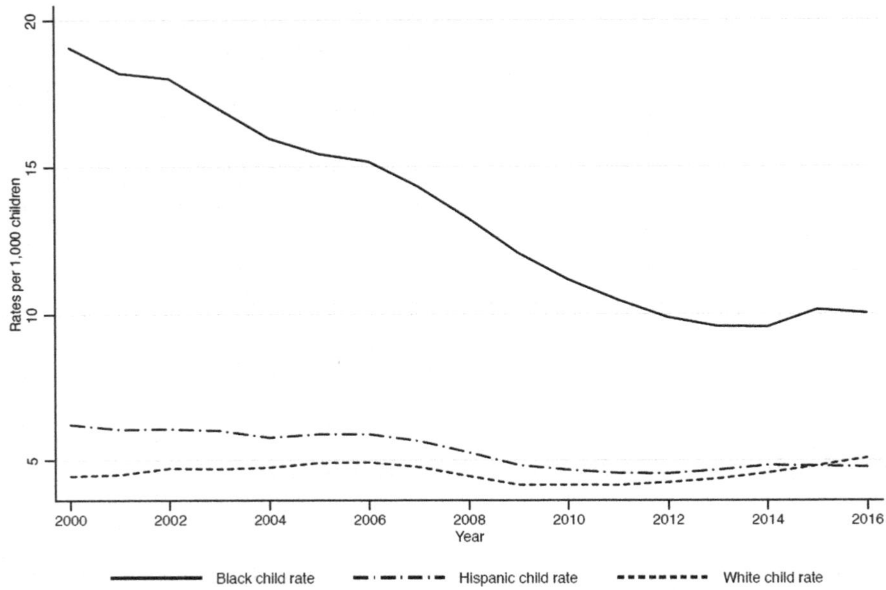

Fig. 1 Black, Hispanic, and white foster care placement rate per 1,000 child population 2000-2016

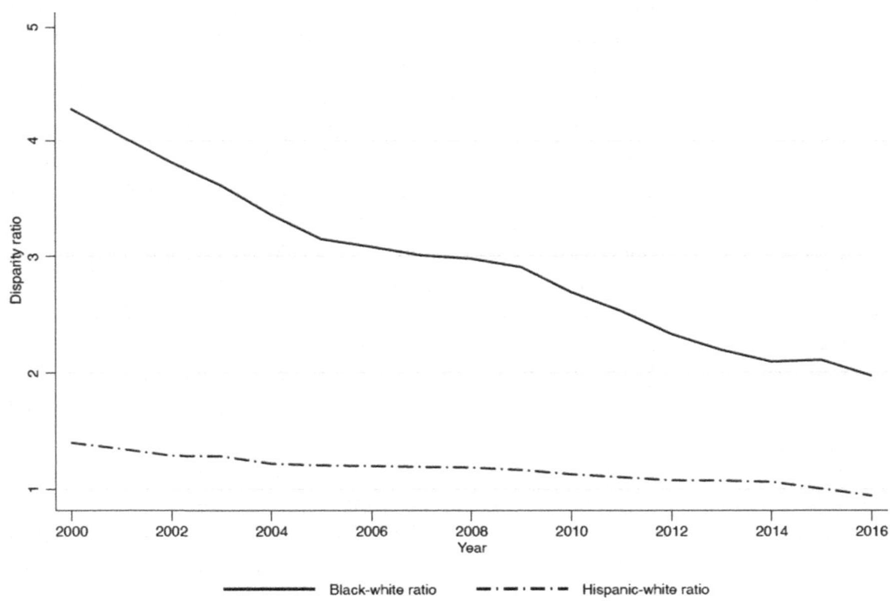

Fig. 2 Black- and Hispanic,-to-white foster care rate disparity ratios, 2000-2016

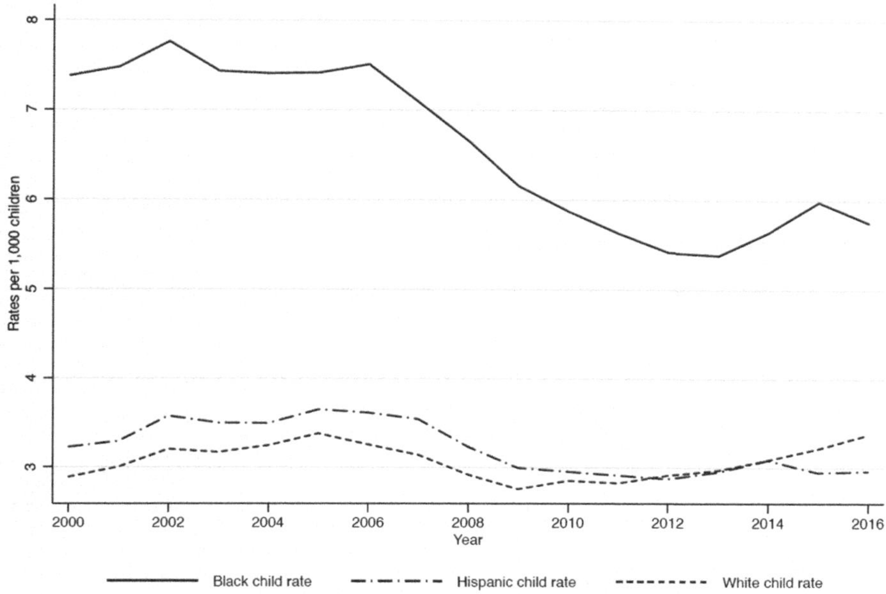

Fig. 3 Black, Hispanic, and white foster care entry rates per 1,000 child population 2000-2016

again in 2016—but after falling from its earlier peak to a low of 2.7 in 2009, it increased linearly to exceed 3.3 in 2016.

The racial and ethnic disparities in foster care entry rates fell, but the fall was not as large as occurred in the foster care placement population. The black-white child foster care entry rate disparity ratio fell from 2.6 to 1.7, with the bulk of the decrease coming after 2006 (Fig. 4). This is the opposite of the pattern occurring in the black-white foster care placement rate disparity. For Hispanic children, the foster care entry rate disparity fell from 1.1 to 0.9. As with foster care placements, by 2015, Hispanic children were entering foster care at lower rates than white children. For both black and Hispanic children, the increase in the white child foster care entry rate over the 2009–2016 period accounted for most of the decrease in disparity. As a result of the increase in the white child foster care entry rate over this period, the disparity ratios fell even during years in which the black or Hispanic child foster care entry rate increased.

The larger decrease in the black child foster care placement than entry rates suggests that the time that black children spent in foster care declined during the study period, as reported by Myers and Sabol (2019).

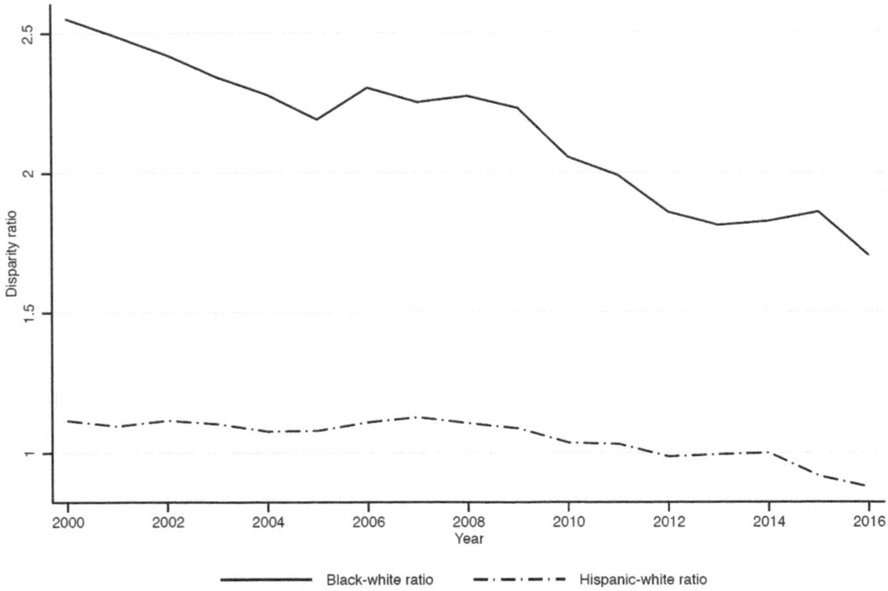

Fig. 4 Black- and Hispanic-to-white foster care entry rate disparity rations 2000-2016

Imprisonment Rate Disparities

In recent years, the Bureau of Justice Statistics has reported on declines in racial disparities in imprisonment (Bronson & Carson, 2019; Carson, 2018). Including state and federal prisoners and males and females combined, the BJS reports show that black imprisonment rates have declined more rapidly than white rates. Underlying the changes in black imprisonment rates are rapid declines for black women.

The imprisonment rate for black women incarcerated in state prisons increased during the 1990s, but beginning in 2000, it declined consistently through 2016. Peaking at nearly 300 per 100,000 black female adults, by 2016, the black female rate fell to 144 per 100,000 (Fig. 5). The Hispanic rate fluctuated around 70 per 100,000 during the late 1990s and early 2000s, but in 2006 it began to decline, and by 2016 it was below the rate for white women. The white female rate increased linearly from 1990 through 2016; from 2000 through 2016, the white female rate increased by nearly 60 percent. These changes in rates resulted in a decrease in the black-white female rate disparity of 6 to 1 in 2000 to 2 to 1 in 2016.

Behind the decline in black-white female imprisonment rates was a shift in the number of black and white women in state prisons for drug crimes. Between 2000 and 2016, the black female drug imprisonment rate fell by nearly 80%, while the white female drug imprisonment rate increased by almost 60% (Sabol et al., 2019).

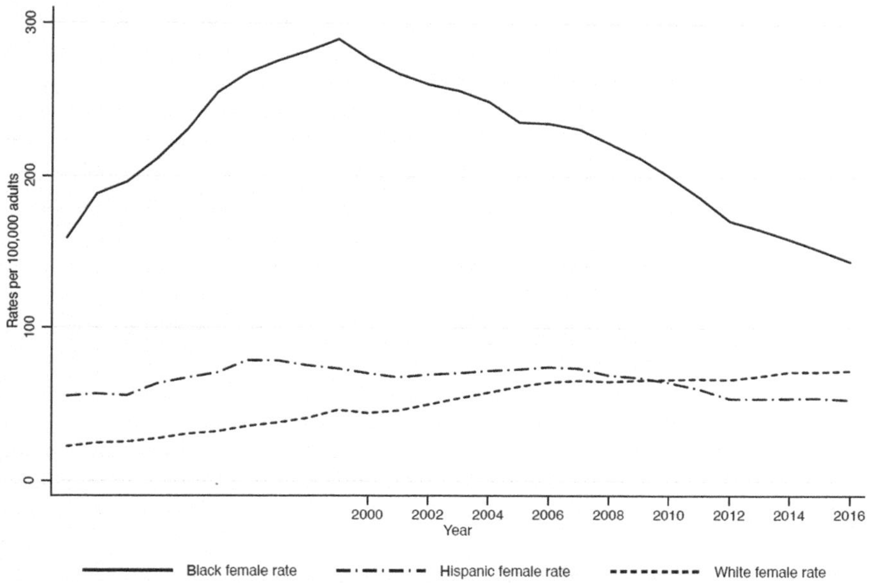

Fig. 5 Black Hispanic, and white female adult imprisonment rates per 100,000, 1990-2016

Relationship Between Incarceration and Foster Care

A large body of research has been done on the consequences of parental, particularly paternal, incarceration on children (Turney & Goodsell, 2018; Wildeman & Anderson, 2017; Wildeman et al., 2016). Much less has been done on the relationship between incarceration and foster care. In one of two such studies, Swann and Sylvester (2006) provided the first comprehensive study of the issue that we could find. Using a state-level panel covering the years 1985 to 2000, they reported that foster care caseloads doubled during that period and that female imprisonment rate growth along with reductions in cash welfare benefits were the two main factors explaining the growth in foster care caseloads over that period. They estimated that female imprisonment rate growth explained more than 30% of the increase in foster care caseloads.

These papers, as well as (Sabol, 2018), describe several ways in which child welfare and criminal justice systems interact and describe mechanisms by which imprisonment and foster care are related. Most immediately, children may be placed out-of-home while the primary caregiver, usually the mother, is incarcerated. In this case, imprisonment precedes and leads to the removal of a child due to the parent's imprisonment. The Adoption and Foster Care Analysis and Reporting System (AFCARS) report for 2016 shows, for example, in about 8% of entries into foster care, parental incarceration was listed among the circumstances leading to foster care entry (AFCARS, 2017). This effect is most likely to be observed among mothers, who generally are the primary caregivers, and children of incarcerated parents are more likely to be removed from home when mothers are incarcerated than when fathers are (Glaze & Maruschak, 2008; Mumola, 2000).

Alternatively, the criminal activity of parents may put children at greater risk of neglect before parents are incarcerated, and this could lead to the removal of the child and subsequent incarceration of a parent. Ross et al. (2004) looked at the chronology of arrest, incarceration, and child placement in NYC and concluded that in the vast majority (90%) of cases in which maternal incarceration overlapped with child placement, the incarceration started after the child placement; similarly, about 85% of the arrests that led to those incarcerations occurred after the child was removed. Their explanation was that removal of the child appeared to accelerate criminal activity among mothers who had prior convictions for drugs, prostitution, petty theft, and crimes related to substance abuse. These behaviors also increased the risk of maltreatment and subsequent removal of children.

Children may remain in foster care after their parents are released from prison, given difficulties that former inmates face in finding housing, getting a job, obtaining substance or mental health treatment, or otherwise demonstrating the capacity to provide for a child (Katz, 1998). The duration of imprisonment can affect whether an incarcerated parent and child are reunified upon a parent's exit from prison. The Adoption and Safe Families Act (ASFA) provides that states may terminate parental rights if a child has been in foster care for 15 of the most recent 22 months (although there are exceptions). As time served in prison generally increased during the 1990s and then remained at the higher levels throughout the 2000s (Travis & Western, 2014), the average mother entering prison on a new commitment for other than a drug crime could expect to serve more than 2 years, thereby raising the specter of ASFA's termination of rights.

High spatial concentrations of imprisonment in small areas could have indirect effects on foster care entry. It is well-documented that incarceration is spatially concentrated (Lynch & Sabol, 2004; Rose & Clear, 1998; Travis & Western, 2014). Such areas may be perceived by child welfare caseworkers as areas that are not safe for children. When child neglect occurs in these areas, a child welfare caseworker may consider the removal of a child for reasons related to a child's safety, even if the mother is not incarcerated. Consistent with ASFA's focus on the safety of a child, incarceration could be viewed as an additional risk factor for further abuse.

From 1980 to 2000, the number of kids with a father in prison or jail increased more than fivefold, as more than five million children have had a parent incarcerated at some point in their lives. According to BJS data, from 1990 to 2017, the number of children (1-day count) with incarcerated parents nearly doubled, from 945,600 to 1,706,600. This amounts to about 2.3% of all minor children having an incarcerated parent. Most parents in prison are men, as are most prisoners, but the majority of incarcerated women (62%) are mothers (Glaze & Maruschak, 2008). Most children lived with their mothers prior to their parents' incarceration. And according to the BJS prison inmate survey data, about 11% of incarcerated mothers reported that their children were in foster care while they were incarcerated. The BJS survey data also reveal the racial disparity among children of incarcerated parents, as slightly less than 1% of white children had an incarcerated parent, while nearly 7% of black children and 2.4% of Hispanic children did.

On the Decline in Racial Disparity in Foster Care Rates

The trends in black-white foster care placement rates that we described above have been given scant attention in the child welfare literature. The Children's Bureau has reported on the decrease in disparity in foster care (Child Welfare Information Gateway, 2016). But much of the empirical work on racial disparities in child welfare outcomes has focused on cross-sectional or single-period analyses that examine the degree to which racial differences in case-level factors vs. child welfare decision-making explain racial disparities. The work is informed by three main arguments about racial disparities. Studies acknowledge the history of discrimination in the USA that contributed to the economic disadvantage faced by black families, but they differ on the mechanisms through which it contributes to disparity and whether this occurs at the caseworker level, at the institutional level (through policies and procedures that are biased against black families), or through the socio-economic disadvantage that leads to higher levels of neglect and abuse that increases the risk of maltreatment (Ards et al., 2003, 2012; Bartholet, 2009; Boyd, 2014; Chand, 2000; Fluke, 2011; Hill, 2004; Kim et al., 2011; Roberts, 2012; Wildeman et al., 2014). In principle, the theories that explain the reasons for disparities could also explain the increase or decrease in disparities in foster care rates. This occurs if the levels of the variables that generate the gaps at the caseworker, institutional, or socio-economic level change.

Studies of disparities focus on child welfare decision points leading to the decision to place a child into foster care. Decision points or stages in the child welfare process include referral, substantiation, and the decision to remove a child from a family (Font & Maguire-Jack, 2015; Graham et al., 2015; Kim et al., 2011; Morton et al., 2011). Myers (2011) distinguished between unconditional and conditional disparities, where conditional disparities measure the probability of transitioning between stages of the child welfare process. Studies that consider child welfare case processing decisions to explain disparities generally find smaller disparities than those that measure the disparities unconditionally (Child Welfare Information Gateway, 2016) but not for all outcomes, such as reunification following parental incarceration (Hayward & DePanfilis, 2007).

The absence of data on the incidence of maltreatment other than through the National Incidence Study of Child Abuse and Neglect (NIS)[2] means that studies of

[2]The NIS estimates the incidence of child abuse and neglect in the USA and provides estimates of the extent of reported and unreported abuse and neglect. Four waves of the NIS have been conducted, with the last wave covering incidents occurring in 2005 and 2006. The national sample design precludes using the data for studies at the subnational level, such as the county, which is the unit of analysis for our proposed project.

the effects of child welfare decision-making on racial disparities generally start with data on reported maltreatment and analyze subsequent decisions.[3] Whether using individual or aggregate data, studies find a strong relationship between poverty and reported maltreatment and that racial differences in poverty rates are a primary driver of the racial disparity in maltreatment (Drake et al., 2009, 2011; Maguire-Jack et al., 2015; Maguire-Jack & Font, 2017).

Although poverty and need may predict maltreatment, it is not immediately clear that they should also predict foster care rates or racial disparities in them. At the state level, changes in socio-economic status do not appear to affect foster care maintenance rates (Goldhaber-Fiebert et al., 2014). But state-level data may mask within-state variation at the county level as Wulczyn (2017), Wulczyn et al. (2013), and Wulczyn and Levy (2007) show in examining the black/white foster care placement gap. They found that county-level measures of poverty and social disadvantage are correlated with county-level variations in the black/white placement gap, but the relationship they found was a negative one: as county-level poverty rates increased, the black/white gap in placement rates narrowed. They explained this somewhat counterintuitive finding by the fact that the relationship between poverty and placement rates depends upon race. Their work suggests that increasing poverty in areas lessens racial disparities in foster care placements.

Consistent with Wulczyn's work, since the late 1990s, poverty has spread geographically, as there has been an expansion in the number of counties in the USA with high poverty rates (Mather & Jarosz, 2016). The number of high-poverty-rate (more than 15.5%) counties increased in all types of counties, but the largest increases between 1989 and 2010/2014 occurred in small–/mid-sized metropolitan areas followed closely by non-metropolitan/rural counties. The increase in urban counties with high poverty rates could contribute to explaining the decrease in racial disparities in foster care if black children in foster care resided in predominantly urban areas, and the child welfare system treated poor children similarly, but the increase in poverty would not necessarily explain the decrease in the black child foster care rate. The increase in high poverty in areas that are largely white—small and rural counties—could help explain the decrease in disparity.

Another plausible explanation for declining racial disparities in foster care is the enhanced federal oversight of child welfare agencies. Since 2000, the Children's Bureau conducted the Child and Family Services Reviews (CFSRs) that established federal standards in child welfare and required states to undertake self-examination and federal audit of their child welfare processes to determine the extent to which they aligned with federal standards. Additionally, the Children's Bureau also undertook several rounds of Title IV-E eligibility reviews to ensure that states met legal requirements for federal funds.

[3] The fourth wave of the NIS reported racial differences in the incidence of maltreatment that were explained by a growing gap between black and white children in economic well-being. Socio-economic status was identified as the strongest predictor of maltreatment rates, and the black-white gap was attributed to lagging black family incomes relative to white family income growth (Sedlak et al., 2010).

During the same time, states could conduct demonstration projects using Title IV-E to develop knowledge about new and innovative child welfare practices. The IV-E waivers gave states flexibility to support alternative services (to foster care) that promoted safety, permanency, and well-being for children in child protection and foster care systems. Between the enactment of the original child welfare waiver authority in 1994 and 2013, 23 states implemented one or more demonstrations involving a variety of service strategies, including:

- Subsidized guardianship/kinship permanence.
- Flexible funding and capped title IV-E allocations to local child welfare agencies.
- Managed care payment systems.
- Services for caregivers with substance use disorders.
- Intensive service options, including expedited reunification services.
- Enhanced training for child welfare staff.
- Adoption and post-permanency services.
- Tribal administration of title IV-E funds (Children's Bureau, 2013).

We expect that states' experimentation with waiver programs reflects their capacity and willingness to try alternative programming that could also lead to reductions in foster care.

Research Questions and Hypotheses

Given prior studies showing that growth in female imprisonment led to growth in foster care, we are interested in whether this relationship holds during a period of declining foster care rates and if there are race-specific effects in this relationship or if the increase in the imprisonment of women accounted for the largest portion of the increase in foster care caseloads during a period of growth in foster-care caseloads, then does the decline in imprisonment for black women account for the decline in foster care caseloads for black children?

More specifically, we ask:

- To what extent do race-specific imprisonment rates explain race-specific *foster care entry rates*, controlling for confirmed maltreatment rates and relevant socio-demographic variables?
- To what extent do race-specific imprisonment rates explain race-specific *foster care placement rates*, controlling for racial differences in the mean expected length of stay in foster care?

Given the literature and patterns in the data that we observed, we speculate that:

- We will observe a positive association between female imprisonment rates and both foster care entry and placement rates and there will be no racial differences in these effects. We base this upon the findings from the prior research we cited.

- We will observe a positive association between male imprisonment rates and foster care entry and placement rates. We view male incarceration as an indication of criminal justice system penetration into a community, and as a consequence of this penetration, the child welfare system will be predisposed to remove children for safety reasons as male incarceration increases.
- We speculate that Title IV-E waiver experimentation will be associated with lower foster care rates.
- We speculate that these relationships will hold controlling for confirmed maltreatment rates.

For our analysis, we take advantage of the differences in black-white female imprisonment rates and black-white foster care entries and placements to examine racial differences in the possible effects of imprisonment on foster care. We have constructed and use an annual, state-level panel covering the years 2000–2015. While we estimate fixed-effects regressions and control for socio-economic variables and state expenditures, our aim is to establish patterns of relationships rather than to estimate causal effects.

Data Sources

Using several sources, we compiled a level, yearly panel dataset covering the years 2000 through 2015 on foster care entries, placements, and exits, confirmed maltreatment cases, incarceration, socio-economic variables, population, state expenditures, and the timing and location (state) of Title IV-E waiver programs. We obtained race- and Hispanic-origin-specific[4] foster care measures from the Adoption and Foster Care Analysis and Reporting System (AFCARS) and race-specific confirmed maltreatment data from the National Child Abuse and Neglect Data System (NCANDS). The foster care measures covered the years 2000 through 2015; the child maltreatment data covered the years 2004–2015, due to data limitations prior to 2004. We downloaded the state-by-year foster care and maltreatment data from the Annie E. Casey Kids Count Database.

We used Bureau of Justice Statistics' (BJS's) National Prisoners Statistics (NPS) data to obtain annual, race-sex-specific counts of persons under the jurisdiction of each state's prison system at year end. The NPS data do not provide race-specific prison admissions data. To calculate race-sex-specific imprisonment rates, we used US Census Bureau inter-census state and county population estimates to generate the denominators of the imprisonment rates. The US Census Bureau's Annual Survey of Government Finance provided the state government expenditure data. Socio-economic data came from the American Communities Survey (ACS).

[4] Henceforth, unless we specify otherwise, we use the phrase "race-specific" to refer to "race- and Hispanic-origin-specific."

The Children's Bureau, Office of Administration for Children and Families within the Department of Health and Human Services compilation of Title IV-E waiver programs, participants, and dates of programs provided the source data on states' participation in IV-E waiver programs.

Measures

Our dependent variables are the race-specific foster care entry and foster care placement rates per 1000 children, within the respective race group. Our main independent variable (or measure of the intervention) was the race-specific adult female and adult male imprisonment rates per 100,000 resident population. Because a child can be removed from a home during the period of incarceration and not just at the point of admission into prison, we measured imprisonment rates based upon the stock of prisoners and not the flow of admissions. We include race-specific measures of male imprisonment rates per adult male. Our third major variable is the confirmed maltreatment rate. Given the centrality of confirmed maltreatment to the foster care process, we included measures of the race-specific confirmed child maltreatment rates per 1000 children in the respective race group.

We added controls for other factors thought to be associated with foster care. State expenditures reflect spending priorities, and shifts in expenditures over time also reflect the relative priorities of different types of state programs. We included per capita state expenditure amounts for several categories of expenditures; these were total state government expenditures, education, public welfare, health, police, and corrections. We expressed all expenditure amounts in constant (2015) dollars. Poverty and socio-economic conditions are known to be associated with child maltreatment and foster care. Consequently, we included race-specific socio-economic measures including teen birth rates, median household income, child poverty rates, and children in families headed by a single person. Household income was measured in constant (2015) dollars.

To address our interest in the possible role of federal child welfare policy, we included measures of states' participation in Title IV-E waiver programs. We measured these using a series of dummy or indicator variables equal to 1 during the years in which a state participated in a program and zero for the other years. We measured four categories of completed waivers, meaning that a state had officially ended a waiver program; these were:

- Subsidized guardianship/kinship permanence: Caregivers or relatives assume legal custody of children who are eligible for a monthly subsidy equal or comparable to monthly foster care payments. Eleven states implemented these between 1996 and 2011. Years of implementation varied among the states.
- Services for caregivers: IV-E monies used to fund services for caregivers with substance use disorders. Three states implemented these between 1996 and 2005; years of implementation varied.

- Managed care payment systems: Tests of alternative managed care financing mechanisms to reduce child welfare costs while improving permanency, safety, well-being, and outcomes for targeted families. Five states implemented these between 1999 and 2003; years of implementation varied among states.
- Intensive service options: States increased the variety and intensity of services to reduce out-of-home placement rates and improve child permanency and safety. Three states implemented these between 1998 and 2008; years varied among states.

We also included a dummy variable for any active waiver demonstrations, that is, wavier demonstrations that were still underway by the end of 2015. We did not classify these into specific program categories due to the diversity of the waiver efforts and multiple foci within states.

Methods

Our general strategy was to use fixed-effects estimators to exploit the within-state variation in imprisonment rates over time. We used state and year fixed effects and weighted the regressions by state population. Standard errors were clustered.

We started by estimating race-specific models of foster care entries on female and male imprisonment rates for the entire 2000–2015 study period. We then estimated regressions adding the several sets of control variables. Second, given the availability of confirmed maltreatment data for 2004–2015 only, we repeated the process for this shorter period. Following the regressions of foster care entry on imprisonment, we then added the confirmed maltreatment rates to the regressions, followed by the additional control and IV-E waiver variables.

The specific progression of the regression models was:

- Female and male incarceration
- Child welfare policy variables: Title IV-E waiver programs
- Sentencing policy variables
- State expenditures per capita (in 2015 dollars)
- Maltreatment rates
- SES covariates

We repeated the process for foster care placement rates.

We used a log-log functional form for the dependent and continuous covariates. The parameters are interpreted as elasticities (the effects of a 1-percent change in a variable on foster care entry rates).

As is well known, regression analysis such as that we have undertaken does not provide a definitive assessment of the causal pathways connecting foster care and imprisonment. It is beyond the scope of the current investigation, however, to test for the direction of causation or to determine whether other factors could explain the trends and patterns we establish.

Results

We focus on the period 2004–2015, for which we have the confirmed maltreatment data. (Results for the 2000–2015 period that exclude maltreatment measures are available upon request of the authors. For brevity, in the tables we show only the estimates for imprisonment and maltreatment and not all of the control variables.)

Black Child Foster Care Entry

The results for black child foster care entry rates show that the effects of imprisonment are not consistent across specifications. In models 1, 2, and 3 in Table 1, the signs on the parameters for both the black female and black male imprisonment rates are positive but not significant. When we introduce confirmed maltreatment rates in models 4 and 5, the signs on the black female imprisonment rate flip and become negative but remain non-significant; however, the signs on the black male imprisonment rate remain positive but reach statistical significance. Across models 4 and 5, the effects of the confirmed maltreatment rate are positive and statistically significant.

The estimated magnitudes of the effects of the black male imprisonment rates are on the same order of magnitude as the effects of the confirmed black child maltreatment rate. In models 4 and 5, the elasticities for these two variables range from about 0.22% to 0.30%, or a 1-percentage-point change in each of the variable results in a combined (additive), roughly half-percentage point change (increase) in the growth of black child foster care entries.

Not shown, participation in IV-E waiver programs reduces the growth in black child foster care entries in models 1–3, but when child maltreatment rates are entered into the equation, only active waiver participation has any effect on black child foster care entry rates, and it exerts a smaller, negative effect on that growth rate than do either black male imprisonment or child maltreatment rates. None of the socio-economic variables has significant effects, and the effects of state expenditures are mixed and small.

White Child Foster Care Entry

For white child foster care entry rates, the white female imprisonment rate is not significant in models 1–3, but when white child maltreatment rates are introduced into the equation, the effect of white female imprisonment rates remains positive and reaches significance (Table 2). A 1-percentage-point change in the white female imprisonment rate results in a 0.16% change in the growth rate of white child foster care entry rates. Conversely, the effects of white male imprisonment rates on white

Table 1 Fixed effects regression estimates of black child foster care entry rates, 2004–2015

(Robust standard errors)										
	Model 1		Mode 2		Model 3		Model 4		Model 5	
Variables	Param	t-stat	Param	t-stat	Param	t-stat	Param	t-stat	Param	t-stat
In(black female imprisonment rate)	0.071	0.048	0.0572	0.048	0.050	0.049	−0.022	0.048	−0.0549	0.0760
In(black male imprisonment rate)	0.027	1.357	0.0082	0.134	0.046	0.136	0.252	0.128 *	0.2981	0.1555 *
In(black child maltreatment rate)							0.234	0.033 **	0.2173	0.0344 **
Controls										
IV-E Waivers	Yes		Yes		Yes		Yes		Yes	
State sentencing policies	Yes		Yes		Yes		Yes		Yes	
State expenditures	Yes		Yes		Yes		Yes		Yes	
SES variables	Yes		Yes		Yes		Yes		Yes	
State & year fixed effects	Yes		Yes		Yes		Yes		Yes	
Notes: *$p < 0.05$; **$p < 0.01$										
N observations	509		509		509		509		509	

child foster care entry go from significant (models 1–3) to insignificant with the introduction of child maltreatment rates (models 4–5).

White child confirmed maltreatment rates have significant, positive effects on white child foster care entry. The white child confirmed maltreatment rate has the largest magnitude of effect (0.2), but the magnitude of the white female imprisonment rate is about the same order of magnitude (0.16).

Two of the measured IV-E waiver programs have significant effects in models 4–5: the intensive service option demonstrations and currently active demonstrations. The effects of these two waiver programs are consistently negative across all five specifications; in models 4 and 5, the combined (additive) effects of these two waiver demonstrations is about −0.2 or the same magnitude (in absolute value) of either the child maltreatment or female imprisonment rate variables.

Among the socio-economic variables, only the white teen birth rate had a significant effect in model 5. White teen birth rates were positively associated with white child foster care entry rates, and the magnitude of the effect (0.27%) was the largest effect on any single variable.

Table 2 Fixed effects regression estimates of white child foster care entry rates, 2004–2015

(Robust standard errors)										
	Model 1		Mode 2		Model 3		Model 4		Model 5	
Variables	Param	t-stat	Param	t-stat	Param	t-stat	Param	t-stat	Param	t-stat
ln(white female imprisonment rate)	0.027	0.071	0.04659	0.071	0.064	0.071	0.161	0.071*	0.1644	0.0722*
ln(white male imprisonment rate)	0.322	0.136*	0.31966	0.135*	0.293	0.134*	0.195	0.135	0.1290	0.1379
ln(white child maltreatment rate)							0.200	0.027**	0.1946	0.0275**
Controls										
IV-E Waivers	Yes		Yes		Yes		Yes		Yes	
State sentencing policies	Yes		Yes		Yes		Yes		Yes	
State expenditures	Yes		Yes		Yes		Yes		Yes	
SES variables	Yes		Yes		Yes		Yes		Yes	
State & year fixed effects	Yes		Yes		Yes		Yes		Yes	
Notes: *$p < 0.05$; **$p < 0.01$										
N observations	536		536		536		536		536	

Hispanic Child Foster Care Entry

The only variable having a significant effect on the Hispanic child foster care entry rates was the Hispanic child confirmed maltreatment rate (Table 3). Its effect was large and positive (0.43%). Neither Hispanic female nor Hispanic male imprisonment rates had a significant effect on Hispanic child foster care entry, although the signs on both imprisonment rates were positive.

Foster Care Placement Rates

Results of the foster care placement rate regressions follow the same general patterns as with the foster care entry rate results, with some important differences. For black and Hispanic children, the effects of female imprisonment on foster care placement are not significant, although for black children the female imprisonment rate effect nears the 0.05 level when confirmed maltreatment is included (Tables 4 and 5). The signs on female imprisonment for blacks and Hispanics are negative,

Table 3 Fixed effects regression estimates of Hispanic child foster care entry rates, 2004–2015

(Robust standard errors)										
Data covering 2004–2015										
	Model 1		Mode 2		Model 3		Model 4		Model 5	
Variables	Param	t-stat	Param	t-stat	Param	t-stat	Param	t-stat	Param	t-stat
ln(Hispanic female imprisonment rate)	−0.015	0.047	−0.0129	0.047	−0.020	0.047	0.036	0.043	0.0600	0.0422
ln(Hispanic male imprisonment rate)	0.059	0.073	0.0568	0.072	0.087	0.072	0.092	0.065	0.1121	0.0677
ln(Hispanic child maltreatment rate)							0.521	0.044 **	0.4281	0.0445 **
Controls										
IV-E Waivers	Yes		Yes		Yes		Yes		Yes	
State sentencing policies	Yes		Yes		Yes		Yes		Yes	
State expenditures	Yes		Yes		Yes		Yes		Yes	
SES variables	Yes		Yes		Yes		Yes		Yes	
State & year fisted effects	Yes		Yes		Yes		Yes		Yes	
Notes: *p < 0.05; **p < 0.01										
N observations	516		516		516		516		516	

implying that increases in their imprisonment rates would lead to decreases in foster care placement rates (and vice versa). For white children, the female imprisonment rate effects are positive and larger than the effects of confirmed maltreatment. While the parameter on the white female imprisonment rate in Table 5 increases (that includes confirmed maltreatment rates), it does not differ statistically from the parameter estimate in Table 4. Hence, conditional upon confirmed maltreatment, there is an effect of female imprisonment rates for white children, but not for black or Hispanic children.

Black male imprisonment rates are positively associated with black child foster care placement rates, but this relationship does not obtain for whites or for Hispanics. For Hispanics, the male imprisonment rate is significant at the lower threshold of 0.01.

Table 4 Race-specific, fixed effects estimates of foster care rates, without confirmed maltreatment rate, 2004–2015

	Black child foster care rate				White child foster care rate				Hispanic child foster care rate			
Variable	Coef.	Std. Err.	t	P > t	Coef.	Std. Err.	t	P > t	Coef.	Std. Err.	t	P > t
Maltreatment rate												
Female imprisonment rate	−0.0966	0.5506	−0.18	0.861	1.7193	0.6067	2.83	0.005	−0.4468	0.5414	−0.83	0.41
Male imprisonment rate	0.1035	0.0789	1.31	0.19	−0.0441	0.1195	−0.37	0.712	0.0728	0.0489	1.49	0.137
Controls												
IV-Waivers	Yes				Yes				Yes			
State sentencing policies	Yes				Yes				Yes			
State expenditures	Yes				Yes				Yes			
SES measures	Yes				Yes				Yes			
State & year fixed effects	Yes				Yes				Yes			
N observations	509				536				516			
N groups	50				50				50			
N years	22				12				12			

Table 5 Race-specific, fixed effects estimates of foster care rates, 2004–2015

	Black child foster care rate				White child foster care rate				Hispanic child foster care rate			
Variable	Coef.	Std. Err.	t	P > t	Coef.	Std. Err.	t	P > t	Coef.	Std. Err.	t	P > t
Maltreatment rate	0.2148	0.0278	7.72	0	0.1030	0.0147	7.02	0	0.2461	0.0233	10.57	0
Female imprisonment rate	−0.8354	0.4691	−1.78	0.076	2.0779	0.6377	3.26	0.001	−0.5635	0.4937	−1.14	0.254
Male imprisonment rate	0.1820	0.0648	2.81	0.005	−0.0857	0.1240	−0.69	0.49	0.0788	0.0465	1.69	0.091
Controls												
IV-Waivers	Yes				Yes				Yes			
State sentencing policies	Yes				Yes				Yes			
State expenditures	Yes				Yes				Yes			
SES measures	Yes				Yes				Yes			
State & year Fixed effects	Yes				Yes				Yes			
N observations	509				536				516			
N groups	50				50				50			
N years	12				12				12			

Discussion

The results on foster care entry rates in model 5 (the preferred model in Tables 1, 2, and 3) and foster care placement (Table 5) show racial differences in the direction and magnitude of effects of the imprisonment variables. For black and Hispanic children, there were no significant effects of female imprisonment rates, but for white children, increases in white female imprisonment rates led to increases in white child foster care entry rates. And only for black children was there an effect of male imprisonment on foster care entry; the black male imprisonment rate had a positive effect on the black child foster care entry rate and the foster care placement rate. The magnitude of the black male imprisonment rate effect is large; its estimated elasticity was almost twice the magnitude of the effect of white female imprisonment rates on white child foster care entry rates.

Confirmed maltreatment rates had positive effects on foster care entry rates for all three racial groups. These effects are consistent with our predictions. Among the socio-economic variables, only white teen birth rates had an effect on foster care entries; the effects of black and Hispanic teen birth rates did not reach statistical significance. State and federal sponsored programs implemented to develop alternatives to foster care do not show any significant effect in reducing foster care rates.

These differential effects suggest that there are different processes at work for black, Hispanic, and white children. The effect of black male incarceration on foster care entry is consistent with the literature that as male incarceration increases, foster care placement increases. However, between 2000 and 2016, the black male imprisonment actually decreased by about 30% (Bronson & Carson, 2019; Sabol et al., 2019). Or, as black men came out of prison in the 2000s, the black child rate of entry into foster care decreased.

Three factors could be at work here. First, the decrease in black male imprisonment rates could be associated with a reduction in the concentration of black male incarceration. We speculated that high-incarceration-rate areas could be perceived by child welfare caseworkers as unsafe for children, thereby hastening their removal to foster care. However, if concentrations of incarceration are lower, child welfare caseworkers' perceptions of them as unsafe could change. Second, these effects could be concentrated in states with less punitive systems or that had more generous welfare programs (Edwards, 2016), a hypothesis that we did not test.

Third, the effect of the declining black male imprisonment rate on foster care entries could be economic. The withdraws of men removes a source of income for black children that in turn affects the remaining caregiver's (mother's) capacity to provide for a child, and then when black male imprisonment rates increase, so too would foster care entry rates. Conversely, when the imprisonment rates decrease, if the income support hypothesis is correct, so too would foster care entry rates. BJS survey data show that the majority of incarcerated fathers report providing primary financial for their child prior to their incarceration, as more than two-thirds of those fathers who lived with the child prior to incarceration provided primary financial support for their minor children (Glaze & Maruschak, 2008). Further, given the difficulties that former prisoners face finding jobs (Bushway et al., 2007; Western, 2006), even if the returning fathers were unable to provide income, to the extent that they provide childcare or other support, this could ease a working mother's efforts to maintain custody of her children.

The effects of white female imprisonment on white child foster care entry rates and placement rates are consistent with our hypotheses, but the absence of effects of black and Hispanic female imprisonment on their respective children's foster care entry rates is not consistent with predictions. The effects of white female imprisonment are generally strengthened by introducing measures of white child confirmed maltreatment rates, suggesting an independent incarceration effect for whites but not blacks or Hispanics.

One plausible explanation for the black-white female imprisonment effects is changes in the types of drugs that were subject to drug enforcement policy. During the 1980 and 1990 period studied by Swann and Sylvester, enforcement of crack cocaine intensified (Travis & Western, 2014), as measured by arrests and imprisonments. Both black drug arrest and black drug imprisonment rates increased during this period along with drug enforcement of crack cocaine. However, since 2000, both black female and black male drug imprisonment rates have coincided with large increases in white female imprisonment rates. As we pointed out, drug crime enforcement explains most of the shift in black-white female imprisonment rates.

Unfortunately, the available criminal justice administrative data systems do not report sufficient detail on drug crimes either to characterize the types of drugs for which persons are arrested or the types of crimes for which they are imprisoned. Consequently, we have to use proxies for these measures. One such proxy for the type of drug of arrest and imprisonment is the drug overdose mortality rate. Under the assumption that high rates of overdose for specific types of drugs indicate involvement or use of types of drugs, changes in drug overdose mortality by type of drug would provide an indication of involvement with different types of drugs. Prescription opioid mortality rates for whites have exceeded those for blacks throughout the 2000s by a factor of two-to-one, and only in recent years have black fentanyl overdose rates reached the levels for whites (Scholl et al., 2018).

The shifts in black-white female drug imprisonment rates are consistent with shifts in the types of drugs enforced. During the 1980s and 1990s, crack cocaine was the focus of enforcement, but during the 2000s, opioids have been. These drug types are associated with racial differences in use and plausibly manufacturing or dealing. Evidence of racial differences in types of drugs comes from drug overdose death rates. Figure 6 shows the state-specific medians, IQRs, and outliers for the white female drug overdose mortality rate, and Fig. 7 shows the same for the black female rate. The white female rate increased linearly throughout the 2000–2016 period, while the black female mortality rate was comparatively flat until about 2015. To the extent that drug overdose rates reflect involvement and use of drug types, the white female rate suggests much higher involvement of white women with opioids.

Unfortunately, the official statistics on drug arrests derived from the Federal Bureau of Investigation's Uniform Crime Reports (UCR) are not available by the

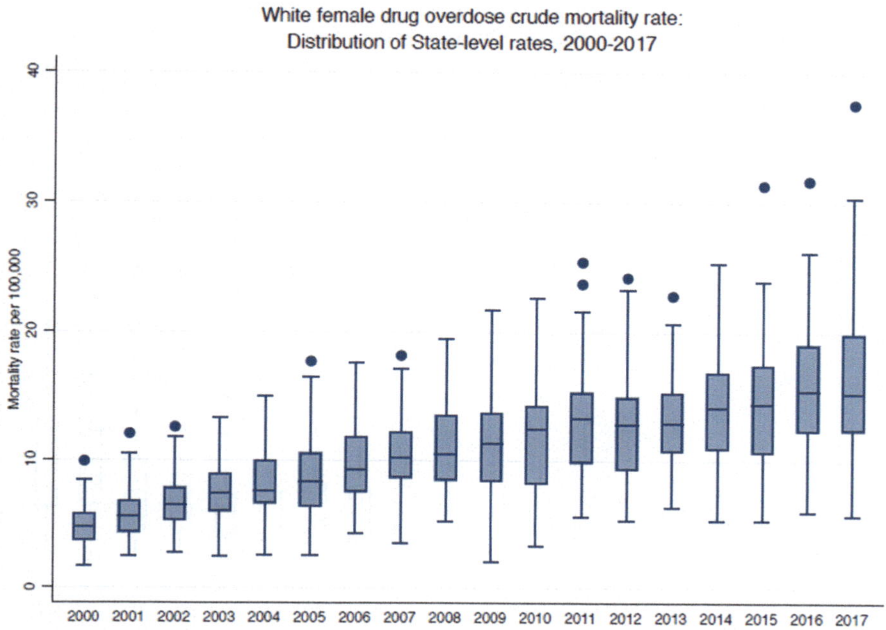

Fig. 6 Sources: Cause of death data: Centers for Disease Control and Prevention, National Center for Health Statistics. Underlying Cause of Death 1999-2017 on CDC WONDER Online Database, released December, 2018. Data are from the Multiple Cause of Death Files, 1999-2017, as compiled from data provided by the 57 vital statistics jurisdictions through the Vitatl Statistics Cooperative Program. Accessed at http://wonder.cdc.gov/ucd-icd10.html on Dec. 14, 2018 3:12:44 PM. Population data: United States Department of Health and Human Services (US DHHS), Centers for Disease Control and Prevention (CDC), National Center for Health Statistics (NCHS), Bridged-Race Population Estimates, United States July 1st population by state, county, age, sex, bridged-race, and Hispanic origin. Compiled from 1990-1999 bridged-race intercensal population estimates (released by NCHS on 7/26/2004); revised bridged-race 2000-2009 intercensal population estimates (released by NCHS on 10/26/2021; and bridged-race Vintage 2017 (2010-2017) intercensal population estimates (released by NCHS on 6/27/2018. Available on CDC WONDER Online Database. Accessed at http://wonder.cdc.bridged-race-v2017.html on Dec 6, 2018 at 9:01:11 AM

combination of race and sex. They are only available by race and by sex. During the 1980s when crack cocaine enforcement increased, the male-female drug arrest rate ratio decreased as the black-white drug arrest rate ratio increased. These patterns are consistent with increasing drug arrest rates for both black men and women. However, since the mid-1990s and continuing through the 2000s, as the male-female arrest rate ratio continued to decline, the black-white arrest rate ratio made a U turn and continued to fall, a pattern that is consistent with increasing arrests of white women for drug crimes and decreasing arrests of black women for drug crimes.

With this enforcement of type of drug explanation, we speculate that there have been increases in the white female drug arrest rate for, first, methamphetamine and second prescription opioids that lead to increases in their drug imprisonment rate.

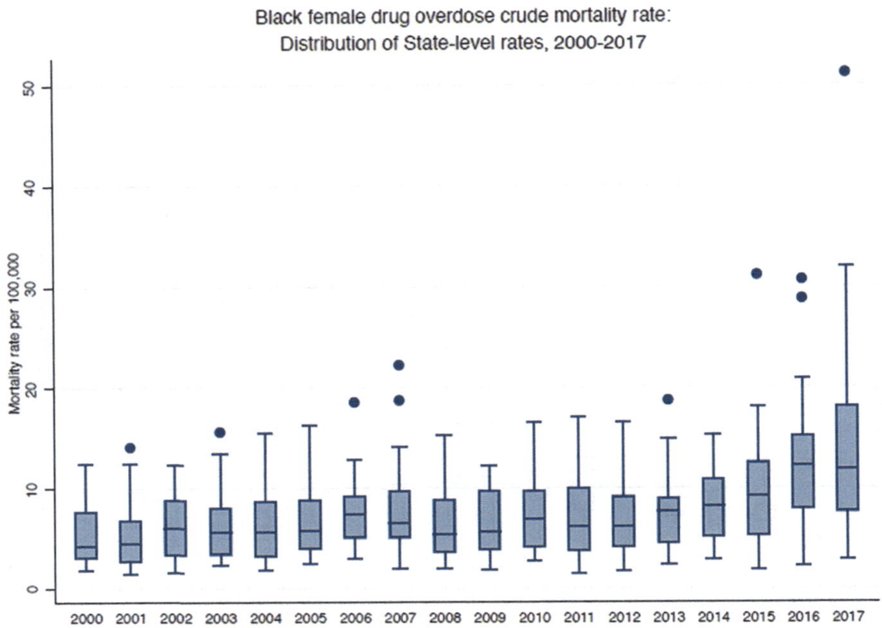

Fig. 7 Sources: Cause of death data: Centers for Disease Control and Prevention, National Center for Health Statistics. Underlying Cause of Death 1999-2017 on CDC WONDER Online Database, released December, 2018. Data are from the Multiple Cause of Death Files, 1999-2017, as compiled from data provided by the 57 vital statistics jurisdictions through the Vitatl Statistics Cooperative Program. Accessed at http://wonder.cdc.gov/ucd-icd10.html on Dec. 14, 2018 3:12:44 PM. Population data: United States Department of Health and Human Services (US DHHS), Centers for Disease Control and Prevention (CDC), National Center for Health Statistics (NCHS), Bridged-Race Population Estimates, United States July 1st population by state, county, age, sex, bridged-race, and Hispanic origin. Compiled from 1990-1999 bridged-race intercensal population estimates (released by NCHS on 7/26/2004); revised bridged-race 2000-2009 intercensal population estimates (released by NCHS on 10/26/2021; and bridged-race Vintage 2017 (2010-2017) intercensal population estimates (released by NCHS on 6/27/2018. Available on CDC WONDER Online Database. Accessed at http://wonder.cdc.bridged-race-v2017.html on Dec 6, 2018 at 9:01:11 AM

By comparison, as the enforcement of crack diminished, there has been a decrease in black female drug arrests and imprisonments.

Under this drug enforcement hypothesis, imprisonment rate change is responsive to drug crimes and the types of drugs enforced. The association between a type of drug and race is important for determining a large portion of the change in imprisonment. This leads to the speculation that as the use of fentanyl increases and is associated with increases in black female drug overdoses, the enforcement effect on black women will increase and so will the effects of drug imprisonment on foster care entries.

Third, we were surprised to find any effect of federal policies and the Title IV-E waiver demonstration participation. We interpret participation in waiver demonstrations as an indication of a state's commitment to improving different aspects of its child welfare system. States that adopted Intensive Service Option (ISO) waiver demonstrations had lower foster care entry rates for whites but did not affect black or Hispanic foster care entry. The ISO waiver (increased the intensity of services to reduce out-of-home placements) had an effect only on the white foster care entry rate (~12% lower than non-ISO states). The three states with ISO waivers (CA, AZ, MS) have diverse populations, and it is not immediately obvious why the effects held only for whites.

States with active waiver demonstrations had lower foster care entry rates for black and white children than states without active waiver programs. The effect was to reduce entry rates by about 7% to 10%. Active waiver demonstrations have been in effect since about 2013; hence their effect on foster care entry rates occurred late in the study period after substantial reductions in FC entry had occurred for black youth. Twenty-four states with active waivers had several different types of demonstrations, including those that focused on "right-sizing" the congregate care system, enhancing assessment and family engagement, flexible funding systems, kinship supports, trauma-informed assessment and services, services for caregivers with substance abuse disorders, and wrap-around and post-unification services. While it would be nice to know if specific types of waiver demonstrations were associated with reductions, the measures and data used are not sufficient to test for these. We point out that states with active waiver demonstrations select themselves into the waiver program; hence, the differences in foster care entry may be due to self-selection and general orientation of the states toward foster care rather than to a specific federal program effect.

Other Explanations and Implications to Consider

We did not explicitly measure changes at the child welfare agency level, especially the racial/ethnic composition of the workforce. Increase in the share of non-white case workers could lead to decreases in confirmed maltreatment and foster care entry. McBreath et al. (2014) suggest that child welfare caseworkers' housing-related service strategies may differ. When caseworkers were culturally similar to clients, caseworkers used more active strategies to connect caregivers to needed housing services.

Ards et al. (2012) used vignettes to show that individual case workers within counties differed in classifying a situation as neglect depending on the randomly assigned race of the child. Ards et al. aggregated these measures of racialized perceptions at the county level and demonstrated that they are predictive of the racial disproportionalities in child maltreatment reports.

Child welfare agency decision-making could be having unobserved effects in decreasing black-white child foster care entry disparities, foster care placement notwithstanding. While state and federal sponsored program showed little effect in reducing rates, kinship care has been used widely in the African-American community (Boyd, 2014). Pryce et al. (2019) found that county agencies in New York state proactively looked for alternatives like family meetings to find "suitable others" before having to take the step to place a child in foster care, and a decade-old program there (Disproportionate Minority Representation (DMR)) was specifically aimed at reducing disparities for black children. A conclusion from this literature is that kinship care could lead to an increase in racial disparity in foster care. Hence, if child welfare agencies are more likely to use kin-care for black children than other children, this would imply increasing the number of black children entering or in foster care, as AFCARS includes children in kinship care among those in foster care. However, the number of black children in foster care fell during the study period, a finding that runs counter to the hypothesis that increased use of kin-care would increase racial disparity in foster care. Among black and Hispanic families, extended family members may be more likely to provide care for children when mothers are unable (Arditi, 2015), and this could lead to lower black foster care placements. Alternatively, faced with budget constraints, child welfare agencies could be less likely to report incidents of abuse for a variety of reasons including fear of misinterpreting cultural practices or perception of the severity of the incident that may be related to the race of the child (Gilbert et al., 2009; Ards et al., 2012). Either or both of these processes would lead to a reduction in black child foster care placements and disparity. Both could also result increased kinship care that would be consistent with the observed reduction in black children in foster care and a desire to have children cared for by kin.

In recent years some states have implemented family-focused approach to sentencing that considers the needs of children and refocuses sentencing to avoid severing the parent-child relationship (Allard, 2006; Feig, 2015). This approach considers alternative sentencing for non-violent offenders where prison time is reduced or eliminated in order to maintain the parental bonds. This approach could potentially help decrease the disparity in entry, placement, and exit rates.

If changes in the racial/ethnic composition of the caseworker workforce or if private efforts such as the Casey-inspired "Places to Watch" and Promising Practices to Address Racial Disparity in Child Welfare have led to changes in or improvements in the culture of child welfare agencies, this could also explain the diminution in the racial disparity in foster care entry (and placements).

Limitations and Future Directions

The state-level unit of analysis masks important within-state variation in the application of child welfare practices, criminal justice system enforcement, and imprisonment. County-level measures would better represent these local processes, but there are limitations on using the child welfare data at the county level. For example, child maltreatment data are available and identifiable to counties with 1000 or more cases. Similarly, incarceration data at the county level are limited by the states that submit such data to the Bureau of Justice Statistics. All told if the black-white differences described herein are due largely to urban-rural differences in the racial distribution of population, the use and enforcement of different drug types, and the child welfare system processes, then the data limitations could limit the extent to which rural practices could be measured and assessed. Nonetheless, we think that examining county-level processes is a worthwhile endeavor.

For example, coincident with the trends in black female imprisonment and black child foster care outcomes has been the spread of poverty throughout the nation. Since the late 1990s, poverty has spread geographically, as there has been an expansion in the number of counties in the USA with high poverty rates (Mather & Jarosz, 2016). The number of high-poverty-rate (more than 15.5%) counties increased in all types of counties, but the largest increases between 1989 and 2010/2014 occurred in small–/mid-sized metropolitan areas followed closely by non-metropolitan/rural counties. The increase in urban counties with high poverty rates could contribute to explaining the decrease in racial disparities in foster care if black children in foster care resided in predominantly urban areas, and the child welfare system treated poor children similarly, but the increase in poverty would not necessarily explain the decrease in the black child foster care rate. The increase in high poverty in areas that are largely white—small and rural counties—could help explain the decrease in disparity.

Identifying the direction of the effects of imprisonment and foster care removal remains a challenge. It is important to know whether incarceration leads to increases in the removal of white children or whether the removal of the child leads to the subsequent incarceration of a mother in order to identify opportunities for improving the welfare of the child. If the incarceration precedes foster care entry, then child welfare systems could assess feasible alternatives. If the removal of the child is due to a pattern of neglect and criminal behavior and precedes incarceration, then more intensive family intervention may be necessary, including interventions that go beyond the scope of child welfare system. For example, drug-abusing mothers may be referred to treatment, but their success in treatment could depend upon a number of factors, including their social support systems. If drug-abusing mothers are embedded in a social support system consisting of other drug users, then removal of the child may be the best option available for the child.

Although we found some effects of federal policies and states' involvement in Title IV-E waivers, the broader scope of federal policy in child welfare needs to be measured. For example, the CFSRs to which we briefly referred established federal standards in child welfare to which states were to adhere. Under the CFSR process, states did self-assessments, and the Children's Bureau audited their practices. Non-compliance with federal standards led to performance improvement plans and subsequently re-reviews. Among the items on which states were assessed were their efforts to address racial disparities. Better measurement of federal policies could implicate them in the reduction in racial disparity in foster care.

Furthermore, the recently implemented Family First Prevention Service Act (NSCL, 2020) combines the Title-E waiver program with tactics similar to the DMR program in New York including finding suitable kinship care before foster care placement. Both programs should be examined further in future research to see whether the data support the qualitative findings by Pryce et al. (2019).

We know little about the processes at work for black women and children and why there are different processes for whites and blacks. The absence of an incarceration effect for black women coincides with the simultaneous decrease in both black female imprisonment and black child foster care rates. This suggests that there may be other variables that are responsible for both trends. The education and economic conditions for black women have improved somewhat over the past decade, but we are not sure that these changes were sufficiently large to generate the observed trends.

This chapter has uncovered unexpected patterns of racially disparate child welfare processes related to imprisonment. They do not necessarily conform to preexisting expectations. It therefore serves as a base for additional research to address some of these issues that we've outlined.

References

Adoption and Foster Care Analysis and Reporting System (AFCARS) (2017). AFCARS report #24. https://www.acf.hhs.gov/sites/default/files/documents/cb/afcarsreport24.pdf

Allard, P. E. (2006). Research to action: Informing policy makers about the needs of mothers and children at risk of separation. *Women & Criminal Justice, 17*(2–3), 27–42.

Arditti, J. A. (2015). A family process perspective on the heterogeneous effects of maternal incarceration on child wellbeing: The trouble with differences. *Criminology & Public Policy, 14*, 1–14.

Ards, S. D., Myers, S. L., Chung, C., Malkis, A., & Haggerty, B. (2003). Decomposing black-white differences in child maltreatment. *Child Maltreatment, 8*, 112–121.

Ards, S. D., Myers, S. L., Jr., Ray, P., Kim, H. E., Monroe, K., & Arteaga, I. (2012). Racialized perceptions and child neglect. *Children and Youth Services Review, 34*(8), 1480–1491. https://doi.org/10.1016/j.childyouth.2012.03.018

Bartholet, E. (2009). The racial disproportionality movement in child welfare: False facts and dangerous currents. *Arizona Law Review, 51*, 871–923.

Billingsley, A., & Giovannoni, J. M. (1972). *Children of the storm: Black children and American child welfare*. Harcourt.

Boyd, R. (2014). African American disproportionality and disparity in child welfare: Toward a comprehensive conceptual framework. *Children and Youth Services Review, 37*, 15–27.

Bronson, J., & Carson, E. A. (2019). *Prisoners in 2017*. Department of Justice, Bureau of Justice Statistics. https://www.bjs.gov/content/pub/pdf/p17.pdf

Bushway, S. D., Stoll, M. A., & Weiman, D. (Eds.). (2007). *Barriers to reentry? The labor market for released prisoners in post-industrial America*. Russell Sage Foundation.

Carson, E. A. (2018). *Prisoners in 2016*. Department of Justice, Bureau of Justice Statistics. https://www.bjs.gov/content/pub/pdf/p16.pdf

Chand, A. (2000). The over-representation of black children in the child protection system: Possible causes, consequences and solutions. *Child & Family Social Work, 5*, 67–78.

Child Welfare Information Gateway. (2016). *Racial disproportionality and disparity in child welfare*. U.S. Department of Health and Human Services, Children's Bureau. https://www.childwelfare.gov/pubpdfs/racial_disproportionality.pdf

Children's Bureau. (2013). *Summaries and profiles of child welfare waiver demonstration projects: Summary table of the completed title IV-E child welfare waiver demonstrations*. Washington,

DC: Administration for Children and Families, Children's Bureau. Available at: https://www.acf.hhs.gov/cb/programs/child-welfare-waivers/completed-projects

Cutuli, J. J., Goerge, R. M., Coulton, C., Schretzman, M., Crampton, D., Charvat, B. J., Lalich, N., Raithel, J. A., Gacitua, C., & Lee, E. L. (2016). From foster care to juvenile justice: Exploring characteristics of youth in three cities. *Children and Youth Services Review, 67*, 84–94.

Drake, B., Lee, S. M., & Jonson-Reid, M. (2009). Race and child maltreatment reporting: Are blacks overrepresented? *Children and Youth Services Review, 31*, 309–316.

Drake, B., Jolley, J. M., Lanier, P., Fluke, J., Barth, R. P., & Jonson-Reid, M. (2011). Racial bias in child protection? A comparison of competing explanations using national data. *Pediatrics, 127*, 471–478.

Edwards, F. (2016). Saving children, controlling families: Punishment, redistribution, and child protection. *American Sociological Review, 81*(3), 575. https://doi.org/10.1177/0003122416638652

Feig, L. (2015). Breaking the cycle: A family-focused approach to criminal sentencing in Illinois. In *University of Chicago, advocates' forum* (pp. 13–26).

Fluke, J. (2011). *Research synthesis on child welfare: Disproportionality and disparities*. Annie E. Casey Foundation. https://www.aecf.org/resources/disparities-and-disproportionality-in-child-welfare/

Font, S. A., & Maguire-Jack, K. (2015). Decision making in child protective services: Influences at multiple levels of the social ecology. *Child Abuse and Neglect, 47*, 70–82.

Gilbert, R., Kemp, A., Thoburn, J., Sidebotham, P., Radford, L., Glaser, D., & MacMillan, H. L. (2009). Recognising and responding to child maltreatment. *The Lancet, 373*, 167–180. https://doi.org/10.1016/S0140-6736(08)61707-9

Glaze, L. E., & Maruschak, L. M. (2008). *Parents in prison and their minor children*. US Department of Justice, Bureau of Justice Statistics. https://www.bjs.gov/content/pub/pdf/pptmc.pdf

Goldhaber-Fiebert, J. D., Babiarz, K. S., Garfield, R. L., Wulczyn, F., Landsverk, J., & Horwitz, S. M. (2014). Explaining variations in state foster care maintenance rates and the implications for implementing new evidence-based programs. *Children and Youth Services Review, 39*, 183–206.

Graham, C. J., Dettlaff, A. J., Baumann, D. J., & Fluke, J. D. (2015). The decision-making ecology of placing a child into foster care: A structural equation model. *Child Abuse & Neglect, 49*, 12–23.

Hayward, R. A., & DePanfilis, D. (2007). Foster children with an incarcerated parent: Predictors of reunification. *Children and Youth Services Review, 29*(10), 1320–1334.

Hill, R. B. (2004). Institutional racism in child welfare. *Race and Society, 7*, 17–33.

Hill, R. B. (2007). *Synthesis of research on disproportionality in child welfare: An update*. Casey-CSSP Alliance for Racial Equity in the Child Welfare System. https://www.aecf.org/resources/synthesis-of-research-on-disproportionality-in-child-welfare-an-update/

Katz, P. C. (1998). Supporting families and children of mothers in jail: An integrated child welfare and criminal justice strategy. *Child Welfare, 77*(5), 495–511.

Kim, H., Chenot, D., & Ji, J. (2011). Racial/ethnic disparity in child welfare systems: A longitudinal study utilizing the Disparity Index (DI). *Children and Youth Services Review, 33*, 1234–1244.

Lawrence, C. R., Carlson, E. A., & Egeland, B. (2006). The impact of foster care on development. *Development and Psychopathology, 18*, 57–76.

Lindquist, M. J., & Santavirta, T. (2014). Does placing children in foster care increase their adult criminality? *Labour Economics, 31*, 72–83.

Lynch, J. P., & Sabol, W. J. (2004). Assessing the effects of mass incarceration on informal social control in communities. *Criminology & Public Policy, 3*(2), 267–294.

Maguire-Jack, K., & Font, S. A. (2017). Intersections of individual and neighborhood disadvantage: Implications for child maltreatment. *Children and Youth Services Review, 72*, 44–51.

Maguire-Jack, K., Lanier, P., Johnson-Motoyama, M., Welch, H., & Dineen, M. (2015). Geographic variation in racial disparities in child maltreatment: The influence of county poverty and population density. *Child Abuse & Neglect, 47*, 1–13.

Mather, M., & Jarosz, B. (2016). *Poverty and inequality pervasive in two-fifths of U.S. Counties*. Population Reference Bureau. https://www.prb.org/poverty-and-inequality-us-counties/

McBeath, B., Chuang, E., Bunger, A., & Blakeslee, J. (2014). Under what conditions does caseworker-caregiver racial/ethnic similarity matter for housing service provision? An application of representative bureaucracy theory. *Social Service Review, 88*(1), 134–165.

Morton, C. M., Ocasio, K., & Simmel, C. (2011). A critique of methods used to describe the overrepresentation of African Americans in the child welfare system. *Children and Youth Services Review, 33*, 1538–1542.

Mumola, C. J. (2000). *Incarcerated parents and their children*. US Department of Justice, Office of Justice Programs, Bureau of Justice Statistics. https://www.bjs.gov/content/pub/pdf/iptc.pdf

Myers, Jr., S. L. (2011). Response to a research synthesis on child welfare disproportionality and disparities. In J. Fluke, B. J. Harden, M. Jenkins, & A Reuhrdanz (Eds.), *Disparities and disproportionality in child welfare: Analysis of the research*. Papers from a Research Symposium Convened by the Center for the Study of Social Policy and The Annie E. Casey Foundation on behalf of the Alliance for Racial Equity Child Welfare (pp. 107–112).

Myers, S. L., Jr., & Sabol, W. J. (1987). Business cycles and racial disparities in punishment. *Contemporary Economic Policy, 5*(4), 36–58.

Myers Jr., S. L., & Sabol, W. J. (2019, January 4). *Determinants of declining racial disparities in female incarceration rates, 2000–2016*. National Economics Association/Allied Social Sciences Association Symposium, Atlanta, GA. https://www.aeaweb.org/conference/2019/preliminary

Myers, S. L., Jr., Sabol, W. J., & Xu, M. (2020). The determinants of declining racial disparities in female incarceration rates, 2000-2015. *Review of Black Political Economy, 40*(3), 231–244.

National Conference of State Legislature. (2020, April 1). *Family First Prevention Services Act*. NCSL. https://www.ncsl.org/research/human-services/family-first-prevention-services-act-ffpsa.aspx

Phillips, S. D., & Dettlaff, A. J. (2009). More than parents in prison: The broader overlap between the criminal justice and child welfare systems. *Journal of Public Child Welfare, 3*, 3–22.

Pryce, J., Lee, W., Crowe, E., Park, D., McCarthy, M., & Owens, G. (2019). A case study in public child welfare: County-level practices that address racial disparity in foster care placement. *Journal of Public Child Welfare, 13*(1), 35–59. https://doi.org/10.1080/15548732.2018.1467354

Roberts, D. E. (2012). Prison, foster care, and the systemic punishment of black mothers. *UCLA Law Review, 59*, 1474–1500.

Rose, D. R., & Clear, T. R. (1998). Incarceration, social capital, and crime: Implications for social disorganization theory. *Criminology, 36*(3), 441–480.

Ross, T., Khashu, A., & Wamsley, M. (2004). *Hard data on hard times: An empirical analysis of maternal incarceration, foster care and visitation*. Vera Institute of Justice.

Rubin, D. M., O'Reilly, A. L., Luan, X., & Localio, A. R. (2007). The impact of placement stability on behavioral well-being for children in foster care. *Pediatrics, 119*(2), 336–344.

Sabol, W. (2018). *Racial differences in incarceration and declines in racial disparities in foster care*. National Children of Incarcerated Parents Conference.

Sabol, W., Johnson, T., & Caccavale, A. (2019). *Trends in correctional control by race and gender*. Council on Criminal Justice. https://doi.org/10.1525/fsr.2020.32.3.157

Scholl, L., Seth, P., Wilson, N., Baldwin, G., Kariisa, M., Wilson, N., & Baldwin, G. (2018). Drug and opioid-involved overdose deaths—United States, 2013-2017. *MMWR. Morbidity and Mortality Weekly Report, 67*(5152). https://doi.org/10.15585/mmwr.mm675152le1

Sedlak, A. J., McPherson, K., & Barnali, D. (2010). *Supplementary analyses of race differences in child maltreatment rates in the NIS-4*. Children's Bureau, Department of Health and Human Services.

Swann, C. A., & Sylvester, M. S. (2006). The foster care crisis: What caused caseloads to grow? *Demography, 43*(2), 309–335. Retrieved from https://search.proquest.com/docview/222972461?accountid=11226

Travis, J., & Western, B. (Eds.). (2014). *The growth of incarceration in the United States: Exploring causes and consequences*. National Academies Press.

Turney, K., & Goodsell, R. (2018). Parental incarceration and children's wellbeing. *The Future of Children, 28*(1), 147–164. https://doi.org/10.2307/26641551

Turney, K., & Wildeman, C. (2013). Redefining relationships: Explaining the countervailing consequences of paternal incarceration for parenting quality. *American Sociological Review, 78*, 949–979.

Western, B. (2006). *Punishment and inequality in America*. Russell Sage Foundation.

Wildeman, C., & Andersen, S. H. (2017). Paternal incarceration and children's risk of being charged by early adulthood: Evidence from a Danish policy shock. *Criminology: An Interdisciplinary Journal, 55*(1), 32–58.

Wildeman, C., & Western, B. (2010). Incarceration in fragile families. *The Future of Children, 20*(2), 157–177. https://doi.org/10.1353/foc.2010.0006

Wildeman, C., Emanuel, N., Leventhal, J. M., Putnam-Hornstein, E., Waldfogel, J., & Lee, H. (2014). The prevalence of confirmed maltreatment among U.S. children, 2004-2011. *JAMA Pediatrics, 168*, 706–713.

Wildeman, C., Turney, K., & Yi, Y. (2016). Paternal incarceration and family functioning: Variation across federal, state, and local facilities. *The Annals of the American Academy of Political and Social Science, 665*(1), 80–97. https://doi.org/10.1177/0002716215625042

Wulczyn, F. (2017). *The black/white placement gap*. Presented to the Administrative Data Research Facilities Network Inaugural Conference.

Wulczyn, F., & Lery, B. (2007). *Racial disparity in foster care admission*. Chapin-Hall Center for Children.

Wulczyn, F., Gibbons, R., Snowden, L., & Lery, B. (2013). Poverty, social disadvantage, and the black/white placement gap. *Children and Youth Services Review, 35*, 65–74.

Yang, J., McCuish, E. C., & Corrado, R. R. (2017). Foster care beyond placement: Offending outcomes in emerging adulthood. *Journal of Criminal Justice, 53*, 46–54.

Language as a Protective Factor: Making Conscious Word Choices to Support Children with Incarcerated Parents

Whitney Q. Hollins and Tanya Krupat

Abstract Language is powerful. Although this may seem obvious, language as a protective factor for children with incarcerated parents has not – to the authors' knowledge – been explored. This chapter discusses the movement toward person-first, humanizing language in general, in the field of criminal justice, and then specifically for children with incarcerated parents. Drawing from the work and words of those directly affected, the authors argue that shifting terminology is important to lessen the stigma and promote children's well-being when a parent is incarcerated. Terms such as "criminal," "inmate," and "offender" should be replaced with "incarcerated person" or "parent who is incarcerated," to acknowledge not only the person behind the alleged law-breaking but also the parent, thereby seeing the child who is affected, too. Other organizations and entities are calling for and have made this shift. Examining the roots of commonplace or field-specific terms and replacing them, as our analysis and understanding evolve, with more accurate, respectful language is critical to ensure that our language does not uphold an oppressive system where racism is baked in. In the field of child welfare, for example, terms such as "visitation" and "freeing children for adoption" should be replaced with "visiting" and "children legally approved for adoption," respectively. The term "minority" is used often to mean "people of color," but it is a term of measurement and comparison; it's continued use functions to remind people of color that they are "less than" even when they are in the majority.

Keywords Children of incarcerated parents · Mass incarceration · Humanizing language · Person-first · Protective factors

---

W. Q. Hollins, Ph.D. · T. Krupat (✉)
Osborne Center for Justice Across Generations, Brooklyn, NY, USA
e-mail: tkrupat@osborneny.org

J. Krysik, N. Rodriguez (eds.), *Children of Incarcerated Parents*, Children of Incarcerated Parents: From Understanding to Impact,
https://doi.org/10.1007/978-3-030-84713-5_6

> "Everybody just thinks people in prison are just bad. Like they say my dad is a bad guy, but he's really not...He's just himself." –Sky, age 14

"A process that humanizes these people/our parents who've made a mistake and are paying for it is essential for the kids and the parents. Labels become something hard to get rid of, so squashing this stigma starts with you, with us, with words." - The Power of Words by Jasmine Robles, Rutgers University Senior and NRCCFI student coordinator of See Us Support Us 2016.

Human beings have an innate need to communicate with one another. We do this in a variety of ways, but one of the most important ways is through language. Language is powerful. Many of us are familiar with the saying "sticks and stones may break my bones, but words will never break/hurt me." The ironic part is that most of us were taught this saying as children to ward off teasing and insults after we were in fact hurt by someone's words. Words can elicit images, feelings, and actions. As Cyrano discovered, words can incite love. The duel between Aaron Burr and Alexander Hamilton showed us that they can also incite hatred. Most of our words fall somewhere in the middle of this spectrum. We use them daily out of necessity and often with automaticity. When something is viewed as important, such as a speech, research article, funding proposal, or graded essay, we may be more careful and conscious of our word choices. However, much of our everyday language comes to us quickly and without thought; terms and phrases become commonplace, and we rarely pause to question where they came from or what alternative terms could be. This can lead people to underestimate the power words hold. Language should not be viewed as neutral or unimportant, nor should it be viewed as rigid or permanent. Language is very powerful for what it does to us subconsciously as well as consciously. We must be willing to constantly analyze and critique it; it must be given room to grow, to change, and to reflect evolving ideas, values, and priorities. This chapter calls for adopting person-first, humanizing language to refer to people and *parents* involved with the criminal legal or justice system both as a matter of asserting our shared humanity and as an under-explored and very important protective factor promoting the well-being of children.

Person-First Language

> "Ultimately, our humanity depends on everyone's humanity… I've come to understand and to believe that each of us is more than the worst thing we've ever done. I believe that for every person on the planet. I think if somebody tells a lie, they're not just a liar. I think if somebody takes something that doesn't belong to them, they're not just a thief. I think even if you kill someone, you're not just a killer. And because of that there's this basic human dignity that must be respected by law." Bryan Stevenson, TED Talk, "We Need to Talk about an Injustice"[1]

[1] https://www.ted.com/talks/bryan_stevenson_we_need_to_talk_about_an_injustice?language=en (2012)

The power of words cannot be lost upon us: words are used as tools to inspire feelings and actions. There have been times where the action is considered heroic – for example, Martin Luther King, Jr.'s famous "I have a Dream Speech" – but just as often words have been used to oppress, marginalize, and dehumanize others. In 1960, Beatrice Wright, an American psychologist, wrote "language is not merely an instrument for voicing ideas, but that it also plays a role in shaping ideas by guiding the experience of those who use it"[2] (p.7). Although Wright was mainly focused on people with disabilities, her thoughts on the power of language and need for person-first language can and have been applied to many other groups. Person-first language has shifted how we think and talk about *people* with disabilities, *people* with mental illness, *people* with addiction, *people* without homes, and *people* who are undocumented.[3] There is a growing movement – begun more than 20 years ago – to adopt people-first language to refer to those who are or have been incarcerated. We assert that this movement is important for their *children's well-being*, as well as for themselves.

Person-first language, which seeks to lessen the marginalization of certain groups by forefronting their humanity, is a response to the power of language. Throughout history, certain groups have been relegated to "less than" status and subjected to dehumanizing treatment, not only through actions but also through language. Language is created intentionally to uphold a system/a set of beliefs; power dynamics, based on race, class, and gender, are invisibly woven into the language we use providing scaffolding for the status quo. In the United States, this includes subtle or explicit terminology that criminalizes/ demonizes people of color and poverty. During slavery in the United States, the dehumanization of Black people by white people occurred not only in the fields but also in print and speech: Black people were often described as indolent, stupid, and lustful, stereotypes that reinforced white supremacy/privilege and persist today. Today, young Black boys and girls are often criminalized – labeled "thugs" and "juveniles" – groups of friends are generalized as "gangs," and school suspension rates remain much higher for students of color.[4]

The roots of today's criminal justice system have been well-traced back to plantation slavery, a way to control and extort labor from people of color and other people viewed as less than in our society.[5] Black people, Latinx people, poor people,

[2] Wright, B. A. (1960). Physical disability--A psychological approach. Harper & Row Publishers

[3] The important shift of language toward "people who are undocumented" and away from "illegal alien" was the result of much advocacy and a public campaign to "drop the 'i' word" and remove "illegal alien" from the APA style guide. This work was led by Race Forward, and the campaign asserted that no human being was illegal nor an alien. https://www.raceforward.org/practice/tools/drop-i-word

[4] "In 2012, for example, Black students made up only 16% of students in the United States, but accounted for 42% of out-of-school suspensions.2 Black students were over three times more likely than White students to be suspended or expelled from school.3" See *Locked Out of the Classroom: How Implicit Bias Contributes to Disparities in School Discipline.*(2017) https://www.naacpldf.org/files/about-us/Bias_Reportv2017_30_11_FINAL.pdf

[5] See M. Alexander (2010), The New Jim Crow and *13th* (2016), the documentary by Ava DuVernay

indigenous people, and people with mental health issues are all overrepresented in US jails and prisons. While these groups are already subjected to dehumanization and the language that often accompanies it (but always supports it), their entrance into the criminal justice system adds an additional layer of oppression. Terms like inmate, ex-con, felon, convicts, and offenders reduce the person to one aspect of a very large and complex life, negating other elements of their identity, including often that of *parent*. In addition, these terms carry stigma. When people hear these terms, they frequently think of a "bad person" who is dangerous in some way. Criminal and other identifiers become the totality of the person. There is no nuance or complexity in these terms. People are reduced to a label based on the worst thing they have ever done and their becoming involved in a system that is inherently racist, cruel, and unfair.

In 2007, Eddie Ellis, founder of the Center for NuLeadership on Urban Solutions, penned an open letter about language, specifically how it relates to those currently and formerly incarcerated.[6] In this letter, Ellis, a formerly incarcerated man and father, emphasized the use of the word PEOPLE, stating:

> When we are not called mad dogs, animals, predators, offenders and other derogatory terms, we are referred to as inmates, convicts, prisoners and felons—all terms devoid of humanness which identify us as 'things' rather than as people. (p.1)

Ellis recognized the power of language, quoting the Bible as saying "Death and life are in the power of the tongue" and calling on all people, but especially those in the media and interested in criminal justice reform to not only adopt these changes but also correct others when they use dehumanizing language. Ellis' call for person-first language was important not only because it highlighted the humanity of those who are justice-involved but also because it is an example of lived experience as expertise. Ellis, using his own experience and that of those who were also formerly incarcerated, asserted that they should be the ones to decide what they would be called. Often decisions, including language and labels, are determined by people from the outside looking in, essentially people who don't have the experience that they are discussing. Ellis pushed back against tradition, stating "We believe we have the right to be called by a name we choose, rather than one someone else decides to use. We think that by insisting on being called 'people,' we reaffirm our right to be recognized as human beings…"(p.1, emphasis in the original). Ellis' push for lived experience as expertise is ever present in today's efforts to transform the criminal justice system.

Adopting humanizing language does not take away from holding someone accountable for their actions, including any harm committed. In fact, even advocates for those who are victims and survivors of crime are joining the call for humanizing language. Danielle Sered, a national leader for restorative justice and healing for victims and survivors of crime, states:

---

[6] https://cmjcenter.org/wp-content/uploads/2017/07/CNUS-AppropriateLanguage.pdf. See also The Center for NuLeadership's website: www.centerfornuleadership.org

> What we need is a criminal justice policy for *people* who commit crime—incarcerated *people*, *people* with felony convictions, *people* on parole, even *people* who have caused great harm and should be held meaningfully accountable. Any truly effective policy solutions will make central the humanity of everyone directly impacted by crime—including those who commit it. *–Danielle Sered, Executive Director, Common Justice, excerpted from The Marshall Project's* **Inmate. Prisoner. Other. Discussed**

Language as a Protective Factor for Children

While Ellis' open letter addressed the need to change the language surrounding currently and formerly incarcerated individuals based on the interests of those who have served time, it is also important to recognize the collateral consequences of mass incarceration. As Wakefield and Wildeman (2014) observe, "Decades of research, in part motivated by the prison boom in the United States, tells us the image of the inmate as an isolated loner is simply false" (p.6).[7] People who are or who have been incarcerated are people first, but they are also other very important roles/ identities such as spouses, siblings, friends, sons, aunties, and, quite often, parents. Over 50% of people currently incarcerated report being parents to minor children.[8] Mothers who are incarcerated were often responsible for the day-to-day care of their children prior to being incarcerated, with 60% living with their children prior to incarceration.[9] These percentages may underestimate the numbers and role of incarcerated parents because stigma and fear of negative repercussions can deter people who are incarcerated from disclosing their parental status on surveys, intakes, or data gathering efforts. Even with this caveat, research reveals 1 in 14 children in the United States have experienced the incarceration of a parent.[10]

Parental incarceration is now recognized by the Centers for Disease Control and Prevention as an adverse childhood experience (ACE).[11] Although the CDC recommends several protective factors that can lessen the risks associated with parental incarceration, language is not discussed and is an area that should be explored. Using language that conveys respect for the humanity of a parent, even while he/ she

[7] Wakefield and Wildeman (2013), Children of the Prison Boom: Mass Incarceration and the Future of American Inequality. Oxford University Press

[8] According to a BJS report, 62% of women and 51% of men in state prison and 63% of men and 56% of women in federal prison report being parents to minor children. Glaze, L.E., and Maruschak, L.M. (2010), *Bureau of Justice Statistics Special Report: Parents in Prison and Their Minor Children*. Bureau of Justice Statistics. https://www.bjs.gov/content/pub/pdf/pptmc.pdf

[9] Ibid.

[10] Murphey, D., and Cooper, P.M. (October 2015). *Parents Behind Bars: What Happens to Their Children?* ChildTrends. https://www.childtrends.org/wp-content/uploads/2015/10/2015-42ParentsBehindBars.pdf

[11] CDC, *Preventing Adverse Childhood Experiences: What Are Adverse Childhood Experiences?* https://www.cdc.gov/violenceprevention/aces/fastfact.html?CDC_AA_refVal=https%3A%2F%2Fwww.cdc.gov%2Fviolenceprevention%2Facestudy%2Ffastfact.html

is incarcerated, signals to a child that you might be someone they could talk to. Utilizing terms such as "inmate" on the other hand reinforces certain perceptions and biases and can have the opposite effect on children. Similar to displaying a rainbow flag in a classroom or office, language can convey a deeper awareness and openness, an acknowledgement of the child's highly stigmatized reality. Shifting our language is perhaps the simplest "do now" intervention we can commit to and implement. Although much of the research surrounding children of incarcerated parents excludes the voices of those with lived experience, it is important to consider children's perspectives and to listen to their analysis and recommendations:

> Understanding that whenever you say inmate or criminal or even prisoner in referring to an incarcerated individual, you <u>are</u> talking about a child's parent, or family member. When we start to use language differently, our actions and feelings about the parents and the children changes." - <u>The Power of Words</u> by Jasmine Robles, Rutgers University Senior and NRCCFI student coordinator of *See Us Support Us 2016*

> Due to the stigma and shame attached to words such as "convict," "inmate," "ex-con" "criminal," "drug offender," many children with incarcerated parents do not often publicize their experience. As a daughter of an incarcerated parent, I did not want to hear my father being referred to as a convict, criminal or drug offender. He was dad in my eyes and I loved him. Was it wrong of me to love my Dad because he was incarcerated? No. He's my dad and will always be my dad, whether he is incarcerated or not. We love and care about our parents and should never feel stigma or ashamed because of their mistakes. Therefore, teachers, caregivers and the general public must be mindful that **#WordsMatter** to children of incarcerated parents. – Ebony Underwood, 2016 Current Founder and Director of We Got Us Now

Children of incarcerated parents have enough stigma and self-questioning to navigate without the additional sting of hearing their parent be referred to as an "inmate" or "criminal." The language we used to talk about their parents is felt as indicative of the child's self-worth and future possibilities. To best support children whose parents are incarcerated, we must acknowledge and connect children with their parent's humanity and strengths. We must view language as a protective factor. Before writing about or discussing any issue related to criminal justice, we must be conscious of the language we use and our intent when using it. We cannot claim to seek reform while refusing to change our outdated terminology. We cannot claim to advocate while simultaneously using language that oppresses.

Here, we can learn much from children's innocence and questioning of everything around them. In a recent article entitled "Aching for Abolition," the author made the following point:

> Children make the best theorists," the critic Terry Eagleton writes in *The Significance of Theory,* "since they have not yet been educated into accepting our routine social practices as 'natural,' and so insist on posing to those practices the most embarrassingly general and fundamental questions, regarding them with a wondering estrangement which we adults have long forgotten. Since they do not yet grasp our social practices as inevitable, they do not see why we might not do things differently.[12]

[12] Felix, Camonghne, *Aching for Abolition: As a Survivor of Sexual Violence, I Know Prison Isn't the Answer*. The Cut (October 1, 2020)

Alternative Terms

One of the authors of this chapter once approached a journalist who was covering a story of a parenting graduation inside a men's prison. The fathers who were graduating that day wore caps and gowns, and some were fortunate to have their family members there, proudly watching them graduate, a testament to their commitment to being the best fathers they could be despite their circumstances. In response to a suggestion to not use the term "inmate," the reporter genuinely asked, "Well, what do you call them, then?" The answer: "People. Parents. Fathers."

Ellis asserted that language such as felon, convict, and criminal essentially freezes a person in a certain space. Not only do these terms fail to understand who the person is but also who they have the potential to be. This type of language is limiting. It also sends indicators to the people who love the incarcerated individual, such as their children, about their own self-worth. With these terms, children hear the parent they love being denied, negated, and erased. One young woman in foster care shared that yes, her father was a "drug addict" and stole but he also helped her with her homework and picked her up from school and tucked her into bed on many nights. Children are able to hold complex realities simultaneously, even when these are confusing; they need support from adults around them to process these, but terms like "criminal" or "inmate" reduce their parent to one thing only and do not allow for this. As a result, those who use these terms signal to children – albeit often unintentionally – to retreat (remove "to retreat") that they will have to grapple with their reality and mixed feelings on their own.

We must actively combat dated, derogatory language. To this, we must first understand the power language holds and then understand the power we hold over language. We can choose what words we use. If we cannot find an appropriate word, we can create a new one. We can make a choice to not only use and model humanizing language but also encourage others to do the same. We can choose to align our language with our ideals and reject any term that goes against our belief in humanity. We can ask people how they prefer to be identified and respect their wishes. We can learn and grow. We can change along with language, and once we do this, we can inspire change in others.

There are several resources available to learn more about language that can serve to bolster the resilience of children whose parents are incarcerated, by acknowledging the humanity and complexity – including strengths – of their parents. The Opportunity Agenda issued a *Criminal Justice Phrase Guide* in 2018. This is an excellent resource and includes a glossary of terms. The Osborne Association's website has a section on Humanizing Language, and Common Justice and The Marshall Project have also taken this up and provide insightful guidance.

As these resources do not focus on the child's perspective or children or family systems, we additionally recommend the following term-shifts:

Intergenerational cycle of racism, trauma, and poverty – **not** of crime or incarceration: the conditions that can be pathways to committing crime (racism, trauma, and poverty) are what can repeat from generation to generation and should be identified and changed at the systemic level. Referring to the "intergenerational cycle of crime or incarceration" seems to infer that individuals or even families and communities are somehow prone to crime and incarceration, caught in a cycle of their own doing. Furthermore, plenty of people who are incarcerated are the first in their families to be incarcerated, so are not part of an intergenerational cycle of incarceration. This has become a phrase that is overused even when it is not accurate and masks the systemic determinants of incarceration which include intentional policy choices to respond to addiction, poverty, and mental illness with incarceration.

Visiting **not** *visitation:* As is often true, wisdom comes "out of the mouths of babes." It was a young man in foster care who shared with one of the authors that "normal people don't visitate with each other," and he called for a change in language. The term "visitation" is only used in systems that separate families–corrections, child welfare, immigration, and juvenile justice. A simple switch to replace this term with "visiting" or "visits" can actually make a significant difference. "Visitation" is a legal, systems-specific term that doesn't lend itself to the love and warmth shared between children and their parents. It is often hard or awkward enough to "visit" with a parent; the least we can do is shift away from the colder terms that remind children that they are subject to the mercy and authority of a disciplinary, punitive system overseeing their very relationship with their parent.

Child legally approved for adoption **not** *"freed" for adoption:* Within the child welfare system, which disproportionately affects Black and Brown families, terms such as "freed" for adoption are common but, when more closely examined, convey a deeper set of views. Children being "freed" from their parents is viewed as a positive and necessary step for their adoption. Systems that separate families in this country disproportionately affect communities of color, and the terminology should be inventoried and revised as many of these same systems now create "disproportionate minority representation" working groups and pledge to undo racism and work for equitable outcomes.

Young person **not** *juvenile:* the term "juvenile" criminalizes young people and sometimes is used to refer to young people even when they have not broken the law. Even when/if they have been arrested, it is critical to remember they are children and young people, not "juveniles" or "delinquents." New research on adolescent brain development underscores the importance of shifting our language to shift our understanding and approach. New research and advocacy in Emerging Adult Justice are infusing development and brain science into how legal and other systems respond to young people whose brains are developing until around age 24.

Replace the term "minority".

The word "minority" is frequently used to describe people of color, but it is a term of measurement and comparison. This term is problematic because it implies a small, less significant group when it usually refers to people of color. People of color will soon be the majority of people in the United States, and these numbers are increasing daily. Depending on the context, people of color may be the majority which causes oxymoronic phrases like "majority minority" to be used. The voices of people of color should hold equal weight in this country. At times, even people of color can be too vague, as various racial and ethnic groups have a very specific experience in this country that informs their relationship with the criminal justice system. For example, while it is true that people of color are disproportionately imprisoned, Black people are incarcerated more than other people of color. This is related to the uniquely heinous history of Black people in the United States, including chattel slavery which viewed them as possessions and thrived on the surveillance and control of Black bodies. When possible, every effort should be made to not only use humanizing language but also speak to the specific experiences of various groups.

A Movement Underway

There is no doubt that using person-first and other humanizing language takes more time than using shorter, loaded terms. However, humanity should never be overlooked for convenience. Many people and organizations – even several correctional institutions and corrections administrators – have already adopted humanizing language. For example, the effective and successful "drop the 'i' word" campaign removed "illegal alien" from the APA style guide and replaced it with "someone who is undocumented."[13] In the special education community, person-first language is quite common. Instead of referring to a student as "disabled" or "impaired," most professionals in this field first refer to the person before addressing the classification, for example, a student with a learning disability or person with autism. The NYS Department of Corrections and Community Supervision recently started replacing "inmate" with "incarcerated individual" in its internal and public-facing memos. NYC Councilmember Daniel Dromm is sponsoring a bill to update NYC Charter language to remove "inmate" and "offender" and replace it with "people who are or were incarcerated."[14]

Although many journalists continue to use the terms "inmate," "convict," and "offender," some are responsive to requests to change these terms. The Style Guide approach of the Trans Journalists Association (TJA) provides a comprehensive model that those who work with children of incarcerated parents could follow in working with and advising the media to responsibly and cover new stories about *people* who are also *parents* who are arrested or incarcerated. As TJA's website explains:

[13] See Footnote 2.

[14] Intro 2038 A Local Law to amend the New York city charter and the administrative code of the city of New York, in relation to the terms "inmate," "prisoner," and "incarcerated individual" and other similar terminology as used therein

> The media bears a great responsibility when it comes to ensuring accurate and sensitive coverage of trans communities. Most of the public's primary source of information on trans topics is likely the media (only about a quarter of people in the United States, for instance, have a close friend or family member who is out as trans), meaning media coverage is critical in shaping how the public talks and thinks about transgender people. Therefore, it's imperative for media outlets to get this coverage right.[15]

Although person-first language has not gone unchallenged, it has become quite common in many circles, often viewed as a sign of respect, especially in reference to groups who have been historically marginalized. Person-first language has encountered some pushback, including some from directly impacted people who believe that person-first language separates them from one of their identifiers and reinforces stigma by making whatever term follows "person with" or "person who" seem negative. In response to this, some advocate for identifier-first language, such as autistic person or incarcerated person. Although there are different approaches, it should be noted that both person-first and identifier-first language acknowledge the humanity of the person being spoken or written about and avoid one-word descriptors which can be particularly loaded. If a person is unsure of whether to use person-first or identifier-first language, it is always prudent to consult the person being described when possible.

Conclusion

One reason people might reject humanizing language is because they are not confident in their ability to use it. When a person is afraid, they may say the wrong thing or believe that they cannot keep up with the changing language, and they may revert to what is familiar and comfortable, but outdated or unexamined terminology. It is imperative to note that language is constantly changing and shifting. What may be considered gold standard terms one day may fall out of favor the next as dialogue and debate influence the way we look at things. In order to inspire confidence, combat stigma, and standardize humanizing terminology, many people and organizations have dedicated themselves to providing resources. We can all stay open to learning, evolving, and listening to those who are being referred to by the terms we are using. Though the terms may change, committing to using language that acknowledges and asserts our common and shared humanity and that considers and cares for children is timeless.

---

[15] https://transjournalists.org/style-guide/

Resources for Humanizing Language[16]

Hashtags to watch: #WeArePeople, #LanguageMatters, #WordsMatter, #PersonFirst, #PeopleFirst, #ThePowerofLanguage, #HumanLanguage, #SeeUsSupportUs.

The Language Letter Campaign

The Center for NuLeadership on Urban Solutions (CNUS).

Includes Downloadable Open Letter to Our Friends on the Question of Language authored by CNUS Founder and social justice leader Eddie Ellis, and 4 Easy Steps To Follow.

Language Guide for Communicating About Those Involved In The Carceral System

The **Underground Scholars Initiative at UC Berkeley** has created this language guide for talking about – and with – people involved in the carceral system.

The Social Justice Phrase Guide

The Advancement Project's Guidelines for Conscientious Communications to help advance a social justice agenda.

Language Matters

Excerpted from the Abolish the Box Student Organizing Toolkit, Education from the Inside Out Coalition. Includes points of reflection and a downloadable language diagram.

Words Matter Guide

Excerpted from The Fortune Society's Reentry Education Project Provider Kit.

Includes guidance on language that is helpful and less helpful in supporting health and well-being, as well as language to use when discussing criminal justice involvement, substance use and mental health, HIV/AIDS, and reproductive health.

"**Inmate. Prisoner. Other. Discussed. What to call incarcerated people: Your feedback**"

The Marshall Project issued a call for responses asking the best way to refer to people behind bars. Here they share a sample of the responses which indicated that of the options they offered, 38 percent of respondents preferred "incarcerated person," 23 percent liked "prisoner" and nearly 10 percent supported use of the word inmate. Thirty percent selected "other" ("person in prison," "man or woman," "the person's name.").

Remembering Eddie Ellis and the power of language

Danielle Sered, Vera Institute of Justice.

This blog honors Ellis' leadership around language sharing Common Justice program's use of the language "harmed party" and "responsible party," throughout their restorative justice practice.

---

[16] These resource list was reprinted with permission from The Osborne Association and can be found at http://www.osborneny.org/resources/resources-for-humanizing-language/

"Names Do Hurt: The Case Against Using Derogatory Language to Describe People in Prison"

Victoria Law and Rachel Roth respond to the language used in RH Reality Check's investigative series, "Women, Incarcerated," referencing The Center for NuLeadership, open letter, and The Fortune Society's "Words Matter "guide.

"Talking Human Services"

A Frameworks MessageMemo.

The Frameworks Institute with support from the Kresge and Annie E. Casey Foundations created this resource to help communicators move beyond the outdated charity-based narrative about human services toward a building wellbeing narrative that emphasizes human services benefit us all.

"Criminal Justice Reform Phrase Guide"

The Opportunity Agenda's Five Tips for Language That Changes Hearts & Minds.

"People first: Changing the way we talk about those touched by the criminal justice system"

The Urban Institute.

This blog includes the Urban Institute's announcement of their commitment to using words that respect the dignity of all people, specifically people affected by the criminal justice system. The Urban Institute has provided economic and social policy research to "open minds, shape decisions, and offer solutions" since 1968.

"The Other F-word"

The Marshall Project.

This blog by Bill Keller, editor-in-chief of The Marshall Project, discusses the evolution of language usage in mainstream media, specifically in reference to people who are incarcerated.

"Labels Like 'Felon' Are an Unfair Life Sentence"

The New York Times.

The New York Times Editorial Board discusses how the stigmatizing way we speak about people who are formerly incarcerated presents a significant barrier when they are reentering their communities.

"Justice Dept. agency to alter its terminology for people who are released from prison or jail"

The Washington Post.

Assistant Attorney General Karol Mason, who has headed the Office of Justice Programs since 2013, announces in a guest post for The Washington Post that her agency will no longer use words such as "felon" or "convict" to refer to people who are released from prison or jail.

"Pennsylvania Dept. of Corrections to discard terms 'offender,' 'felon' in describing formerly incarcerated people"

The Washington Post The head of the Department of Corrections in Pennsylvania, Secretary John E. Wetzel announces his decision to join the movement to use people-first language when referring to people who are affected by the criminal justice system.

Part III
The Exo System

Development and Implementation of an Attachment-Based Intervention to Enhance Visits Between Children and Their Incarcerated Parents

Margaret L. Kerr, Pajarita Charles, Michael Massoglia, Sarah Jensen, Jennifer Wirth, Kerrie Fanning, Karen Holden, and Julie Poehlmann-Tynan

Abstract Parental incarceration is a significant cause of relationship disruption for millions of children across the United States. Despite their elevated risk for attachment insecurity, behavior and health problems, cognitive delays, and academic difficulties, few interventions exist for children with incarcerated parents, and even fewer are rigorously evaluated. This chapter focuses on the Enhanced Visits Model (EVM), an attachment-based intervention for children with incarcerated parents, developed by a transdisciplinary team in partnership with a local jail. The EVM focuses on improving incarcerated parent-child relationships and parental reflective functioning through facilitating in-home video chat and visit coaching, which supports children through helping incarcerated parents and caregivers identify positive attachment-focused connections with children. In this chapter, we describe the theoretical background and conceptualization of the EVM, the design, development, and feasibility of implementing the model, including assessment of individual and family well-being and relationships, and provide an illustrative case study. We discuss implications for families involved with the criminal justice system and those seeking to develop an innovative and replicable intervention model that supports attachment needs and rights in children with incarcerated parents that may help them heal from disruptions caused by parent-child separation.

M. L. Kerr (✉) · J. Wirth · K. Fanning · J. Poehlmann-Tynan
Human Development and Family Studies, School of Human Ecology, University of Wisconsin-Madison, Madison, WI, USA
e-mail: margaret.kerr@wisc.edu

P. Charles
School of Social Work, University of Wisconsin-Madison, Madison, WI, USA

M. Massoglia · S. Jensen
Department of Sociology, University of Wisconsin-Madison, Madison, WI, USA

K. Holden
Consumer Science, School of Human Ecology, University of Wisconsin-Madison, Madison, WI, USA

J. Krysik, N. Rodriguez (eds.), *Children of Incarcerated Parents*, Children of Incarcerated Parents: From Understanding to Impact,
https://doi.org/10.1007/978-3-030-84713-5_7

Keywords Attachment · Caregiver · Child · Incarceration · Jail · Parent · Visits

More than five million, or 1 in 14, US children have had a resident parent leave for jail or prison (Murphey & Cooper, 2015), with low-income children of color disproportionately affected (Glaze & Maruschak, 2008; Western & Wildeman, 2009). Parent-child separation resulting from parental incarceration is a significant attachment disruption for many children, and controlling for other risks, children with incarcerated parents (CIP) are more likely to experience behavior and health problems, attachment insecurity, cognitive delays, and academic difficulties than their peers (Wakefield & Wildeman, 2013; Wildeman, 2009). Moreover, studies have found that incarcerated mothers experience challenges in reflective functioning, likely because of their trauma histories (Sleed et al., 2013). Because parental reflective functioning is related to the type of sensitive parenting that can facilitate children's attachment security (Fonagy et al., 2002; Slade et al., 2005), increasing parental reflective functioning in incarcerated parents is critical (Sleed et al., 2013). Interventions for CIP and their families are critically needed, as few interventions exist, and even fewer have been empirically investigated (Wildeman et al., 2017). Although visits with incarcerated parents are a key opportunity to maintain and build parent-child relationships, they can be stressful for children, especially when they occur behind glass (Poehlmann-Tynan et al., 2017). Some scholars argue that child visits in corrections facilities might recreate traumatic separation because of elements like uniformed officers with guns, metal detectors, razor wire, locked doors, and glass walls (Arditti, 2003). Moreover, many at-home caregivers experience stress before, during, and after children's visits to corrections facilities and often view visits negatively (Tasca, 2014). Because family visits are not only a key factor in reducing recidivism but can lead to closer parent-child relationships post-release (Arditti, 2003; Duwe & Clark, 2013; Visher, 2013), it is important that visits are helpful to children *and* parents and are supported by caregivers. In this chapter, we describe the theoretical conceptualization of the Enhanced Visits Model (EVM), the design, development, and feasibility of implementing the model, and provide a case study to illustrate our approach that works toward building positive family relationships and attachment representations in a vulnerable population.

Development of the Enhanced Visits Model

A transdisciplinary team, with input from corrections administrators and families affected by incarceration, designed the EVM. The team was comprised of scholars from multiple fields including developmental and clinical psychology, social work, criminology, sociology, economics, and design studies. The EVM promotes supported in-home video chat between children and their incarcerated parents, with special attention to children's attachment relationships as well as family, community, and policy contexts. Importantly, the EVM was originally designed to complement and enhance in-person visits and other forms of communication between children and their incarcerated parents, not replace them.

Focus on Visits

There are several reasons we focused on visits. First, visits are generally the only time that family members come together during a parent's incarceration (Poehlmann et al., 2010). Second, the emotional nature of visits and desire for children to have a positive experience may make families more receptive to interventions that focus on visits rather than general parenting (e.g., Arditti, 2003; Poehmann-Tynan et al., 2017). Third, visits are associated with positive outcomes for incarcerated individuals but mixed outcomes for children, calling for improved visit quality for children (Bales & Mears, 2008; Poehlmann et al., 2010). Fourth, video visits take advantage of several child developmental competencies, making video chat preferable to phone calls (Borelli et al., 2020). Finally, caregivers often resist bringing children to visits for a variety of reasons, including expense, time, distance, conflicted relationships, and stigma (e.g., Tasca, 2014).

For incarcerated parents, more contact with children—including visits—is associated with less distress (Roxburgh & Fitch, 2014), fewer depressive symptoms (Poehlmann, 2005), less parenting stress, and more coparenting with at-home caregivers (Beckmeyer & Arditti, 2014). Conversely, stress about lack of contact with children relates to more depressive symptoms as well as higher rates of institutional misconduct (Houck & Loper, 2002). In addition, incarcerated individuals who receive more visits are less likely to experience post-release convictions and reincarcerations (e.g., McKay et al., 2019; Visher, 2013). Contact with children during incarceration, as well as more engagement immediately post-release, is associated with more successful post-release outcomes such as working more hours per week, no criminal behavior or supervision violations, and less depression (Borelli et al., 2020; Visher, 2013). Importantly, fathers who had more contact with their children during incarceration were more likely to be engaged with their children post-release (McKay et al., 2019; Visher, 2013).

Studies have reported mixed findings regarding the relation between parent-child contact during parental incarceration and children's behavioral adjustment. For example, more visits with jailed parents are associated with elevated behavior problems and role reversal in children's drawings (Dallaire et al., 2012; Dallaire et al., 2015), whereas child-friendly visiting is associated with positive child outcomes (Poehlmann et al., 2010). In addition, video visiting is perceived as a more normative experience for children compared to other types of corrections visiting (Tartaro & Levy, 2017) and, when done remotely from the home, also makes use of child development competencies, such as children's tendency to gesture when talking, refer to objects that they can see, and engage in play, making video more advantageous for children than phone calls (Borelli et al., 2020). Indeed, video chat is the only type of digital activity recommended for children of all ages by the American Academy of Pediatrics (2016).

Focus on Jails

We focus on local jail incarceration for several reasons. Most importantly, the majority of US incarceration occurs in jails, with more than 10.7 million annual admissions (Zeng, 2020). About 27% return to jail within the same year, with repeat incarcerations more likely among individuals who are poor or Black or have substance abuse or mental health problems (Jones & Sawyer, 2019). Despite these high numbers, few programs are offered in jails compared to prisons (Jones & Sawyer, 2019). In addition, the 3163 jails across the United States are embedded in communities (Sawyer & Wagner, 2019), relatively close to where families live compared to prisons, which are often located far from population centers. This makes it more likely for incarcerated parents to receive visits from their families compared to prisons (Shanahan & Agudelo, 2012). Finally, whereas prisons typically offer contact visits, where visitors can hug each other at the beginning and end of visits and hold hands, jails most often offer non-contact visits (Shlafer et al., 2015), including barrier visits (e.g., plexiglas). Non-contact visits can be stressful for family members, including children (Arditti, 2003; Poehlmann-Tynan et al., 2015).

Theoretical Basis of the Model

Attachment Theory According to attachment theory (Ainsworth et al., 1978; Bowlby, 1973), infants and children develop secure or insecure relationships with their parents and other caregivers based on how well the attachment figure protects the child, alleviates distress, and fosters exploration. In addition, early attachment quality has implications for emotional, relational, and behavioral outcomes throughout the lifespan (Cassidy & Shaver, 2018). This is particularly important for CIP—as separation from a parent often disrupts a child's attachment system and a parent's caregiving system (Bowlby, 1973). Further, many CIP face additional chronic stressors, including poverty, residential instability, and family conflict (e.g., Wildeman et al., 2017). Theoretically, it is beneficial to strengthen the attachment between the child and incarcerated parent because secure relationships with parents can buffer negative impacts of adversity on lifespan development (Werner, 2000).

Relational Savoring Relational savoring, primarily informed by attachment theory, holds that enhancing feelings associated with experiences of safety and security experienced within early relationships can increase socioemotional health over the lifespan (Borelli et al., 2020). Savoring is the process of prolonging and appreciating the positive emotions attached to experiences (Bryant & Veroff, 2007), and *rela-*

tional savoring focuses specifically on memories of responding sensitively to others' needs. Savoring interventions are linked with more positive affect and greater life satisfaction across diverse populations (e.g., Hurley & Kwon, 2011).

One goal of implementing relational savoring in the EVM is to strengthen parent-child bonds via priming feelings related to attachment security and caregiving (e.g., Mikulincer & Shaver, 2007). Through relational savoring, parents and caregivers can magnify positive moments that are often overshadowed by everyday concerns or by more negative experiences that tend to grab one's attention (Kiken & Shook, 2011). This may be particularly true for incarcerated parents who may focus more on their negative experiences (e.g., separation from their families, isolation, criminal charges) than the few positive ones they can enjoy (e.g., moments of connection with their children). Similarly, children's at-home caregivers may focus on stressors associated with their caregiving role or strain in their relationship with the incarcerated parent and may not have an opportunity to focus on the more positive aspects—such as the bond they have with the child or the importance of providing stable and reliable care for the child. Relational savoring serves to create opportunities to help parents and caregivers attend to positive moments with their children and intentionally focus on the meaning of these experiences (Borelli et al., 2020; Burkhart et al., 2015).

Further, relational savoring aims to increase the capacity for reflective functioning by encouraging parents and caregivers to consider links between emotions and behaviors in both themselves and their children. Practicing these skills when in a positive state of mind, such as when reflecting on or anticipating moments of connection together, enhances learning and adaptive reuse of those skills (Fredrickson & Joiner, 2002). Given that reflective functioning is an important precursor to parenting sensitivity (Fonagy et al., 2002; Slade et al., 2005), encouraging this reflective thinking through the coaching process may help parents consider how their children feel during video visits or why they act in certain ways and in turn help them respond sensitively and appropriately before, during, and after visits.

Ecological Theory In addition to attachment theory, the EVM relied on Bronfenbrenner's (1979) ecological model, with the child at the center of the model. The EVM is designed to affect several contexts of children's development, including their dyadic interactions and relationships with parents and caregivers (microsystem), parenting (exosystem), coparenting relationships (mesosystem), family connections to community resources (exosystem), and corrections and criminal justice policies that affect justice involved parents (macrosystem) and aspects of the visiting process (microsystem). While we focus on changing children's proximal processes at the center of the ecological model, multiple contexts of development need to be addressed for microsystem change to occur. Please see Poehlmann et al. (2010) and Poehlmann-Tynan et al. (2019) for more detailed descriptions of how the ecological model applies to CIP.

By fostering responsive parent-child interactions through supported video chats and helping improve the reflective functioning and positive emotions of incarcerated parents and caregivers through visit coaching, we aim to affect the child's proximal processes or the daily interactions considered to be the primary drivers of development (Bronfenbrenner & Ceci, 1994). Because a cornerstone of the EVM involves strengthening parent-child relationships through visiting, attachment theory supplied much of the intervention content (i.e., relational savoring during visit coaching). Other important processes occurred within the microsystem, mesosystem, and exosystem to make change at the microsystem level possible.

One advantage of the EVM is that it focuses on the larger family system beyond just the parent-child dyad, including the triadic relationship between the child, incarcerated parent, and at-home caregiver and the coparent relationship. The triadic and coparent relationships become particularly important following parental incarceration (McHale et al., 2013). During visits, the caregiver may facilitate conversations between parent and child, help the child pay attention, and regulate the child's time and behavior—and even turn taking in the case of multiple children. The pre- and post-visit coaching process is intended to help support and strengthen these triadic interactions. An integrated ecological family systems theory has been the basis of family policy work over the past several decades (e.g., Ooms, 2019) and provides a lens from which we work with corrections administrators and community organizations that provide support services to families. Although the centerpiece of the EVM is supported visits, this is often only possible within the context of working with the child's exosystem and mesosystem because the corrections facility needed to change their visit policies to support the intervention, and the administration and wider systems needed to accept supporting families as a programming focus.

The Enhanced Visits Conceptual Model

The EVM was designed with two primary active intervention components: supported technology combined with attachment-based visit coaching (see Fig. 1). This integrated approach enables children to access digital technology, including in-home video chat, and supports them in efforts to have positive video visits with the incarcerated parent. The EVM is conceptualized as being embedded in a larger context that accounts for parental, family, community, and criminal justice factors that are known to influence CIP and the triadic parent-child-caregiver relationship. The model recognizes the economic and racial inequities experienced by most CIP and attempts to provide leverage against this by increasing children's access to technology and educational apps (Rideout & Katz, 2016), including free Internet access if needed. We also provide no-cost in-home video chat to foster positive family connections regardless of family income (Rubenstein et al., 2019).

In the short term, we expect improvements in several proximal processes as the result of technology use and visit coaching. As a result of the technology, we expect to observe increases in three areas: (a) opportunities for contact and communication between jailed parents and children because of access to technology, (b) frequency

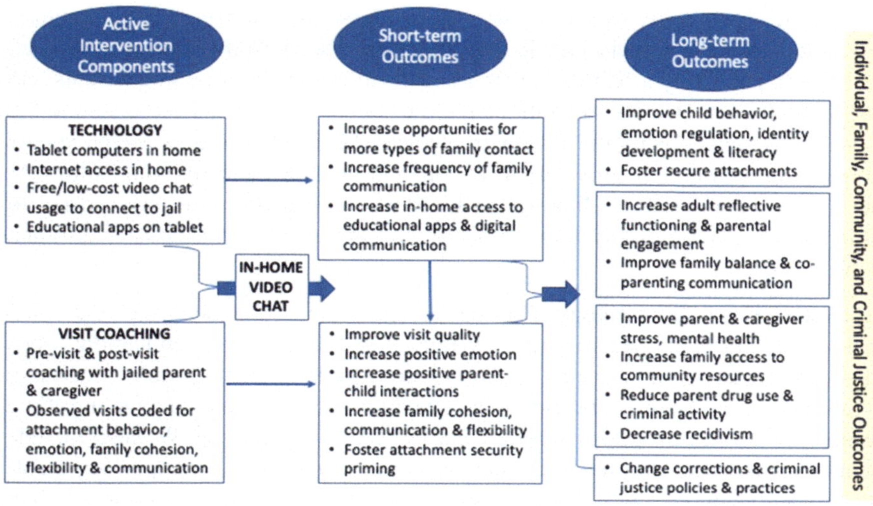

Fig. 1 Enhanced visits model for children with incarcerated parents

of communication because the costs of video contact were reduced or eliminated, and (c) access to digital apps that could foster learning. As a result of visit coaching, we expect to observe (a) increased positive emotions in children and adults; (b) increased attachment priming and caregiving priming or exposure to thoughts and memories that activate both safe haven and secure base aspects of children's and adults' internal working models—for example, increases in a sense of comfort, safety, responsiveness, and reflective functioning; (c) improved visit quality using the technology and skills learned from the coaching; and (d) increased capacity to have positive parent-child interactions because of guidance around how to conduct the visit, what to focus on, what activities to engage in, and the types of questions to ask the child.

Proximal processes are predicted to have short- and longer-term impacts on children across multiple contextual levels (Bronfenbrenner & Ceci, 1994). At the microsystem level, we expect improved child adjustment in the longer term (e.g., reduced behavior problems) and more secure attachments between children and their parents because some of the disruptive aspects of parental incarceration are mitigated through regular use of supported technology and visit coaching. Relational savoring further enhances the opportunity to experience positive emotions during the visit and promotes positive parent-child relationship quality. In the child's exosystem, we expect positive changes in adult adjustment (e.g., increased hopefulness and motivation, increased reflective functioning, reduced depression and anxiety), as well as increased access to community resources (e.g., child and family support, food, clothing, housing, medical, mental health, reentry). For example, the provided technology may help families locate community resources that meet their needs. Based on prior research focusing on family visits, we also expect that the EVM, when used with fidelity over time, will lead to less parental drug use, criminality, and recidivism (e.g., arrests, convictions, reincarceration). At the mesosystem level, we hope to positively affect the coparenting relationship. In providing parents and caregivers the opportunity to facilitate child-centered video visits and encouraging coordination and cooperation as they implement the EVM strategies, we anticipate increases in their collaborative alliance, coparenting skills, and communication. At the macrosystem level, facilitating the EVM's proximal processes is expected to influence the corrections system we operate in and longer-term, broader criminal justice policies.

Innovative Use of Technology Families receive a tablet preloaded with the video chat software used by the corrections system, as well as children's educational apps chosen to foster learning, self-regulation, social skills (e.g., mindfulness, Daniel Tiger), and understanding of parental incarceration and accompanying feelings (i.e., Sesame Street's *Little Children, Big Challenges: Incarceration*). We also include caregiver apps that promote sleep, meditation, and yoga, email, and apps on parenting, education, and science. There is also an app that assists with monitoring tablet usage, an encouraged practice for everyone (Tang et al., 2018).

At our first home visit, we assess ease of use with technology (e.g., smart phones, tablets) and software (e.g., email, browsers) and whether an Internet connection meeting the speed requirements for video visits exists. If not, we provide the family with a home-based hotspot, or they can use locations with free Internet access (e.g., library, restaurant). We provide 3 months of free video chat for the family to use. The family can continue the video chats afterward if the parent is still incarcerated in the same jail, but the cost at the present time is prohibitive (about $13 for a 45-minute visit). The jail changed its policy on frequency of video visits (previously a maximum of twice per week onsite) to accommodate our model. The change thus allows two video visits per week at the jail, plus up to one daily video chat through our study. Each remote video visit is scheduled for 45 minutes, and families can use as much of that time as they want or need.

Visit Coaching Based on the premise that increased access to visits alone is not enough to support families (Poehlmann-Tynan & Pritzl, 2019), we developed an attachment-based coaching protocol to accompany in-home video visits between children and their jailed parents. The 10- to 15-minute coaching activity is designed to help caregivers and jailed parents support children through the visiting process, comfort the child when distressed, and see the visit "through the child's eyes." This is achieved through an adaptation of relational savoring or the process of guiding individuals to focus on memories of intense positive connection with a close loved one (Borelli et al., 2020).

We complete visit coaching with both the jailed parent and the at-home caregiver at least twice during the study participation—once in preparation for a visit that is focused on anticipating what the visit will be like for both the child and the parent and once following a visit that focuses on savoring the positive moments of connection during the visit. The coaching for the caregiver focuses on identifying and savoring moments when they were able to be a source of comfort for the child. Because these visits can be challenging and full of intense emotions, the goal of the coaching is to maximize opportunities for the visits to be positive for both parent and child and to help at-home caregivers recognize the importance of their role in supporting the child and the parent-child relationship. When parents and caregivers have a difficult time recalling or reflecting on positive memories or moments of connection and wish to discuss loss, conflict, or trauma, we listen and gently redirect them to a more positive memory. If this trend persists, we offer an additional coaching session.

Connections to Community Resources At the initial visit to the child's home and during the incarcerated parent interview, we provide a community resource guide to give incarcerated parents and caregivers information about food pantries, child care, substance abuse recovery, housing, respite services, parenting support services, and stress hotlines.

A history of domestic violence, often resulting in no-contact orders between incarcerated parents and caregivers, can be a significant barrier to parent-child contact, as is having an open child abuse case. These issues are more common in families with an incarcerated parent than in other families in the community (Western & Pettit, 2010). In families where there is an open child protective case (but no prior child abuse conviction), we contact the child protective services caseworker for the child and determine if remote visits can be facilitated. If so, we discuss if and how the visits will be supervised and keep a log of all parent-child contacts.

In families where there is a no-contact order between the incarcerated parent and the caregiver (but not other household members), we ask the family if there is someone else who can facilitate the visits, such as a grandparent. If not, we pay for the services of a local nonprofit organization that specializes in supervising visits for the state Department of Children and Families. Either the trained family resource center worker travels to the family's home to facilitate the visit, or the family travels to the resource center.

Implementation of the Feasibility Study

We began implementing the EVM through a pilot feasibility study. Although not yet completed, we plan to enroll 100 children with parents incarcerated in the local county jail. The study consists of a consenting process, initial interview and data collection, technology support, visit coaching sessions, and a 3-month follow-up visit. A 1-year follow-up is planned.

In light of the current COVID-19 pandemic, adjustments to our ongoing study are in process. For instance, we obtained permission from the sheriff's office to conduct interviews via remote video visits. In an era of increased physical distancing, it is more critical than ever to examine the feasibility, benefits, and consequences of using video visits to help jailed parents and their families stay connected. Therefore, we plan to continue the pilot study although the sample size, timelines, and methods for collecting data may be different than expected.

Recruitment and Enrollment Following IRB approval, which includes an NIH Certificate of Confidentiality, the jail put study information on tablets used in the jail housing units. A list of interested parents is provided to the study team weekly. Families are eligible to participate if the incarcerated parent has at least one child or stepchild between 3 and 12 years of age; the parent speaks and reads English; the child lives within an hour of the jail; the parent has not been convicted of child maltreatment; and the child's at-home caregiver agrees to participate. After consent, we check public records to confirm the child abuse criterion (see Borelli et al., 2020).

We collect children's caregivers' names and contact information from incarcerated parents, followed by separate meetings with the incarcerated parent and the caregiver to review and discuss the study in more detail, answer questions, and invite them to participate. Written consent is obtained from both adults, plus verbal or written assent from the children, depending on their age. Because the project requires the participation of the incarcerated parent and caregiver, some family-level attrition occurs. On average, we successfully enroll one caregiver for every three incarcerated parents. Reasons for caregiver non-participation include conflicted caregiver-incarcerated parent relationships, inability to locate caregivers (e.g., incorrect or disconnected phone, incorrect address, homelessness), caregivers' distrust of the criminal justice system, and no-contact court orders between caregivers and jailed parents. To date, we have consented and enrolled 44 incarcerated parents. Of those, we currently have 33 families that include the incarcerated parent, at-home caregiver, and one or more children. Please see Table 1 for a description of incarcerated parent and caregiver demographics.

Initial Interview and Assessments Consistent with our conceptual model, most assessments are at the child or parent level but also include observed dyadic and triadic family interactions and some systems-level data. We ask parents and caregivers to report on individual health and stress; dyadic communication and relationship quality; parenting behaviors and satisfaction; reflective functioning and attachment history; adult addiction; residential instability; prior incarcerations; and use of programs/services in the jail and community. We also ask parents and caregivers to report on children's behavior problems, adverse experiences and trauma symptoms, and relationships. For children, we administer a vocabulary assessment and a family drawing and take a hair sample to analyze children's cumulative stress hormones; for children age 7 and up, we assess children's self-reported trauma symptoms, adverse experiences, depressive symptoms, and attachment security with parents and caregivers. We videotape caregiver-child interactions in the home and code them with the Early Relational Assessment (Clark, 1985/2018). We conduct 5-minute speech samples and code them for parental reflective functioning (Adkins & Fonagy, 2017). We also observe children's visits, coding children's affect and

Table 1 Incarcerated parent and caregiver sample characteristics

	Parent in jail			At-home caregiver		
Variables	*n*	*%/M*	*SD*	*n*	*%/M*	*SD*
Age (years)	31	33.6	7.8	32	36.8	12.8
Sex	31			32		
Male		80.6			9.4	
Female		19.4			90.6	
Education	31			32		
Less than high school degree		9.7			9.4	
High school degree or equivalent		38.7			31.2	
Greater than high school degree		51.7			59.4	
Race	31			31		
White		38.7			54.8	
Black		51.6			41.9	
American Indian or Alaskan native		3.2			–	
Native Hawaiian and other Pacific islander		3.2			–	
Other		3.2			3.2	
Hispanic, Latino, Spanish origin	31			32		
Yes		6.5			6.3	
No		93.5			93.8	
Household income	31			31		
Less than $10,000		29.0			16.1	
$10,000–$34,999		35.5			45.1	
$35,000 or above		29.0			29.0	
Prefer not to answer		6.4			9.7	
Number of children	31	3.0	1.9	–	–	–
Sentenced	30	35.3		–	–	–

attachment behaviors using the Jail/Prison Observation Checklist, an attachment-based measure developed for CIP (Poehlmann-Tynan et al., 2017). Finally, we collect public administrative records of child protective involvement, convictions, institutional infractions, and recidivism over time.

Three-Month Follow-Up At the follow-up visit, we conduct another interview with the incarcerated parent (who may be in the community, still in jail, or transferred to a prison) and the child's caregiver. This includes a second administration of some initial self-report measures and questions about the perceived benefits and challenges of the intervention. Data on tablet usage is collected to learn about which applications are used and for how long. We also obtain information on the number and length of visits directly from the company that facilitates the video visits, as well as public records reflecting any new parental (or caregiver) convictions.

Feedback from Families and Agencies We have received positive feedback about the EVM from incarcerated parents, children, at-home caregivers, corrections administrators, and community organizations. Initial interest in the project was very high. During the first week, more than 60 incarcerated individuals signed up, which is higher than the 3–5 individuals per week we have screened in previous projects. Incarcerated parents have asked if they can continue the video visits if they are transferred to another facility. Attorneys have contacted us asking to have their clients enrolled, and recently a judge allowed an incarcerated father to serve the remainder of his time in the jail that we work with (instead of another jail) so that he could continue video visits with his children. The state agency in charge of foster care has asked us to include foster children in our program as well as children living in kinship care.

Many incarcerated parents, especially those with younger children, indicated that book reading was a favorite activity during visits. We have seen examples of joint play, such as a child dressed up in dinosaur costume, pretending to go to sleep; the incarcerated parent played along, pretending to sleep by the "dinosaur," with the parent and child jointly singing a lullaby. Children have shown their artwork, demonstrated new skills such as cartwheels and playing an instrument, and shown their pets, new toys, or video games to their parent. The incarcerated parent has engaged in parenting behaviors, such as supervising children brushing their teeth; helping with homework; limit setting; and participating in bedtime routines. The incarcerated parent has been virtually engaged in daily routines (e.g., cooking, mealtimes, watching a movie) and special occasions (e.g., birthday party at a roller rink, thanksgiving celebration at grandmother's home, decorating the Christmas tree). Most observed interactions have been quite positive. We have also coded some negative interactions, especially early in the program, such as parents swearing at the child, arguing with each other, or children not being available to chat. In one case, there was inappropriate parental behavior that led to the jail terminating visits for that parent (<1% of families). These visits prompted us to add guidelines related to language and appropriate use of video chat, as well as to give families a copy of the jail's standard visiting rules.

Most incarcerated parents interviewed say that having regular video contact with their children is "what keeps them going" and is the best part of their day. They have stated that they are motivated to stay out of jail in the future because of their strengthened relationships with their children. Caregivers have indicated positive effects as well, such as daily visits helping the parent stay more "in the loop" with the child and home. One mother said that her child was having school trouble because he regularly pretended to call his incarcerated father on an imaginary phone and melted down when teachers tried to redirect him. Since participating in the EVM, the child is no longer pretending to call his father, and the mother attributes this to her son being able to video visit with his father. Several older children (7 to 12 years) said that they did not like going to the jail because it was stressful to check in, go through locked doors, and visit behind glass. Moreover, they said visits were boring because only one person could hear at a time (as there is only one telephone receiver per family). One child said that her mother spent most of the in-jail visits talking to her father, so she spent most of the time waiting; but during the in-home video visit, she could curl up on the couch with a blanket and her cat and could talk to her dad without any waiting or interruptions. Although she did not use the word "stigma," she described an experience that reduced the stigma of going to the jail.

During the 3-month follow-up, we also received positive feedback on the visit coaching. Several parents and caregivers mentioned that the coaching helped them identify tools to help children stay engaged during visits, plan ahead by thinking of conversation topics, and reflect on their role in supporting children. One father said that the coaching helped him to focus on more positive things with his child during visits, while another mentioned that he gained insight into his own and his children's feelings.

Case Study

In this section, we present a representative case study to illustrate how the EVM works in practice. To help protect individual and family confidentiality, we combined details from two different families and changed names and other potentially identifying details.

James is a 33-year-old African American man serving a 4-month sentence for a revocation involving possession of illegal substances. James has had multiple incarcerations and separations from his son, Mason, who is 6 years old. James has been involved with the criminal justice system since he was 16 years old, struggling with addiction and mental health concerns. These issues have made it difficult for him to hold a steady job and make child support payments, leading to a conflicted relationship with his son's mother, Stephanie. James expresses a strong desire to "clean up his act" and "be there" for Mason, but his mental health and substance use have made it difficult for him to be a consistent and present father. James shared how important being a father is to him and how badly he wants to be there for his son, especially because of the absence of his own father when he was growing up.

Stephanie is a 35-year-old White woman. She lives in a modest subsidized apartment with her three children. She works full-time at a local fast food chain. She receives SNAP benefits and Medicaid but, however, still finds it difficult to make ends meet. Her mother lives nearby and helps Stephanie with the children and occasionally with bills and groceries. Stephanie says that she and her mother have been the biggest influences and supports in Mason's life. Stephanie is devoted to her children, mentioning that "it has always just been me and them." Stephanie shared that Mason recently started asking more questions about where his father is and when he will see him again. She wants James to be in Mason's life but resents the emotional drain that comes with it.

Mason is a talkative and energetic 6-year-old. He was recently diagnosed with attention-deficit/hyperactivity disorder and oppositional defiant disorder and receives reading and speech services. Although Stephanie's and Mason's interactions seemed positive during study visits, and Stephanie appeared sensitive to Mason's cues, Stephanie said she struggles with his behavioral issues, such as whining, hitting, and fighting at school. She feels like she does not know how to handle them and becomes frustrated and angry. Mason often talks about his father saying he "misses him so much." However, Stephanie feels that contact with James exacerbates Mason's challenging behaviors.

At first, Stephanie was hesitant about the EVM project. She wanted Mason to have contact with his father but reports that supporting Mason after visits is challenging because she also has to manage her own emotional reactions. She decided to participate because Mason could visit his father from home without Stephanie needing to interact with James.

During their initial coaching sessions, James and Stephanie expressed concerns about keeping Mason's attention for a 45-minute visit. James brainstormed topics to discuss with Mason such as school and music. During the first coaching session, he envisioned what Mason might be wearing and what he might say and feel when he first saw his dad. Stephanie reflected on how important she is in supporting Mason's connection with James and discussed a time that she comforted Mason when he was upset about an incident at school. She struggled at times to separate her own complicated relationship with James from the relationship that James and Mason have but ultimately resolved to act as a source of support for Mason. She also identified ways she could prepare Mason for visits by suggesting activities at school that he could share with James.

After starting the video visits, Stephanie reported that Mason developed "a routine" of video visiting every Wednesday after school. During the visits, James talked to Mason about the "countdown" to his release and made plans for his return to the community. Sometimes James helped Mason with his homework, reviewing his spelling words and listening to Mason read books. Other times, Mason propped up the tablet and showed his dad the family dog or toys that he likes. One time they played a game together, with Mason moving the game pieces following his father's instructions. During post-visit coaching, Stephanie reflected that she thought the visits were helpful as they gave her son the opportunity to connect with his father and involve him in Mason's daily life.

During a 3-month follow-up visit with James, he described how the video visits allowed him to "stay relevant" in his son's life even when physically separated. Mason spoke positively about the visits, comparing them to FaceTime with relatives. Stephanie shared that Mason has been doing better in school since beginning the video visits. She said: "I really think this change is due to Mason being able to see his dad every week. He still asks about him and when he is coming home, but it's less so now." Stephanie also shared that Mason's behavior following visits had improved. Though he still whines and sometimes cries and runs to his room, she reports it as "less frequent and less intense now." She said that she feels more confident in her ability to comfort Mason when he is upset, assuring him that it is okay to miss his dad and that they will be together again soon. Stephanie acknowledged the role she plays in her son's life as his primary caregiver but also recognized the importance of her son's relationship with his father, saying that she will encourage them to stay connected.

Conclusion

Our EVM has implications for CIP and their families, as well as those seeking to develop an innovative and replicable intervention that takes attachment-based and social justice approaches. CIP are often invisible and highly vulnerable, calling for a recognition of their needs and rights, as has been done by the San Francisco Children of Incarcerated Parents Partnership. In 2003, they published the Bill of Rights for CIP, with the hope that decisions affecting affected children consider their well-being. The eight rights outlined state: I have the right to be kept safe and informed at the time of my parent's arrest; I have the right to be heard when decisions are made about me; I have the right to be well cared for in my parent's absence; I have the right to speak with, see, and touch my parent; I have the right to support as I face my parent's incarceration; I have the right not to be judged, blamed, or labeled because my parent is incarcerated; I have the right to a lifelong relationship with my parent. In line with attachment theory and research, EVM supports children's attachment needs and rights to engage in positive close relationships with their incarcerated parents during incarceration and in the future. It may help children heal from the disruption caused by parent-child separation during parental incarceration.

References

Adkins, T., & Fonagy, P. (2017). *Coding reflective functioning in parents using the five minute speech sample procedure: Version 2*. Unpublished Manuscript.

Ainsworth, M., Blehar, M., Waters, E., & Wall, S. (1978). *Patterns of attachment: A psychological study of the strange situation*. Hillsdale, NJ: Erlbaum.

American Academy of Pediatrics. (2016). Media and young minds. *Pediatrics, 138*(5), e20162591. https://doi.org/10.1542/peds.2016-2591.

Arditti, J. A. (2003). Locked doors and glass walls: Family visiting at a local jail. *Journal of Loss and Trauma, 8*(2), 115–138.

Bales, W. D., & Mears, D. P. (2008). Inmate social ties and the transition to society: Does visitation reduce recidivism? *Journal of Research in Crime and Delinquency*, 287–321.

Beckmeyer, J. J., & Arditti, J. A. (2014). Implications of in-person visits for incarcerated parents' family relationships and parenting experience. *Journal of Offender Rehabilitation, 53*(2), 129–151.

Borelli, J. L., Smiley, P. A., Kerr, M. L., Hong, K., Hecht, H. K., Blackard, B., Falasiri, E., Cervantes, B. R., & Bond, D. K. (2020). Relational savoring: An attachment-based approach to promoting interpersonal flourishing. *Psychotherapy*. Advance online publication. https://doi.org/10.1037/pst0000284.

Bowlby, J. (1973). *Attachment and loss, Vol. 2: Separation*. New York, NY: Basic Books.

Bronfenbrenner, U. (1979). *The ecology of human development*. Boston, MA: Harvard University Press.

Bronfenbrenner, U., & Ceci, S. J. (1994). Nature-nurture reconceptualized in developmental perspective: A bioecological model. *Psychological Review, 101*(4), 568–586.

Bryant, F. B., & Veroff, J. (2007). *Savoring: A new model of positive experience*. Mahwah, NJ: Lawrence Erlbaum.

Burkhart, M. L., Borelli, J. L., Rasmussen, H. F., & Sbarra, D. (2015). Cherish the good times: Relational savoring in parents of infants and toddlers. *Personal Relationships, 22*, 692–711.

Cassidy, J., & Shaver, P. (Eds.). (2018). *Handbook of attachment: Theory, research, and clinical applications* (3rd ed.). New York, NY: Guilford Press.

Clark, R. (1985/2018). *The early relational assessment*. University of Wisconsin-Madison.

Dallaire, D., Ciccone, A., & Wilson, L. C. (2012). The family drawings of at-risk children: Concurrent relations with contact with incarcerated parents, caregiver behavior and stress. *Attachment & Human Development, 14*(2), 161–183.

Dallaire, D., Zeman, J., & Thrash, T. (2015). Differential effects of type of children's contact with their jailed mothers and children's behavior problems. In J. Poehlmann-Tynan (Ed.), *Children's contact with incarcerated parents* (pp. 23–38). Springer International.

Duwe, G., & Clark, V. (2013). Blessed be the social tie that binds: The effects of prison visitation on offender recidivism. *Criminal Justice Policy Review, 24*(3), 271–296.

Fonagy, P., Gergely, G., Jurist, E., & Target, M. (2002). *Affect regulation, mentalization and the development of the self.* New York, NY: Other Press.

Fredrickson, B. L., & Joiner, T. (2002). Positive emotions trigger upward spirals toward emotional Well-being. *Psychological Science, 13*, 172–175.

Glaze, L., & Maruschak, L. (2008). *Incarcerated parents and their minor children*. D.C., Bureau of Justice Statistics: Washington.

Houck, K. D., & Loper, A. B. (2002). The relationship of parenting stress to adjustment among mothers in prison. *American Journal of Orthopsychiatry, 72*(4), 548–558.

Hurley, D. B., & Kwon, P. (2011). Results of a study to increase savoring the moment: Differential impact on positive and negative outcomes. *Journal of Happiness Studies, 13*(4), 579–588.

Jones, A., & Sawyer, W. (2019). *Arrest, release, repeat: How police and jails are misused to respond to social problems*. Prison Policy Initiative. Retrieved from https://www.prisonpolicy.org/reports/repeatarrests.html.

Kiken, L. G., & Shook, N. J. (2011). Looking up: Mindfulness increases positive judgments and reduces negativity bias. *Social Psychological and Personality Science, 2*(4), 425–431.

McHale, J. P., Salman, S., Strozier, A., & Cecil, D. K. (2013). Triadic interactions in mother-grandmother coparenting systems following maternal release from jail. *Monographs of the Society for Research in Child Development, 78*(3), 57–74.

McKay, T., Comfort, M., Lindquist, C., & Bir, A. (2019). *Holding on: Family and fatherhood during incarceration and reentry*. University of California Press.

Mikulincer, M., & Shaver, P. R. (2007). *Attachment in adulthood: Structure, dynamics, and change*. New York, NY: Guilford Press.

Murphey. D., &Cooper, P. M. (2015). Parents behind bars: What happens to their children? Child Trends. Retrieved from https://www.childtrends.org/publications/parents-behind-bars-what-happens-to-their-children.

Ooms, T. (2019). The evolution of family policy: Lessons learned, challenges, and hopes for the future. *Journal of Family Theory & Review, 11*, 18–38.

Poehlmann, J. (2005). Incarcerated mothers' contact with children, perceived family relationships, and depressive symptoms. *Journal of Family Psychology, 19*, 350–357.

Poehlmann, J., Dallaire, D., Loper, A. B., & Shear, L. D. (2010). Children's contact with their incarcerated parents: Research findings and recommendations. *American Psychologist, 65*, 575–598.

Poehlmann-Tynan, J., & Pritzl, K. (2019). Parent–child visits when parents are incarcerated in prison or jail. In J. M. Eddy & J. Poehlmann-Tynan (Eds.), *Handbook on children with incarcerated parents* (pp. 131–147). Springer.

Poehlmann-Tynan, J., Runion, H., Burnson, C., Maleck, S., Weymouth, L., Pettit, K., & Huser, M. (2015). Young children's behavioral and emotional reactions to Plexiglas and video visits with jailed parents. In J. Poehlmann-Tynan (Ed.), *Springer briefs in psychology. Children's contact with incarcerated parents: Implications for policy and intervention* (pp. 39–58). Springer International Publishing. https://doi.org/10.1007/978-3-319-16625-4_3.

Poehlmann-Tynan, J., Burnson, C., Runion, H., & Weymouth, L. A. (2017). Attachment in young children with incarcerated fathers. *Development and Psychopathology, 29*, 389–404. https://doi.org/10.1007/978-3-319-16625-4.

Rideout, V. J. & Katz, V.S. (2016). *Opportunity for all? Technology and learning in lower-income families*. A report of the Families and Media Project. NY: The Joan Ganz Cooney Center and Sesame Workshop.

Roxburgh, S., & Fitch, C. (2014). Parental status, child contact, and Well-being among incarcerated men and women. *Journal of Family Issues, 35*, 1394–1412.

Rubenstein, B. Y., Toman, E. L., & Cochran, J. C. (2019). Socioeconomic barriers to child contact with incarcerated parents. *Justice Quarterly, 36*, 1–27.

Sawyer, W., & Wagner, P. (2019). *Mass incarceration: The whole pie 2019*. Prison Policy Initiative. Retrieved from https://www.prisonpolicy.org/reports/pie2019.html.

Shanahan, S., & Agudelo, S.V. (2012) The family and recidivism. *American Jails*. https://www.prisonpolicy.org/scans/vera/the-family-and-recidivism.pdf.

Shlafer, R. J., Loper, A. B., & Schillmoeller, L. (2015). Introduction and literature review: Is parent–child contact during parental incarceration beneficial? In J. Poehlmann-Tynan (Ed.), *Children's contact with incarcerated parents* (pp. 1–21). Cham: Springer.

Slade, A., Grienenberger, J., Bernbach, E., Levy, D., & Locker, A. (2005). Maternal reflective functioning, attachment, and the transmission gap: A preliminary study. *Attachment & Human Development, 7*(3), 283–298.

Sleed, M., Baradon, T., & Fonagy, P. (2013). New beginnings for mothers and babies in prison: A cluster randomized controlled trial. *Attachment & Human Development, 15*(4), 349–367.

Tang, L., Darlington, G., Ma, D. W., & Haines, J. (2018). Mothers' and fathers' media parenting practices associated with young children's screen-time: A cross-sectional study. *BMC Obesity, 5*(1), 37.

Tartaro, C., & Levy, M. P. (2017). Inmate visitation: Visitor preferences regarding the best visitation modality for children. *Corrections, 2*(1), 20–40.

Tasca, M. (2014). *"It's not all cupcakes and lollipops": An investigation of the predictors and effects of prison visitation for children during maternal and paternal incarceration*. (Doctoral dissertation, Arizona State University).

Visher, C. A. (2013). Incarcerated fathers: Pathways from prison to home. *Criminal Justice Policy Review, 24*(1), 9–26.

Wakefield, S., & Wildeman, C. (2013). *Children of the prison boom: Mass incarceration and the future of American inequality*. Oxford University Press.

Werner, E. E. (2000). Protective factors and individual resilience. In J. P. Shonkoff & S. J. Meisels (Eds.), *Handbook of early childhood intervention* (2nd ed., pp. 115–132). New York, NY: Cambridge.

Western, B., & Pettit, B. (2010). Incarceration & social inequality. *Daedalus, 139*(3), 8–19.

Western, B., & Wildeman, C. (2009). The black family and mass incarceration. *The Annals of the American Academy of Political and Social Science, 621*(1), 221–242.

Wildeman, C. (2009). Parental imprisonment, the prison boom, and the concentration of childhood disadvantage. *Demography, 46*(2), 265–280.

Wildeman, C., Haskins, A. R., & Poehlmann-Tynan, J. (Eds.). (2017). *When parents are incarcerated: Interdisciplinary research and interventions to support children*. Washington, DC: American Psychological Association.

Zeng, Z. (2020). *Jail inmates in 2018*. Washington, DC: U.S. Department of Justice, Bureau of Justice Statistics.

Poehlmann, J., Dallaire, D., Loper, A. B., & Shear, L. D. (2010). Children's contact with their incarcerated parents: Research findings and recommendations. American Psychologist, 65(6), 575-598. https://doi.org/10.1037/a0020279

Poehlmann-Tynan, J., & Pritzl, K. (2019). Parent–child visits when parents are incarcerated in prison or jail. In J. M. Eddy & J. Poehlmann-Tynan (Eds.), Handbook on children with incarcerated parents (2nd ed., pp. 131–147). Springer International Publishing. https://doi.org/10.1007/978-3-030-16707-3_10

A Review of Reentry Programs and Their Inclusion of Families

J. Mark Eddy, Hyo-Mi Pak, Claudia Reino, and Andrea Reino

Abstract Reentry, the period before and after release from incarceration, is considered a critical period in terms of the long-term success of formerly incarcerated individuals. Unfortunately, recidivism in the USA is more common than not, and occurrences of recidivism have negative implications not only for the safety and health of society at large but also for the families and children of the those who recidivate. Social connection, support, and access to resources have long been thought to be crucial for reentry success and particularly when these come from family. In this chapter, we review the research literature on reentry programs that engage families. We discuss our findings, the urgent need for high-quality research, and recommendations for future program development and outcome studies.

Keywords Reentry · Prison · Parents · Parent management training · Visiting · Children · Caregivers · Incarceration

Thanks to our colleagues Kimberley Gonzalez-Quiles, Gabriella Damewood, Jean Schumer, and Jean Kjellstrand for their assistance in preliminary work related to this chapter. Correspondence should be sent to J. Mark Eddy, Department of Educational Psychology and Department of Kinesiology and Health Education, College of Education, University of Texas at Austin, Austin, TX, mark.eddy@austin.utexas.edu.

J. M. Eddy (✉) · H.-M. Pak · C. Reino
University of Texas at Austin, Austin, TX, USA
e-mail: mark.eddy@austin.utexas.edu

A. Reino
Princeton University, Princeton, NJ, USA

J. Krysik, N. Rodriguez (eds.), *Children of Incarcerated Parents*, Children of Incarcerated Parents: From Understanding to Impact,
https://doi.org/10.1007/978-3-030-84713-5_8

A Review of Reentry Programs and Their Inclusion of Families

Although the USA accounts for just 5% of the world's population, it houses 25% of the world's incarcerated population (Deady, 2014). Over 2.3 million people—roughly 1 in every 100 adults in the USA —are currently confined in local jails, state and local prisons, immigration detention facilities, state psychiatric hospitals, military prisons, or prisons (Sawyer & Wagner, 2020). Most who are incarcerated are eventually released, and thus the flow of adults out of these institutions is substantial. Over 825,000 people are released from prison each year (Sabol & Minton, 2008), and many more are released from jail. Returning home is the pivot point of the "reentry" process, which encompasses a period that begins sometime before release (e.g., in prisons, often 6–9 months prior) and continues after release for as long as 1, 3, or even 5 years, depending on the conceptualization of the particular system (National Institute of Corrections, 2017). As the numbers of incarcerated individuals in the USA grew over the past several decades, momentum has built among local and state policymakers to find effective strategies that help formerly incarcerated men and women succeed. In recent years, the dialogue around reentry has shifted from one dominated by shifting ideologies (e.g., Eddy & Swanson-Gribskov, 1998) to one that is focused on programmatic, evidence-based solutions (Visher, 2007). Driving the discussion has been an ongoing concern with recidivism.

Recidivism

What happens for formerly incarcerated individuals during reentry depends not only on them and their personal relationships and resources, but also on the decisions and actions of the judicial and corrections systems that are connected to their case as well as characteristics within their local context, including the availability of resources, services, and opportunities. Once released from prison, a formerly incarcerated individual may face a wide variety of obstacles to successful integration, including, but not limited to, a lack of jobs, affordable housing, and prosocial supports (Morgan et al., 2012; Esparza Flores, 2018; Li, 2018). Failing to overcome these obstacles may ultimately lead to recidivism—being convicted of a new crime and returning to jail or prison. Like incarceration itself, recidivism in the USA is higher than in most other countries, estimated at a staggering rate of over 63% of formerly incarcerated adults over the 9-year period after release (Yukhnenko et al., 2019). Rates of return are quite high beginning early in the post-release period, with 28% of men reincarcerated within 6 months, 58% within the first year, and 77% within the first 5 years (Durose et al., 2014). This compares to rates in other Western countries of 59% in 5 years in France, 51% in 3 years in Ireland, 48% in 2 years in the Netherlands, and 29% in 2 years in Denmark (Fazel & Wolf, 2015).

Recidivism in the USA is a notable concern for several reasons. Recidivism follows continued offending and thus reflects new instances of victimization. High recidivism is thus a threat to public safety at large. Recidivism is often followed by continued hardships of various types for the families of the incarcerated, lost connections within the community, and decreases in civic participation (Visher, 2007; Ahalt et al., 2013). All told, the financial costs of recidivism are expansive. According to the Bureau of Justice Statistics (BJS), total state expenditures to operate corrections systems in the USA is $81 billion US dollars annually, not including policing and court costs, with a substantial sum of those dollars spent on incarcerating repeat offenders (Kyckelhahn, 2015; Eisen, 2015).

Families and Recidivism

Common predictors of recidivism include risk factors such as offense type, drug involvement, neighborhood variables, and spatial contagion (i.e., the proximity to others who recidivate) (e.g., Stahler et al., 2013). Researchers in the reentry field have often suggested that the most promising programs to mitigate recidivism begin during incarceration and extend well past release as a formerly incarcerated man or women gets his or her foothold in a new life on the outside (James, 2014). Over the years, a key target within reentry programs has been strengthening a host of protective factors against recidivism, including social connections and support and access to needed basic resources (Visher et al., 2004; La Vigne et al., 2005; Maruna & Toch, 2005; Morenoff & Harding, 2014). In this regard, finding ways to shore up protective factors *over the long run* seems like a particularly promising strategy, and accomplishing this goal requires working within social structures that both already exist and have the potential to remain in place. The family is one such structure. Not surprisingly, many men and women do turn to their families for assistance during reentry. Subsequently, families may become the "front line" for reentry, providing critical material and emotional support that may either make or break a successful transition from incarceration to home (Bobbitt & Nelson, 2004; Brooks-Gordon & Bainham, 2004; Brown & Bloom, 2009).

An important precursor to obtaining support and reducing recidivism is thought to be what happens during prison. A variety of studies over the years have found that visits before release are related to a lower likelihood of recidivism (e.g., Holt & Miller, 1972; Bales & Mears, 2008; Duwe & Clark, 2013). Family visits have received particular attention in the literature in recent years (e.g., Poehlmann, Dallaire, Loper, & Shear, 2010), and particularly visits between incarcerated parents and their children and families (see Eddy & Poehlmann-Tynan, 2019). Over 60% of women and 50% of men in prison, for example, are parents (Glaze & Maruschak, 2008). Parent-child contact during incarceration, which is most typically due to positive parent-caregiver contact, is associated with a variety of important long-term outcomes, including more engaged parent-child relationships after release and less recidivism (e.g., McKay et al., 2019; Thomas et al.,, 2020; Visher et al., 2013; Duwe & McNeeley, 2020).

Unfortunately, while families hold much potential to assist during reentry, they may be in a comprised state. The loss of their family member may have reduced their family income significantly, which may reverberate into a host of negative consequences, such as an unstable housing situation, a loss of childcare and limited employment opportunities, transportation difficulties, hunger, and child protective services involvement (e.g., Schwartz-Soicher et al., 2011; Sugie, 2012; Wildeman et al., 2016; Wakefield & Wildeman, 2018; Slack et al., 2017). In one study, the poverty status of a formerly incarcerated adult increased the odds of rearrest by a factor of 4.6 and the odds of a supervision violation by a factor of 12.7 (Holtfreter et al., 2004). On the interpersonal level, parental incarceration is associated with a heightened risk for negative adjustment outcomes for children, most notably conduct problems (Murray et al., 2012; cf. Eddy & Poehlmann-Tynan, 2019), which in turn are related to a host of other problems both for children (e.g., academic failure, substance use and abuse) and for their families.

Thus, while family connection and support may hold promise in helping reduce recidivism, what a formerly incarcerated adult can contribute to his or her family after release is critical. Reentry programs have the potential to play a role in increasing the chances that men and women are in a position to make significant contributions. Certainly, a place to start is around family communication, both between parent and child and between parent and caregivers, and finding ways to do this in positive ways seems congruent with the findings on visits while in prison and reduced recidivism. However, this is just a starting place. For example, in one study, state-sponsored support to address short-term needs (e.g., housing) for women reduced the odds of recidivism by 83% (Holtfreter et al., 2004). Without a foothold in a new life outside, it is difficult to get a new start. However, more is needed than just a foothold. Over the long run, stable employment is one of the strongest predictors of post-release success, including reduced recidivism, but finding employment is one of the greatest barriers to successful reintegration for offenders and ex-offenders (Varghese & Cummings, 2012). Thus, programs to assist in finding and retaining employment are vital to reentry success (Visher & Travis, 2011). In short, given the potentially important role of families during reentry, as well as the plethora of needs that may go beyond what families can provide, reentry programming may be vital to success for many releasing men and women. In this chapter, within the scientific literature, we examine the extent to which children and families have been considered a part of such programming and, when they have, what other elements have been included to try to maximize reentry success.

Method

Reentry studies were identified through a multiple-step process. To begin, an Internet-based literature search was conducted that focused on reentry programs that targeted parents and were delivered either in prison, jail, or a community setting and that included direct interaction with children and/or caregivers. We did not limit the time frame for reentry—it could start upon the start of lock-up and continue for years past release, as long as the conceptual frame in the paper was the provision of service during "reentry" or some such synonym. Our search was done through multiple queries to PubMed, Tandfonline, Web of Science, Publons, and other search engines available through the University of Texas at Austin Library as well as to Google, including Google Scholar. Examples of search words of interest included parental incarceration, prisoners, prison, jail, reentry, caregiver, caretaker, guardian, parent, child, pilot study, comparison group study, and randomized controlled trial. For each individual search using a unique combination of words, text generated from the first 100 findings were screened. Relevant articles were downloaded and scanned for additional references, which were also downloaded for review. Documents retained for further review included reports on findings from randomized controlled trials on programs delivered during the reentry period for fathers and mothers that included a variable for children, caregivers, and/or family members. Finally, prior reviews of the literature that focused on reentry or closely related issues, such as parenting while incarcerated, were searched, and relevant articles retained. All articles were reviewed initially to ensure that they were published in a peer-reviewed journal in the past two decades, that participants were approaching release or recently released, that the reentry intervention that was examined included a caregiver and/or child oriented component, and that either a pre-post (one sample) or a comparison group study was conducted and outcomes were examined.

Results

Our search process ultimately yielded 16 articles, 10 of which, upon further review, fully met all criteria (see Table 1). However, it is important to note that a broader set of articles were found but suffered from lack of specification regarding important aspects of the search, including what was actually done in a family component, let alone how many people actually received that component. Given the confusion we found in the literature (and the resulting confusion we had in coding some programs), we view the articles we retained as a sampling of the literature, rather than a comprehensive listing. Notably, we found very few articles that met our criteria published in the past decade.

Among the articles that we retained, 80% focused on parenting education. Most of these (88%) also included some type of direct family contact component, most often relatively brief parent-child visits. One of these programs was a prison nursery, where babies lived with their mothers. Only 20% of programs involved a more comprehensive approach to reentry. Most programs took place in lock-up, rather than across the reentry period. Further, most programs were studied with a comparison group design , and most analyses revealed some positive outcomes. However, most reported outcomes were on incarcerated parents, rather than family members. One program, and the most comprehensive of the bunch (i.e., Wilson & Davis, 2006), reported iatrogenic effects for recidivism.

Table 1 Reentry intervention studies with family components

Study	Intervention Program Description			Research Design	Example Impacts of Intervention on Variables Related to Family
	Incarcerated Parent	Caregiver	Child		
Anderson (2002)	In community, tailored intervention (e.g., substance abuse education and treatment, survival skills, GED prep, cognitive restructuring, anger management, employment skills, parenting and family reintegration)	Possible involvement in parenting and family reintegration group (unclear)	None specified (unclear)	Comparison group (randomized)	Significant positive effects concerning the acquisition of knowledge of appropriate parenting techniques as well as significantly lower recidivism
Wilson & Davis (2006)	Multimodal tailored in-prison program (e.g., job readiness, relapse prevention, drug treatment readiness, practical living skills), links to community-based resources, facilitating relationship with parole officer	Family counselor and family specialist available to work with family before release	None specified (except as part of work with caregiver)	Comparison group (randomized)	Significantly higher recidivism (iatrogenic effect)
Miller et al. (2014)	Parent training program focused on parenting attitudes	Several family sessions (in community)	Weekly parent-child sessions	Intervention group only	Significant reductions in inappropriate developmental expectations and in endorsement of corporal punishment

(continued)

Table 1 (continued)

Study	Intervention Program Description			Research Design	Example Impacts of Intervention on Variables Related to Family
	Incarcerated Parent	Caregiver	Child		
Harris & Landreth (1997)	Parent training program focused on child-centered play skills	None specified	Bi-weekly 30-minute parent-child sessions	Comparison group (not randomized)	Significant increases in empathic behavior and perceived acceptance of child
Landreth & Lobaugh (1998)	Parent training program focused on child-centered play skills	None specified	Weekly 30-minute structured parent-child visits	Comparison group (randomized)	Significantly higher attitude of acceptance and empathic behavior toward child and increased self-concepts of children
Moore & Clement (1998)	Parent training program focused on parent and child development education, follow-up support groups	None specified	Several all-day contact visits, additional parent-child visits	Comparison group (randomized)	Significant acquisition of knowledge of appropriate parenting techniques
Sandifer (2008)	Parent training program focused on effective parenting with extended visits from children to practice parenting skills	None specified	Monthly, day-long structured and unstructured visitation time	Comparison group (not randomized)	Significant reduced preference for physical force to discipline children, increased ownership of responsible parent role and empathy towards children's feelings and needs
Sleed et al. (2013)	Parent training program focused on attachment	None specified	Weekly 2-hour sessions with babies	Comparison group (randomized)	Significant effect on the quality of dyadic behavior

(continued)

Table 1 (continued)

Study	Intervention Program Description			Research Design	Example Impacts of Intervention on Variables Related to Family
	Incarcerated Parent	Caregiver	Child		
Goshin et al. (2014)	Parent training focused on child development, coping and access to prison nursery	None specified	Prison nursery (infants live with mothers)	Intervention group only	Three years after release, vast majority of women remained in the community ; of the few who did not, most returned to prison for parole violation rather than a new conviction
Eddy et al. (2013)	Parent management training (PMT) specifically designed for incarcerated parents	PMT materials sent home to caregiver upon request	None specified	Comparison group (randomized)	Significant effect on positive parent-child interaction

Discussion

Despite the relation between family contact and positive concurrent and future outcomes for incarcerated fathers and mothers, in the research literature, we found very few examples of reentry programs that actively include caregivers and/or children. Those we did find typically included elements that were rather limited in scope, such as a few parent-child visits (including up to all-day contact visits) or a planned family discussion. The major exception is prison nurseries, of which there are only a few around the country (cf. Byrne, 2019). The findings reported for the various programs suggest some positive impacts, but most of the available information concerns outcomes and parent perceptions at the end of the program, rather than concrete situations or events (e.g., living with family, not returning to prison) over the long run. Most studies were lacking in scientific rigor. In short, the literature on reentry programs for incarcerated parents and their families is in its infancy.

Clearly, more research is needed, but where might be the most useful place to begin such work? We suggest that a good place to start given what we know about the reentry period and success would be with a reconsideration of what "parenting" means within the context of corrections. For the past two decades, our research team has been advocating for the idea of broadening the scope of what is targeted in reentry parenting programs (e.g., Eddy et al., 2008, 2010, 2019; Eddy et al., 2013; Shortt et al., 2014; Kjellstrand, 2018; Burraston & Eddy, 2017; Eddy & Burraston, 2018; Eddy & Schumer, 2018). The basic rationale is that being a parent after release involves more than knowing certain pieces of knowledge or being exposed to certain types of communication skills—the typical target in most prison-based parenting programs. Rather, it involves getting support for actually using those skills while in prison and then employing the gained knowledge and skills within family relationships on a day-to-day basis in the community after release. It involves taking care of oneself, finding a place to live, finding a job, and repairing and nurturing existing relationships with prosocial adults (e.g., caregivers, intimate partners, relatives), but also making wise choices about the new relationships that one enters into with new friends and partners. It also involves making wise choices after release in terms of the relationships that one had with peers and family members that were not healthy (and possibly supported criminal behavior) prior to incarceration.

The frame we use for this approach in relation to parents and their children is illustrated in Fig. 1. The ideas are grounded in the theoretical work of Bronfenbrenner (e.g., Bronfenbrenner, 1979) and in Patterson and colleagues (e.g., Patterson, 1982; Reid et al., 2002), which emphasize the importance, and nesting, of multiple levels of influence on child and family development. From our reading of the research literature and our work on the ground, we focus on eight key targets in our work on reentry parenting programs. The first set we call the "little four." These targets are centered within the relationship between the parent and child: positive involvement, supervision and monitoring, guidance and discipline, and problem-solving. The second set we call the "Big Four." These targets are vital elements of the context that surround the parent-child relationship. These include parent mental and physical health, safe and stable housing, a living wage job, and the quality of parent-other adult relationships.

With this frame in mind, over the past 5 years, we have collaborated with the Reentry and Correctional Industries Division of the Washington State Department of Corrections (DOC) on the creation and refinement of the *Strength in Families* (SIF) program (Eddy et al., 1). This work has been supported through the DOC and a grant from the federal Administration for Children and Families. The program is place-based, focusing on fathers incarcerated in specific institutions in southwestern Washington who are returning to nearby counties. SIF begins in prison and continues back in the home communities of fathers for up to 1 year after release.

SIF is a multimodal, multilevel, tailored approach designed to prepare and support parents for their return back to their communities and to their families. The process and content of the core components of the program are informed by multiple sources, including the research literature on incarcerated parents and their children and families in general (Eddy & Poehlmann, 2010; Eddy & Poehlmann-Tynan, 2019) as well as on incarcerated fathers and reentry in specific (Eddy & Burraston, 2018); the experiences of incarcerated fathers; the experiences of practitioners, correctional officers, counselors, and administrators in Washington State who have worked with criminal justice-involved parents; and our own experiences working with fathers before and after release.

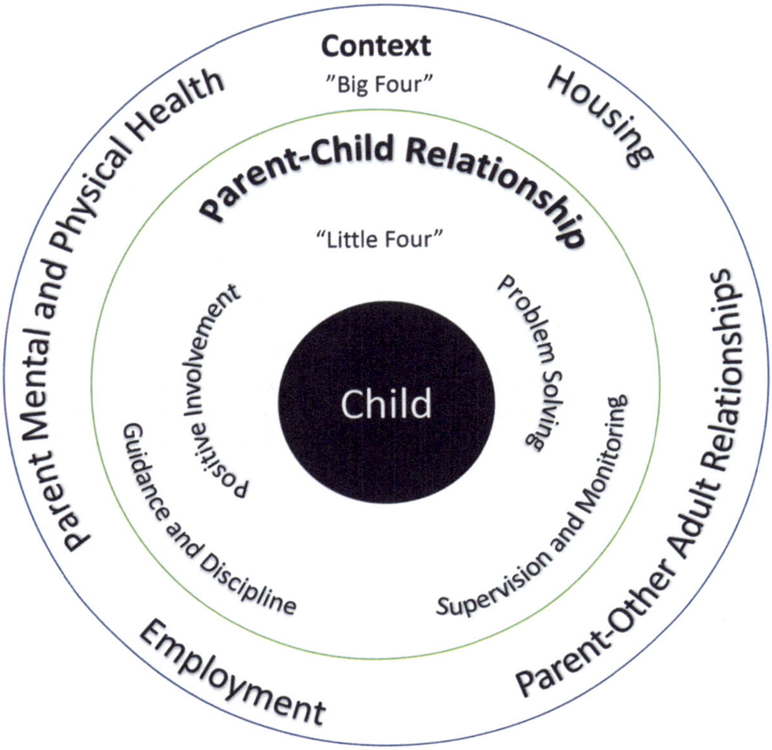

Fig. 1 The Big four little four model

SIF is a voluntary program that links together a series of evidence-based or evidence-informed skills training programs. Interested fathers who enroll are first invited to participate in *Walking the Line* (WTL; Einhorn et al., 2008; Erlacher, 2010), a group-based cognitive-behavioral intervention that centers on the development of knowledge and skills that support positive and lasting intimate partner relationships. WTL is a second-generation adaptation of the evidence-based PREP program (e.g., Halford et al., 2008; Markman et al., 1993).

At the conclusion of WTL, fathers are invited to enroll in *Parenting Inside Out* (PIO; Eddy et al., 2013). PIO is a second-generation adaption of the evidence-based *Parent Management Training* (PMT) program developed by the research group at the Oregon Social Learning Center (see Reid et al., 2002) and focuses on the development of knowledge and skills that support positive and constructive parent-caregiver and parent-child relationships.

Along the way, fathers are invited to enroll in *Job Seeking Skills* (JSS), a program developed by the Washington State Employment Security Department and DOC Offender Employment Services. JSS develop "soft" skills related to finding and keeping a job, as well as developing needed products such as a resume. Each of these three skills training programs is taught by trained and supervised SIF instructors. These individuals are DOC employees, rather than outside contractors. Many are individuals with extensive experience working in other capacities within prisons, including correctional officers and counselors.

While going through these programs, a father begins to work with a trained and supervised Case Manager as well as a trained and supervised Education and Employment Navigator. Each of these individuals helps a father set the stage for their return to their community using a *Solutions-Based Casework* (Christensen et al., 1999) approach. Case Managers and fathers develop a plan that is grounded in meeting basic needs such as housing and transportation and obtaining community-based support tailored to each father's strengths and challenges. Case Managers also facilitate opportunities for contact and problem-solving between fathers and their families, including video visiting and brief family counseling. In contrast, Navigators focus on assisting fathers in developing and carrying out a plan to obtain employment and/or enter a job skills training or education program after release.

We view a program such as this as an ideal candidate for research. It is grounded in an expanded definition of what it means to be a parent during and after prison—not only showing love and providing guidance but also taking care of your own well-being, providing a safe and stable home, earning solid income through prosocial means, fostering and maintaining healthy relationships with other adults, and not engaging in and staying away from criminal activity. We posit that a vital part of programs that take a holistic view of parenting like this is the involvement of family members in the program, both during and after incarceration.

One of the impediments to research such as this, however, is the difficulty for systems to get access to high-quality programs for families. Many such programs now exist for families living in at-risk or high-risk situations and have been or are undergoing testing, particularly in terms of parenting skills (for a review of programs for incarcerated parents, see Eddy & Poehlmann-Tynan, 2019). However, as is true in other areas of intervention and prevention practice, most programs are expensive and require purchasing not only materials but also training and supervision. At least part of the intent behind these costs are well meaning, such as the desire to maintain quality and the need for resources to do such, and the perceived importance of program fidelity and the recognition that obtaining and maintaining fidelity take work and focus. A key problem is that many systems don't have the financial resources to enter the market without grant funding, and grant funding in this area is quite limited given the sheer numbers of people in corrections systems in the USA that are in need of reentry services. An additional problem is that often a program does not quite fit the needs of a system and/or the needs of the people being served by that system and needs to be changed in a variety of ways. A common area in this regard is related to the cultural fit of a program to the client population.

A few years ago, we were approached by partners in a jurisdiction we were working in regarding this very problem and came up together with a potential solution—the creation of high-quality materials for parents and families that from inception were intended to be "open source"—available for free on the Internet and adaptable, as long as the adaptation was also shared back. We see great promise in this type of approach. It is certainly something that has caught on in other fields, such as computer software development, with some success. Our hope is that it can also become standard within this field. We took this idea and employed it within the context of a recent GIZ (a German-based NGO)-funded international collaboration. The result is that a family- and school-based youth violence prevention program was created, *Miles de Manos*, that has not only been disseminated widely in four countries in Central America but is also being studied within the context of a newly launched National Institutes of Health-funded randomized controlled trial in Honduras (Martinez et al., 2020). The program caught the attention of other international NGOs and countries, and adaptations are now being attempted in Sri Lanka and the Philippines. Opening up family interventions for innovation and dissemination, and then studying such interventions using rigorous scientific methods, seems like a much more useful strategy to use than the rather closed system of distribution that exists today.

Connecting and supporting incarcerated adults with their families seem like a promising strategy for improving outcomes during reentry. It is time to move the field forward and find optimal ways to fulfill such a promise. To do this requires trying not only to include families in reentry programming but to study outcomes using research designs that provide answers, rather than suggestions, to whether or not something "works." In this chapter, we attempted to find more rigorous studies of reentry programs, and even when we set the bar low in this regard, we found few. We did find a broader set of work, not discussed here, that was not peer reviewed and included studies of utilization and process, rather than of outcomes. This type of work is commonly required in large-scale federal funding initiatives, for example, but falls short of providing the plethora information needed to guide the field forward.

A more promising route for the field to take would be a combination of optimization and experimentation. A prime example of a method for such work is the Multiphase Optimization Strategy (MOST) of Collins and colleagues (Wilbur et al., 2016). The fundamental idea is that before a rigorous research design, such as a randomized controlled trial, is used to examine the impact of an intervention, work must be done to find out what intervention elements maximize effects on desired outcomes. To make optimization useful, rigor (in bringing the existing findings from science to bear in the early stages of program development) and specificity (in clarifying the theoretical model that underlies the work) during the development of a reentry program are required. A combination of a broader approach to what parents, children, and families need to succeed during reentry *with* new ways to access intervention materials *with* promising research approaches such as MOST has the potential to make a real difference in both the reduction of recidivism and the improvement of the health of parents, children, families, and society at large.

References

Ahalt, C., Trestman, R. L., Rich, J. D., Greifinger, R. B., & Williams, B. A. (2013). Paying the price: The pressing need for quality, cost and outcomes data to improve correctional healthcare for older prisoners. *Journal of the American Geriatrics Society, 61*(11), 2013–2019.

Anderson, J. L. (2002). Overview of the Illinois DOC high-risk parolee re-entry program and 3-year recidivism outcomes of program participants. *Cognitive-Behavioral Treatment Review, 11*(1-2), 4–6.

Bales, W. D., & Mears, D. P. (2008). Inmate social ties and the transition to society: Does visitation reduce recidivism? *Journal of Research in Crime and Delinquency, 45*(3), 287–321.

Bobbitt, M., & Nelson, M. (2004). *The front line: Building programs that recognize families' role in reentry*. New York, NY: Vera Institute of Justice.

Bronfenbrenner, U. (1979). *The ecology of human development: Experiments by nature and design*. Cambridge, MA: Harvard University Press.

Brooks-Gordon, B., & Bainham, A. (2004). Prisoners' families and the regulation of contact. *Journal of Social Welfare and Family Law, 26*(3), 263–280.

Brown, M., & Bloom, B. (2009). Reentry and renegotiating motherhood: Maternal identity and success on parole. *Crime & Delinquency, 55*(2), 313–336.

Burraston, B. O., & Eddy, J. M. (2017). The moderating effect of living with a child prior to incarceration on post-release outcomes related to a prison-based parent management training program. *Smith College Studies in Social Work, 87*(1), 94–111.

Byrne, M. (2019). Interventions in prison nurseries. In J. M. Eddy & J. Poehlmann-Tynan (Eds.), *Handbook on children with incarcerated parents: Research, policy, and practice* (2nd ed., pp. 167–182). New York, NY: Springer.

Christensen, D., Todahl, J., & Barrett, W. C. (1999). *Solution-based casework: An introduction to clinical and case management skills in casework practice*. New York, NY: Routledge.

Deady, C. W. (2014). *Incarceration and recidivism: Lessons from abroad*. Newport, RI: Salve Regina University.

Durose, M. R., Cooper, A. D., & Snyder, H. N. (2014). *Recidivism of prisoners released in 30 states in 2005: Patterns from 2005 to 2010* (No. 244205; p. 31). US Department of Justice.

Duwe, G., & Clark, V. (2013). Blessed be the social tie that binds: The effects of prison visitation on offender recidivism. *Criminal Justice Policy Review, 24*(3), 271–296.

Duwe, G., & McNeeley, S. (2020). Just as good as the real thing? The effects of prison video visitation on recidivism. *Crime & Delinquency*. Advance online publication.

Eddy, J. M., & Burraston, B. O. (2018). Promoting the successful reentry of fathers coming home from jail or prison. In C. Wildeman, A. R. Haskins, & J. Poehlmann-Tynan (Eds.), *When parents are incarcerated: Interdisciplinary research and interventions to support children* (pp. 109–131). Washington, DC: American Psychological Association.

Eddy, J. M., & Poehlmann, J. (Eds.). (2010). *Children of incarcerated parents: A handbook for researchers and practitioners*. Washington, DC: Urban Institute Press.

Eddy, J. M., & Poehlmann-Tynan, J. (Eds.). (2019). *Handbook on children with incarcerated parents: Research, policy, and practice* (2nd ed.). New York, NY: Springer.

Eddy, J. M., & Schumer, J. (2018). Parents in prison: Promoting success during reentry to the community. In W. T. Church & D. W. Springer (Eds.), *Serving the stigmatized: Working within the incarcerated environment* (pp. 114–137). New York, NY: Oxford University Press.

Eddy, J. M., & Swanson-Gribskov, L. (1998). Juvenile justice and delinquency prevention in the United States: The influence of theories and traditions on policies and practices. In T. P. Gullota, G. R. Adams, & R. Montemayor (Eds.), *Delinquent violent youth* (pp. 12–52). Thousand Oaks, CA: Sage.

Eddy, J. M., Martinez, C. R., Jr., Schiffmann, T., Newton, R., Olin, L., Leve, L., Foney, D. M., & Shortt, J. W. (2008). Development of a multisystemic parent management training intervention for incarcerated parents, their children and families. *Clinical Psychologist, 12*(3), 86–98.

Eddy, J. M., Kjellstrand, J., Martinez, C. R., Jr., & Newton, R. (2010). Theory-based multimodal parenting intervention for incarcerated parents and their families. In J. M. Eddy & J. Poehlmann (Eds.), *Children of incarcerated parents: A handbook for researchers and practitioners*. Washington, DC: Urban Institute Press.

Eddy, J. M., Martinez, C. R., & Burraston, B. (2013). A randomized controlled trial of a parent management training program for incarcerated parents: Proximal impacts. *Monographs of the Society for Research in Child Development, 78*(3), 75–93.

Eddy, J. M., Kjellstrand, J. M., Martinez, C. R., Jr., Newton, R., Herrera, D., Wheeler, A., Shortt, J. W., Schumer, J. E., Burraston, B. O., & Lorber, M. F. (2019). Theory-based multimodal parenting intervention for incarcerated parents and their children. In J. M. Eddy & J. Poehlmann-Tynan (Eds.), *Handbook on children with incarcerated parents: Research, policy, and practice* (2nd ed., pp. 219–236). New York, NY: Springer.

Eddy, J. M., Kjellstrand, J. M., Goff, D., McElravy, T., & House-Higgins, C. (2021). *Strength in Families: Development of a multimodal, reentry-focused parenting intervention for fathers releasing from state prison*. Manuscript in preparation.

Einhorn, L., Williams, T., Stanley, S. M., Markman, H. J., & Eason, J. (2008). PREP inside and out: Marriage education for inmates. *Family Process, 47*, 341–356.

Eisen, L. B. (2015). *Charging inmates perpetuates mass incarceration*. New York, NY: Brennan Center for Justice.

Erlacher, J. (2010). *Walking the line: PREP's curriculum for incarcerated men*. Greenwood Village, CO: PREP.

Esparza Flores, N. (2018). Contributing factors to mass incarceration and recidivism. *Themis: Research Journal of Justice Studies and Forensic Science, 6*, 4.

Fazel, S., & Wolf, A. (2015). A systematic review of criminal recidivism rates worldwide: Current difficulties and recommendations for best practice. *PLoS One, 10*(6), e0130390.

Glaze, L. E., & Maruschak, L. M. (2008). *Parents in prison and their minor children*. US Department of Justice. Bureau of Justice Statistics, Special Report. NCJ, 222984.

Goshin, L. S., Byrne, M. W., & Henninger, A. M. (2014). Recidivism after release from a prison nursery program. *Public Health Nursing, 31*(2), 109–117.

Halford, W. K., Markman, H. J., & Stanley, S. M. (2008). Strengthening couples' relationships with education: Social policy and public health perspectives. *Journal of Family Psychology, 22*, 497–505.

Harris, Z. L., & Landreth, G. L. (1997). Filial therapy with incarcerated mothers: A five-week model. *International Journal of Play Therapy, 6*(2), 53–73.

Holt, N., & Miller, D. (1972). *Explorations in inmate-family relationships*. Sacramento, CA: California Department of Corrections.

Holtfreter, K., Reisig, M. D., & Morash, M. (2004). Poverty, state capital, and recidivism among women offenders. *Criminology & Public Policy, 3*(2), 185–208.

James, N. (2014). *Offender reentry: Correctional statistics, reintegration into the community, and recidivism* (No. 7–5700; RL34287, p. 37). Congressional Research Service.

Kjellstrand, J. M. (2018). Building a tailored, multilevel prevention strategy to support children and families affected by parental incarceration. In M. Harris & J. M. Eddy (Eds.), *Children of incarcerated parents: Challenges and promise* (pp. 111–128). New York, NY: Routledge.

Kyckelhahn, T. (2015). *Justice expenditure and employment extracts, 2012—preliminary* (No. 248628; Justice Expenditure and Employment Series). U.S. Department of Justice.

La Vigne, N. G., Naser, R. L., Brooks, L. E., & Castro, J. L. (2005). Examining the effect of incarceration and in-prison family contact on prisoners' family relationships. *Journal of Contemporary Criminal Justice, 21*(4), 314–335.

Landreth, G. L., & Lobaugh, A. F. (1998). Filial therapy with incarcerated fathers: Effects on parental acceptance of child, parental stress, and child adjustment. *Journal of Counseling & Development, 76*(2), 157–165.

Li, M. (2018). *From prisons to communities: Confronting re-entry challenges and social inequality*. Washington, DC: American Psychological Association.

Markman, H. J., Renick, M. J., Floyd, F., Stanley, S., & Clements, M. (1993). Preventing marital distress through communication and conflict management training: A four- and five-year follow-up. *Journal of Consulting and Clinical Psychology, 62*, 70–77.

Martinez, C. R., Eddy, J. M., McClure, H., & Nelson, J. (2020). *Miles de Manos: A randomized controlled trial*. Austin, TX: University of Texas at Austin.

Maruna, S., & Toch, H. (2005). The impact of incarceration on the desistance process. *Prisoner reentry and public safety in America*, 139–178.

McKay, T., Comfort, M., Lindquist, C., & Bir, A. (2019). *Holding on: Family and fatherhood during incarceration and reentry*. Berkeley, CA: University of California Press.

Miller, A. L., Weston, L. E., Perryman, J., Horwitz, T., Franzen, S., & Cochran, S. (2014). Parenting while incarcerated: Tailoring the strengthening families program for use with jailed mothers. *Child and Youth Services Review, 44*, 163–170.

Moore, A. R., & Clement, M. J. (1998). Effects of parenting training for incarcerated mothers. *Journal of Offender Rehabilitation, 27*(1-2), 57–72.

Morenoff, J. D., & Harding, D. J. (2014). Incarceration, prisoner reentry, and communities. *Annual Review of Sociology, 40*, 411–429.

Morgan, R. D., Kroner, D. G., & Mills, J. F. (2012). *Re-entry: Dynamic risk assessment* (Technical Report No. 238075; p. 129). Texas Department of Criminal Justice.

Murray, J., Farrington, D. P., & Sekol, I. (2012). Children's antisocial behavior, mental health, drug use, and educational performance after parental incarceration: A systematic review and meta-analysis. *Psychological Bulletin, 138*(2), 175–210.

National Institute of Corrections. (2017). *Offender reentry/transition*. Washington, DC: National Institute of Corrections.

Patterson, G. R. (1982). *Coercive family process*. Eugene, OR: Castalia.

Poehlmann, J., Dallaire, D., Loper, A. B., & Shear, L. D. (2010). Children's contact with their incarcerated parents: Research findings and recommendations. *American Psychologist, 65*(6), 575–598.

Reid, J. B., Patterson, G. R., & Snyder, J. (2002). *Antisocial behavior in children and adolescents: A developmental analysis and model for intervention*. Washington, DC: American Psychological Association.

Sabol, W. J., & Minton, T. D. (2008). *Jail inmates at midyear 2007* (No. 221945; p. 11). U.S. Department of Justice.

Sandifer, J. L. (2008). Evaluating the efficacy of a parenting program for incarcerated mothers. *The Prison Journal, 88*(3), 423–445.

Sawyer, W., & Wagner, P. (2020). *Mass incarceration: The whole pie 2020*. Northhampton, MA: Prison Policy Initiative.

Schwartz-Soicher, O., Geller, A., & Garfinkel, I. (2011). The effect of paternal incarceration on material hardship. *The Social Service Review, 85*(3), 447–473.

Shortt, J. W., Eddy, J. M., Sheeber, L., & Davis, B. (2014). Project home: A pilot evaluation of an emotion-focused intervention for mothers reuniting with children after prison. *Psychological Services, 11*, 1–9.

Slack, K. S., Font, S., Maguire-Jack, K., & Berger, L. M. (2017). Predicting child protective services involvement among low-income U.S. families with young children receiving nutritional assistance. *International Journal of Environmental Research and Public Health, 14*(10), 1197.

Sleed, M., Baradon, T., & Fonagy, P. (2013). New beginnings for mothers and babies in prison: A cluster randomized controlled trial. *Attachment & Human Development, 15*(4), 349–367.

Stahler, G. J., Mennis, J., Belenko, S., Welsh, W. N., Hiller, M. L., & Zajac, G. (2013). Predicting recidivism for released state prison offenders. *Criminal Justice and Behavior, 40*(6), 690–711.

Sugie, N. F. (2012). Punishment and welfare: Paternal incarceration and families' receipt of public assistance. *Social Forces: A Scientific Medium of Social Study and Interpretation, 90*(4), 1403–1427.

Thomas, A., Wirth, J., Poehlmann-Tynan, J., & Pate, D.J. (2020). *"When she says Daddy": One year desistance after jail reentry among African American fathers*. Manuscript submitted for publication.

Varghese, F. P., & Cummings, D. L. (2012). Introduction: Why apply vocational psychology to criminal justice populations? *The Counseling Psychologist, 41*, 961–989.

Visher, C. A. (2007). Returning home: Emerging findings and policy lessons about prisoner reentry. *Federal Sentencing Reporter, 20*(2), 93–102.

Visher, C. A., & Travis, J. (2011). Life on the outside: Returning home after incarceration. *The Prison Journal, 91*(3), 102S–119S.

Visher, C. A., Kachnowski, V., La Vigne, N. G., & Travis, J. (2004). *Baltimore prisoners' experiences returning home*. Washington, DC: Urban Institute.

Visher, C. A., Bakken, N. W., & Gunter, W. D. (2013). Fatherhood, community reintegration, and successful outcomes. *Journal of Offender Rehabilitation, 52*(7), 451–469.

Wakefield, S., & Wildeman, C. (2018). How parental incarceration harms children and what to do about it. *National Council on Family Relations, 3*(1), 6.

Wilbur, W., Kolanowski, A. M., & Collins, L. M. (2016). Utilizing MOST frameworks and SMART designs for intervention research. *Nursing Outlook, 64*(4), 287–289.

Wildeman, C., Turney, K., & Youngmin, Y. (2016). Paternal incarceration and family functioning: Variation across federal, state, and local facilities. *The Annals of the American Academy of Political and Social Science, 665*(1), 80–97.

Wilson, J. A., & Davis, R. C. (2006). Good intentions meet hard realities: An evaluation of the project greenlight reentry program. *Criminology and Public Policy, 5*(2), 303–338.

Yukhnenko, D., Sridhar, S., & Fazel, S. (2019). A systematic review of criminal recidivism rates worldwide: 3-year update. *Welcome Open Research, 4*, 28.

Gender Differences and Implications for Programming During the Reentry of Incarcerated Fathers and Mothers Back into Their Communities

Jean M. Kjellstrand, J. Mark Eddy, Kimberley Gonzalez-Quiles, Gabriella Damewood, and Jean Schumer

Abstract Over the past several decades, the population of incarcerated women in the United States increased multifold, surpassing the growth rate of men during the same period. A majority of these individuals are also parents to minor children. Recent findings highlight gender differences in the incarcerated population particularly around issues related to family circumstances, family history, trauma, poverty, criminality, and substance abuse issues. Given both the increasing incarceration rate of women and the differences in risks facing men and women, gender-specific information is needed to inform the development of gender-responsive reentry strategies to help inmates navigate specific challenges they face as they reintegrate back into their communities and families.

In this chapter, we review existing literature on the backgrounds of incarcerated fathers and mothers. We then address critical gaps in our knowledge by examining a representative sample of incarcerated parents who were randomly selected from Oregon prisons on key background characteristics as well as pre- and post-release needs related to parenting. Following this, we review existing evidenced-based reentry interventions for men and women, specifically parents, and explore the degree that knowledge about potential issues related to gender informed the development of these programs. Lastly, we conclude with an examination of the extent to

J. M. Kjellstrand (✉)
University of Oregon, Eugene, OR, USA
e-mail: jeank@uoregon.edu

J. M. Eddy
University of Texas at Austin, Austin, TX, USA

K. Gonzalez-Quiles
Independent Researcher, New York, NY, USA

G. Damewood
St. Johns University, New York, NY, USA

J. Schumer
Private Practice, Corvallis, OR, USA

J. Krysik, N. Rodriguez (eds.), *Children of Incarcerated Parents*, Children of Incarcerated Parents: From Understanding to Impact,
https://doi.org/10.1007/978-3-030-84713-5_9

which existing gender-responsive programs address established differences between incarcerated men and women.

Keywords Incarcerated parents · Needs · Gender-responsive · Reentry · Programs

Since 1970, the number of incarcerated adults in the United States has increased significantly. Currently, the United States leads the world both in the number and the percent of incarcerated citizens (Walmsley, 2009). Policymakers, practitioners, and researchers alike worry about the social, psychological, and economic impact of this "mass" incarceration not only on the incarcerated individuals but also on the children and families who have been left behind. In this regard, the most recent estimates indicate that over half of all men and women held in state or federal prison are parents to an estimated 1.7 million minor children (e.g., Maruschak & Mumola, 2010). However, the number of children who are currently experiencing parental incarceration (including in jail, prison, or an immigration detention facility) or who have experienced parental incarceration in the past far exceeds this count. Regardless, the majority of children with incarcerated parents are in situations where it is likely that their parent's incarceration has at least some direct impact on family functioning through such issues as family disruption, financial strain, or the stigma of having an incarcerated family member (Eddy et al., 2019). After long being ignored, research interest in children with incarcerated parents and their families has increased in the past several decades. Findings from a variety of studies now point to the increased likelihood, but not certainty, for at least some problematic outcomes for children with incarcerated parents compared to their peers (e.g., Kjellstrand & Eddy, 2011a, Kjellstrand & Eddy, 2011b; Murray & Farrington, 2005; Myers et al., 1999; Phillips et al., 2002; Johnston, 1995).

The growth in incarceration in the United States has resulted not only in more individuals being imprisoned but also more people being released back into their communities after incarceration. For example, of the 1.5 million Americans who are incarcerated in state and federal prisons in a given year, approximately 640,000 are released (Carson & Anderson, 2016). Not surprisingly, this movement of men and women away from and then back into their homes and communities has piqued interest in how to best support a successful "reentry." Unfortunately, rigorous research has not kept up with policy and practice innovations around reentry practices and programs. This lack of scholarly progress has put states, communities, and agencies in the unfortunate position of having to implement reentry interventions and strategies based on a limited body of empirical evidence about "what works."

While most incarcerated individuals are men, and much of the research knowledge base about people in prison focuses on men, the number of incarcerated women rapidly increased across the past few decades. Between 1980 and 2002 alone, the population of incarcerated women in the United States increased eightfold, surpassing the growth rate of men during the same period (Harrison & Karberg, 2004; Lapidus et al., 2004). Researchers attribute this to the proliferation of certain types of drug laws, particularly those that implemented mandatory sentences even for what had previously been considered "lower-level" drug offenses (Bloom et al., 2004; Javdani et al., 2011). Importantly, recent research findings have highlighted gender differences in the incarcerated population, particularly around issues related to family history, trauma exposure, poverty, corrections involvement, substance abuse, mental health problems, and current family circumstances (Glaze & Maruschak, 2008; Greenfeld & Snell, 1999; James & Glaze, 2006; Kjellstrand et al., 2012; Mumola, 2000). Given the increasing rate of incarceration of women, and the emerging evidence on differences between incarcerated men and women, evidence-based "gender-responsive" reentry strategies that build on the strengths of each gender while helping men and women navigate the gender-specific challenges they are likely to face as they reintegrate back into their families and communities seem warranted.

In this chapter, we review the existing literature on the backgrounds of incarcerated men and women. We address critical gaps in knowledge by examining a representative sample of incarcerated parents who were randomly selected from the general prison population in Oregon to participate in a survey on key background characteristics as well as pre- and post-release needs related to parenting. We review existing evidenced-based reentry interventions for men and women, and parents in specific, and explore the degree that knowledge about potential issues related to gender have informed the development of these programs. We conclude with an examination of the extent to which existing gender-responsive programs address established differences between incarcerated men and women and provide suggestions for future work.

Backgrounds of Incarcerated Men and Women

For many men and women, arrest and incarceration are the cumulation of a set of adverse events in an already difficult life and one that for many has involved some combination of poverty, unstable living situations, substance abuse and mental health problems, and traumatic personal and family relationships (Travis et a., 2004; Johnston 1995; Nichols & Loper 2012). Exposure to any one of these problems can pose significant challenges; exposure to several in concert can be overwhelming. While many of these problems are common for both incarcerated mothers and fathers, on average, gender differences exist in the prevalence of issues, parenting roles, pathways into crime, and length and frequency of incarceration across the life course.

Overall, corrections-involved women tend to come from more challenging backgrounds than men (Dallaire, 2007; Greenfeld & Snell, 1999; James & Glaze, 2006; Kjellstrand et al., 2012; McClellan et al., 1997). For many individuals who are incarcerated – women or men – problems started early. Roughly a third had parents who abused substances (drugs or alcohol), a fifth had been physically or sexually abused in their childhood, and a fifth had parents who had also been incarcerated (James & Glaze, 2006). While incarcerated men are more likely to become involved in the justice system as juveniles, women are more likely to have experienced family difficulties, especially in the area of abuse during childhood (e.g., Kjellstrand et al., 2012).

Challenges from childhood often reverberate into adulthood for many corrections-involved individuals, but especially for women. Historically, incarcerated women tend to have higher rates of unemployment and lower levels of income than men (Greenfeld & Snell, 1999; Kjellstrand et al., 2012; McClellan et al., 1997; Mumola, 2000). Recent studies have revealed unemployment rates for incarcerated mothers prior to imprisonment that are nearly twice the prior unemployment rate for incarcerated fathers (e.g., Kjellstrand et al., 2012). Moreover, while incomes prior to prison were low for the majority of people in prison, employed fathers on average earned substantially more than employed mothers (Mumola, 2000; Kjellstrand et al. 2012). This, coupled with the fact that incarcerated women were frequently single parents before prison, amplifies the impact of low incomes and unemployment, leading to higher poverty rates for women and their children before incarceration.

Substance abuse is another area within which incarcerated men and women frequently struggle. Up to 93% of incarcerated individuals report prior drug and alcohol abuse or addiction, over half used drugs during the 3 months prior to their arrest, and roughly a third were under the influence of drugs or alcohol when they were arrested (Kjellstrand et al., 2012; Mumola, 2000). However, there are gender differences in the usage and type of substances used by individuals prior to incarceration (Fedock et al., 2013; Kjellstrand et al., 2012; McClellan et al., 1997, Mumola, 2000). Incarcerated mothers are more likely than incarcerated fathers to report drug usage both in the month prior to their arrest and at the time of arrest (Mumola, 2000). The types of substances used also vary between the genders. Women report a higher incidence of past illicit drug use or dependence than men, especially in the use of hard drugs such as heroin and crack cocaine, while men report a higher incidence of past alcohol abuse or dependence (Binswanger et al., 2010; Kjellstrand et al., 2012; McClellan et al., 1997).

Unfortunately, for women, abusive and violent relationships that were prevalent during childhood may continue into adulthood. Several studies have found that incarcerated women are more likely than incarcerated men to have been sexually abused, to have experienced mental/emotional abuse, and to have felt unsafe or in danger as adults (Kjellstrand et al., 2012; McClellan et al., 1997). This combination of poverty, abuse, and substance abuse can contribute to propelling women down a pathway of criminality (Bloom et al., 2004).

Given this backdrop, it is not surprising that physical and mental health is another area where incarcerated men and women frequently have problems. Again, however, as with substance abuse, there are differences for women versus men. Incarcerated women are more likely to report more physical health problems (e.g., asthma, arthritis, hypertension, heart problems, HIV) and mental health issues (e.g., depression, bipolar, posttraumatic stress) than incarcerated men (Adams et al., 2013; Binswanger et al., 2010; Fedock et al., 2013; Kjellstrand et al., 2012; Magaletta et al., 2009; James & Glaze, 2006; Steadman et al., 2009).

While most individuals held in state or federal prison are parents, the prevalence and parenting circumstances differ by gender. Within state prisons, over 50% of incarcerated men are fathers to minor children, while over 60% of incarcerated women are mothers to minor children (Glaze & Maruschak, 2008). Mothers are more likely to have lived with their children prior to police arrest than fathers (i.e., 73% versus 46%) and are more likely to be parenting alone (i.e., 52% versus 19%). Upon release, many incarcerated parents will serve in some parenting role with at least one of their children. However, this is more frequently the case for mothers than fathers (Eddy & Poehlmann, 2010; Kjellstrand et al., 2012).

A final area where there appears to be gender differences is around criminality patterns, including rates of involvement, the types of crimes committed, and personal criminal histories. Men have higher rates of involvement in the criminal justice system and commit a higher percentage of violent crimes and fewer drug offenses than women (Carson & Anderson, 2016; Van Dieten et al., 2014). Further, drug offenses committed by women tend to be non-violent in nature (e.g., drug-related charges, fraud), and violence charges tend to be less severe (Steffensmeier et al., 2006; Van Dieten et al., 2014). In terms of criminal histories, men tend to have more frequent and longer involvement with the criminal justice system than women (Kjellstrand et al., 2012). Not only are men more likely to be involved with the juvenile justice system and tend to be younger when first arrested as an adult; they are also sentenced more frequently and for longer periods of time.

Given this plethora of differences, pathways to criminality and to prison frequently differ by gender (Daly, 1994). For men, involvement in interpersonal aggression and other antisocial behaviors such as lying, cheating, and stealing during childhood and early adolescence may play a role in the development of men's criminality. However, for women, past abuse and trauma can be precursors to future mental health issues, substance use, and addiction. These, in turn, may lead to the commission of a variety of criminal behaviors including prostitution, drug dealing, robbery, and violence later in adolescence or early adulthood (El-Bassel et al., 2001; Grella et al., 2005; Surratt et al., 2004).

State-Wide Survey of Men and Women

While there are accruing data on men and women in prison and their background characteristics, information about mothers and fathers in prison per se (versus women and men) is still scant. To increase our knowledge of this significant subpopulation of prisoners, a total of 3078 incarcerated men and women from the general populations within 13 Oregon Department of Corrections (DOC) facilities were invited to participate in a family and visitation experiences survey, including all women and randomly selected men. During the window of time that the survey was administered, 2216 of those invited to participate attended an informed consent meeting (on average, $M = 74.31\%$ [$SD = 16.72$], within a facility). Of these men and women, 1582 (on average, $M = 73.92\%$ [$SD = 14.20$], within a facility) consented to participate and completed the survey anonymously. The final sample of 814 comprised those participants who indicated that they had children under 18 years of age (51% of all participants, 48% of all the men, and 63% of all the women).

Sample

Participants (see Table 1) included 598 incarcerated fathers (73%) and 216 incarcerated mothers (27%). The majority of participants were White (64%). Participants ranged in age from 17 to 67 years (M = 34.00 years, SD = 8.39). Their sentence lengths ranged from 0.5 to 50.8 years, with an average length of 6 years (M = 6.48, SD = 6.22). Participants had been in prison on average 1.73 times (SD = 1.58), with a range of 1 to 15 times.

Table 1 Sample Characteristics (N = 814)

	%	*M (SD)*
Age		34.00 (8.39)
Gender		
Men	73.5	
Women	26.5	
Education		
Did not graduate HS	40.0	
Received HS diploma, GED	32.2	
Some college	27.8	
Race/culture		
White	64.1	
Black/African American	8.8	
Native American	6.0	
Latino	10.7	
Asian	1.0	
Biracial	7.0	
Multiracial	1.0	
Childhood community		
City	37.2	
Suburb	15.1	
Small town	30.5	
Rural	17.1	
Took Spanish version of survey	3.8	
Arrested as juvenile	48.9	
Mother criminality	19.9	
Mother incarcerated	14.0	
Father criminality	43.2	
Father incarcerated	35.5	
Any family members incarcerated	68.6	
Number of children		2.77 (1.85)
Lived with child before prison	71.9	
Will live with child after prison	66.5	

Measures

The survey was conducted as part of the development process for the parent management training program, *Parenting Inside Out* (see Eddy et al., 2008, 2010, 2013), and included self-report questions about key characteristics and personal experiences of participants, including questions about family of origin, pertinent childhood and adult experiences, systems involvement across life, and the amount and type of contact with friends and family. As is the case for most of the research on gender differences for criminal justice involved men and women, most constructs of interest were measured with one-item, face valid questions. While most questions had fixed choice responses, a few questions were open-ended and focused on participant views on what they need (pre- and post-release) to help them parent their children. Categories were developed which captured the various topics that emerged in these responses. Responses to open-ended questions were coded and aggregated.

Analytic Strategy

Chi-square tests for independence (with Yates' continuity correction when relevant) and independent-samples *t*-tests were used to compare males and females in the sample. In the *t*-tests, Levene's test of significance was used to consider whether equal variance could be assumed in each bivariate relationship. Effect sizes, using a phi coefficient (for chi-square tests) or Cohen's *d* (for *t*-tests), were calculated.

Results

Incarcerated fathers and mothers in this sample were similar to one another in several ways (see Table 2). They were from similar racial/ethnic backgrounds, with a majority being White (reflecting the racial/ethnic demographics of the state at that time of the survey). They also had similar educational backgrounds; slightly less than half of the participants did not complete high school, and less than a third obtained any education beyond high school. Nearly a quarter had spent time in foster care, a fifth had spent time in a group home, and over a third had spent time in lock-up. In terms of family histories, over a third had a parent who had been incarcerated. Typically, this had been a father. Nearly three quarters had at least one family member who had been incarcerated. Parents typically had a total of three children (including biological and stepchildren). Nearly three quarters of parents had lived with their children prior to prison, and a majority hoped to live with their children after prison.

While there were several similarities, with most variables having small effect sizes, mothers and fathers differed significantly from one another on a number of

Table 2 Characteristics and experiences of inmates

	All (*N* = 814)	Fathers (*n* = 598)		Mothers (*n* = 216)				
		%	*M (SD)*	%	*M (SD)*	X^2	*t*	*Effect size* [a]
Demographics								
Age	33.99 (8.37)		34.39 (8.72)		32.90 (7.24)		2.46**	0.18
Education								
Did not graduate H.S.	40.2	41.2		37.4		2.75		0.06
Received H.S. diploma/GED	32.2	32.7		30.6				
Some college	27.6	26.1		32.0				
Early system involvement								
Spent time in foster care	22.9	21.8		26.1		1.49		−0.05
Spent time in group home	20.8	21.5		19.2		0.37		0.02
Spent time in lock up	37.0	39.0		31.7		3.34^{t}		0.07
Adverse events: Family history of corrections involvement and substance abuse								
Parent incarcerated	39.1	38.2		41.6		0.62		0.03
Mother corrections involvement	19.7	18.3		23.7		2.79^{t}		0.06
Mother incarcerated	13.9	13.3		15.5		0.50		0.03
Father corrections involvement	43.4	43.5		42.9		0.00		−0.00
Father incarcerated	35.6	35.5		35.6		0.00		0.00
Other relatives in jail/prison	61.3	62.2		58.9		2.73		0.06
Any family member incarcerated	68.6	69.1		67.1		0.21		−0.02
Mother abused drugs/alcohol	26.0	23.0		34.4		10.42**		0.12
Father abused drugs/alcohol	42.6	40.4		48.6		4.43^{t}		0.07
Other relatives abused drugs/alcohol	65.1	63.2		70.3		11.07**		0.11

(continued)

Table 2 (continued)

	All (N = 814)	Fathers (n = 598)		Mothers (n = 216)				
		%	*M* (*SD*)	%	*M* (*SD*)	X^2	*t*	*Effect size* [a]
Other adverse events and health issues								
Physically/ sexually abused as child	44.2	37.9		61.6		35.83***		0.21
Physically abused as child	38.0	34.9		46.6		8.83**		0.11
Sexually abused as child	22.9	13.3		49.3		116.02***		0.38
Physically/ sexually abused by partner	36.5	20.9		79.5		234.65***		0.54
Physically abused by romantic partner	35.6	20.3		77.6		228.05***		0.53
Sexually abused by romantic partner	14.0	3.7		42.5		197.61***		0.50
Substance abuse	72.0	69.8		78.1		5.10*		0.10
Living on streets	41.8	40.2		46.1		2.08^{t}		0.05
Live in temporary housing situation	53.0	48.8		64.4		14.96***		0.14
Mental health problems	25.7	21.1		38.4		24.16***		0.18
Physical health problems	14.6	12.6		20.1		6.59**		0.09
Deportation	2.1	1.7		3.2		1.19		0.05
Other	3.9	3.5		5.0		0.64		0.04
Total number of problems	3.24 (2.30)		2.70 (2.01)		4.71 (2.38)		−11.16***	0.91
Corrections system experiences								
Length of sentence	6.48 (6.22)		7.14 (6.55)		4.64 (4.87)		5.74***	0.43
Number of times in prison	1.73 (1.58)		1.85 (1.71)		1.38 (1.03)		4.81***	0.33
Ever arrested at juvenile	51.2	56.6		36.1		26.38***		−0.18
Age first detained by police as teen	14.06 (2.11)		14.06 (2.19)		14.09 (1.76)		−0.11	0.02
Age first arrested as adult	23.06 (7.41)		22.53 (7.55)		24.43 (6.79)		−3.35***	0.26

(continued)

Table 2 (continued)

	All (*N* = 814)	Fathers (*n* = 598)		Mothers (*n* = 216)				
		%	*M* (*SD*)	%	*M* (*SD*)	X^2	*t*	*Effect size* [a]
Experiences as a parent								
Age first became a parent	20.94 (5.04)		21.43 (5.25)		19.54 (4.05)		5.42***	0.40
Number of bio children	2.26 (1.63)		2.14 (1.60)		2.64 (1.65)		−3.85***	0.31
Number of step children	0.73 (1.41)		0.79 (1.42)		0.55 (1.34)		2.25*	0.17
Total number of children	2.77 (1.85)		2.75 (1.89)		2.89 (1.78)		−0.97	0.08
Before prison, lived w/any child under 18	71.9	71.9		71.7		0.00		−0.00
Before prison, number of children lived w/ under 18 years	1.58 (1.60)		1.53 (1.50)		1.76 (1.91)		−1.62*	0.13
Will live with children under 18 after prison	66.5	62.8		76.7		13.35***		0.13
After release, number of children hope to live with under 18 years	1.30 (1.37)		1.18 (1.65)		1.65 (1.44)		−4.25***	0.30
Happy w/contact w/children			4.15 (1.32)		3.76 (1.52)		3.31***	
Received any parent education before current prison term	26.9	22.1		40.1			25.40***	−0.18
Received any parent education during current prison term	24.6	18.0		42.6			50.23***	−0.25
Child's other parent received parent education	26.1	28.7		18.9			24.8***	0.18

Note. * = $p < 0.05$, ** = $p < 0.01$, *** = $p < 0.001$. *Phi* and Cohen's *d* were used to evaluate the effect sizes for chi-square tests and t-tests respectively key issues. Mothers were younger than fathers. Mothers were more likely to have mothers with at least some corrections involvement in her past, as well as to have parents and other relatives who abused drugs or alcohol. Mothers also faced substantially more challenges than fathers. They were more likely to have substance abuse, mental health, and physical health problems. In terms of living situations, they were much more likely to have lived in a temporary housing situation or lived on the streets prior to prison. Finally, they were much more likely than fathers to have been physically and sexually abused, both during childhood (i.e., 62% versus 38%) and during adulthood (i.e., 80% versus 21%).

As parents, mothers had first become a parent at a younger age than fathers and, on average, had more biological children than fathers. Over three quarters of all mothers planned to live with their children after prison (as opposed to 63% of fathers), and roughly a quarter had received parenting education prior to or during their current prison term. In contrast, fathers tended to have more involved criminal histories, including involvement with the juvenile justice system. While the age of first police detainment as a teenager was similar for fathers and mothers ($M = 14.1$, $SD = 2.11$), fathers tended to be slightly younger than mothers when first arrested as an adult. Finally, fathers had greater involvement in the criminal justice system, including more bouts of incarceration and for longer periods of time per bout.

Finally, parents were asked what they needed pre- and post-release to assist them in their roles as parents (see Table 3). There were a wide variety of opinions on what

Table 3 Parents' views on pre- and post-release programming needs regarding parenting

	All ($N = 814$)	Fathers ($n = 598$)	Mothers ($n = 216$)		
	%	%	%	X^2	*Effect size*
Pre-release needs					
Contact with children & family	24.1	24.1	24.1	0.000	0.00
Parenting education	23.6	23.4	24.1	0.01	0.01
Counseling	6.9	5.0	12.0	11.14***	0.12
Other programs	4.9	4.0	7.4	3.22[t]	0.07
Inmate actions	4.4	5.0	2.8	1.39	−0.05
Better DOC policies	2.3	2.7	1.4	0.66	−0.04
Other	13.6	12.7	16.2	1.36	0.04
Post-release needs					
Basic needs	13.5	11.5	19.0	6.90**	0.10
Relationships	11.3	12.5	7.9	3.00[t]	−0.06
Inmate actions	7.0	8.2	3.7	4.25*	−0.08
Emotional support	6.9	5.7	10.2	4.34*	0.08
Legal support	6.8	7.2	5.6	0.44	−0.03
Parenting education	6.5	5.7	8.8	2.04	0.06
Counseling	6.3	4.7	10.6	8.63**	0.11
Other	15.1	14.5	16.7	0.40	0.03

was needed, with no areas being endorsed by even close to a majority of mothers or fathers. Pre-release, parents most frequently identified increasing communication or contact with their children and receiving more parenting education as key needs. Post-release, parents most frequently identified needing assistance with basic needs and relationships. While many needs were similarly identified in terms of importance across genders, mothers were more likely to identify basic needs, emotional support, and counseling, while fathers were more likely to identify their own actions and, at a trend level, relationships. However, the few differences that were found all had small effect sizes. Table 3

Discussion

With the increasing number of men and women prisoners releasing back to their communities, the expanding population of parents who have been imprisoned, and the growing reentry service needs for all, more research-based evidence is needed particularly around effective interventions to help support incarcerated parents and their families both while the parent is in prison and once they are released back into their communities and their families. The results of this state-wide survey help inform the development of gender-specific reentry interventions for parents by providing key statistics on the characteristics and experiences of incarcerated mothers and fathers and examining what the parents identify as needs across the reentry continuum.

Most striking of all were the similarities between mothers and fathers. Consistent with prior studies, many incarcerated fathers and mothers came from backgrounds marked by little formal education, exposure to traumatic events including physical abuse, family difficulties with substance abuse, and family criminality. Many parents struggled with personal substance abuse, homelessness, and mental and physical health problems. Regardless of gender, these issues can pose serious challenges to a man or a woman when they serve in a parental role. Given this, attempts to increase the well-being of parents and children and to improve the likelihood of reentry success need to take the scope of these contextual pieces into consideration. Programming which takes a multifaceted approach seems most likely to succeed. Specifically, programs that focus on education or vocational training, employment, past trauma, substance use, healthy relationships, and mental and physical health problems seem particularly appropriate.

It was not surprising that when mothers and fathers were queried about what would help them as parents while in prison, they responded in ways that were congruent with past research findings. Pre-release, parents saw communication/contact with their children as most critical followed closely by parenting education. Increasingly, research shows the importance of relationships and social support especially as individuals reenter their communities after incarceration (Mowen & Visher, 2013). By building this support network, nurturing family relationships, and improving parent-child relationships while in prison, parents are better equipped to start a new life more quickly once they released. Building, maintaining, and/or improving connections can be helpful for both the parent and child alike.

When returning to their communities, parents noted that what would assist them most in their role as a parent would be in the area of basic needs (e.g., through having a job and a place to live) as well as with the development and maintenance of positive adult relationships. Most strikingly, there were very few differences in how mothers and fathers perceived these needs. The transition from prison to home can be a stressful and difficult time for many returning parents. Many are released with only a bus ticket home and a few dollars in their pocket. Resettling and reestablishing themselves in their community without any resources can be a daunting task. Providing parents, whether mothers or fathers, with the skills, means, resources, and support needed to address their basic needs while also addressing the complexity of their other social-emotional-physical needs could be vital to success for many individuals.

The major differences found between mothers and fathers were in the extent to which certain problems had been experienced. The most notable of these were differences in experiences of physical and sexual abuse – and undoubtedly other types of abuse that were not queried – during childhood and adulthood. Clearly, more mothers were abused than fathers, a finding reported elsewhere (Dallaire, 2007; Glaze & Maruschak, 2008; Kjellstrand et al., 2012). Additionally, more mothers experienced mental health, physical health, and substance abuse problems, a finding that also has been reported elsewhere (Mumola, 2000; Dallaire, 2007; Glaze & Maruschak, 2008; Kjellstrand et al., 2012). Further, on average, the total number of problems experienced by mothers was greater than that experienced by fathers. While many fathers had also experienced these issues, the prevalence was less. In contrast, fathers were more likely to have been involved in juvenile justice and had more criminal justice involvement overall, including having had been to prison more times and currently serving a longer sentence. This again replicates findings from other researchers (e.g., Mumola, 2000; Dallaire, 2007; Glaze & Maruschak, 2008; Kjellstrand et al., 2012). Even so, both mothers and fathers averaged over 4 years for their current sentence, many mothers had served more than one prison sentence, and many mothers also had juvenile justice involvement.

Gender-Responsive Intervention

While all parents are likely to accrue some benefit by a general approach within reentry interventions, given the observed differences between mothers and fathers, tailoring such an approach for each gender may improve outcomes. Fedock and Covington (2017) suggested six guiding principles as part of a framework for a gender-responsive approach: (1) acknowledging that gender makes a difference; (2) creating an environment based on safety, respect, and dignity; (3) developing policies, practices, and programs that are relational and promote healthy connections to children, family members, significant others, and the community; (4)

addressing substance abuse, trauma, and mental health issues through comprehensive, integrated, and culturally relevant services and appropriate supervision; (5) providing opportunities to improve individuals' socioeconomic status; and (6) creating a system of comprehensive and collaborative community services. Certainly, each of these is relevant for working with both fathers and mothers. However, in our experience working within several corrections systems around the United States, "gender-responsiveness" is a term that is often used to refer to "women's programs." Not surprisingly, the frame in Covington's papers on this topic has focused on women and has highlighted two central issues that appear to be more common for women than men (at least based on self-report): abuse and histories of trauma.

Gender-Responsiveness in Existing Programs

Given the accruing evidence on gender differences was well as the potential importance of gender-responsive programming to long-term success, we were interested in whether and how *existing* reentry programs for fathers and mothers have been construed to be gender-responsive. To answer these questions, we conducted a multi-stage search of the peer-reviewed literature. First, an online search was conducted for articles that focused on fathers or mothers who were in prison, jail, and in community corrections settings. Various search engines and databases (e.g., PsycINFO, Google Scholar, EBSCO) were used with relevant search terms (e.g., "incarceration," "reintegration," "reunification," "reentry," "returning," "recidivism"). Articles were downloaded and examined for additional references, which were also downloaded. If a study appeared to be relevant to discussing a problem delivered during the reentry period (broadly defined, within a year before or after release) for fathers or mothers, it was retained for further review. Finally, relevant literature reviews, including chapters, on reentry and incarceration were scanned for additional references. Because this strategy yielded few articles, we repeated the search with a broader focus on men or women.

Once a pool of articles was assembled, the following criteria were required for an article to be retained for review for this chapter: (1) the study of interest in the article was conducted in the United States, (2) the article was published in a peer-reviewed journal in the year 1990 or beyond, (3) the study focused either on men or on women (but not both), (4) the study included a program of interest which was delivered to adults (all 18 years and older) who were approaching release or who had recently been released from incarceration, (5) the program of interest was intended to impact behavior and adjustment prior to and after release, and (6) data were collected on participant outcomes, at least at the end of the program period, within at least two conditions (program versus control or another active condition; randomized or not). In short, we were interested not only in programs for men or for women but programs for which outcomes had been examined in an experimental or quasi-experimental study. From our initial pool, we located 26 articles (on 23 programs) that focused on men and 10 articles (on 9 programs) that focused on women that met each of our criteria.

Once relevant articles were identified, each was coded as "gender-responsive" in terms of several criteria: (1) the program targets the gender of focus, (2) the program is stated to be "gender-responsive" (or a synonym), (3) the program was developed by a person of the target gender, (4) the program was developed with the help of people of the target gender, (5) the study relied on research on gender to inform content and/or process, (6) the study relied on a theory of gender to inform content and/or process, and (7) the intervention had a targeted focus that had specific and different implications for each gender (i.e., sexual health, pregnancy). Each of these criteria was chosen by the research team as important to code because they reflect different strategies to address the issue of gender within a program. For example, including a program developer that is the target gender and otherwise including members of the target gender in contributing to program development signal attempt to include perspectives from representatives of the target gender in decision-making about the content and process of the program. As such, "getting a seat at the table" would demonstrate a serious consideration of gender and thus be considered, in our collective opinion, a gender-responsive strategy (Table 3).

Programs for Men

Gender-responsiveness was not something that was discussed in the reentry literature for men (see Table 4). While men contributed as authors in a majority of the programs reviewed, very few of the programs that were studied were stated to have been influenced by findings from gender research and none by theories on gender in an attempt to better address the needs of men during reentry. Additionally, none of the programs reviewed incorporated a targeted gender focus. For example, although

Table 4 Gender responsive literature review

	Program targets men	Program targets women	Stated to be "gender responsive" or synonym	Developed by target gender	Developed with the help of targeted gender	Relied on research on gender to inform content or process	Relied on theory on gender to inform content or process	Intervention had a targeted gender-relevant focus
Men	23	–	0	15	1	2	0	0
	–	–	0%	65%	0.04%	0.08%	0%	0%
Women	–	9	2	8	6	7	2	6
	–	–	22%	88%	66%	77%	22%	66%

a few programs focused on strengthening incarcerated men's romantic relationships and/or their relationships with their children, we did not rate this as a gender-responsive approach per se unless additional information was provided that documented how such an approach was addressing specific research-based issues or factors for men or fathers. Along these lines, a program pitched as a "fatherhood" program required more than just this label to be considered "gender-responsive."

Programs for Women

In contrast to programs for fathers, gender-responsiveness was referred to in a variety of ways in programs developed for women (see Table 4). Most programs for women were developed by women researchers and practitioners, and many sought input from women clients. Most did refer to research on gender as an influence in program content or process, but few relied on theoretical notions on gender. The content of programs that cited gender as a consideration ranged widely in topics, from a focus on abstinence or reduction of drug use and HIV-risk behaviors to a focus on trauma symptomology and mental health. Over half of programs did have some gender-relevant focus. Several programs that attempted a gender-responsive approach did appear to be promising. For example, in a study by Messina et al. (2010), women in a gender-responsive program focused on substance abuse treatment reported reductions in drug use over time, which were significantly greater than reductions in drug use for women in the control group of a therapeutic community program. Treatment was delivered by a women-only intervention staff. Unfortunately, whether or not gender-responsive reentry interventions lead to superior outcomes to programs that are not attempting such strategies is unknown.

What Might Gender-Responsive Programming Look like for Fathers and for Mothers?

Clearly, the majority of reentry programming that has been researched is not designed to be gender-responsive, at least not in an overt sense. Given this, what would a gender-responsive approach to reentry look like? Based on the observed differences between men and women in the collective literature, as well as in the survey results reported in this chapter, and combined with potentially different pathways into prison, correctional involvement, and societal norms and expectations of being a mother versus a father in our society, we posit that a gender-responsive approach requires varying the content, delivery, and degree to which certain topics are addressed.

In general, fathers might be best served by programs that address parenting both directly and from afar, establishing healthy relationships with the child's caregiver, addressing potentially longer histories of criminal behavior patterns, and developing plans to mitigate common challenges, including meeting basic needs such as housing and employment. If not addressed, each of these challenges has the potential to diminish the likelihood of successful reentry for men in general and fathers in particular. Further, based on the father participants' views on the importance of individual actions, focusing on issues related to empowerment and independence could be a key component in programming for men.

In contrast, and again in general, mothers might especially benefit from programs that guide them in living with and providing a home for their children, discuss expectations and challenges for mothers and women in our society, and address traumatic pasts of abuse, substance use, and physical/mental health issues. The amount of trauma faced by many women suggests trauma-informed interventions could be especially appropriate for women. Finally, based on our results, providing emotional support and counseling seem likely to be well received by mothers. This is not to imply that many mothers are not in need of having their basic needs addressed through reentry programs. They frequently need this type of support as well.

What most strikes us at the end of this search is the great deal of overlap in the experiences of fathers and mothers on a wide variety of topics. Most notably, both men and women need to find a safe and stable place to live after release and reliable employment that provides wages that are sufficient to support themselves and their families. These are challenging tasks to complete in the housing and job markets of today, and innovative strategies and supports are needed. Further, providing individual tailoring elements appropriate to a given individual and family within a gender-responsive program structure seems warranted. For example, issues related to trauma and substance use and the need for emotional support and counseling may be absolutely critical elements for many women but also for many men. In our own recent work on reentry with the Washington State Department of Corrections (Eddy et al., 2019), for example, we have found keen interest from incarcerated fathers in brief, problem-solving-focused family counseling in the hopes that participating in such would assist them in reconnecting with their families, particularly with their middle school- and high school-aged children.

Conclusions

As men and women reenter their communities after prison, many face the same challenges they experienced prior to incarceration, particularly poverty, conflictual relationships, substance abuse, and health issues (Mumola, 2000; Travis et al., 2004). Having been convicted and imprisoned, reentering individuals often find it difficult to secure safe housing and livable wage employment. Further, many have learned new deviant behaviors, developed an extended group of antisocial contacts, and experienced additional trauma while in prison. Given this constellation of issues, it is not surprising that a majority (77%) end up rearrested within their first 5 years out of prison. Of these men and women, almost half return to prison (Durose et al., 2014).

Our findings emphasize the complexity involved in many parents' lives and the nuances that can exist between incarcerated mothers and fathers specifically. Providing parenting information and promoting healthy parent-child and family relationships can be important to the eventual success of parents reestablishing themselves in their communities and within their families. However, careful attention also must be given to the contextual influences that can alter these relationships including past trauma, limited formal education, mental health and substance abuse issues, and close relationships with peers involved in criminal behavior. Most of all, the basic needs of mothers and fathers after release must be front and center when considering key components of a reentry program. Creating comprehensive, multimodal programs that begin working with parents and their families while in prison and continue supporting parents and families once released hold great promise in preventing the revolving door in and out of prison and improving the well-being of both parents and their children.

While the findings here shine light on some of the issues and differences that exist for mothers and fathers, more research is needed to understand specific reentry practices, programs, and strategies that might help address these as well as the multiple issues confronting incarcerated individuals. Understanding what works best for whom and during what point in the reentry process is a vital question that has not been well explored (see Paul, 1967; Eddy & Burraston, 2018) and can only be answered with a systematic research program that is coordinated across sites. Only through such exploration can we develop targeted effective strategies for meeting the needs of both mothers and fathers alike during incarceration and post-release. Building an infrastructure of positive social supports combined with programs addressing education, employment, housing, substance abuse, mental/physical health, healthy relationships, and criminality might provide an especially powerful way to assist parents in reintegrating successfully back into their communities and families.

To our surprise, we did not find research on programs that delved into gender roles, although we are well aware that this type of approach is a common element within programs that are perceived within the field to be gender-responsive. From our experience, how this issue plays out within a particular program is often based not on research but on the points of view that program developers and/or program deliverers have about men and women or fathers and mothers within the home, within the workplace, or within society at large. Unfortunately, programs that are grounded in cultural beliefs or practices such as this are not yet reflected in the more rigorous research base that we examined for this chapter.

We suggest that researchers and practitioners developing reentry programs for parents who are incarcerated take into consideration the wide array of issues and challenges that surround men and women both during prison and upon release. Gender-responsive programming may increase the likelihood that efforts are relevant and successful by reducing specific incarceration and reentry difficulties. To find out if there is any support for this idea, rigorous studies are needed of reentry programs that are designed with gender in mind. We hypothesize that the more that program developers appropriately tailor interventions toward the strengths, needs, and challenges *both* of specific subpopulations of the incarcerated (e.g., men, women) *and* of individuals within those subpopulations, the better the long-term success in reducing recidivism and criminal activity while improving outcomes for all. This seems like a reasonable guess based on the available data, but one very much in need of testing and replication.

Acknowledgments Part of this chapter reports results from a state-wide survey. We thank the incarcerated men and women who participated, as well as the superintendents, program staff members, and correctional officers within each of the 13 participating facilities institutions and the research department staff members and administrators within the headquarters of the Oregon Department of Corrections who made the conduct of the survey possible. Correspondence concerning this chapter should be addressed to Jean Kjellstrand, College of Education, University of Oregon, Eugene, OR 97405. Contact: jeank@uoregon.edu

References[1]

Adams, L. M., Kendall, S., Smith, A., Quigley, E., Stuewig, J. B., & Tangney, J. P. (2013). HIV risk behaviors of male and female jail inmates prior to incarceration and one-year post-release. *AIDS and Behavior, 17*(8), 2685–2694. https://doi.org/10.1007/s10461-011-9990-2

*Anderson, J. (2002). Overview of the Illinois DOC high-risk parolee re-entry program and 3-year recidivism outcomes of program participants. *Cognitive-Behavioral Treatment Review,* 11(1/2), 4–6.

Binswanger, I. A., Merrill, J. O., Krueger, P. M., White, M. C., Booth, R. E., & Elmore, J. G. (2010). Gender differences in chronic medical, psychiatric, and substance-dependence disorders among jail inmates. *American Journal of Public Health, 100*(3), 476–482. https://doi.org/10.2105/ajph.2008.149591

*Block, S., Brown, C. A., Barretti, L. M., Walker, E., Yudt, M., & Fretz, R. (2014). A mixed-method assessment of a parenting program for incarcerated fathers. *Journal of Correctional Education,* 65(1), 50–67.

Bloom, B., Owen, B., & Covington, S. (2004). Women offenders and the gendered effects of public policy. *Review of Policy Research, 21*(1), 31–48. https://doi.org/10.1111/j.15411338.2004.00056.x

Carson, E. A., & Anderson, E. R. (2016). *Prisoners in 2015*. Bureau of Justice Statistics. Office of Justice Programs. US Department of Justice: Washington, D.C.

*Clark, V. A. (2015). Making the most of second chances: An evaluation of Minnesota's high-risk revocation reduction reentry program. *Journal of Experimental Criminology,* 11(2), 193–215. doi: https://doi.org/10.1007/s11292-014-9216-5.

*Cook, P. J., Kang, S., Braga, A. A., Ludwig, J., & O'Brien, M. E. (2015). An experimental evaluation of a comprehensive employment-oriented prisoner re-entry program. *Journal of Quantitative Criminology,* 31(3), 355–382. doi: https://doi.org/10.1007/s10940-014-9242-5.

Dallaire, D. H. (2007). Incarcerated mothers and fathers: A comparison of risks for children and families. *Family Relations, 56*(5), 440–453. https://doi.org/10.1111/j.1741-3729.2007.00472.x

Daly, K. (1994). *Gender, crime, and punishment*. Yale University Press.

[1] *Notes*. *Included in men's programs review. **Included in women's programs review.

Durose, M. R., Cooper, A. D., & Snyder, H. N. (2014). *Recidivism of prisoners released in 30 states in 2005: Patterns from 2005 to 2010*. US Department of Justice, Office of Justice Programs, Bureau of Justice Statistics Washington, DC.

Eddy, J. M., & Burraston, B. O. (2018). Programs promoting the successful reentry of fathers from jail or prison to home in their communities. In C. Wildeman, A. Haskins, & J. Poehlmann-Tynan (Eds.), *When parents are incarcerated: Interdisciplinary research and interventions to support children* (pp. 109–131). American Psychological Association. https://doi.org/10.1037/0000062-006

Eddy, J. M., Kjellstrand, J. M., Martinez, C. R., & Newton, R. (2010). Theory-based multi-modal parenting intervention for incarcerated parents and their families. In J. M. Eddy & J. Poehlmann (Eds.), *Children of incarcerated parents: Multidisciplinary perspectives on research, intervention, and policy* (pp. 237–264). Urban Institute Press. https://doi.org/10.1037/0000062-006

Eddy, J. M., Kjellstrand, J. M., Martinez, C. R., Newton, R., Herrera, D., Wheeler, A., Shortt, J. W., Schumer, J. E., Burraston, B. O., & Lorber, M. F. (2019). Theory-based multi-modal parenting intervention for incarcerated parents and their children. In J. M. Eddy & J. Poehlmann-Tynan (Eds.), *Children of incarcerated parents: Research, policy, and practice* (2nd ed., pp. 219–235). Springer. https://doi.org/10.1007/978-3-030-16707-3_15

Eddy, J. M., Martinez, C. R., Jr., Schiffman, T., Newton, R., Olin, L., Leve, L., et al. (2008). Development of a multisystemic parent management training intervention for incarcerated parents, their children and families. *Clinical Psychologist, 12*(3), 86–98. https://doi.org/10.1080/13284200802495461

Eddy, J. M., Martinez, C. R., Jr., & Burraston, B. (2013). A randomized controlled trial of a parent management training program for incarcerated parents: Proximal impacts. *Monographs of the Society for Research in Child Development, 78*(3), 75–93. https://doi.org/10.1111/mono.12022

Eddy, J. M., & Poehlmann, J. (2010). *Children of incarcerated parents: A handbook for researchers and practitioners*. Urban Institute Press. 2100 M Street NW, Washington, DC 20037.

El-Bassel, N., Simoni, J. M., Cooper, D. K., Gilbert, L., & Schilling, R. F. (2001). Sex trading and psychological distress among women on methadone. *Psychology of Addictive Behaviors, 15*(3), 177–184. https://doi.org/10.1037/0893-164x.15.3.177

Farrell, A. (2000). Women, crime and drugs: Testing the effect of therapeutic communities. *Women & Criminal Justice, 11*(1), 21–48. https://doi.org/10.1300/j012v11n01_02

Fedock, G., & Covington (2017). Correctional programming and gender. In Oxford *Research Encyclopedia of Criminology*, https://doi.org/10.1093/acrefore/9780190264079.013.89 from https://oxfordre.com/criminology/view/10.1093/acrefore/9780190264079.001.0001/acrefore-9780190264079-e-89?rskey=GzUBt3&result=1

Fedock, G., Fries, L., & Kubiak, S. P. (2013). Service needs for incarcerated adults: Exploring gender differences. *Journal of Offender Rehabilitation, 52*(7), 493–508. https://doi.org/10.1080/10509674.2012.759171

Glaze, L. E. & Maruschak, L.M. (2008). *Parents in prison and their minor children* (U.S. Department of Justice, Trans.): Bureau of Justice Statistics.

*Gordon, M. S., Kinlock, T. W., Schwartz, R. P., & O'Grady, K. E. (2008). A randomized clinical trial of methadone maintenance for prisoners: Findings at 6 months post-release. *Addiction*, 103(8), 1333–1342. https://doi.org/10.1111/j.1360-0443.2008.002238.x.

*Gordon, M. S., Kinlock, T. W., Couvillion, K. A., Schwartz, R. P., & O'Grady, K. (2012). A randomized clinical trial of methadone maintenance for prisoners: Prediction of treatment entry and completion in prison. *Journal of Offender Rehabilitation,* 51(4), 222–238. https://doi.org/10.1080/10509674.2011.641075.

*Gottfredson, D. C., Najaka, S. S., & Kearley, B. (2006). Effectiveness of drug treatment courts: Evidence from a randomized trial. *Criminology and Public Policy,* 2(2), 171–196. https://doi.org/10.1111/j.1745-9133.2003.tb00117.x.

Greenfeld, L. A., & Snell, T. L. (1999). *Women offenders* (U.S. Department of Justice, Trans.) (pp. 14). Office of Justice Programs.

Grella, C. E., Stein, J. A., & Greenwell, L. (2005). Associations among childhood trauma, adolescent problem behaviors, and adverse adult outcomes in substance-abusing women offenders. *Psychology of Addictive Behaviors, 19*(1), 43–53. https://doi.org/10.1037/0893-164x.19.1.43

*Grommon, E., Davidson II, W. S., & Bynum, T. S. (2013). A randomized trial of a multimodal community-based prisoner reentry program emphasizing substance abuse treatment. *Journal of Offender Rehabilitation,* 52(4), 287–309. https://doi.org/10.1080/10509674.2013.782775.

Guydish, J., Chan, M., Bostrom, A., Jessup, M. A., Davis, T. B., & Marsh, C. (2011). A randomized trial of probation case management for drug-involved women offenders. *Crime and Delinquency, 57*(2), 167. https://doi.org/10.1177/0011128708318944

Hall, E. A., Prendergast, M. L., Wellisch, J., Patten, M., & Cao, Y. (2004). Treating drug-abusing women prisoners: An outcomes evaluation of the forever free program. *The Prison Journal, 84*(1), 81–105. https://doi.org/10.1177/0032885503262456

*Harrison, K. (1997). Parental training for incarcerated fathers: Effects on attitudes, self-esteem, and children's self-perceptions. *The Journal of Social Psychology,* 137 (5), 588–593. https://doi.org/10.1080/00224549709595480.

Harrison, P. M., & Karberg, J. C. (2004). *Prison and jail inmates at midyear 2003.* Bureau of Justice Statistics.

James, D. J., & Glaze, L. E. (2006). *Mental health problems of prison and jail inmates.* Bureau of Justice Statistics.

Javdani, S., Sadeh, N., & Verona, E. (2011). Gendered social forces: A review of the impact of institutionalized factors on women and girls' criminal justice trajectories. *Psychology, Public Policy, and Law, 17*(2), 161–211. https://doi.org/10.1037/a0021957

Johnston, D. (1995). Effects of parental incarceration. In K. Gabel & D. Johnston (Eds.), *Children of incarcerated parents* (pp. 59–88). Lexington Books.

*Kinlock, T. W., Gordon, M. S., Schwartz, R. P., Fitzgerald, T. T., & O'Grady, K. E. (2009). A randomized clinical trial of methadone maintenance for prisoners: Results at 12 months post-release. *Journal of Substance Abuse Treatment, 37,* 277–285. (15) https://doi.org/10.1016/j.jsat.2009.03.002

*Kinlock, T. W., Gordon, M. S., Schwartz, R. P., O'Grady, K., Fitzgerald, T. T., & Wilson, M. (2007). A randomized clinical trial of methadone maintenance for prisoners: Results at 1-month post-release. *Drug and Alcohol Dependence,* 2, 220. https://doi.org/10.1016/j.drugalcdep.2007.05.022.

*Kinlock, T. W., Gordon, M. S., Schwartz, R. P., & O'Grady, K. E. (2008). A study of methadone maintenance for male prisoners: 3-month post release outcomes. *Criminal Justice and Behavior,* 35(1), 34–47. doi: https://doi.org/10.1177/0093854807309111.

Kjellstrand, J. M., Cearley, J., Eddy, J., Foney, D., & Martinez, C. R. (2012). Characteristics of incarcerated fathers and mothers: Implications for preventive interventions targeting children and families. *Children and Youth Services Review, 34*(12), 2409–2415. https://doi.org/10.1016/j.childyouth.2012.08.008

Kjellstrand, J. M., & Eddy, J. (2011a). Mediators of the effect of parental incarceration on adolescent externalizing behaviors. *Journal of Community Psychology, 39*(5), 551–565. https://doi.org/10.1002/jcop.20451

Kjellstrand, J. M., & Eddy, J. (2011b). Parental incarceration during childhood, family context, and youth problem behavior across adolescence. *Journal of Offender Rehabilitation, 50*(1), 18–36. https://doi.org/10.1080/10509674.2011.536720

*Lattimore, P. K., & Visher, C. A. (2013). The impact of prison reentry services on short-term outcomes: Evidence from a multisite evaluation. *Evaluation Review,* 37(3–4), 274–313. https://doi.org/10.1177/0193841X13519105.

*Landreth, G. L., & Lobaugh, A. F. (1988). Filial therapy with incarcerated fathers: Effects on parental acceptance of child, parental stress, and child adjustment. *Journal of Counseling and Development,* 76, 157–165. https://doi.org/10.1002/j.1556-6676.1998.tb02388.x.

Lapidus, L., Luthra, N., Verma, A., Small, D., Allard, P., & Levingston, K. (2004). *Caught in the net: The impact of drug policies on women and families*. American Civil Liberties Union Drug Law Reform Project: American Civil Liberties Union.

Magaletta, P. R., Diamond, P. M., Faust, E., Daggett, D. M., & Camp, S. D. (2009). Estimating the mental illness component of service need in corrections: Results from the mental health prevalence project. *Criminal Justice and Behavior, 36*(3), 229–244. https://doi.org/10.1177/0093854808330390

Maruschak, L. M., & Mumola, C. J. (2010). Incarcerated parents and their children: Findings from the Bureau of Justice Statistics. In J. M. Eddy & J. Poehlmann (Eds.), *Children of incarcerated parents: A handbook for researchers and practitioners* (pp. 33–54). Urban Institute Press. https://doi.org/10.1007/978-3-030-16707-3_11

McClellan, D. S., Farabee, D., & Crouch, B. M. (1997). Early victimization, drug use, and criminality: A comparison of male and female prisoners. *Criminal Justice and Behavior, 24*(4), 455–476. https://doi.org/10.1177/0093854897024004004

*Menting, A. T. A., Bram Orobio de Castro, Leoniek D. N. V. Wijngaards-de Meij & Walter Matthys (2014). A trial of parent training for mothers being released from incarceration and their children, *Journal of Clinical Child & Adolescent Psychology,* 43*(3)*, 381–396, https://doi.org/10.1080/15374416.2013.817310.

Messina, N., Calhoun, S., & Warda, U. (2012). Gender-responsive drug court treatment: A randomized controlled trial. *Criminal Justice and Behavior, 39*(12), 1539–1558. https://doi.org/10.1037/e701002011-001

Messina, N., Grella, C. E., Cartier, J., & Torres, S. (2010). A randomized experimental study of gender-responsive substance abuse treatment for women in prison. *Journal of Substance Abuse Treatment, 38*(2), 97–107. https://doi.org/10.1016/j.jsat.2009.09.004

Mowen, T. J., & Visher, C. A. (2013). Drug use and crime after incarceration: The role of family support and family conflict. *Justice Quarterly, 32*(2), 337–359. https://doi.org/10.1080/07418825.2013.771207

Mumola, C. J. (2000). *Incarcerated parents and their children*. Bureau of Justice Statistics Special Report (pp. 13).

Murray, J., & Farrington, D. P. (2005). Parental imprisonment: Effects on boys' antisocial behaviour and delinquency through the life-course. *Journal of Child Psychology and Psychiatry, 46*(12), 1269–1278. https://doi.org/10.1111/j.1469-7610.2005.01433.x

Myers, B. J., Smarsh, T. M., Amlund-Hagen, K., & Kennon, S. (1999). Children of incarcerated mothers. *Journal of Child and Family Studies, 8*(1), 11–25. https://doi.org/10.1023/A:1022990410036

Nichols, E. B., & Loper, A. B. (2012). Incarceration in the household: Academic outcomes of adolescents with an incarcerated household member. *Journal of Youth and Adolescence, 41*(11), 1455–1471. https://doi.org/10.1007/s10964-012-9780-9

Paul, G. L. (1967). Strategy of outcome research in psychotherapy. *Journal of Consulting Psychology, 31*, 109–118. https://doi.org/10.1016/b978-0-08-019506-3.50019-6

Phillips, S. D., Burns, B. J., Wagner, H., Kramer, T. L., & Robbins, J. M. (2002). Parental incarceration among adolescents receiving mental health services. *Journal of Child and Family Studies, 11*(4), 385–399. https://doi.org/10.1023/A:1020975106679

*Prendergast, M. L., Hall, E. A., & Wexler, H. K. (2003). Multiple measures of outcome in assessing a prison-based drug treatment program. *Journal of Offender Rehabilitation,* 37(3–4), 65–94. https://doi.org/10.1300/J076v37n03_04.

*Prendergast, M. L., Hall, E. A., Wexler, H. K., Melnick, G., & Cao, Y. (2004). Amity prison-based therapeutic community: 5-year outcomes. *The Prison Journal,* 84(1), 36–60. doi: https://doi.org/10.1177/0032885503262454.

*Rainforth, M. V., Alexander, C. N., & Cavanaugh, K. L. (2003). Effects of the transcendental meditation program on recidivism among former inmates of Folsom prison: Survival analysis of 15-year follow-up data. *Journal of Offender Rehabilitation,* 36(1–4), 181–203. https://doi.org/10.1300/J076v36n01_09.

*Robbers, M. L. (2005). Focus on family and fatherhood: Lessons from Fairfax County's responsible fatherhood program for incarcerated dads. *Justice Policy Journal,* 2(1), 1–27.

Sacks, J. Y., McKendrick, K., & Hamilton, Z. (2012a). A randomized clinical trial of a therapeutic community treatment for female inmates: Outcomes at 6 and 12 months after prison release. *Journal of Addictive Diseases, 31*(3), 258–269. https://doi.org/10.1080/10550887.2012.694601

*Sacks, S., Chaple, M., Sacks, J. Y., McKendrick, K., & Cleland, C. M. (2012b). Randomized trial of a reentry modified therapeutic community for offenders with co-occurring disorders: Crime outcomes. *Journal of Substance Abuse Treatment,* 42(3), 247–259. https://doi.org/10.1016/j.jsat.2011.07.011.

Scott, C. K., & Dennis, M. L. (2012). The first 90 days following release from jail: Findings from the recovery management checkups for women offenders (RMCWO) experiment. *Drug and Alcohol Dependence, 125*(1–2), 110–118. https://doi.org/10.1016/j.drugalcdep.2012.03.025

*Shamblen, S. R., Arnold, B. B., McKiernan, P., Collins, D. A., & Strader, T. N. (2013). Applying the creating lasting family connections marriage enhancement program to marriages affected by prison reentry. *Family Process,* 52(3), 477–498. https://doi.org/10.1111/famp.12003.

*Shamblen, S. R., Kokoski, C., Collins, D. A., Strader, T. N., & McKiernan, P. (2017). Implementing creating lasting family connections with reentry fathers: A partial replication during a period of policy change. *Journal of Offender Rehabilitation,* 56(5), 295–307. https://doi.org/10.1080/10509674.2017.1327917.

**Shortt, J. W., Eddy, J. M., Sheeber, L., & Davis, B. (2014). Project home: A pilot evaluation of an emotion-focused intervention for mothers reuniting with children after prison. *Psychological Services,* 11(1), 1–9. https://doi.org/10.1037/a0034323.

Steadman, H. J., Osher, F. C., Robbins, P. C., Case, B., & Samuels, S. (2009). Prevalence of serious mental illness among jail inmates. *Psychiatric Services, 60*(6), 761–765. https://doi.org/10.1176/appi.ps.60.6.761

Steffensmeier, D., Zhong, H., Ackerman, J., Schwartz, J., & Agha, S. (2006). Gender gap trends for violent crimes, 1980 to 2003: A UCR-NCVS comparison. *Feminist Criminology, 1*(1), 72–98. https://doi.org/10.1177/1557085105283953

Surratt, H. L., Inciardi, J. A., Kurtz, S. P., & Kiley, M. C. (2004). Sex work and drug use in a subculture of violence. *Crime & Delinquency, 50*(1), 43–59. https://doi.org/10.1177/0011128703258875

Travis, J., Waul, M., & Geraghty, T. F. (2004). Prisoners once removed: The impact of incarceration and reentry on children, families, and communities. *Journal of Criminal Law and Criminology, 94*(4), 1149–1162.

Van Dieten, M., Jones, N. J., & Rondon, M. (2014). *Working with women who perpetrate violence: A practical guide*. National Resource Center on Justice Involved Women.

*Van Voorhis, P., Spruance, L. M., Ritchey, P. N., Listwan, S. J., & Seabrook, R. (2004). The Georgia cognitive skills experiment: A replication of reasoning and rehabilitation. *Criminal Justice and Behavior, 31*(3), 282–305. https://doi.org/10.1177/0093854803262506

Walmsley, R. (2009). *World prison population list.* Retrieved from http://www.kcl.ac.uk/depsta/law/research/icps/downloads/wppl-8th_41.pdf

*Welsh, W. N., Zajac, G., & Bucklen, K. B. (2014). For whom does prison-based drug treatment work? Results from a randomized experiment. *Journal of Experimental Criminology,* 10(2), 151–177. https://doi.org/10.1007/s11292-013-9194-z.

*Wexler, H. K., De Leon, G., Thomas, G., Kressel, D., & Peters, J. (1999). The Amity prison TC evaluation: Reincarceration outcomes. *Criminal Justice and Behavior,* 26(2), 147–167. https://doi.org/10.1177/0093854899026002001.

*Wexler, H. K., Melnick, G., Lowe, L., & Peters, J. (1999b). Three-year reincarceration outcomes for Amity in-prison therapeutic community and aftercare in California. *The Prison Journal,* 79(3), 321–336. https://doi.org/10.1177/0032885599079003003.

*Wilczak, G. L., & Markstrom, C. A. (1999). The effects of parent education on parental locus of control and satisfaction of incarcerated fathers. *International Journal of Offender Therapy and Comparative Criminology,* 43 (1), 90–102. https://doi.org/10.1177/0306624x99431009.

*Wilson, J. A., & Davis, R. C. (2006). Good intentions meet hard realities: An evaluation of the project greenlight reentry program. *Criminology & Public Policy,* 5(2), 303–338. https://doi.org/10.1111/j.1745-9133.2006.00380.x.
*Wilson, J. A., & Zozula, C. (2012). Risk, recidivism, and (re) habilitation: Another look at project greenlight. *The Prison Journal,* 92(2), 203–230. https://doi.org/10.1177/0032885512438870.
*Wolitski, R. J., & Project START Writing Group. (2006). Relative efficacy of a multisession sexual risk–reduction intervention for young men released from prisons in 4 states. *American Journal of Public Health,* 96(10), 1854–1861. https://doi.org/10.2105/AJPH.2004.056044.
Zlotnick, C., Johnson, J., & Najavits, L. M. (2009). Randomized controlled pilot study of cognitive-behavioral therapy in a sample of incarcerated women with substance use disorder and PTSD. *Behavior Therapy, 40*(4), 325. https://doi.org/10.1016/j.beth.2008.09.004

Part IV
The Macro System

We Are Not Collateral Consequences: Arrest to Reentry Policy Solutions for Children of Incarcerated Parents

Isabel Coronado

Abstract Finding the right solutions to decrease the traumatic experiences children of incarcerated parents (COIP) face is not a singular issue. The spectrum of needs varies by child, family, and community. Nonetheless, having an incarcerated parent is a major hardship that many children in the United States endure. With absence of continual action to create solutions for COIP, the trauma will continue to perpetuate harmful outcomes in COIP's lives and communities. The policies listed in this chapter do not address mass incarceration or systemic solutions, but rather the day-to-day gaps in policy addressing the problems COIP experience. The policy solutions range from arrest to reentry, including solutions for healthcare, caregivers, and the foster care system. To be clear, the solutions addressed in this chapter are not the structural changes needed to end mass incarceration, poverty, racism, or the Jim Crow era of criminal justice policy. That, however, does not mean they are not worth pursuing. They address necessary changes to be made, such as the way COIP experience the arrest of their parents, their lack of educational opportunities and availability of counseling services, and many other gaps in services. These are solutions meant to identify the oppressive system COIP encounter once their parents come into contact with the justice system.

Keywords Children of incarcerated parents · Trauma · Policy · Incarceration

This chapter includes a series of policies that the federal, state, and local governments can implement to better support COIP. Some of these policy solutions have come from existing programs and policies that states and local communities have already implemented; others are from the input and ideas of resilient COIP and are based on my own unique experience as a COIP. Collectively, they are meant to address the challenges we COIP experience. In this chapter, eight areas are addressed in which we must better support COIP through their parent's arrest, sentencing,

I. Coronado (✉)
Next100 Policy Entrepreneur and citizen Mvskoke Nation, Okmulgee, OK, USA
e-mail: Isabel-Coronado@outlook.com

J. Krysik, N. Rodriguez (eds.), *Children of Incarcerated Parents*, Children of Incarcerated Parents: From Understanding to Impact,
https://doi.org/10.1007/978-3-030-84713-5_10

incarceration, and reentry. For each area, potential policy solutions that various levels of government can implement are identified, including examples where possible.

Children of Color and Community Needs

- Level: Local, state, tribal, and federal
- Challenge: Children of incarcerated parents are disproportionately children of color. Black children are seven times more likely to have an incarcerated parent than white children, and Latinx children are twice as likely (The Sentencing Project, 2009). Although data for Native children of incarcerated parents is not available nationally, in Oklahoma, the data show that Native children are twice as likely as white children to have an incarcerated parent while, in both the Dakotas, they are about five times more likely (The Annie E. Casey Foundation, 2018).

- For Native children, the Indian Child Welfare Act (ICWA) is particularly important to allow Native COIP to stay within their culture and tradition. The Act gives custody priority to first people in the child's family, then their community, and then people outside the community. From years of forced removal of children from their tribal nations, ICWA seeks to reconcile those past traumas by ensuring they stay where their community is located. Efforts have been made to dismantle ICWA because of claims that it is a race-based policy. Native children are critical to carry on the generational tradition, culture, and language. In addition, Black and Latinx COIP also deserve attention to their community needs. The racist criminal justice system has had the same generational impacts – from Jim Crow and redlining impacting Black children and anti-immigration and negative stereotypes impacting Latinx children, we need policies that are tailored to our communities.

Policy Solutions to Implement

- Strengthening the Indian Child Welfare Act: The positive outcomes for Native children are being within their community and not transplanting them to a foreign community. This means strengthening ICWA to ensure those who oppose the legislation do not have grounds to call it a "race-based policy"; instead Tribal nations have the authority to ensure the citizens of their Tribe are protected.
- Building Inclusive Community Programs: Creating community services that can cater to more inclusive programs for COIP with varying racial backgrounds and community practices. Those programs are best run when staff mirror the people they are serving.
- Increasing Professional Competence Through Broad-Based Training: Staff in every agency of the justice system, as well education, social services, and healthcare, should be trained on ACEs (adverse childhood experiences), trauma including the trauma of systemic racism, brain development, and undoing racism/implicit bias so that youth are not criminalized, increasing their own likelihood of involvement with the justice system. Training should consider the diversity

within communities of color as well as understanding the impact of separation for a child when a parent is incarcerated.

Protecting the Well-Being of Children During Arrest

- Level: Local, state, tribal, and federal
- **Challenge:** The number of children who have witnessed the arrest of their parents and the scenes they have witnessed are gut-wrenching. One study estimated that of all parents arrested, 67% were handcuffed in front of their children, 27% reported weapons drawn in front of their children, 4.3% reported a physical struggle, and 3.2% reported the use of pepper spray (Phillips, 1998). These incidents invoke years of trauma in a child's life. It is telling that there has not been a more recent study published on this topic, reflecting the reality that children remain largely invisible at the time of a parent's arrest.

Policy Solutions to Implement
Child-Sensitive Arrest Protocols: These protocols have been successfully implemented in several states and localities such as Albany, San Francisco, and New York City. Law enforcement at all levels should adopt arrest protocol and provide training to minimize the harm to children at the time of parental arrest. Such protocol includes:

- Look for signs of children as part of every arrest protocol
- Ensure the safety, respect, and well-being of children during the arrest of their parents
- Allow for physical proximity or contact if appropriate, e.g., letting a child give their parent a hug and kiss before departing from them during arrest
- Allow parents to arrange alternative care for their child and aid them in making such arrangements

Maintaining Children's Connections to Their Parents

- Level: Local, state, and federal
- **Challenge:** Whether a parent is in jail or prison, and regardless of the length of the stay, it is important that children be able to stay connected through phone calls and visits. When children cannot see their parents, phone calls are an important way to stay in touch, but can be costly. A report released from Forward Together, the Ella Baker Center for Human Rights, and Research Action Design reports the results of a year-long survey of 712 formerly incarcerated people and 368 of their family members across 14 states (deVuono-Powell et al., 2015). It found that the costs of incarceration extend far beyond the incarcerated person. The difficulties continue as families try to stay in touch with their family member. More than one-third had to go into debt to pay for phone calls and visits

alone. Just as phone calls are important to stay in contact with parents, being able to see parents in person is even more important for children. Most jails only offer visiting through glass (non-contact visits) which is upsetting for children. A number of facilities have installed video call cameras which is also costly to the families.

Policy Solutions to Implement

- Free Phone Calls: Although the Federal Communications Commission (FCC) has ended $1-per-minute phone calls, the cost of calls is a barrier that should be removed altogether from the incarcerated person. New York City has free phone calls for persons who are incarcerated due to legislation passed in 2018 and implemented in 2019.
- Child-Friendly Visits: Some prisons throughout the country have implemented specific positive events for parents and children such as father/daughter dances, arts and craft activities, and even sleepovers for children to be able to spend the night with their parents. Not only is it important for the environment to be child friendly, but the people who come into contact with the children, such as correctional officers and administrative staff, should be trained on child-friendly approaches including respectful and trauma-informed communication techniques.
- Visit Format: Ensure in-person visiting is not replaced with video conference calls. The Urban Institute released an important report that outlines visit type, structure, frequency/length of visits, and many other recommendations for facilities to integrate into their protocol to better facilitate child visits (Cramer et al., 2017).
- Visit Area: Ensure waiting areas, screening protocols, and visiting rooms are family friendly for children of all ages.

Include Children in Decision-Making Regarding Their Living Situation and Support Caretakers

- Level: Local, state, tribal, and federal
- **Challenge:** Child custody is sometimes left to the court's discretion. Family and dependency courts examine the "the best interest of the child," but many often never actually hear what the child wants and believes is in her/his/or their best interest. Caretakers are crucial to the quality of life and well-being of COIP. Caretakers include parents, grandparents, aunts/uncles, sisters/brothers, and even the greater community including foster parents. Caretakers take on a huge responsibility to care for COIPs. The foster care system accounts for at least 4.5 percent of children who have incarcerated parents. It is critical that foster parents understand the complexities of fostering a child with incarcerated parents (Human Impact Partners and Free Hearts, 2018).

Policy Solutions to Implement

- Expand the Use of Family Impact Statements: Implement and expand practices that allow for children's voices to be heard and considered in decision-making. Family impact statements made in family court that involve the child in the decision-making process about their care situation would truly mean decisions are made "in the best interests of the child." Family impact statements allow children to make statements regarding the challenges their parent's incarceration may have on them. This is an important strategy to ensure judicial personnel understand the full impact of incarceration on children and families and needs to be adhered to and expanded. A holistic approach to ensuring children are considered would include information about the parent's responsibilities, even if it came from sources other than the child, and may include the impact various sentencing decisions would have on the child. Criminal courts do not need to take the impact of children into consideration which is why pre-plea and pre-sentencing memorandums should include a family impact statement, and criminal courts should be required to consider them. Illinois passed such a law in 2019; HB2444 of the 101st General Assembly amends Illinois Code of Criminal Procedure, 725 ILCS 5/110-5.3 and 730 ILCS 5/5-5-3.1. This law became effective January 1, 2020.
- Support for Caregivers/Foster Families: By assisting caregivers, there is an additional positive impact on the child. Caregivers deserve the added help and benefits to properly care and provide for the COIP in their custody. Informal and kinship caregivers should have access to a monthly stipend/ financial assistance outside of the foster care system. Providing information and fostering the strengthening of relationships between COIP and their parent who is incarcerated are pertinent for the child's well-being. Children should have a right to, and arrangements should be made for, visits and calls with the incarcerated parent. If it is determined that contact is not appropriate for a child, then ongoing assessment is needed as the situation may change over time.
- Training: Ensure foster parents and kinship caregivers attend training on experience with COIP, including facilitating child-friendly visits in jail/prison.

Sentencing: Parent and Caregiver Alternative Sentencing and Prison Proximity

- Level: State and federal
- **Challenge:** When a parent is removed, the child often loses all normalcy resulting in many additional consequences from mental and physical health issues to unstable financial assurance. Prisons are often in rural areas; one report showed 63 percent of people in state prisons serve their sentences in facilities more than 100 miles from home. For federal prisons, the average distance is 500 miles or more (Rabuy & Kopf, 2015).

Policy Solutions to Implement

- Parent and Caregiver Alternative Sentencing: It is possible to divert parents from serving prison time and instead use alternatives to incarceration such as the Washington parent alternative sentencing. Its aim is to divert parents from prison and keep them home with their children under community supervision and with community resources.
- Prison Proximity: If alternative sentencing is not an option, then parents who are sentenced should serve their sentence in the prison closest to their child's location. In 2019, legislators in New York introduced Bill A4339 that would establish a pilot project to prioritize placing incarcerated parents near their children (https://www.nysenate.gov/legislation/bills/2019/a4339).
- Alternative Sentencing: Ensure judges have the option to grant alternatives to incarceration at sentencing, or consider imposing community supervision along with conditions for treatment and programming, services which are more likely to address the roots of the law-breaking while maintaining parent-child ties. Washington State has research that shows such a program is successful https://www.doc.wa.gov/corrections/justice/sentencing/parenting-alternative.htm.

Support Educational Opportunities for COIP

- Level: Local, state, and tribal
- **Challenge:** On average, children spend 34 hours a week at school, a substantial amount of time (National Center on Education and the Economy, n.d.). This means that teachers play a crucial role of support in children's lives, including COIP – but educators are not always equipped nor do they have the tools to best support COIP. Emotional development, which also happens in schools, is also important to the development of a child. And yet too often, COIP are not comfortable sharing their full selves at school. COIP often create cover stories about the whereabouts of their parents in fear of bullying, embarrassment, and simply not wanting to disclose such personal information. Currently, incarcerated parents have very little input or communication of any with their children's teacher, resulting in low participation in their child's education. Many schools discourage parents who have been justice involved from volunteering at school events or field trips. Education at any point, vocational, community college, or four-year university college, has a positive impact on long-term outcomes, yet only two percent of children with an incarcerated mother earn a college degree.

Policy Solutions to Implement

- School Training: Teachers, staff, and school administrators should undergo training to understand the trauma induced when a child's parent is incarcerated, implicit bias training about those who are incarcerated, and strategies for how to create affirming spaces for students with incarcerated parents.

- Scholarship and Supportive Opportunities: Creating scholarships specifically for COIP students would help decrease educational disparities, similar to opportunities for children in the foster care system. ScholarCHIPS (https://www.scholarchipsfund.org) is an example of a college scholarship program started by daughter of incarcerated parent, Yazzmine Arrington, in the DC, Maryland, Virginia area. Youth need opportunities for emotional as well as financial support to succeed in college.
- Parental Involvement from Prison and After: Schools should issue a directive to make involvement in a child's education accessible for incarcerated parents. The support should continue after the parent has reentered society by encouraging them to volunteer and support their child at school functions.
- Community Involvement: Children do not just encounter teachers throughout their days. Dance teachers, coaches, music instructors, etc. need the same training to understand the challenges COIP face.

Healthcare: Mental and Physical Health

- Level: Local, state, and tribal

- **Challenge:** Healthcare has proven difficult for COIP, which means long-term health outcomes are in jeopardy. Children experiencing the trauma of forced separation from their parent or parents due to incarceration may have significant mental health needs they struggle to address. One issue that is often missing from the conversation about COIP is the topic of sexual health. Today's barriers to birth control for children under 18 – even with a parent's consent – are substantial. It is extremely difficult for any young person to navigate the health system – whether that be, for instance, understanding co-payments and deductibles, the laws around abortion, or parental and pediatric care – to protect their bodies; and doing so with an incarcerated parent who is unable to offer emotional or physical support makes things even harder.

Policy Solutions to Implement

- Training: Counselors and therapists should receive training on working with COIP. Most clinicians do not receive any training on COIP and, as a result, may carry their own biases and misunderstandings and "treat" this complicated loss as if it were an abandonment or divorce when it is unique.
- Counseling/Therapy: Providing accessible and affordable counseling/therapy aids in the COIP's life to find healthy coping and grieving mechanisms.
- Health Insurance: Providing healthcare to COIP during the incarceration of their parent through, for example, the expansion of Medicaid is critical to decreasing long-term health consequences.

Reentry Assistance

- Level: Local, state, and tribal
- **Challenge:** The formerly incarcerated have many barriers to reentry including housing, jobs, education, and transportation. One of the most important barriers for parents to overcome is gaining custody of their children or reestablishing themselves as a parent in their children's lives. As reported by The Marshall Project in 2018, at least 32,000 parents who were incarcerated had their parental rights terminated, even though they had not been accused of maltreatment (The Marshall Project, 2018). This has proven difficult for both parents and COIP; it is a complex issue, layered on top of many other challenges.

Policy Solutions to Implement

- Counseling/Therapy Resources: Building and preparing for the reentry is a process that should begin not just with the parent but for the children as well, preparing them both in advance for reunification.
- Counseling/Therapy Sessions: This should begin 18–24 months prior to release of the incarcerated parent for the parent and the child and last beyond the immediate release of a parent.
- Navigating Release: Many parents come home from being incarcerated and then are on parole. Prior to release parents should be supported in regaining custody and re-assuming parental responsibilities. Funding is needed to inform and guide parents to regain custody of their children, adjust child support payments, and reduce fine/fees for parents. Local, state, and tribal entities should provide funds to assist incarcerated parents with navigating custody hearings.

Summary

Some of the policy recommendations in this chapter have been implemented in states, and some states are looking to pass these kinds of policy reforms. We need to accelerate these types of reforms to limit the negative impact on children of incarcerated parents. We can continue to move the needle on criminal justice reform and include COIP in the efforts or continue down a path that is harmful both to children and communities.

Acknowledgments I want to thank my advisory board and those who provided input and suggested edits. Thank you for the work you do every day that impact and help COIP. I would like to dedicate these policy solutions to the future children who may never have to experience having an incarcerated parent and the past resilient children of incarcerated parents who grew up with more strength than people realize.

References

Cramer, L., Goff, M., Peterson, B., & Sandstrom, H. (2017, April). *Parent-child visiting practices in prisons and jails*, Urban Institute. Retrieved from https://www.urban.org/sites/default/files/publication/89601/parent-child_visiting_practices_in_prisons_and_jails_0.pdf

deVuono-Powell, S., Schweidler, C., Walters, A., & Zohrabi, A. (2015). *Who pays? The true cost of incarceration on families*. Oakland, CA: Ella Baker Center, Forward Together, Research Action Design. Retrieved from http://whopaysreport.org/wp-content/uploads/2015/09/Who-Pays-FINAL.pdf

Human Impact Partners and Free Hearts. (2018, February). Keeping kids and parents together: A healthier approach to sentencing in Tennessee. Oakland, CA. Retrieved from https://humanimpact.org/wp-content/uploads/2018/02/HIP_PrimaryCare-TN-Report.pdf

National Center on Education and the Economy. (n.d.) Statistic of the month: How much time do students spend in school? Retrieved from https://ncee.org/2018/02/statistic-of-the-month-how-much-time-do-students-spend-in-school/

Phillips, S. D. (1998). Programming for children of female offenders. Proceedings from 4th National Head Start Research Conference, Washington, DC, quoted from The Osborne Association, A Call to Action: A Report of the New York Initiative for Children of Incarcerated Parents, May 2011, 17. 7.

Rabuy, B., & Kopf, D. (2015, October). *Separation by bars and miles: Visitation on state prisons*. Prison Policy Initiative. Retrieved from http://www.prisonpolicy.org/reports/prisonvisits.html

The Annie E. Casey Foundation. (2018). *Kids count data book*. Retrieved from https://www.aecf.org/resources/2018-kids-count-data-book/

The Marshall Project. (2018, December). How Incarcerated Parents Are Losing Their Children Forever. Retrieved from https://www.themarshallproject.org/2018/12/03/how-incarcerated-parents-are-losing-their-children-forever

The Sentencing Project. (2009, February). *Incarcerated parents and their children: Trends 1991-2007*. Author.

Towards a Critical Race Analysis of Positive Youth Development for Adolescents of Color Experiencing Parental Incarceration

Alexandria S. Pech and Kevin Lawrence Henry Jr

Abstract Five million children (7% of US children) have had a parent they were living with go to jail or prison at some point during their lives (Murphey & Cooper, Parents behind bars: What happens to their children: 2015). Drawing on several lines of scholarship, the authors use a critical race theoretical framework to deconstruct how the impact of parental incarceration differentially unfolds for adolescents of color. We theorize the ways that parental incarceration, which is rooted in mass incarceration and systemic oppression, might hinder opportunities for positive youth development, especially for adolescents of color. We argue for the utilization of counterstorytelling as a powerful tool to unveil systemic racism experienced by adolescents of color who must navigate through their adolescence as sons and daughters of incarcerated parents.

Keywords Adolescence · Counterstories · Critical race theory · Parental incarceration · Positive youth development · Punishment system

Background

When the punishment system incarcerates a human life, whether that person is a mother, father, or other type of caregiver, it does not mean that the impact is solely on the individual behind bars. Five million children (7% of US children) have had a parent they were living with go to jail or prison at some point during their lives (Murphey & Cooper, 2015). Compared with parental divorce or separation,

A. S. Pech (✉)
Family Studies and Human Development, The University of Arizona, Tucson, AZ, USA
e-mail: alexandriapech@email.arizona.edu

K. L. Henry Jr
Department of Educational Leadership and Policy Analysis, University of Wisconsin-Madison, Madison, WI, USA

J. Krysik, N. Rodriguez (eds.), *Children of Incarcerated Parents*, Children of Incarcerated Parents: From Understanding to Impact,
https://doi.org/10.1007/978-3-030-84713-5_11

researchers have found that parental incarceration was more strongly associated with behavior problems in children (Turney, 2014). For example, exposure to parental arrest/incarceration predicted kindergarteners' scores on both aggression, hyperactivity, and withdrawal behavior (Ziv et al., 2010). Children with formerly incarcerated fathers face elevated risks for a variety of behavior problems, including ADHD, hyperactivity, oppositional problems, self-control issues, and internalizing and externalizing problems (Emory, 2018; Wildeman & Turney, 2014). While a well-established positive association between parental incarceration and child behavior problems exists, what is less known is how the effects of parental incarceration differentially unfold for adolescents.

In this paper, critical race theory (CRT) is used to analyze and deconstruct the experiences of parental incarceration for adolescents of color. Critical race theory is a theoretical, pedagogical, and methodological tool to problematize how parental incarceration hinders opportunities for positive youth development because it centralizes how the role of race and racism is embedded in all of adolescents' proximal and distal contexts, introduces the idea of interest convergence, criticizes how liberalism perpetuates slow efforts in social transformation, highlights systemic forms of oppression experienced by individuals with multiple intersectional identities, and utilizes counterstorytelling as a powerful tool to unveil systemic racism experienced by people of color, resulting in a call to action for change.

Situating Adolescents of Color with Incarcerated Parents in Positive Youth Development

Adolescence is a developmental period of growth across multiple domains. Adolescents experience changes in their cognition (e.g., decision-making), their biology in relation to pubertal timing, and socioemotional domains in relation to forming intimate relationships with peers (Arnett, 2014). All these changes are known to influence key developmental tasks like autonomy, intimacy, identity, sexuality, and achievement (Arnett, 2014). Various theoretical frameworks and paradigms exist to understand changes that occur across the adolescent developmental time period, such as positive youth development. Positive youth development (PYD) frameworks, derived from dominant theories found in the developmental science field, posit that all youth, no matter their background or circumstances, have inherent strengths (Silbereisen & Lerner, 2007). PYD frameworks move toward promoting healthy outcomes in adolescents instead of solely reducing risky behaviors. Thus, when adolescents' individual strengths are aligned with ecological strengths available within their familial, educational, and community contexts, they possess the potential to thrive across the adolescent developmental time period (Zaff et al., 2016). Positive youth development frameworks situate youth in bidirectional, reciprocal relationships with their contexts. That is, an adolescent is its own developmental system that consists of multiple levels of context ranging from an individual's physiological levels to familial contexts, schools, communities, and structural levels such as culture and history (Bronfenbrenner & Morris, 2006). Therefore, it would be important to look at the multiple relations between the adolescent and their school context, the adolescent and their peers and familial context, the adolescent and their community contexts, as well as the adolescent and their institutional contexts (i.e., government, public policy, criminal justice system) (Lerner et al., 2002). In this way, adolescents are agentic beings in that their cognitive, behavioral, and socioemotional skills contribute to their role as active co-producers of their own development (Lerner et al., 2011). While positive youth development frameworks are optimistic in nature, there is a lack of research that critically examines how the punishment system acts as an oppressive structural context that impacts youth with incarcerated parents across their multiple everyday contexts such as school, family, and community, especially youth who identify as Black, Latinx, Asian, Native Hawaiian/Pacific Islander, and/or Native American. That is, we know little about the population of youth who navigate their adolescence by means of indirect carceral supervision via parental incarceration.

While positive youth development is regarded as the ultimate goal, it is important to deconstruct the structural barriers that exist to hinder youth with incarcerated parents from experiencing healthy development. For example, in one study of 1303 young adults (ages 24–34), those who first experienced parental incarceration before birth or age 1 reported 15% higher depressive symptom scores in young adulthood in comparison to young adults without any parental incarceration histories (Gaston, 2016), suggesting there are long-term implications of parental incarceration for young adults. Given that positive youth development frameworks optimistically view human development, such frameworks may inadvertently render invisible the lived experiences (i.e., adverse childhood experiences) of adolescents experiencing parental incarceration.

Parental Incarceration as an Adverse Childhood Experience

Parental incarceration is conceptualized as one of eleven adverse childhood experiences (ACEs), which are "traumatic experience that serves as pathway for social, emotional, and cognitive neurodevelopmental impairments" (Arditti, 2012, p. 181). The consequences of adverse childhood experiences are known to extend beyond childhood into adolescence and adulthood (Felitti et al., 1998), such as increased risk for sexually transmitted infections, increase in the odds of mental illness, and increased history of substance abuse (Wade Jr. et al., 2016). The other 10 ACEs include physical, sexual, and emotional abuse, physical and emotional neglect, intimate partner violence, violent treatment against mother, substance misuse within household, household mental illness, or parental separation or divorce.

Recent reports and studies have started to document the prevalence of adverse childhood experiences for children of incarcerated parents with some studies breaking down the findings by race/ethnicity and age. A 2015 Child Trends report found that children exposed to parental incarceration experienced almost three additional adverse childhood experiences compared to children not exposed to the experience of parental incarceration. Similarly, Turney (2018) found that children of incarcerated parents were up to seven times more likely to experience an additional ACE compared to their counterparts. By age, adolescents aged 13 to 17 with incarcerated parents experienced the highest number of ACEs. The number of exposures to ACEs was disproportionately concentrated among Black children, followed by multiracial and Hispanic children. Therefore, we intend to also use critical race theory to explore in what ways experiencing parental incarceration across multiple intersectional identities, held especially by youth of color (i.e., Black, Latinx, Asian, Native Hawaiian/Pacific Islander, and Native American youth), contributes to multiple forms of oppression for youth of color as well as the long-term implications (i.e., the successful transition from adolescence to adulthood) it has for adolescent development.

Situating Adolescents and their Families within Punishment System

Researchers, youth programs, schools, and communities must place importance in their understanding of how adolescents of incarcerated parents and their families are embedded in the structural context of the punishment system if they are truly committed to promoting positive youth development. In the last two decades, the US incarceration rate has shown a linear trend upward since 1980–2006 (Pratt, 2018) with small increases in 2014 (Kaeble et al., 2015); therefore adolescents with an incarcerated parent have had to adapt to structural inequalities set forth by mass incarceration such as housing and financial instability, high recidivism rates, and systemic racism as seen in the disproportionate number of incarcerated Black and Latinx mothers and fathers compared to incarcerated White parents (Durose et al., 2014; Geller et al., 2011; Wakefield & Uggen, 2010). Consequently, these structural inequalities can place adolescents of color and their families at risk for experiencing enduring stress (Green et al., 2006). Geographically, the prevalence of parental incarceration across US states has demonstrated how prisons and jails are concentrated in places like Kentucky that held the highest percentage of children with an incarcerated parent at 13%, followed by Indiana with 11% and Alaska, Michigan, New Mexico, Ohio, Oklahoma, and Tennessee with 10% of children who have had a residential parent become incarcerated.

In a concerted effort to bring in youth voices in studies about parental incarceration, Young and Smith (2019) interviewed 14 college students to examine how earlier experiences of parental incarceration and reentry during childhood may impact their current lives as adults. The incarceration of a parent produces a multitude of complex and nuanced types of parent-adult child relationships. For example, while one young adult held a permanently nonexistent relationship with their incarcerated parent, others held temporarily nonexistent relationships with their incarcerated parents such that they were open to building relationships with their incarcerated parent in the future, or other young adults held ongoing, but unstable relationships, or active, but with boundary types of relationships with their previously or currently incarcerated parent (Young & Smith, 2019). This type of relationship continuum allowed for change to occur, such that relationships between young adults and their incarcerated parent moved from negative to sometimes positive (Young & Smith, 2019). Young adults also voiced the ramifications of their parent's incarceration for building trusting relationships with others, such as romantic partners and working through negative emotions such as anger, sadness, and self-doubt that is fueled by stigma associated with one's parental status (Young & Smith, 2019). While not fully unpacked, a small number of young adults were able to develop critical consciousness around structural issues that are associated with incarceration (Young & Smith, 2019).

Researchers have examined the longitudinal effects of paternal incarceration across childhood into young adulthood and found that young adults who reported their father's incarceration were more likely to report a diagnosis of depression or anxiety, were less likely to graduate from college, and simultaneously report lower levels of satisfaction with their personal level of educational attainment (Miller & Barnes, 2015). Further, young adults who experienced paternal incarceration during childhood were more likely to receive public assistance as an adult (Miller & Barnes, 2015). Similarly, mass incarceration as a public health issue has shown that incarceration of a loved one contributes to poorer health in children (and female partners) and may very well contribute to racial health disparities (Wildeman & Wang, 2017).

Further, the US prison boom has altered family dynamics where we have seen a rise in single motherhood (Turney, 2014), economic inequality for men and women, and an overall concentration of childhood disadvantage, especially among Black children and children of parents with lower educational attainment (Wildeman, 2009). Across a 6-year time span (1994–1999), almost 1 in 7 Black children, ages 12–17 years old, experienced parental incarceration (Murphey & Cooper, 2015). Further, Black children were twice as likely to have experienced parental incarceration compared to White children (Murphey & Cooper, 2015). One study highlighted that Latinx children living in California were 2.5 times more likely to experience the incarceration of a family member than their White peers (Forster et al., 2019). In one study that retrospectively examined the prevalence of adverse childhood experiences in American Indian/Alaskan Native incarcerated women, 69% of the women reported having an immediate family member incarcerated (De Ravello et al., 2008). While it is difficult to locate data on Native American adolescents who have experienced parental incarceration, what we do know is that Native American adults were admitted to prison at over 4 times the rate of White adults (Hartney & Vuong, 2009). More specifically, Native American women were 6 times more likely than White females to be admitted to prison (Hartney & Vuong, 2009). The State of Hawaii, for example, has an overrepresentation of Asian and Pacific Islander persons in their state prison, but it should be noted how data tends to aggregate all Asians into one group, ignoring the subgroups that exist within Asia (Hartney & Vuong, 2009). An example of disaggregated data illuminates how out of a sample of 240 Native Hawaiian women under parole supervision, 85% were mothers to nearly 600 children in the state of Hawaii (Brown & Bloom, 2009). Taken together, the implications of parental incarceration on young adult's health and educational and economic outcomes provide a deeper picture of what it means to be positioned as a collateral consequence of mass incarceration, in which the separation between an incarcerated parent, their child(ren), and their families is an informal consequence of conviction (Genty, 2003; Kirk & Wakefield, 2018) .

Adolescents, Parental Incarceration, and COVID-19

In Spring 2020, the USA was hit by a global pandemic caused by coronavirus (COVID-19), an illness caused by a virus that can spread from person to person and led to a pandemic (Centers for Disease Control and Prevention, 2020). While much of the nation took precautions to stay home and practice social distancing to stop the spread, the nature of prisons made social distancing impossible for people incarcerated. Masks, basic hygiene supplies, and testing were not readily available for people incarcerated. Small cells, communal spaces, limited medical care, and staff coming to and from prisons were additional factors that helped to spread the infectious disease inside prison walls, endangering both incarcerated people (especially immunocompromised and elderly people) and staff.

In response, young people, families, communities, and justice-oriented organizations, on behalf of their incarcerated loved ones, mobilized to demand safety, release, and disinvestment from prisons. While many people asked what services and resources could help youth with incarcerated parents, we argue that the best plans in place were the same plans that youth had already created. That is, young people were leading efforts and demands that best served as the blueprint for how the department of corrections must proceed. An example by We Got Us Now, an organization built by, led by, and about children of incarcerated parents, released the following open letter demanding:

1. Immediate clemency for elderly and sickly parents who are the most vulnerable for contracting COVID-19, pose no safety risk, and have aged out of criminality.
2. Free communications (i.e., free phone calls, email, postage mail, and tablet use) in lieu of family visiting that was shut down when COVID-19 hit.
3. A free mobile notification system that provides families in real time updates on prison closures and lockdowns to reduce stress, worry, and trauma in children and families.
4. Safe and sanitary measures for our incarcerated loved ones to receive free medical care, hygiene products, sanitary and clean living environments, and no medical co-pays.

Similarly, over 50 criminal justice reform organizations and coalitions signed a letter demanding the following:

1. Prevent the spread of disease by way of reducing jail, prison, and detention center populations before an outbreak occurs, stopping the cycle of people in and out of jails and detention centers by drastically reducing admissions and holds.
2. Protect, don't exploit, incarcerated people by way of providing people incarcerated with protective gear, an option to opt out of labor that makes them at risk for contracting COVID-19, and pay people, who are in prison, minimum wage.
3. Do not use public health orders to criminalize Black and Brown communities (i.e., stealing supplies and resources for survival).

Even at the state level, organizations fighting for safety, release, and disinvestment from carceral institutions in Arizona (i.e., ReFraming Justice Project, Mass Liberation Arizona, Puente Human Rights Movement) created campaigns demanding release of all people in jails, prisons, and detention centers; suspension of revocations to prison for technical probation and parole violations (e.g., nonpayment of fines); suspension of the number of prison admissions for low-level drug offenses or other short-term, low-risk individuals; and transparency by demanding COVID-19 data to be collected and released publicly and by releasing to the public the existing plan and procedures in place to address COVID-19 within state and federal prisons, jails, and detention centers.

Theoretical Framework

Critical race theory emerged out of critical legal studies (CLS). Law school personnel and culture was predominately White and held conservative notions of racial justice (Crenshaw et al., 1995; Delgado & Stefancic, 2017). Increasingly, law students and law professors in the late 1970s engaged in intellectual inquiries that moved beyond conservative and liberal views of the law to establish CLS as a "political, philosophical and methodological movement in legal academia" (Crenshaw et al., 1995, p. 17). Although CLS was a critical intellectual movement that analyzed class dynamics within a capitalist system, growing frustrations occurred, as scholars of color desired a framework that was attentive to racism and racial power. As such, CRT developed in response to both conservative and liberal ellisons of race and racism. Notably, the underpinnings of CRT have seamlessly crossed over into fields such as education (Ladson-Billings & Tate, 1995). Whereas family science has been slower to the cross-over, scholars like Few (2007) have challenged family science scholarship to move toward integrating Black feminist and critical race feminist frameworks alongside mainstream family theories in order to create culturally sensitive intervention approaches and center the experience of families that have intimately experienced marginalization. While other fields such as family studies and human development have made initial attempts to integrate CRT frameworks into family science (Burton et al., 2010; Few, 2007; Few-Demo, 2014), little progress has been made in other fields such as applied developmental science and positive youth development frameworks to integrate CRT frameworks. However, Clonan-Roy, Jacobs, and Nakkula (2016) are a notable exception by problematizing if the well-known five competencies of positive youth development (i.e., competence, confidence, character, connection, caring, and contribution) are culturally relevant for adolescent girls of color. Their work is necessary to combat how girls of color are differentially viewed outside of the well-established competencies within the positive youth development frameworks. For example, Morris (2016) describes how girls who embody confidence by expressing themselves through their clothing are often hypersexualized and/or sexually harassed via the male gaze and arbitrary dress codes in school settings. Other competencies such as the character competency, defined as youth who possess standards of correct behaviors (Lerner et al., 2005), position Black girls as being labeled as what Morris (2016) describes as "willfully defiant" where adults subjectively label their actions as misbehaviors when Black girls are often just engaging in a notable skill of "standing up for oneself" (Morris, 2016, p. 70). Unfortunately, willfully defiant behaviors often put Black girls at risk for suspension or other means of reprimand (Morris, 2016).

The authors revise the model to include resistance and resilience as additional competencies needed for healthy development in adolescent girls of color as well as situating critical consciousness as a core competency through which all other competencies manifest during and across adolescence (Clonan-Roy et al., 2016).

Major theorists suggest the following tenets are central to critical race theory: (a) the permanency of race and racism in American society; (b) the challenge to dominant ideologies that argue for objectivity, meritocracy, neutrality, and colorblindness; (c) the centrality of experiential knowledge and utilization of counterstorytelling derived from persons of color; (d) revisionist interpretations of history and argues to unveil and deconstruct US race relations law; (e) integrating interdisciplinary perspectives to analyze various forms of oppression across racial, gender, sexual orientation, and class identities; (f) a commitment to social justice and dismantling systems of racial oppression; and (g) intersectionality frameworks to analyze how subjugation and harm are a result of the multiple identities held by women of color that intersect or overlap at one crossroad.

First, critical race theory is cognizant of the role of race and racism in that both are foundational to how the USA is built and functions (Winant, 2007) and infiltrates across micro- and macro-levels of life for non-White persons of color. Critical race theorists hold true to the fact that race is socially constructed to create hierarchies of superior and inferior categories of people such that White people are on top of the hierarchy and people of color are at the lowest level of the hierarchy (Smedley & Smedley, 2005). CRT posits that racism is not random, individual, nor a set of isolated events; rather racism is permanent and an everyday reality of people of color (Bell, 1992; Bonilla-Silva, 1997). Racial realism doesn't take on colorblind notions of all human beings treated equal nor does it endorse the reality that the USA morphed into a post-racial society after the election of Barack Obama, the first

African American president (Delgado & Stefancic, 2017). Second, critical race theory critically deconstructs and challenges dominant liberal ideologies that attempt to argue that large institutions embody objectivity, meritocracy, neutrality, and colorblindness, often referred to as a "a critique of liberalism" (Ladson-Billings & Tate, 1995; Mills, 2008; Milner IV, 2008). For example, notions of objectivity and neutrality construct an argument that laws and legal policies are impartial and apolitical (Parker & Lynn, 2002). Further, colorblind explanations of meritocracy posit that merit does not discriminate by race, ethnicity, nationality, gender, and sexuality. However, a critical race theoretical lens would propel CRT theorists or "Crits" to provide a critique of liberalism, such that the secondary effects of parental incarceration on children, youth, and families call into question how the punishment system is considered impartial, fair, or just, whether it is families adapting to the prison culture while visiting loved ones inside prisons (Comfort, 2008); the disproportionate number of women who bear the financial, physical, and emotional costs associated with having an incarcerated loved one (Clayton et al., 2018); or the way public policy works to exclude women, with felony convictions, from housing, employment, and nutritional assistance, which denies them of providing care for their children (Bloom, Owen, & Covington, 2004). Third, critical race theory holds true to the principle where people of color are valued and humanized for their experiential knowledge (Yosso, 2006). Therefore, people of color must be at the forefront of analyzing law and systems of oppression as it directly relates to their lived experiences; this concept is also called legal storytelling (Delgado & Stefancic, 2017). Counterstorytelling or counterstories are real-life stories that are told by groups of people who have historically experienced marginalization at the hands of dominant groups (Delgado, 1989). Counterstories function to disrupt the status quo and counterbeliefs, stereotypes, and ideologies that the dominant group often imposes on marginalized groups of people (Delgado, 1989; Espino 2012; Solórzano & Bernal, 2001). It is important to note that counterstories do not merely respond to dominant or majoritarian storytelling because doing so would re-center dominant stories (Yosso, 2006). Instead, counterstories function to record the experiences of racism from the perspectives of people harmed by its enduring impacts as well as document how people of color resist racist practices, discourses, and institutions and strive to a world that is rid of social and racial injustices (Yosso, 2006). In this way, counterstories have the potential to transform everyday environments and institutions that people of color navigate (Bernal, 2002).

Fourth, critical race theory is rooted in revisionist interpretations of history and argues that history plays a central role in unveiling and deconstructing US race relations law (Delgado & Stefancic, 2013). Critical race theorists denounce an ahistorical approach in analyzing social phenomenon, such as the school-to-prison pipeline, racial profiling, and the disproportionate number of people of color who are incarcerated, because by doing so, ahistorical interpretations of history ignore the ways the social construction of race and racism contributed to the creation of dominant and subjugated groups of people via historical events such as school desegregation, war on drugs, and privatization of prisons (Delgado & Stefancic, 2017).

Fifth, critical race theory utilizes an interdisciplinary perspective that allows for collaboration across multiple fields of knowledge to interrogate "racism, classism, sexism, and homophobia" (Yosso, 2006, p. 8). In this way, critical race theory is open to being applied across disciplines such as education, criminology, and family studies. In fact, CRT may be a theoretical tool to bridge fields together that are not commonly connected such as developmental science and criminology. Sixth, critical race theory challenges theorists to be committed to social justice that is conceptualized as society rid of racial oppression that often intersects with other forms of subordination (Matsuda, 1991). In many ways, critical race theory seeks not only to deconstruct systems of oppression but also to disrupt and ultimately dismantle systems of oppression.

Finally, the seventh theme rooted in CRT looks at how, historically, Black women have been subjected to courts of law that refused to acknowledge that the intersection of both sex discrimination and race discrimination is one in the same, reinforcing the problematic message that Black women do not merit protection (Crenshaw, 1989). In legal settings, the notion of either/or had negative implications for Black women who sought to challenge policies and practices that uniquely discriminated against them based on both race and sex because their claims of race and sex discrimination were seen as exclusionary against white women or divisive against Black men (Crenshaw, 1989). Thus, intersectionality was coined by Kimberlé Crenshaw (1989) to examine how women are marginalized because of their dual identity of both women *and* women of color. Notably, the history of intersectionality emerged from a collective group of Black feminists, known as the Combahee River Collective, who actively fought for an end to multiple oppressions (i.e., racial, sexual, class oppression) and argued in their 1977 statement for an examination of how these multiple oppressions work in tandem to contribute to multifaceted social inequalities in Black women's lives (Taylor, 2017). A deeper examination into the history of intersectionality uncovers how Chicana feminists in the 1970s and 1980s engaged in intersectional discourses through anthologies alongside women of color from different race, class, gender, ethnic, linguistic, national, religious, and sexual orientation backgrounds (Hill Collins & Bilge, 2016). In the early 1970s and late 1980s, Asian American feminism used intersectional principles to deconstruct the lived experiences of Asian American women from various ethnic and national backgrounds (Hill Collins & Bilge, 2016). Further, indigenous feminisms integrated discourses on how colonialism, alongside patriarchy, white supremacy, poverty, and heteronormativity, worked to create social and structural inequalities faced by Indigenous/Native women, who actively resisted against (settler) colonialism since 1492 (Hill Collins & Bilge, 2016).

Moreover, intersectionality challenges "single issue analyses" and, instead, critically analyzes how subjugation and harm are a result of the multiple identities of Black women that intersect or overlap at one crossroad (Crenshaw, 1989). Today, an intersectional analysis goes beyond antiracist and feminist perspectives by demonstrating how intersections of multiple oppressions create systemic policies and practices that reinforce the subordination of women of color through the lack of "collective support and social justice advocacy on their behalf" within the punishment system, for example (Crenshaw, 2012, p. 26).

Counterstories as Theory, Praxis, and Pedagogy

While these tenets are often parallel to each other, we focus on the importance of experiential knowledge embedded within adolescents of color who experience parental incarceration to unveil how systemic racism acts as a barrier to positive youth development, the primary dominant framework within developmental science. Further, within counterstories, we focus on the unique experiences of adolescents of color navigating parental incarceration and construct an argument that parental status (i.e., incarcerated versus non-incarcerated parent) further subjugates adolescents of color. It is our hope that utilizing counterstories through a CRT lens acts as a pedagogical (i.e., striving for racial realist accounts of parental incarceration through adolescents' counterstories), methodological (i.e., person-centered approaches to centering the intersectional identities of adolescents of color; Huber, 2009), and theoretical tool (i.e., critiquing liberalism's notions of objectivity, neutrality, and interest convergence) that contributes to the elimination of systemic oppression that has positioned adolescents of color as collateral consequences of mass incarceration, which is historically built on and upheld by racial oppression. That is, critical race theory refutes an ahistorical view of the arrival, development, and expansion of prisons. Instead, a critical race theoretical lens unveils the link between slavery and modern-day punishment systems such that after US slavery was abolished, the construction of black codes in the US South subjectively criminalized Black people for possessing firearms, missing work, breaking job contracts, and vagrancy (Davis, 2013). These oppressive codes contributed to the newly constructed criminal justice system and convict lease system that incarcerated free Black people in the US South that many considered the "reincarnation of slavery" (Davis, 2013, p. 29). In the 1980s, politicians argued for tough on crime policies that included longer prison sentences and harsher formats of imprisonment (i.e., super maximum-security prisons) to pander to people's desire to have lowered crime rates in their communities (Davis, 2013). Instead, tough on crime policies drastically increased the prison population and led to the expansion of more prison facilities to accommodate the growing population of incarcerated people (Davis, 2013). Further, the rapid expansion of prisons morphed the US prison system into the prison industrial complex because of the ways corporations were involved in the "construction, provision of goods and services, and use of prison labor" (Davis, 2013, p. 12). The arrival, development, and expansion of the US prison system have disproportionally impacted Black, indigenous, people of color and can be traced back to the chattel slavery system that enslaved African people (Wacquant, 2002).

The Real(Ist) Counterstory of Adolescents of Color Experiencing Parental Incarceration

Racial realism requires individuals with subordinate status to recognize that race and racism are in multiple forms, extend beyond the individual, and are embedded in all spaces. Those who hold subordinate statuses are advised to adopt a racial realist mentality to (1) avoid hopelessness and (2) to liberate their minds as means to reimagine the world and enact strategies that resist against racist structures in a way that brings about "fulfillment and even triumph" (Bell, 1992, p. 373). The words that Derrick Bell wrote provide a straightforward perspective of examining the ways the punishment system continues to be upheld, despite temporal peaks and subsequent lulls in progress, and how racial realist accounts can emerge from counterstories told by adolescents of color experiencing parental incarceration. For example, scholars have documented the reality that one in nine Black children has a parent behind bars on any given day and 25% Black children will experience their parent being incarcerated for at least 1 year (Sykes & Pettit, 2014). This disproportionate number of parental incarcerations experienced by Black children and children of parents without a high school education demonstrates how the punishment system perpetuates race and class inequality.

For youth of incarcerated parents, incarceration reproduces complex families in ways that can reproduce childhood disadvantage (Sykes & Pettit, 2014). For example, given that noncustodial incarcerated parents are unable to financially contribute to their child's well-being during incarceration, this puts strain on the romantic relationship between the incarcerated and non-incarcerated parent and can result in relationship dissolution (Sykes & Pettit, 2014), thus altering a child's family dynamic. Similarly, youth with formerly incarcerated parent(s) are also more likely to experience financial instability because system-involved parents often experience reduced employment and economic opportunities (Uggen et al., 2004). Researchers have further documented how youth with incarcerated mothers are more likely to enter the foster care system when their mother is convicted (Kirk & Wakefield, 2018).

To this end, adopting a racial realist approach through counterstories may allow adolescents of color to be fully aware of the punishment system's regime and thus create strategies to resist racial oppression.

However, it is important to ensure that adolescents of color do not fall into despair once they become aware of their subordinate status as children of incarcerated parents. From a pedagogical standpoint, racial realism can be taught alongside the concept of critical hope for adolescents. Critical hope is conceptualized as going beyond traditional notions of hope to engage youth and adults in a process that interrogates the root of systemic oppressions, examines and validates pain, and looks to transform it in the communities around them (Duncan-Andrade, 2009). Rooted in critical pedagogy in urban schools that are located in under-resourced and underserved communities, critical hope is used as a tool and a practice for educators to teach their students to link their experiences of systemic oppression to actionable responses that provide relief from suffering (Duncan-Andrade, 2009). The transformative aspect of critical hope explicitly rejects despair that is often associated with understanding social inequalities (Duncan-Andrade, 2009). Further, critical hope challenges the overly optimistic perspectives of positive youth development as fleeting and instead positions adolescents of color, experiencing parental incarceration, in the active struggle against systems of oppressions. To this end, we argue that racial realism, in conjunction with critical hope, can be used as a pedagogical tool when constructing counterstories with adolescents of color who have experienced parental incarceration.

Interest Convergence and the Transition to Adulthood for Youth of Incarcerated Parents

Earlier scholarship on interest convergence, a principle of critical race theory, is applied to teacher education (Milner IV, 2008) and school desegregation law (Bell, 1980). In relation to the punishment system, the principle of interest convergence can be a useful "analytical, explanatory, and conceptual tool" (Milner IV, 2008), to examine policies and practices in youth programs that aim to promote positive youth development in adolescents of color who experience parental incarceration. Interest convergence argues that racial equality and equity for persons of color will only be achieved when it converges with the interests, beliefs, and values of White people (Milner IV, 2008). Consequently, this reality contributes to change that is deliberately incremental with the dominant group in power often acting as the architect of such gradual progression (Milner IV, 2008). We argue that reform to the criminal justice system has been incremental, at best, for incarcerated parents and their children and families.

While the notion of interest convergence offers some appeal with respect to how changes for racial equity may occur, Guinier (2004) reframes the notion of interest convergence to what she terms "interest divergence." In Guinier's estimation interest divergence most accurately captures how ultimately short-lived and limited racial reforms are. More precisely, interest divergence illustrates how laws and policies may be contrary to transformative racial justice, reproducing or reimagining the inequalities they purport to address. For instance, Delgado and Stefancic (2007) discuss how the war on drugs was a failure. While drug rehabilitation and needle exchange programs were known to be more cost-effective and yield more positive outcomes in comparison to mandatory-minimum sentencing protocols that devastated Black and Brown communities, such treatment and programs did not converge with White people's morals of law-abiding citizen versus criminal (Crenshaw, 1988), the financial interests of private prisons run by corporations, or political parties who relied on voter disenfranchisement (Delgado & Stefancic, 2007).

While under the carceral gaze of the punishment system, research has illuminated how parental incarceration further complicates, penalizes, and disrupts adolescents' transition to adulthood through experiences that maintain inequality such that adolescents experience an accelerated life course (Turney & Lanuza, 2017), significantly lowered earnings, higher mental health problems, and decreased probability in achieving higher education in comparison to young adults who do not experience parental incarceration (Mears & Siennick, 2016). Further, scholars have examined the sociopolitical consequences of familial incarceration in that the punishment system operates as an agent of political socialization and threatens civic engagement for young adults with incarcerated parents (Lee et al., 2014). More specifically, young adults of incarcerated parents are less likely to have voted in the last election, have little trust in government entities, and perceive discrimination on a daily basis (Lee et al., 2014).

Yet, while understanding that a group of adolescents will experience inequality or inequity, efforts to pass common sense sentencing reform legislation, abolish current policies that terminate parental rights for incarcerated parents whose children are placed in foster care for longer than 15 months (i.e., Adoption and Safe Families Act), and implement the Children of Incarcerated Parents Bill of Rights across all settings that youth interact with do not converge with the interests of White people in power. It is plausible to think that White people in power feel that rights given to adolescents of color with incarcerated parents may alter the status or rights of adolescents who do not experience incarceration.

We extend our argument to deconstruct how youth programs that serve adolescents of color with incarcerated parents may be at risk for being complicit in upholding the interests of the punishment system. For example, youth programs provide just enough resources for Black, Latinx, Asian, Native Hawaiian/Pacific Islander, and Native American youth and their families to deal with parental incarceration. However, these resources are not enough to contribute to decarceration of parents, abolish notions of second-class citizenship upon reentry, and eradicate policies that funnel parents into the prison industrial complex in the first place, as such resources do not converge with the interests of private prison corporations, tough on crime legislators, and leaders within the punishment system. That is, liberation for adolescents of color who have experienced parental incarceration does not serve the interest of those in power. As well intentioned as positive youth development programs are structured, true liberation from the punishment system is kept at bay as the nonprofit industrial complex forces many organizations to prioritize funding sources over satisfying their mission to pursue social justice (Samimi, 2010). Historically, marginalized groups who sought to create nonprofit organizations to alter systems of power and achieve social justice for their respective communities were denied authorization to exist, as doing so did not converge with the government's interest to preserve religious, racial, and gender oppression (Samimi, 2010). It is plausible to think that nonprofits dedicated to serving adolescents of color who have incarcerated parents have a harder time receiving funding to sustainably exist given that dominant society strategically labels incarcerated parents as felons, ex-cons, prisoners, and inmates that only serve to devoid them and their children of humanness. Scholars argue that grassroots coalitions that are member-led and community-based and replace traditional funding sources with grassroots funding techniques are better equipped to address the root causes of structural violence and promote social justice (Fox & Turner, 2016; Samimi, 2010).

The Intersectional Lived Experiences of Adolescents Experiencing Parental Incarceration

Counterstories act as a methodological tool that adopts person-centered approaches to centering the intersectional identities of adolescents of color. For example, because adolescent girls of color with incarcerated parents can be harmed as a woman and as a woman of color, we argue that adults have a responsibility to think critically about intersectional components of identity and power that "contribute to the surveillance, punishment, and mass incarceration of women of color" (Crenshaw, 2012, p. 23). While liberalism would have us believe that the law is neutral and objective, Kimberlé Crenshaw (2012) unveils how intersectional points of oppression for Black girls are tragically intertwined alongside their Black mothers such that minor drug offenses often result in Black mothers having their parental rights terminated under the guise of 1997 Adoption and Safe Families Act. That is, the punishment system violently spills over into the lives of daughters by imposing its structural violence onto their bodies. Thus, identifying as an adolescent girl of color along with the identity as a daughter of an incarcerated parent(s) gives evidence to how adolescents are positioned as informal collateral consequences in the age of mass incarceration. Therefore, counterstories using an intersectional lens help to debunk myths that adolescents of color with incarcerated parents are a homogenous group of adolescents. For example, Davis and Shlafer (2017) examined mental health outcomes by comparing young adults (on average, students were 14 years old) with currently incarcerated parents, young adults with formerly incarcerated parents, and young adults with no history of parental incarceration. Mental health outcome variables included measures on suicide ideation, suicide attempt, self-injury behaviors, and diagnosis of a mental, emotional, or behavior problem. The authors found that girls of incarcerated parents were at greater risk for poor mental health outcomes. Further, scholars have used a gendered pathway lens to unpack the nuance of parental incarceration for young adults and found that maternal incarceration was more predictive of adult daughters' contact with the punishment system (i.e., arrest, conviction, and incarceration) than paternal incarceration (Burgess-Procter et al., 2016) whereas paternal incarceration was more predictive of sons' contact with the punishment system (i.e., arrest, conviction, and incarceration) than maternal incarceration (Burgess-Procter et al., 2016).

As a theoretical and pedagogical tool, it is critical for positive youth development programs to adopt and implement an intersectional lens in working with adolescents of color experiencing parental incarceration as there is variation in how different adolescents experience parental incarceration across their many identities. Positive youth development programs emphasize and seek to cultivate healthy adult-youth relationships that are supposed to be culturally bound and individualized across age, gender, and adolescents' prior experiences (Eccles & Gootman, 2002). Intersectionality can be a pedagogy where directors, coordinators, and adult staff are explicitly taught how to be a resource to adolescents of color experiencing parental incarceration in a way that recognizes how these adolescents negotiate systems of oppression across their life course (Few-Demo, 2014). For adolescents of color, harm can be a result of various intersectional identities such as race, class, gender, and sexual orientation, to name a few. However, we argue that parental status (i.e., mother and/or father is a current or former incarcerated parent) is another identity that intersects with race, gender, and sexuality to further subjugate sons and daughters during, across, and beyond adolescence. That is, intersectionality frameworks position positive youth development programs to be cognizant about how adolescents are situated by multiple social locations especially with how their social identity as a son or daughter of an incarcerated parent(s) overlaps in different contexts (Few-Demo, 2014). As a methodological tool, adolescents of color experiencing parental incarceration can create counterstories that use an intersectional lens to analyze various forms of oppression across racial, gender, sexual orientation, and class identities. For example, Maisha T. Winn's (2010a) work with formerly incarcerated Black girls utilizes practices, such as writings and performing arts, to center girls' voices who are directly impacted by incarceration. In this way, creating and sharing stories that embody the lived experience of Black and Brown girls' contact with punishment systems can mobilize individuals to "respond, organize and act" (Winn, 2010a, p. 315). That is, "writing, reading, speaking, and performing" stories transcend girls from both in real time and figurative notions of incarceration (Winn, 2010b) by providing Black girls opportunities to critically analyze the punishment systems that confine them and re-imagine their futures outside of youth punishment facilities. An important caveat that Winn (2010a) unpacks is the reality that while storytelling through writing and performing provides opportunities for Black and Brown girls to "rewrite lives and perform possible futures," Black and Brown girls must have access to educational, economic (i.e., safe and affordable housing), and employment resources as means to build power rather than prioritize building programs.

(Counter)stories that expose the realities of what it means to navigate the world possessing identities that are multiplicative can disrupt dominant narratives that try to paint the picture that the law, especially criminal (in)justice systems, are neutral, objective, and fair for all.

Positive Youth Development and the Criminal (in)Justice System

Critical race theorists call into question notions of equality, objectivity, and neutrality that are supposed to be achieved through law (Greene, 1989). We argue that parental incarceration further entrenches adolescents of color in systems of oppression. Parental incarceration is rooted within a state punishment and policy regime that is often referred to as the US criminal justice system. As such, scholars have investigated how exclusionary practices imposed on youth with incarcerated parents are produced by calculated social policies that have intergenerational effects between parent and child especially during the child's transition from childhood to adulthood; unfold across multiple institutions such as economic, school, and labor markets; and are intersectional in that the gender and racial/ethnic identities interact with parental incarceration to produce various social inequalities (Foster & Hagan, 2015). For example, schools can act as sites of surveillance that may instill fear in parents who may have histories of contact with the law because students are tracked via formal records of their personal and academic history, the presence of school resource officers (i.e., police officers) and security is pervasive, and families are closely linked to local agencies (Haskins & Jacobsen, 2017). Parental fear may contribute to a reduction in parental academic involvement (Haskins & Jacobsen, 2017). The reality is that adolescents of color are at higher risk for being subjected to social exclusion that is structurally set up to shut them out of society (Foster & Hagan, 2015), providing more evidence to the way liberalism is racialized (Mills, 2008), such that individual rights and freedoms are only afforded to White adolescents and families even in the context of parental incarceration.

More importantly, the lived experiences of adolescents of color experiencing incarceration refute the claim that the same law that imprisons parents is a law that is neutral, impartial, or equal. For example, Comfort (2003, 2008) explains how family members of incarcerated loved ones experience secondary prisonization where they are subjected to the similar stringent regulations, invasive surveillance, and physical imprisonment, especially during visiting. In this way, adolescents and family members are indirectly prisonized in that they are "both captive and free" (Comfort, 2008, p. 16) and are forced to "adapt to carceral norms and structures of prison and jail" even as legally free individuals (Aiello & McCorkel, 2018). Refusing to acknowledge this reality is negligent in the struggle toward liberation.

While it can be argued that the creation of the 2003 Children of Incarcerated Parents Bill of Rights gave equal rights alongside scholarship that argues children and adolescents of incarcerated parents have a constitutional right to a parental relationship with their mother and/or father (Boudin, 2011), counterstories may be a tool for adolescents of color to unveil the truths of how their rights have or have not been considered across school, positive youth development programs, and of course within carceral settings. Counterstories may also be a tool to ask what an alternative justice system or anti-punishment system looks like for adolescents who have formerly or currently incarcerated family members. It is plausible that adolescents may use their counterstories to reimagine what justice looks like without mass incarceration. Instead, they may cultivate demands and solutions that require full investment into their overall well-being (i.e., mental, physical, economic, and emotional well-being). Similarly, adolescents may demand full investment (i.e., money and time) into their own leadership development in ways that position them to create policy, direct non-profits, and cultivate grassroots organizations to organize against the social issue of mass incarceration or congregate a network of directly impacted children of incarcerated parents.

Counterstories can position adolescents of color as subject matter experts to advocate for the intersectional needs of adolescents with currently and formerly incarcerated parents and to put into action alternatives to punishment plans that youth have already helped to co-create with communities (i.e., Young Women's Freedom Center, Northern CA; Youth Justice Coalition, Southern, CA; and Puente Youth Program, AZ).

Discussion

The current paper attempted to analyze and deconstruct the experiences of parental incarceration for adolescents who identify as Black, Latinx, Asian, Native Hawaiian/Pacific Islander, and Native American from a critical race theory lens. In particular, we sought to identify gaps located within heavily popularized positive youth development frameworks that often fail to recognize how systems of oppression act as a barrier for adolescents who have been historically marginalized. While positive youth development should be attainable by all youth, questioning the ways that the punishment system impedes and excludes adolescents of color with incarcerated parents from engaging in this developmental process is necessary. Given that adolescence is a developmental time period ripe with changes needed to achieve autonomy, identity, and intimacy, among other key developmental tasks, it is necessary to investigate how the stigma and second-class citizenship imposed on incarcerated parents (Uggen et al., 2004) can also be imposed on adolescents of color. For example, researchers have detailed how feelings of shame and embarrassment about their parent's incarceration interfere with adolescents' attempts to develop friendships (Cochran et al., 2018). Consequently, adolescents of incarcerated parents, grappling with feelings of stigma, may have difficulty forming their identity and can put them at risk for experiencing social exclusion or isolation from their peers (Saunders, 2018).

To this end, we argued for the utilization of counterstorytelling as a powerful tool to unveil systemic racism experienced by adolescents of color who must navigate through their adolescence as sons and daughters of incarcerated parents. Stovall (2016) challenges us, especially as a directly impacted researcher (e.g., the first author), to be cognizant that our liberation will not be achieved by a theoretical construct or by a single person. We argue that the challenge is also applied to youth programs, practitioners, and academia that can often exist in silos. In contrast, it will be a coalition of adolescents, their families, local communities, positive youth development programs, and progressive research institutes, who are collectively devoted to engaging in both action and reflection (Stovall, 2016). We use critical race theory to carry out a form of subversive scholarship that "contests, refutes, and offers a different reality" (Stovall, 2016, p. 282) than the realities set forth by the punishment system.

References

Aiello, B. L., & McCorkel, J. A. (2018). 'It will crush you like a bug': Maternal incarceration, secondary prisonization, and children's visitation. *Punishment & Society, 20*(3), 351–374.

Arditti, J. A. (2012). Child trauma within the context of parental incarceration: A family process perspective. *Journal of Family Theory & Review, 4*(3), 181–219.

Arnett, J. J. (2014). *Adolescence and emerging adulthood*. Pearson Education.

Bell, D. A. (1980). Brown v. Board of Education and the interest-convergence dilemma. *Harvard Law Review, 93*, 518–533.

Bell, D. (1992). Racial realism. *Connecticut Law Review, 24*, 363–379.

Bernal, D. D. (2002). Critical race theory, Latino critical theory, and critical raced-gendered epistemologies: Recognizing students of color as holders and creators of knowledge. *Qualitative Inquiry, 8*(1), 105–126.

Bloom, B., Owen, B., & Covington, S. (2004). Women offenders and the gendered effects of public policy. *Review of Policy Research, 21*(1), 31–48.

Bonilla-Silva, E. (1997). Rethinking racism: Toward a structural interpretation. *American Sociological Review, 62*(3), 465–480.

Boudin, C. (2011). Children of incarcerated parents: The child's constitutional right to the family relationship. *Journal of Criminal Law & Criminology, 101*, 77–118.

Bronfenbrenner, U., & Morris, P. A. (2006). The bioecological model of human development. In W. Damon & R. M. Lerner (Eds.), *Handbook of child psychology: Theoretical models of human development* (6th ed.). Wiley.

Brown, M., & Bloom, B. E. (2009). Colonialism and carceral motherhood: Native Hawaiian families under corrections and child welfare control. *Feminist Criminology, 4*(2), 151–169.

Burgess-Proctor, A., Huebner, B. M., & Durso, J. M. (2016). Comparing the effects of maternal and paternal incarceration on adult daughters' and sons' criminal justice system involvement: A gendered pathways analysis. *Criminal Justice and Behavior, 43*(8), 1034–1055.

Burton, L. M., Bonilla-Silva, E., Ray, V., Buckelew, R., & Hordge Freeman, E. (2010). Critical race theories, colorism, and the decade's research on families of color. *Journal of Marriage and Family, 72*(3), 440–459.

Clayton, G., Richardson, E., Mandlin, L., & Farr, B. (2018). *Because She's powerful: The political isolation and resistance of women with incarcerated loved ones*. Essie Justice Group.

Clonan-Roy, K., Jacobs, C. E., & Nakkula, M. J. (2016). Towards a model of positive youth development specific to girls of color: Perspectives on development, resilience, and empowerment. *Gender Issues, 33*(2), 96–121.

Cochran, J. C., Siennick, S. E., & Mears, D. P. (2018). Social exclusion and parental incarceration impacts on adolescents' networks and school engagement. *Journal of Marriage and Family, 80*(2), 478–498.

Comfort, M. L. (2003). In the tube at san Quentin: The "secondary prisonization" of women visiting inmates. *Journal of Contemporary Ethnography, 32*(1), 77–107.

Comfort, M. (2008). *Doing time together: Love and family in the shadow of the prison*. The University of Chicago Press.

Crenshaw, K. W. (1988). Race, reform, and retrenchment: Transformation and legitimation in antidiscrimination law. *Harvard Law Review, 101*, 1331–1387.

Crenshaw, K. (1989). Demarginalizing the intersection of race and sex: A black feminist critique of antidiscrimination doctrine, feminist theory and antiracist politics. *University of Chicago Legal Forum, 1989*, 139–167.

Crenshaw, K. W. (2012). From private violence to mass incarceration: Thinking intersectionally about women, race, and social control. *UCLA Law Review, 59*, 1418–1472.

Crenshaw, K., Gotanda, N., Peller, G., & Thomas, K. (1995). *Critical race theory: The key writings that formed the movement*. The New Press.

Davis, A. Y. (2013). *Are prisons obsolete?* Seven Stories Press.

Davis, L., & Shlafer, R. J. (2017). Mental health of adolescents with currently and formerly incarcerated parents. *Journal of Adolescence, 54*, 120–134.

De Ravello, L., Abeita, J., & Brown, P. (2008). Breaking the cycle/mending the hoop: Adverse childhood experiences among incarcerated American Indian/Alaska native women in New Mexico. *Health Care for Women International, 29*(3), 300–315.

Delgado, R. (1989). Storytelling for oppositionists and others: A plea for narrative. *Michigan Law Review, 87*(8), 2411–2441.

Delgado, R., & Stefancic, J. (2007). Critical race theory and criminal justice. *Humanity and Society, 31*(2–3), 133–145.

Delgado, R., & Stefancic, J. (2013). Discerning critical moments. In *Handbook of critical race theory in education* (pp. 43–53). Routledge.

Delgado, R., & Stefancic, J. (2017). *Critical race theory: An introduction*. NYU Press.

Duncan-Andrade, J. (2009). Note to educators: Hope required when growing roses in concrete. *Harvard Educational Review, 79*(2), 181–194.

Durose, M. R., Cooper, A. D., & Snyder, H. N. (2014). *Recidivism of prisoners released in 30 states in 2005: Patterns from 2005 to 2010*. US Department of Justice, Office of Justice Programs, Bureau of Justice Statistics.

Eccles, J. S., & Gootman, J. A. (2002). Features of positive developmental settings. In J. S. Eccles & J. A. Gootman (Eds.), *Community programs to promote youth development* (pp. 86–118). National Academy Press.

Espino, M. M. (2012). Seeking the" truth" in the stories we tell: The role of critical race epistemology in higher education research. *The Review of Higher Education, 36*(1), 31–67.

Emory, A. (2018). Explaining the consequences of paternal incarceration for children's behavioral problems. *Family Relations, 67*, 302–319. https://doi.org/10.1111/fare.12301.

Felitti, V., Anda, R., Nordenberg, D., Williamson, D., Spitz, A., Edwards, V., et al. (1998). Relationship of childhood abuse and household dysfunction to many of the leading causes of death in adults: The adverse childhood experiences (ACE) study. *American Journal of Preventive Medicine, 14*, 245–258.

Few, A. L. (2007). Integrating black consciousness and critical race feminism into family studies research. *Journal of Family Issues, 28*(4), 452–473.

Few-Demo, A. L. (2014). Intersectionality as the "new" critical approach in feminist family studies: Evolving racial/ethnic feminisms and critical race theories. *Journal of Family Theory & Review, 6*(2), 169–183.

Forster, M., Davis, L., Shlafer, R., & Unger, J. B. (2019). Household incarceration and salient emerging adult role transitions: Findings from an urban sample of Hispanic youth. *Emerging Adulthood, 7*(1), 3–11.

Foster, H., & Hagan, J. (2015). Punishment regimes and the multilevel effects of parental incarceration: Intergenerational, intersectional, and interinstitutional models of social inequality and systemic exclusion. *Annual Review of Sociology, 41*, 135–158.

Fox, K. H., & Turner, R. (2016). Shifting the locus of power in public engagement: The revolution will not be funded by the non-profit industrial complex. *Mitchell Hamline Law Review, 42*, 1508–1518.

Gaston, S. (2016). The long-term effects of parental incarceration: Does parental incarceration in childhood or adolescence predict depressive symptoms in adulthood? *Criminal Justice and Behavior, 43*(8), 1056–1075.

Geller, A., Garfinkel, I., & Western, B. (2011). Paternal incarceration and support for children in fragile families. *Demography, 48*(1), 25–47.

Genty, P. M. (2003). Damage to family relationships as a collateral consequence of parental incarceration. *Fordham Urban Law Journal, 30*, 1671–1684.

Green, K. M., Ensminger, M. E., Robertson, J. A., & Juon, H. S. (2006). Impact of adult sons' incarceration on African American mothers' psychological distress. *Journal of Marriage and Family, 68*(2), 430–441.

Greene, L. S. (1989). Race in the 21st century: Equality through law. *Tulane Law Review, 64*, 1533–1538.

Hartney, C., & Vuong, L. (2009). *Created equal: Racial and ethnic disparities in the US justice system*. National Council on Crime and Delinquency.

Haskins, A. R., & Jacobsen, W. C. (2017). Schools as surveilling institutions? Paternal incarceration, system avoidance, and parental involvement in schooling. *American Sociological Review, 82*(4), 657–684.

Hill Collins, P. H., & Bilge, S. (2016). *Intersectionality*. Polity.

Huber, L. P. (2009). Disrupting apartheid of knowledge: Testimonio as methodology in Latina/o critical race research in education. *International Journal of Qualitative Studies in Education, 22*(6), 639–654.

Kaeble, D., Glaze, L., Tsoutis, A., & Minton, T. (2015). *Correctional populations in the United States, 2014*. US Department of Justice, Bureau of Justice Statistics.

Kirk, D. S., & Wakefield, S. (2018). Collateral consequences of punishment: A critical review and path forward. *Annual Review of Criminology, 1*, 171–194.

Ladson-Billings, G., & Tate, W. F. (1995). Toward a critical race theory of education. *Teachers College Record, 97*(1), 47.

Lee, H., Porter, L. C., & Comfort, M. (2014). Consequences of family member incarceration: Impacts on civic participation and perceptions of the legitimacy and fairness of government. *The Annals of the American Academy of Political and Social Science, 651*(1), 44–73.

Lerner, R. M., Brentano, C., Dowling, E. M., & Anderson, P. M. (2002). Positive youth development: Thriving as the basis of personhood and civil society. *New Directions for Youth Development, 95*, 11–34.

Lerner, R. M., Almerigi, J. B., Theokas, C., & Lerner, J. V. (2005). Positive youth development: A view of the issues. *The Journal of Early Adolescence, 25*(1), 10–16.

Lerner, R. M., Lerner, J. V., & Benson, J. B. (2011). Positive youth development: Research and applications for promoting thriving in adolescence. In *Advances in Child Development and Behavior* (pp. 1–17).

Matsuda, M. J. (1991). Voices of America: Accent, antidiscrimination law, and a jurisprudence for the last reconstruction. *Yale Law Journal*, 1329–1407.

Mears, D. P., & Siennick, S. E. (2016). Young adult outcomes and the life-course penalties of parental incarceration. *Journal of Research in Crime and Delinquency, 53*(1), 3–35.

Miller, H. V., & Barnes, J. C. (2015). The association between parental incarceration and health, education, and economic outcomes in young adulthood. *American Journal of Criminal Justice, 40*(4), 765–784.

Mills, C. W. (2008). Racial liberalism. *PMLA, 123*(5), 1380–1397.

Milner, H. R., IV. (2008). Critical race theory and interest convergence as analytic tools in teacher education policies and practices. *Journal of Teacher Education, 59*(4), 332–346.

Morris, M. (2016). *Pushout: The criminalization of black girls in schools*. The New Press.

Murphey, D., & Cooper, P. M. (2015). *Parents behind bars: What happens to their children*. Child Trends. Retrieved from http://www.childtrends.org/wpcontent/uploads/2015/10/2015-42ParentsBehindBars.pdf

Parker, L., & Lynn, M. (2002). What's race got to do with it? Critical race theory's conflicts with and connections to qualitative research methodology and epistemology. *Qualitative Inquiry, 8*(1), 7–22.

Pratt, T. C. (2018). *Addicted to incarceration: Corrections policy and the politics of misinformation in the United States*. Sage Publications.

Samimi, J. C. (2010). Funding America's nonprofits: The nonprofit industrial complex's hold on social justice. *Columbia Social Work Review, 1*, 17–25.

Saunders, V. (2018). What does your dad do for a living? Children of prisoners and their experiences of stigma. *Children and Youth Services Review, 90*, 21–27.

Silbereisen, R. K., & Lerner, R. M. (2007). Approaches to positive youth development: A view of the issues. In R. K. Silbereisen & R. M. Lerner (Eds.), *Approaches to positive youth development* (pp. 3–30). Sage Publications.

Smedley, A., & Smedley, B. D. (2005). Race as biology is fiction, racism as a social problem is real: Anthropological and historical perspectives on the social construction of race. *American Psychologist, 60*(1), 16.

Solórzano, D. G., & Bernal, D. D. (2001). Examining transformational resistance through a critical race and LatCrit theory framework: Chicana and Chicano students in an urban context. *Urban Education, 36*(3), 308–342.

Stovall, D. (2016). Out of adolescence and into adulthood: Critical race theory, retrenchment, and the imperative of praxis. *Urban Education, 51*(3), 274–286.

Sykes, B. L., & Pettit, B. (2014). Mass incarceration, family complexity, and the reproduction of childhood disadvantage. *The Annals of the American Academy of Political and Social Science, 654*(1), 127–149.

Taylor, K. Y. (Ed.). (2017). *How we get free: Black feminism and the Combahee River collective*. Haymarket Books.

Turney, K. (2014). Stress proliferation across generations? Examining the relationship between parental incarceration and childhood health. *Journal of Health and Social Behavior, 55*(3), 302–319.

Turney, K. (2018). Adverse childhood experiences among children of incarcerated parents. *Children and Youth Services Review, 89*, 218–225.

Turney, K., & Lanuza, Y. R. (2017). Parental incarceration and the transition to adulthood. *Journal of Marriage and Family, 79*(5), 1314–1330.

Uggen, C., Manza, J., & Behrens, A. (2004). 'Less than the average citizen': Stigma, role transition and the civic reintegration of convicted felons. In S. Maruna & R. Immarigeon (Eds.), *After crime and punishment: Pathways to ex-offender reintegration* (1st ed., pp. 258–290). Willan Publishing.

Wacquant, L. (2002). From slavery to mass incarceration: Rethinking the 'race question' in the US. *New Left Review, 13*, 41–60.

Wade, R., Jr., Cronholm, P. F., Fein, J. A., Forke, C. M., Davis, M. B., Harkins-Schwarz, M., … Bair-Merritt, M. H. (2016). Household and community-level adverse childhood experiences and adult health outcomes in a diverse urban population. *Child Abuse & Neglect, 52*, 135–145.

Wakefield, S., & Uggen, C. (2010). Incarceration and stratification. *Annual Review of Sociology, 36*, 387–406.

Wildeman, C. (2009). Parental imprisonment, the prison boom, and the concentration of childhood disadvantage. *Demography, 46*(2), 265–280.

Wildeman, C., & Turney, K. (2014). Positive, negative, or null? The effects of maternal incarceration on children's behavioral problems. *Demography, 51*(3), 1041–1068.

Wildeman, C., & Wang, E. A. (2017). Mass incarceration, public health, and widening inequality in the USA. *The Lancet, 389*(10077), 1464–1474.

Winant, H. (2007). The dark side of the force: One hundred years of the sociology of race. In C. Calhoun (Ed.), *Sociology in America: A history*. The University of Chicago Press.

Winn, M. T. (2010a). 'Our side of the story': Moving incarcerated youth voices from margins to center. *Race Ethnicity and Education, 13*(3), 313–325.

Winn, M. T. (2010b). 'Betwixt and between': Literacy, liminality, and the celling of black girls. *Race Ethnicity and Education, 13*(4), 425–447.

Yosso, T. J. (2006). Why use critical race theory and counterstorytelling to analyze the Chicana/o educational pipeline? In T. J. Yosso (Ed.), *Critical race counterstories along the Chicana/Chicano educational pipeline* (pp. 1–20). Taylor & Francis Group.

Young, D. S., & Jefferson Smith, C. (2019). Young adult reflections on the impact of parental incarceration and reentry. *Journal of Offender Rehabilitation, 58*(5), 421–443.

Zaff, J. F., Donlan, A. E., Pufall Jones, E., Lin, E. S., & Anderson, S. (2016). Comprehensive community initiatives creating supportive youth systems: A theoretical rationale for creating youth-focused CCIs. In J. F. Zaff, E. Pufall Jones, A. E. Donlan, & S. Anderson (Eds.), *Comprehensive community initiatives for positive youth development* (pp. 1–16). Routledge/ Taylor & Francis Group.

Ziv, Y., Alva, S., & Zill, N. (2010). Understanding head start children's problem behaviors in the context of arrest or incarceration of household members. *Early Childhood Research Quarterly, 25*(3), 396–408.

Programmatic and Policy Responses to Mothers Who Are Incarcerated

Judy Krysik and Natalia Vasiliou

Abstract Women who are incarcerated constitute a unique, poorly understood population. Knowledge of these women is lacking, and programs and facilities designed for them have largely been extensions of those designed for males who are incarcerated. Women housed in our nation's prisons and jails face challenges different from men that often arise prior to incarceration and continue after release. This paper describes trends in modern-day female incarceration, theories to explain those trends, the population of females who are incarcerated in the United States, and an overview of problems specific to mothers who are incarcerated. Treatment of women by the judicial system and implications for programs and policies are provided.

Keywords Incarceration · Women · Mothers · Policy · Interventions

Women have accounted for the fastest-growing population in federal and state prisons across the United States. In fact, the rate of growth for female incarceration has been double that of men since 1980 (The Sentencing Project, 2020). "Between 1980 and 2019, the number of women who are incarcerated increased by more than 700%, rising from a total of 26,378 in 1980 to 222,455 in 2019" (The Sentencing Project, 2020). Although actual numbers indicate that there are still far fewer women incarcerated in prisons than men, the ratio of men to women has shifted considerably from 30:1 in 1971 to 14:1 in 2005 (Bureau of Justice Statistics, 2008). As the overall number of adults in prison started to decline at the end of 2016, the rate of decline for women was lower compared to that of men (Bronson & Carson, 2019).

In addition to the increase in the number of women incarcerated, there a difference between men and women in the types of crime for which they are incarcerated. Violence and drug trafficking account for 62% of female incarcerations in state and federal prisons (Bronson & Carson, 2019). In 2018, the majority of women in state

J. Krysik (✉) · N. Vasiliou
Center for Child Well-Being, Arizona State University, Phoenix, AZ, USA
e-mail: Judy.krysik@asu.edu

J. Krysik, N. Rodriguez (eds.), *Children of Incarcerated Parents*, Children of Incarcerated Parents: From Understanding to Impact,
https://doi.org/10.1007/978-3-030-84713-5_12

and federal prisons were incarcerated because of drug and property offenses, whereas men were more likely to be incarcerated for violent crime (The Sentencing Project, 2020). Not only has the number of females incarcerated increased much more rapidly than that of men, but the types of offenses women commit have changed as well. Two contemporary theories explain the increase and change in type of offenses committed in opposite ways.

Contemporary Theories of Women's Criminal Behavior

Convergence of opportunity theory suggests that distinctions of *typical* male and female crimes are becoming less clear. Women appear to be committing crimes more like those committed by men. Adler (1975) contended that these changes may be due to the weakening of the boundaries between traditionally male and female spheres. As gender boundaries weaken, women's opportunities for legitimate activities increase. As women's legitimate opportunities increase to be more similar to those of men, so too do their illegitimate opportunities. In other words, as women participate more in the public sphere of business and politics, opportunities for criminal behavior increase, and those behaviors will be more similar to those of men (Simon & Landis, 1991). Gang activity, for example, was formerly a behavior that was thought to be predominantly male. We have since seen young, female gang members whose activities are similar to those of their male counterparts (Jankowski, 1991).

Feminist scholars have argued that the increase of women in prison is best explained by women's position in the patriarchal structure of our society (Chesney-Lind, 1978; Freidan, 1989; Smart, 1977). Feminist criminologists contend that the male-dominated justice system is more concerned with punishing women for deviating from traditional gender roles, rather than for their criminal behavior. Discriminatory control theory views there to be a definition of morality for women that is different from that for men, and social control dynamics place women in a *double bind* position. For example, mothers who find it necessary to be employed to support their children are often labeled ineffective because the roles of provider and caring for children are viewed as antithetical. Women are often caught in a no-win situation, not only due to female specific attribution but also because of the hierarchical valuation among the genders. Figueira-McDonough and Sarri (1987), for example, commenting on the classic experiment of Boverman, concluded: "If women had good mental health, something was wrong with their womanhood; if they were well adjusted to the gender role, they had poor mental health" (p. 23). Should a woman step outside of the gender-prescribed roles within the patriarchal order, she is labeled deviant (Schur, 1983). Although these two theories may explain sociological factors in defining women's behavior as criminal, they do not address the individual characteristics common to women in prison.

Characteristics of Women in Prison

Although women in prison represent a diverse population who are incarcerated for a variety of crimes, they do share some compelling similarities. The profile of the female commitment that emerges in study after study is that of a young, often minority, single mother. In 1998, the median age of the female prisoner was 33 years in state institutions and 36 years in federal institutions (Beck, 2000). In that same year, 67% of women in state and 71% of women in federal prisons were minority, the majority of whom were Black (Beck, 2000). The majority of women in state and federal prisons have never been married, 47% and 34%, respectively. Sixty-five percent of women in state prisons and 59% in federal had dependent children. Together these women were mothers to some 110,264 minor children (Beck, 2000), emphasizing the importance of focusing on the children of incarcerated parents.

Special Problems Encountered by Women in Prison

Miller (1977) reported that female offenders were not a priority in the prison system. Consequently, still today programs targeted to the prisoner often do not reflect an understanding of the complexities of the problems and needs of the female who is incarcerated.

History of Abuse Almost 60% of women living in state prisons reported being sexually or physically abused at some point in their lives (Beck, 2000). Patterns of such abuse often result in low self-esteem, a precursor to drug and alcohol dependence. According to Young (1995) and Colman and Widom (2004), early childhood abuse may also result in depression and problematic and abusive relationships. We now recognize these as symptoms of traumatic experiences (van der Kolk, 2014). Women in prison who have a history of sexual abuse have been shown to be twice as likely to be committed for violent crimes than other women in prison (Bloom et al., 1994). Approximately one-third of women in prison have been abused in the past by an intimate partner, and one-quarter reported abuse by a family member (Beck, 2000). Thus, it is not surprising that women are much more likely to kill a partner than to kill anyone else, whereas men are much more likely to perpetrate homicides against individuals outside the intimate relationship. For instance, from 1976 to 1997, 44% of murders committed by women were against a spouse or intimate compared to 11% for men, and of those murdered by women, 10.4% were their children or stepchildren compared to 2.2% of those murdered by men (Beck, 2000).

Substance Abuse Women in prison report more drug use before commitment than do men. Almost one out of four women reported their crime was a means to obtaining drugs as compared to one out of six men (Beck, 2000). In contrast, 29% of women in state prisons and 15% in federal prisons reported using alcohol at the time of their offenses. On all measures of drug use (ever used, using regularly, using in the month before, and at time of offense), women report higher rates of use than men, whereas men report greater alcohol use (Beck, 2000).

Health A recent study found 3% of women in federal prisons, 4% in state prisons, and 5% in local jails were pregnant when admitted (Daniel, 2019). For women who are incarcerated while pregnant, the essentials for a healthy pregnancy such as nutritional meals, fresh air and exercise, sanitary conditions, extra vitamins, and prenatal care are lacking. A California Department of Health Study indicated that one-third of all prison pregnancies ended in late term miscarriages (Kurshan, 1988). In the *Life* issue of October, 1997, a photograph by Jane Evelyn Atwood depicted a woman prisoner giving birth with handcuffs on her wrist and shackles on her ankles. Although there are now national standards condemning this practice, 12 states have not provided any policy to limit restraints during birth (Daniel, 2019). For women who do manage to deliver a healthy newborn, forced separation usually comes within 24 to 72 hours (Kurshan, 1988).

Poverty Twenty-seven percent of women in federal prison and 44% of women in state prison lack a high school education which sentences them to a lifetime of low wage labor. When comparing male and female commitments in state prisons, 60% of women were unemployed at the time of their offense compared to 40% of males. Thirty percent of all female offenders received public assistance prior to their arrest (Bureau of Justice Statistics, 1999). This may partially explain why many women prisoners have a history of poverty. In a society in which money is power, the poor woman with children is placed in a catch-22 situation. Unable to economically care for herself or her children, she is labeled an inadequate mother. On the other hand, if imprisoned for attempting to gain economic power through criminal means, she places herself in a position to be further degraded. She is viewed as an unfit mother who should not be permitted to take care of her children.

Children From 1991 to 2007, the number of children with a mother in prison more than doubled (Glaze & Maruschak, 2010). Koban (1983) found that prior to imprisonment, females have closer relationships with their children than do males. More children, therefore, are affected by the forced separation due to incarceration from their mothers than their fathers, since the majority depend on their mothers for economic and emotional support and as the primary caretaker. Not only do mothers who are in prison report feeling of depression and despair regarding their unavailability to parent their children; they often are consumed with fear that the state will assume care for their children. About 33% of mothers do not have relatives who are willing or able to take care of their children and therefore require child protective services or other agencies to help with out-of-home placement (Smith, 1993). Women prisoners are five times more likely than male prisoners to report that their children are in foster care (Glaze & Maruschak, 2010).

Stigma Stigma is an issue for both men and women who are incarcerated; however, stigma is assumed to be experienced differently by males and females. Lombroso (1920) first made the assumption that the role of criminal is more congruent with the adventurous, risk-taking, violent identity that coexists with the male identity and which is not a part of the female identity. Once a woman has entered the prison system, her defining status is that of *deviant*. From the moment that she is so labeled, observers tend to attribute to her a devalued identity, and her overall character and ensuing behaviors will be interpreted through such lenses. According to Schur (1983), all of her past behavior is then reconstructed to fit the new label. This will occur first within the prison system and later as she exits. These problems may be compounded for the minority woman who is thrice stigmatized; she is a woman, her skin color is not white, and she is labeled a "convict" or a "felon." The children of parents who are incarcerated also experience the stigma of having a parent incarcerated, especially when it is a mother.

Impact of Incarceration on Parenting

In the United States, there are more children with parents who are incarcerated than there are people in prison (Shlafer et al., 2019). From 1991 to 2007, the number of children with at least one parent incarcerated grew from 860,300 to 1,427,500; and the largest growth period occurred between 1991 and 1997 when the number grew by over 40% (Glaze & Maruschak, 2010). "Women in state prison (62%) were more likely than men (51%) to report being a parent" compared to 63% of males and 56% of female in federal prisons (Glaze & Maruschak, 2010). At the time of a 2004 survey, the majority of those incarcerated in state (52%) and federal (63%) prisons reported having at least one minor child, a quarter of whom were under the age of 5 years; and one-third of these children will turn 18 while their parent is still incarcerated (Glaze & Maruschak, 2010).

It is difficult to quantify the devastating personal loss experienced by parental incarceration. Additionally, incarceration presents a myriad of difficulties for the individual as well as the family they have left behind. It can be said that the incarceration of a mother may introduce issues of immediacy less present compared with paternal incarceration. Of those incarcerated in state institutions who reported being a parent, 88% of males reported that their child(ren) were currently being cared for by the other parent compared to only 37% of females (Glaze & Maruschak, 2010). Of those females incarcerated in state prisons, 42% named the child's grandmother as current caregiver (Glaze & Maruschak, 2010). Therefore, maternal imprisonment may result in immediate effects on the child such as sudden changes in living arrangements, separation of siblings, financial instability, and child welfare involvement. It is important to understand that many of these changes may not be temporary; one study found that only 1 in 11 older children of parents who were incarcerated had lived continuously with a primary caregiver since birth (Simmons, 2000).

Impact of Policy Although the woman who is incarcerated has individual circumstances and history, it is important to understand the ways in which public policy has impacted women who are incarcerated and their children. In order to explain the rampant increase in female incarceration, it is necessary to address the "War on Drugs." President Nixon signed into effect the National War on Drugs in 1972; it continued to gain public and governmental support through the 1980s (Amundson et al., 2014). The War on Drugs resulted in tougher sentencing, such as minimum sentences, prison expansions, and mandatory drug testing (Amundson et al., 2014). Public support for the "War" was based on largely misguided inference; the rise in incarceration was not a symptom of rising crime, but rather the result of an emphasis on punishment (Bloom et al., 2004). Women, namely, poor women of color, were disproportionately affected by the harsh policies of the War on Drugs. By the end of 1996, the number of women in state prisons serving sentences for drug-related crimes had jumped to 23,700, up from 2370 in 1986 (Beck, 2000).

Bloom, Chesney-Lind, and Owen (1994) discussed the harsh, lasting societal effects of the War on Drugs:

> Instead of a policy of last resort, imprisonment has become the first order response for a wide range of women offenders that have been disproportionately swept up in this trend. This politically motivated legislative response often ignores the fiscal or social costs of imprisonment. Thus, the legislature has missed opportunities to prevent women's crime by cutting vitally needed social service and educational programs to fund ever-increasing correctional budgets. (p. 2)

The War on Drugs set a precedent for further social policies that largely criminalized women. President Clinton's Welfare Reform Act of 1996 introduced a lifetime ban on cash assistance and food stamps for anyone with a prior state or federal drug-related charge. Although many states have now recognized the ban as harmful and have taken steps to remove it, the Act kept necessary aid from many of the most vulnerable families (Thompson, 2019). Additionally in 1996, "the federal government implemented the 'One Strike Initiative,' authorizing local Public Housing Authorities (PHA) to obtain from law-enforcement agencies the criminal conviction records of all adult applicants or tenants" (Bloom et al., 2004). This initiative not only created lasting barriers to housing for formerly incarcerated individuals but further strengthened a culture of sustained criminalization of poverty.

Public policy has also impacted the ability for children to be reunified with their parent after incarceration. The Adoption and Safe Families Act of 1997 (ASFA) was created with the purpose of attempting to shorten the length of time a child would be placed in temporary care as well as addressing the child welfare system's alleged practice of reunifying children and parents too quickly, resulting in reoccurring maltreatment (Humphrey et al., 2006). In order to achieve this, "ASFA mandated that a permanency planning hearing be held within 12 months of a child entering foster care," 6 months shorter than the previous mandate (Humphrey et al., 2006, p. 114).

Additionally, ASFA also added time limits to reunification services such as counseling, mental health treatment, substance abuse treatment, domestic violence services, temporary childcare, and transportation accommodations (Humphrey et al.,

2006). If the permanency hearing finds that reunification with a child's family of origin is not possible, the plan must state whether a child will be referred for adoption or legal guardianship; if it is determined that the child will be referred for adoption, the state will file a petition for the termination of parental rights (Humphrey et al., 2006, p. 114).

ASFA has garnered harsh criticism for the impact the policy has on parents who are incarcerated and their families (D'Andre & Valdez, 2012). Many incarcerated parents are forced to terminate their parental rights before even being released from prison. Often, incarcerated parents are not even able to participate in the permanency hearing at all. Sherry (2010) identifies various communication breakdowns between the prison system and child welfare agencies as possible reasons for this, "Sometimes the [court] order does not make it to the prison on time or the inmate may have transferred to another prison" (p. 385). Of note, although a parent may be able to access reunification services while incarcerated, this access is not guaranteed, and the services vary in quality, target population, and staffing (Tuerk & Loper, 2006). A 2006 study on the effects of ASFA on families found that important decision-making time was shortened, reducing families' access to services that could result in reunification (Humphrey et al., 2006).

ASFA also brings to light the gaps that exist between the child welfare system and kinship care, the care of children by family members or fictive kin. "Placement of children with relatives, which would avoid the harsh ASFA mandate, is hampered by state policies that provide less financial aid to relatives who are caregivers than to nonrelative foster caregivers" (Bloom et al., 2004, p. 41). Although financial assistance varies across states, this assistance "may equate to less than one half of what foster care providers receive" (Wu & Snyder, 2019, p. 163).

Maintaining Connections Through Incarceration One way for incarcerated parents to facilitate a parenting relationship with their child(ren) is through visits and communication such as phone calls and letter writing. However, current practices, apart from the pandemic which shut down in-person visiting, make it extremely difficult for families to maintain constant, meaningful contact with their loved one during incarceration. A survey on prison visiting policies by Yale Law School found that state policies regarding visits vary greatly in approach and outcome (Boudin et al., 2013). Several states place limitations on how long visitors are allowed to visit, while other states have policies to ensure a "minimum number of days or hours visits must be made available" (Boudin et al., 2013 p. 161). Visitation rights may also be impacted on the security classification of the person who is incarcerated, which is dependent on crimes and behavior within the prison (Boudin et al., 2013). These policies sometimes extend beyond the individual who is incarcerated; "policies often exclude individuals with criminal records from visiting" (Boudin et al., 2013, p. 165). Fifty-eight percent of mothers in state prison reported having a family member who has been incarcerated (Glaze & Maruschak, 2010). For children of incarcerated parents currently in the care of family or friends, this rule may impact their ability to ever visit their parent.

Family visits for females who are incarcerated are more problematic than for males, simply because there are fewer prisons for women and distance from home may make visits impossible. A 2015 report by prisonpolicy.org showed that among people incarcerated less than 50 miles from home, 50 percent received one visit in a month (Rabuy & Kopf, 2015). When the number of miles increased to between 50 and 100, the percent who received one visit per month dropped to 40 percent; and between 101 and 500 miles, only 25 percent were visited (Rabuy & Kopf, 2015). This poses a challenge for mothers who, on average, are incarcerated 160 miles from their children (Travis et al., 2005). A national study revealed that only about 8% of mothers had visits from their children once a week, 35% reported weekly telephone contact, 35% had weekly mail contact, and 58% reported never receiving a visit from their children throughout their incarceration (Glaze & Maruschak, 2010). Due to distance, telephone communication and letter writing may serve as the only feasible avenue to maintain familial connections. However, for people incarcerated in jails or private prisons, phone or video calls can be very expensive (Wagner & Jones, 2019).

Discussion

When considering program and policy responses to address the issues faced by women who are incarcerated and their children, it is important to begin with a wide variety of research and theory. The research, such as that presented in this chapter, helps to establish the issue as a social problem, i.e., a condition that affects a sizable number of people, that threatens established societal values and that inspires a collective action with an associated commitment of resources to better the condition.

The presentation of data in this chapter supports that the number of women who are incarcerated in jails and prisons has grown rapidly, and together these women are mothers to a large number of children, many of whom are very young. Theory and research contribute to a multidimensional, nuanced understanding of the problem. The theories presented in this chapter that help explain the increase in the incarceration of women are grounded in gender. For instance, convergence of opportunity theory suggests that activities that were previously outside of the prescribed gender roles for females, e.g., participation in gang and illicit drug activity, have become more acceptable and available for women. At the same time, the focus on punishment for stepping outside prescribed gender roles was emphasized with the War on Drugs and spread into other policy areas including mandatory minimum sentencing, child welfare, public housing, and income support programs. Research on the characteristics of women who are incarcerated, i.e., predominantly poor, single, minority, and lacking education, helps to understand the pull toward illegitimate opportunities.

Research also shows that women who are incarcerated are also more likely than their nonincarcerated peers to have histories of abuse, which can lead to the use of illicit substances as a means of coping and involvement in emotionally and physically abusive relationships. Early abuse histories are associated with a host of adverse health and mental health behaviors and adverse consequences. These conditions make women vulnerable to participation in activities that can lead to incarceration, such as participation in domestic violence, drug use, and other crimes of survival.

In its focus on punishment, courts have long ignored women's caretaking roles and responsibilities and have not considered the consequences on millions of children, separated from their main caretaker and left in the care of relatives or placed in the care of strangers.

An approach that is focused on well-being, as well as accountability, would include both prevention and intervention. Primary prevention would target the prevention of abuse during childhood, to avoid the adverse childhood experiences associated with risk behaviors and their consequences. Secondary prevention would target emotional healing and healthy coping strategies for those who have experienced early abuse and neglect or other forms of childhood trauma such as the separation from a parent through death, divorce, or incarceration. Prevention would also target enhanced education and employment skills, especially in depressed areas that lead to a living wage, with opportunities for women to earn a living through legitimate means and the provision of support for family caregiving responsibilities.

Some states have passed policies to help reduce the traumatic experiences of arrest of a parent through law officer training and the development of arrest protocols such as asking adults if they are parents of minor children who may be at risk due to the arrest and considering children during sentencing procedures. For those women who are incarcerated, approaches to sentencing should consider their caretaking responsibilities, with alternatives to incarceration for nonviolent and low-level offenses, especially when incarceration would make ongoing contact with children unlikely due to distance, cost, and the availability of a third party to facilitate visits. All policy should be considered in terms of its impact on the well-being of children, for instance, policies that regulate rates for calling services, the receipt of mail by incarcerated individuals (e.g., postcard only mail rules), and child-friendly visit rules and settings.

When children enter the child welfare system due to parental incarceration, courts and child welfare agencies should make additional efforts to ensure the parent who is incarcerated is represented in the dependency hearings and case planning. Engaging parents who are incarcerated in decisions about their children's care can make the difference between the child being placed in stranger foster care in an unknown family and even culture and community, to care with friends and family members who can help maintain the parent/child bond and cultural and community connections over the course of incarceration. This requires protocol, training, and assessment, with the option of promoting legislation if the outcomes are not as expected.

While incarcerated, women need opportunities to increase their education and parenting knowledge and skills and interventions to help them heal from past traumas. The best approaches build on cultural strengths and when possible incorporate cultural practices. It is through these opportunities that women are able to work through the shame and stigma of incarceration, value themselves as positive parents, even if that means making the decision that someone else should parent their children through guardianship or adoption.

Pregnancy is not a rare event among incarcerated women, and these women need access to healthy foods, prenatal vitamins, and medical care to increase their chances to safely deliver healthy infants. Some states have banned the practice of shackling during delivery, and some programs allow women to bond with their babies until they reach a certain age. These programs are few and little is known about their outcomes. Women who are reentering society post incarceration need support for housing and employment so that they can be reunified with their children if safely possible and to help them avoid opportunities to recidivate. Important reentry policies include the "ban the box" initiative that ensures prospective employees are considered on their merits rather than discriminated against on the basis of their criminal history.

Efforts to continue data collection to understand the magnitude of social problem should be ongoing. Until recently, the number, characteristics, and experiences of women who are incarcerated and their children have remained largely hidden. In general, much more research is needed on policies and interventions prior to, during, and post incarceration. Although there is a cost associated with prevention and rehabilitative interventions, it would be recouped in healthier children beginning in early childhood and the future productive involvement of the women.

Acknowledgments The authors gratefully acknowledge contributions to this chapter by Dr. Patti J. Flanagan and Dr. Josefina Figueira-McDonough.

References

Adler, F. (1975). *Sisters in crime: The rise of new female criminals*. New York: McGraw-Hill.

Amundson, K., Zajicek, A., & Hunt, V. (2014). Pathologies of the poor: What do the war on drugs and welfare reform have in common? *Journal of Sociology and Social Welfare, 41*(1), 5–28.

Beck, A. J. (2000, August). *Prisoners in 1999*. Bureau of Justice Statistics Bulletin. Retrieved from https://www.bjs.gov/content/pub/pdf/p99.pdf

Bloom, B., Chesney-Lind, M., & Owen, B. (1994). *Women in California prisons: Hidden victims of the war on drugs*. San Francisco: Center on Juvenile and Criminal Justice.

Bloom, B., Owen, B., & Covington, S. (2004). Women offenders and the gendered effects of public policy. *Review of Policy Research, 21*(1), 31–48.

Boudin, C., Stutz, T., & Littman, A. (2013). Prison visitation policies: A fifty-state survey. *Yale Law & Policy Review, 32*(1), 150–189.

Bronson, J., & Carson, A. (2019, April). Prisoners in 2017. Bureau of Justice Statistics. Retrieved from https://www.bjs.gov/content/pub/pdf/p17.pdf

Bureau of Justice Statistics (1999). *Criminal offender statistics*. Retrieved from http://www.ojp.usdoj.gov/bjs/crimoff.htm

Bureau of Justice Statistics. (2008). *Census of state and federal correctional facilities, 2005*. Retrieved from https://www.bjs.gov/content/pub/pdf/csfcf05.pdf

Chesney-Lind, M. (1978). Young women in the arms of the law. In L. Bowker (Ed.), *Women, crime and the criminal justice system*. D.C. Heath: Lexington, MA.

Colman, R. A., & Widom, C. S. (2004). Childhood abuse and neglect and adult intimate relationships: A prospective study. *Child Abuse & Neglect, 28*(11), 1133–1151.

D'Andrade, A. C., & Valdez, M. (2012). Reunifying from behind bars: A quantitative study of the relationship between parental incarceration, service use, and foster care reunification. *Social Work in Public Health, 27*(6), 616–636.

Daniel, R. (2019, December). Prisons neglect pregnant women in their healthcare policies. Prison Policy Initiative. Retrieved from www.prisonpolicy.org/blog/2019/12/05/pregnancy/

Figueira-McDonough, J., & Sarri, R. (1987). *The trapped woman: Catch-22 in deviance and control*. Newbury Park, CA: Sage.

Freidan, B. (1989). *The fountain of age*. New York: Simon and Schuster.

Glaze, L. E., & Maruschak, L. M. (2010). *Parents in prison and their minor children*. Washington, DC: Bureau of Justice Statistics. Retrieved from http://www.bjs.gov/index.cfm?ty=pbdetail&iid=823.

Humphrey, K. R., Turnbull, A. P., & Turnbull, H. R., III. (2006). Impact of the adoption and safe families act on youth and their families: Perspectives of foster care providers, youth with emotional disorders, service providers, and judges. *Children and Youth Services Review, 28*(2), 113–132.

Jankowski, M. S. (1991). *Islands in the street: Gangs and American urban society*. Oakland, CA: University of California.

Koban, L. (1983). Parents in prison: A comparative analysis of the effects of incarceration in the families of men and women. *Research in Law, Deviance and Social Control, 5*, 171–183.

Kurshan, N. (1988). *Women and Imprisonment in the U.S.: History and current reality*. International Global Communications. Retrieved from http://www.igc.org/justice/prisons/women

Lombroso, C. (1920). The female offender. Appleton. (Original work published 1903).

Miller, E. E. (1977). The woman offender and community corrections. In E. E. Miller & M. R. Montilla (Eds.), *Corrections in the community: Success models in correctional reform* (pp. 145–152). Reston, VA: Reston Publishing.

Rabuy, B., & Kopf, D. (2015, October). *Separation by bars and miles: Visitation in state prisons*. Prison Policy Initiative. Retrieved from www.prisonpolicy.org/reports/prisonvisits.html

Schur, E. M. (1983). *Labeling women deviant: Gender, stigma and social control*. Philadelphia: Temple University.

Sherry, S. (2010). When jail fails: Amending the ASFA to reduce its negative impact on children of incarcerated parents. *Family Court Review, 48*(2), 380–397. https://doi.org/10.1111/j.1744-1617.2010.01316.x.

Shlafer, R., Duwe, G., & Hindt, L. (2019). Parents in prison and their minor children: Comparisons between state and national estimates. *The Prison Journal, 99*(3), 310–328.

Simmons, C. W. (2000, March). *Children of Incarcerated Parents*. CRB Note 7(2).

Simon, R. J., & Landis, J. (1991). *The crimes women commit, the punishments they receive*. Lexington Books/D. C. Heath and Com.

Smart, C. (1977). *Women, crime and criminology: A feminist critique*. London: Routledge.

Smith, V. (1993). Special needs of women in the criminal justice system. Center for Substance Abuse Treatment, *TIE Communique* (pp. 31–32). U.S. Department of Health and Human Services.

The Sentencing Project. (2020, November). *Incarcerated women and girls*. Retrieved from https://www.sentencingproject.org/publications/incarcerated-women-and-girls/

Thompson, D. (2019). No more double punishments: Lifting the ban on SNAP and TANF for people with prior felony drug convictions. Retrieved from https://www.clasp.org/sites/default/files/publications/2019/04/2019.03.15%20No%20More%20Double%20Punishments.pdf

Travis, J., McBride, E. C., & Solomon, A. L., (2005). Families left behind: The hidden costs of incarceration and reentry. Urban Institute Justice Policy Center. Retrieved from www.urban.org/sites/default/files/publication /50461/310882-Families-Left-Behind.pdf

Tuerk, E., & Loper, A. (2006). Contact between incarcerated mothers and their children: Assessing parenting stress. *Journal of Offender Rehabilitation, 43*(1), 23–43.

van der Kolk, B. A. (2014). *The body keeps the score: Brain, mind, and body in the healing of trauma*. Viking.

Wagner, P. & Jones, A. (2019, September). *The biggest priorities for prison and jail phone justice in 40 states*. Prison Policy Imitative. Retrieved from www.prisonpolicy.org/blog/2019/09/11/worstatesphones

Wu, Q., & Snyder, S. (2019). Factors associated with the decision-making process in kinship diversion. *Journal of Family Social Work, 22*(2), 161–186.

Young, E. (1995). The role of incest issues in relapse and recovery. In A. M. Washton (Ed.), *Psychotherapy and substance abuse: A Practitioner's handbook* (pp. 451–469). New York: Guilford.

Incarcerated Parents and Their Children: Perspectives from the Smart Decarceration Social Work Grand Challenge

Pajarita Charles, Amy Blank Wilson, Branden McLeod, Aaron Gottlieb, and Melissa Villodas

Abstract Over half of people incarcerated in state prisons and over three-fifths of people incarcerated in federal prisons were parents to minor children (Glaze & Maruschak, 2010). Families of incarcerated parents are negatively impacted and burdened by mass incarceration, increasing family instability, economic hardship, substance use, and mental health challenges. The staggering economic, social, and human costs to society resulting from mass incarceration call for research and evidence to inform "Smart Decarceration" policies and practices that reduce imprisonment, support well-being, and promote justice. Therefore, this chapter brings attention to the cross section of families and the Smart Decarceration Social Work Grand Challenge. In so doing, this chapter illustrates the need for "smart" policies and practices that meaningfully take these experiences and contexts into account and aim to reduce the criminal justice system's reach while building community and social institutions' supportive capacity. This chapter explores different types of family-focused programming that is available to incarcerated parents and their families and concludes with a discussion about Smart Decarceration efforts that inform and support the development of partnerships, programs, and policies fostering resiliency and improving outcomes for impacted families.

Keywords Incarcerated parents · Children of incarcerated parents · Jail · Prison · Smart Decarceration Grand Challenge

---

P. Charles (✉)
Sandra Rosenbaum School of Social Work, University of Wisconsin-Madison, Madison, WI, USA
e-mail: paja.charles@wisc.edu

A. B. Wilson · M. Villodas
School of Social Work, The University of North Carolina at Chapel Hill, Chapel Hill, NC, USA

B. McLeod · A. Gottlieb
Jane Addams College of Social Work, University of Illinois Chicago, Chicago, IL, USA

J. Krysik, N. Rodriguez (eds.), *Children of Incarcerated Parents*, Children of Incarcerated Parents: From Understanding to Impact,
https://doi.org/10.1007/978-3-030-84713-5_13

Estimates show that 52% of people incarcerated in state prison and 63% incarcerated in federal prison were parents to minor children (Glaze & Maruschak, 2010). Consequently, over five million US children under the age of 14, or 7% of all children who resided with their parent, have been separated because of prison or jail (Murphey & Cooper, 2015). An important aspect of incarceration in the United States is the large racial disparities in the US criminal justice system. Compared to their white counterparts, African American children are six times more likely to have an incarcerated parent (11.4% compared to 1.8%), while Latinx children (at 3.5%) are approximately two times more likely (The Pew Charitable Trusts, 2010).

The staggering economic, social, and human costs to society resulting from mass incarceration call for research and evidence to inform "Smart Decarceration" policies and practices that reduce imprisonment, promote safety and well-being, champion justice, and support communities most impacted by mass incarceration. Social Work's Smart Decarceration Grand Challenge addresses mass incarceration by reducing the criminal justice system's reach and working toward outcomes that reduce racial, behavioral health, and LGBTQ-related disparities in the criminal justice system (Epperson & Pettus-Davis, 2017).

Families of incarcerated parents are one of the groups most impacted and burdened by mass incarceration, increasing family instability, economic hardship, substance use, and mental health challenges (Arditti, 2012; Schwartz-Soicher et al., 2011; Sugie, 2012; Wakefield & Uggen, 2010; Wakefield & Wildeman, 2018). Consequently, parental incarceration has been consistently associated with negative outcomes for children, including increased behavioral and mental health problems, cognitive delays, homelessness, academic difficulties, and exposure to other adverse childhood experiences (ACEs), adjusting for a range of characteristics (Gottlieb, 2016; Turney, 2018; Wakefield & Wildeman, 2014; Wildeman, 2009). These unique challenges call for action that addresses families' needs in innovative ways. The social work profession is well positioned to lead these innovation efforts with a focus on decarcerating parents and proposing actions that maximize child and family well-being (Pettus-Davis, 2012).

Given the staggering effects of mass incarceration on American families, this chapter aims to bring attention to the intersection of incarcerated parents and children and the Smart Decarceration Grand Challenge. We do this by focusing on variation within the criminal justice system itself and on contexts that shape the experience of families during and after parental incarceration, including differences in prison and jail settings, variation in programs and services, and ways of maintaining parent-child contact. We conclude with recommendations informed by the Smart Decarceration Grand Challenge about partnerships, programs, and policies that aim to foster resiliency and improve outcomes for impacted families.

Do Differences in Prisons and Jails Matter for Families?

Prisons are defined as long-term confinement facilities that typically hold people convicted of crimes serving sentences of more than 1 year (Bronson & Carson, 2019). The United States operates 50 state prison systems and one federal prison system, collectively housing 1,833 separate state prisons and 110 federal prisons (Sawyer & Wagner, 2020). Estimates also suggest that 28 states incarcerate people in privately operated prisons (The Sentencing Project, 2019). Differences in prison rules and operations between states, and even between facilities within states, can have implications for children and families. The type of prison facility where a person is incarcerated can affect the physical proximity of a child to their incarcerated parent, the regulations that dictate visiting options, the type of contact children and parents can have during visits, and the availability of family-friendly or parent-focused services for the incarcerated parent (Shlafer et al., 2015; Turney & Goodsell, 2018).

In contrast to prisons, jails are local correctional facilities designed for individuals awaiting trial and those serving short-term sentences, typically 1 year or less. Jails include city and county correctional facilities, work release programs, and temporary holding or lock-up facilities (Bronson & Carson, 2019). According to the Bureau of Justice Assistance, there are 3,134 local jails and 80 Indian country jails in the United States (Sawyer & Wagner, 2020). The size, physical structure, and purpose of these correctional facilities vary widely. Over 50% of jails house 100 people or less, with 33% housing less than 50 people. On the other hand, 4% of jails house 1,000 to 2,500 individuals, and 1% (or 30 correctional institutions) house more than 2,500 people (Zeng, 2019), with the largest jail systems housing up to 19,000 individuals—a capacity that is larger than the entire correctional population of 24 state correctional systems (Bronson & Carson, 2019).

Since people incarcerated in prison serve longer sentences than those in jails, prisons admit and release fewer people each year compared to jails and generally have more formalized policies pertaining to contact with children and other family members, as well as different types of services and programs (Poehlmann-Tynan, 2015). In 2017, for instance, 10.6 million people entered jail compared to 600,000 admitted to prison (Bronson & Carson, 2019; Zeng, 2019). Over 745,000 individuals, or one-third of the correctional population, were being held in jails in 2017, an estimated two-thirds of whom were awaiting trial; additionally, over 50% of the jail population turns over each week with an average stay of 26 days (Zeng, 2019). This dynamic leads to "churning" in and out of jails, resulting in considerably higher jail admission rates compared to prisons.

Although incarceration in the United States occurs most frequently in jails with higher rates of people entering and exiting than in prisons, research on incarcerated parents and their children most commonly focuses on prisons or does not differentiate between the different types of corrections settings (Eddy & Poehlmann-Tynan, 2019). Consequently, less is understood about jails and the implications for children whose parents cycle in and out of local correctional institutions and as a result are removed from the home for frequent, but short periods of time (Siegel & Luther, 2019). Unlike prisons, jails are local correctional facilities and as such are generally found in or near the communities they serve. Because of this, children and caregivers may live in closer proximity to the incarcerated parent resulting in more opportunities to visit than if the parent was held in a prison. However, there is considerable variation within jails in the type of visiting options available. A survey of 50 jails, one from each state in the United States, found significant differences in visit types across jails, including barrier visits using plexiglass (most common), on-site video visits, off-site video visits, and face-to-face or contact visits (least common). In the case of one jail (located in Wisconsin), visits by minors were prohibited all together (Shlafer et al., 2015).

Distinctions between jails and prisons are important because most jails are not designed to incarcerate people for long periods of time and, as a result, lack the space and resources needed to support face-to-face visitation and programming for parents and children (Shlafer et al., 2015). This applies especially to smaller jails because their size and construction place physical limitations on available visitation and programming space, even when opportunities to develop such services are available through community collaborations. While some research has suggested that families are more likely to visit jailed parents because they live in closer proximity to the jail (Arditti et al., 2003), other evidence finds that phone calls are the most common form of contact between children and their jailed parents (Shlafer et al., 2020).

Since prisons are designed to confine people for longer periods of time, they may have the staff and infrastructure needed to provide incarcerated individuals with opportunities for family contact and programming that promotes parent-child interactions and communication during the incarceration stay. Yet, even within a single prison system (e.g., within the same state), actual prison facilities vary widely in terms of number, size, location, programming, and policies as related to visitation and other forms of contact with families (Shlafer et al., 2015).

Programs and Services for Incarcerated Parents

To address the negative consequences of incarceration on children and to improve parents' life outcomes, programs have been developed to assist parents with various aspects of their family life and parenting role in correctional and community settings. Although research is limited, parenting programs in corrections have been linked to improvements in adjustment and misconduct during incarceration (Cochran, 2012; Eddy et al., 2013; Pierce et al., 2018), increases in parenting knowledge and improvements in parent-child relationship quality (Armstrong et al., 2017), and reductions in recidivism and better employment and mental health outcomes for the parent upon release (Duwe & Clark, 2013; Visher, 2013). However, widespread adoption of such programs—in particular, practices that promote parent-child contact—have been limited as a consequence of corrections administrators' safety and security concerns (Peterson et al., 2019) and a lack of rigorously evaluated evidence-based models (Loper et al., 2019).

To the extent that parenting education and visitation programs exist in prisons and jails, they tend to differ widely along several dimensions, including when services are delivered (during or after incarceration), where they are offered (inside corrections institutions or in the community), and who delivers them (corrections staff, volunteers, social service providers). Treatment models and the level of assessed risk for recidivism also influence whether someone is offered parenting-related services at all. For prisons that rely on Andrews and Bonta's (2010) Risk-Need-Responsivity (RNR) model (one of the most widely used and influential treatment planning tools in corrections), higher-risk individuals may be offered programs unavailable to lower-risk individuals because the model is designed so that higher-risk individuals receive more intensive services than those with lower risk (Batastini et al., 2018). However, even treatment for high-risk individuals may not include family-focused services since parenting skills and family relationships are considered of only moderate relevance to reducing criminal behavior (Andrews & Bonta, 2010). Thus, correctional systems' use of the RNR model may be leading to less uptake of potentially beneficial services for parents in two ways. First, low-risk parents simply may not be offered potentially stabilizing services (e.g., parenting or relationship skill building classes) that promote pro-social behavior. Second, high-risk parents are limited to treatments that are considered of higher relevance for future recidivism. Because the RNR model may not adequately assess the full range of treatment needs of incarcerated individuals (Ward, 2015), alternative ways of prescribing treatment plans that include assessing parents' needs for parent-child contact and parenting skills and knowledge may be an area for future consideration (e.g., Veeh et al., 2018).

Programs available to incarcerated parents may also differ based on the parents' correctional facility setting. For instance, curriculum-based programs with modules or lessons that build on one another in successive classes may be offered in prisons but not jails because individuals tend to serve longer, more predictable sentences in prisons. For example, the *Parenting Inside Out* parent management training program (Eddy et al., 2013) offers 60–90 hours of curriculum content for prisons usually delivered over the course of 12–18 weeks. A 24-hour jail version does exist in order to increase feasibility of delivery over a short period of time. Indeed, some jails do have the capacity to offer regular and comprehensive programming. Two examples include jails in San Francisco, California, and Allegheny County, Pennsylvania, which offer parenting classes based on manualized curricula to fathers and mothers (Peterson et al., 2015). These locations partner with local social service agencies who help provide parenting classes and other services that promote parent-child contact and bonding.

Other variations in family-focused programming, both within and between correctional settings, include delivery format (group meetings vs. one-on-one sessions), length of the program (number of sessions), and frequency of groups (e.g., biweekly, weekly). Significant variation in program structure centers around the type and scope of family-focused practices that correctional facilities incorporate into their daily operations. For instance, the only family related programming in prisons and jails might be an assessment at intake to evaluate immediate parental needs because of the parent's incarceration (e.g., are children safe, does the parent need to make a call about the child). However, in comparison, the assessment at intake might instead gauge interest in family-focused and parenting classes, which could then be provided during incarceration (Peterson et al., 2019).

Corrections settings also vary widely in terms of the information provided to family members who want to visit in person or communicate by way of mail, email, or video. There is little research on correctional practices related to how family members are notified of visiting rules and other inmate communication guidelines or how to make a visit appointment. Furthermore, practices vary within and between correctional facilities related to sharing information about where incarcerated people are located and when they are transferred between facilities. Additionally, there is no consistency in how incarcerated individuals and their families are notified about family-focused programs that will be offered to the parent in prison or jail or information about resources that could be helpful to affected children and caregivers in the community.

Contact and Communication

Services and policies that promote contact and communication between children and their incarcerated parents have the potential to positively influence parent-child relationships during incarceration (Poehlmann et al., 2010) and strengthen relationship bonds important to parental involvement and residence with children after release (Charles et al., 2021). However, the type of contact and the frequency with which it occurs varies significantly across correctional settings with implications for the well-being of children and parents. Moreover, not all incarcerated parents and families have equal access to these forms of contact, highlighting the economic disparities that incarcerated individuals and their families often face. Evidence suggests that financially vulnerable families find it hard to afford the costs associated with maintaining contact with their incarcerated family members. Expenses related to travel and transportation (Christian, 2005; Clark & Duwe, 2017; Cochran et al., 2016), calls, and mail to correctional facilities can prove prohibitive (Christian et al., 2006) making it difficult or impossible for children to talk with, see, or otherwise communicate with their parent.

Variations in visiting patterns among children and family members exist for a myriad of reasons. Traveling long distances, inadequate and unfriendly visiting spaces for children, and unclear visiting policies (e.g., what to wear, when to visit, what can be brought into the facility) all contribute to the barriers that families face when considering visitation opportunities (Schirmer et al., 2009). A fifty-state review of visiting policies in state prisons and the federal prison system revealed similarities, as well as wide-spread differences across systems with no clear understanding or explanation as to the source of the policies (Boudin et al., 2013). For instance, North Carolina restricts visits to weekly, 2-hour sessions, while New York allows for visiting 365 days a year. South Dakota restricts who can be on an incarcerated person's visiting list (two people plus family members), while California allows individuals to list any number of people. In the case of jails, evidence suggests that family members may be more likely to visit because they live closer to the facility (Arditti et al., 2003). However, jail visitation policies often vary more than they do within state prison systems because of the discretion that local administrators have on visiting policies.

Letters represent the most frequent and common form of communication and contact between incarcerated parents and their children (Shlafer et al., 2015) for various reasons (e.g., affordable, can be saved and re-read). However, there are certain drawbacks as well. For instance, mail correspondence is less instantaneous, and the frequency and sensitivity of certain life-events may not be communicated in letters. Also, younger children often rely on their caretakers to assist with reading the letter and corresponding (Shlafer et al., 2015).

While phone calls are the second most common form of communication, they present monetary and privacy challenges, where the correctional facility environment can make it difficult to share personal matters (Shlafer et al., 2015). Email correspondence or electronic messaging is a potentially lower-cost option for some incarcerated parents and their loved ones; however, computer and Internet availability vary across facilities, nearly all messaging services charge fees, and many institutions block messages, limit the length of messages, and restrict attachments (Raher, 2016).

This said, innovative strategies have been developed in some states that offer family support services, including various types of contact between children and incarcerated parents (McKay et al., 2010). For example, some correctional facilities provide child-friendly visiting services specifically for children and their incarcerated mothers (Peterson et al., 2019), such as a Texas prison's implementation of the "Sesame Street Goes to Prison" curriculum (Poehlmann-Tyan et al., 2020) or the New Jersey Department of Corrections' case managers who assist with visitation barriers (McKay et al., 2010). Case managers help arrange travel plans, submit documentation, and schedule visits. While research has found that settings with supportive services are more likely to have a positive effect on children and incarcerated parents (Poehlmann et al., 2010), some correctional environments facilitate less secure attachment between children and their parents. Often seen in jail settings, these facilities permit visits through plexiglass and provide minimal to no opportunity for children and their parents to hug, hold hands, or interact naturally (Loper et al., 2009; Poehlmann-Tyan & Pritzl, 2019).

A more recent method of communication that is drawing increased attention in both prisons and jails is the use of video chat through platforms similar to Zoom or Skype. While the evidence in this area is not well understood, research is underway to develop and test enhanced parent-child visits that include a combination of supportive visit coaching with jailed parents and at home caregivers and video chat technology, Internet access, and other family-friendly educational apps (e.g., health, finances, and parenting).

Recommendations from a Smart Decarceration Perspective

Our review points to evidence that interactions between parents and children in prisons and jails vary widely. Drawing from this information, we conclude with a set of recommendations that reflect the Smart Decarceration Grand Challenge goals put forth to help shape the identification, implementation, and evaluation of innovative strategies aimed at undoing decades of mass incarceration. The goals, which include (1) substantially reducing the incarcerated population in jails and prisons, (2) redressing existing social disparities among the incarcerated, and (3) maximizing public safety and well-being, act as guideposts to help ensure that we achieve effective, sustainable, and socially just decarceration (Epperson & Pettus-Davis, 2017). With these goals in mind, there are three pathways we hypothesize would be advantageous to pursue in promoting child and family well-being for incarcerated parents and their children. The first is to consider alternative sentencing or diversion away from prison or jail for parents. The second is to develop and test parenting programs inside corrections settings and support services for children and families in the community. The third is to ensure that parents and children are provided opportunities for contact and communication during incarceration.

Alternative Sentencing

One mechanism to decarcerate parents is to employ alternative sentencing strategies, an approach already used with certain groups through specialized courts (e.g., drug courts, mental health courts), typically used for individuals convicted of low-level offenses and implemented through time served under community supervision or probation (Tyuse & Linhorst, 2005). These alternative sentencing models often combine social services (e.g., mental and behavioral health treatment), with close monitoring and restrictions in the community to address various needs and disorders while maximizing public safety. The empirical evidence on the success of these alternative sentencing strategies is mixed. However, findings from the use of drug courts suggest favorable effects (i.e., reductions in recidivism and substance abuse), as do the use of mental health courts (i.e., decreases in recidivism) (Honegger, 2015). But, many of the studies are fraught with methodological problems limiting the degree to which conclusions can be drawn, pointing to the need for improvements in research in order to rigorously assess their impacts (Epperson et al., 2014).

Despite the mixed findings about these more established alternative court models, early evidence about alternative programs geared toward *parents* suggests promising findings and is a strategy receiving increased attention (Goldman, et al., 2019). For example, Washington state's Community Parenting Alternative program, which allows for a parent to serve their last year of incarceration in the community with monitoring and a sponsor, shows that the odds of recidivism are reduced by over 70% compared to similar non-participating parents (Agular & Leavell, 2017).

Oklahoma instituted an alternative sentencing program for incarcerated mothers with substance abuse disorders in 2009 through a partnership between the George Kaiser Family Foundation and a community-based organization serving children and families. Research from this program shows promising effects on children with mothers who had an alternative sentence compared to mothers who served their sentence in prison with children performing better on externalizing behavior problems, parental trust, parental alienation and communication, and parent-child attachment (Fry-Geier & Hellman, 2017).

Oregon also instituted a model in 2016, the Family Sentencing Alternative Pilot Program, under House Bill 3503. This program serves parents with non-violent offenses facing a prison sentence whose children are at risk of entering foster care. Early evidence shows a range of positive outcomes including increased patience with children, motivation to succeed while on probation, and enthusiasm for the future (Oregon Department of Human Services, 2019). While probation agents attribute these early findings to more intensive and specialized supervision and interaction with participants and increased resources geared toward meeting families' needs (e.g., parenting classes, substance abuse treatment, mental health services, life skills classes), more time is needed to assess outcomes on recidivism and housing and employment stability (Oregon Department of Human Services, 2019).

While the number of studies evaluating the effects of alternative sentencing models in the United States are limited, evidence from other countries suggest a clearer picture of potential promise for positive outcomes among parents and their children. Analyses from a longitudinal data registry of the Danish population suggest a range of encouraging findings (see Goldman et al., 2019, for a more extensive discussion). Evidence about children of incarcerated parents indicates lower risk of foster care place (Andersen & Wildeman, 2014) and a decreased likelihood of being charged with a criminal offense in early adulthood (Wildeman & Andersen, 2017). Research about parental outcomes finds a reduction in social welfare dependence (Andersen & Andersen, 2014) and some indication of lower recidivism in the short run (Andersen, 2015).

Family-Focused Programming and Strategies

Alternative sentences that allow parents to remain in the community should be matched with programs and services that promote rehabilitation and address underlying conditions linked to criminal justice system involvement during and after incarceration in cases where getting locked up cannot be avoided. Programs and services should address individual needs (e.g., trauma, mental illness, substance abuse disorders, parenting skills, and family connections) and contextual factors if possible (e.g., poverty, housing instability, child welfare system involvement). Differences in the proximity of prisons and jails to family members and children, as well as variation in services and programs in different types of institutions, should be accounted for when implementing models that are family friendly.

Jails, whose location closer to families makes visits less onerous, generally have fewer programs and services. As such, they could be the focus of models to support parenting and child connections. For example, Dane County Jail in Wisconsin recently instituted a screener at booking, which can be used to identify individuals who are parents that then trigger referrals and services (C. Jones, personal communication, October 30, 2020). The screener questions include "Are you a primary caregiver for any child(ren) under the age of 18?" "Do you have any concerns about your child's safety and well-being right now?" (If yes, the parent is offered a free phone call to confirm the child's location and safety.) "Would you like your information shared with the Dane County Jail Family Connections Social Worker who can follow up with you to provide information and resources for family services available at the jail?" And finally, "Are you interested in information about how to communicate and visit with your family and child(ren) while you are housed at the jail?" If yes, they are offered information about a tablet for communication (e.g., video visits, messaging, photo sharing), setting up a phone account for calls, and details on visiting policies. Instituting screeners like this at the front end of incarceration, combined with assessments to determine other needs before release from jail or prison, are necessary to link parents to services that match the support they require to be successful in the long run.

Research suggests that parents are interested in programs that focus on rebuilding relationships with caregivers and family members, maintaining child contact, and strengthening parenting skills, as well as programs that offer counseling and treatment to address trauma and behavioral and mental health disorders (Charles et al., 2019; Dworsky et al., 2020). Strengthening parenting skills and knowledge, and increasing family connections while separated, can help ease the transition to the community and to parenting once released (Miller et al., 2014). Drawing from an ecological systems approach (Holmes et al., 2010), interventions in the community can also work to support family members (e.g., partners, relatives, children) of those currently and formerly incarcerated so that their needs are also addressed (Pettus-Davis, 2021). An example of how to engage loved ones of formerly incarcerated parents in programming is to offer similar services to both family members. For example, instead of solely providing parenting services to the formerly incarcerated parent, invite the other caregiver (e.g., mother, grandparent) of the child to participate as well. Complementing parenting services with other needed supports such as counseling and support groups so that fathers, mothers, as well as their partners and relatives can share experiences, offer support to one another, and build knowledge and skills, is also critical (Eddy et al., 2013; Fontaine et al., 2017).

In addition, evidence shows that inadequate housing, lack of education, and unemployment top the list of needs that parents have when asked about the supports required to keep them from being incarcerated in the future (Muentner & Charles, 2020). While continued research is needed to build evidence about parenting programs, findings suggest promise when these services are combined with other critically needed supports. Termed "multimodal" (Eddy et al., 2019), this approach aims to address the range of needs that people have (Western, 2018). Services that can be useful cut across multiple domains including employment training and job placement assistance, transitional and permanent housing, guaranteed drug treatment and healthcare services, mentoring or peer support, and case management.

These programs and services should be provided through a linked service delivery system that begins upon entry to prison or jail and continues after release by using "in-reach" with community staff or volunteers who go into the prison and jail to assess needs and develop a reentry plan pre-release that continues with consistent transitional support once a person returns to the community (Miller & Miller, 2010). Moreover, these services should be comprehensive (i.e., meeting multiple needs), evidence-based, and social justice focused (i.e., use strategies that keep children and families safe while making opportunities available to justice-involved individuals so they can meaningfully transform their lives) (Poehlmann-Tynan & Eddy, 2019; Epperson & Pettus-Davis, 2015).

Maintaining Connections during Incarceration

In addition to the need for family-focused services and programs, it is important for children and parents to directly communicate with one another during incarceration in order to maintain parent-child bonds. While in-person contact is preferred by many people including incarcerated parents and advocates, there are circumstances that make visits with direct contact not possible or unsafe (e.g., distance, COVID-19) and instances when parents and caregivers simply prefer to not have their children visit a corrections setting.

Traditional forms of communication including in-person or contact visits, telephone, and letter writing have largely been associated with a range of positive outcomes for parents, although conclusions are uncertain owing to variability in the rigor of studies on the topic (see De Claire & Dixon, 2017, for a review of in-person visits). This said, available evidence suggests promise for incarcerated individuals who have contact with loved ones including improved mental health post-release (Folk, et al., 2019), successful future employment, lower levels of substance use (Visher, et al., 2013), and less recidivism (Duwe & Clark, 2013). It is important to note, however, that the quality of visits can impact the range of outcomes experienced by incarcerated parents, children, and family members (Poehlmann-Tynan & Pritzl, 2019). For instance, without supportive interventions that accompany visits to help children and parents have positive interactions (Poehlmann, et al., 2010), when plexiglass is used to separate children from their parents (Poehlmann-Tynan, et al., 2015), when visiting spaces are unfriendly for children (Dworksky et al., 2020), and when noisy, public, controlling visiting environments prohibit hugging and sharing of personal experiences and feelings, contact between parents and their children can lead to more, not less, problems. For instance, studies have found in some circumstances, contact (via plexiglass) leads to increased child anxiety and behavior problems (Poehlmann-Tynan et al., 2015) and less parent-child closeness (Beckmeyer & Arditti, 2014). As such, support services and parenting programs that include in-person contact when feasible, child-friendly visiting spaces, and family-focused visiting practices that promote closeness and bonding are needed so that parents have the greatest chance of fulfilling their parenting role (Peterson et al., 2019).

A newer, but now exploding form of communication owing to COVID-19 is video chat or video visitation. Prior to the coronavirus pandemic, video chat was being used or explored by approximately 500 institutions across the United States in some way (Rabuy & Wagner, 2015). While research is needed to obtain an accurate estimate of where video visitation is being used, how frequently, and at what cost today, the evidence is beginning to build and suggests that when implemented with appropriate supports, video visits can offer significant benefits to children and their parents as a supplement to in-person contact visits (McLeod & Bonsu, 2018; Skora Horgan & Poehlmann-Tynan, 2020; and see chapter in this volume on enhanced child visits).

Conclusion

The family-related consequences of incarceration are widespread impacting children, parents, relatives, and entire communities in ways that are often lost in the shadows of the criminal justice system. The Smart Decarceration Grand Challenge seeks to bring light to those shadows by transforming programs, policies, and research efforts so that the incarcerated population is reduced, and evidence-driven strategies take the place of unjust, unsafe, and unsustainable practices. Smart Decarceration offers an opportune way to prioritize the needs of incarcerated parents, to make changes to systems to promote child well-being, and to work toward preventing future generations of parents behind bars.

References

Agular, C. M., & Leavell, S. (2017). A statewide parenting alternative sentencing program: Description and preliminary outcomes. *Smith College Studies in Social Work, 87*(1), 1–16.

Andersen, S. H. (2015). Serving time or serving the community? Exploiting a policy reform to assess the causal effects of community service on income, social benefit dependency and recidivism. *Journal of Quantitative Criminology, 31*(4), 537–563.

Andersen, L. H., & Andersen, S. H. (2014). Effect of electronic monitoring on social welfare dependence. *Criminology & Public Policy, 13*(3), 349–379.

Andersen, S. H., & Wildeman, C. (2014). The effect of paternal incarceration on children's risk of foster care placement. *Social Forces, 93*(1), 269–298.

Andrews, D. A., & Bonta, J. (2010). Rehabilitating criminal justice policy and practice. *Psychology, Public Policy, and Law, 16*(1), 39–55.

Arditti, J. A. (2012). Child trauma within the context of parental incarceration: A family process perspective. *Journal of Family Theory & Review, 4*(3), 181–219.

Arditti, J. A., Lambert-Shute, J., & Joest, K. (2003). Saturday morning at the jail: Implications of incarceration for families and children. *Family Relations, 52*(3), 195–204.

Armstrong, E., Eggins, E., Reid, N., Harnett, P., & Dawe, S. (2017). Parenting interventions for incarcerated parents to improve parenting knowledge and skills, parent Well-being, and quality of the parent–child relationship: A systematic review and meta-analysis. *Journal of Experimental Criminology, 14*, 279–317.

Batastini, A. B., Hill, J. B., Repke, A., Gulledge, L. M., & Livengood, Z. (2018). Approaching correctional treatment from a programmatic standpoint: Risk-needs-responsivity and beyond. In M. Ternes, P. Magaletta, & M. Patry (Eds.), *The practice of correctional psychology* (pp. 283–303). Springer.

Beckmeyer, J. J., & Arditti, J. A. (2014). Implications of in-person visits for incarcerated parents' family relationships and parenting experience. *Journal of Offender Rehabilitation, 53*(2), 129–151.

Boudin, C., Stutz, T., & Littman, A. (2013). Prison visitation policies: A fifty-state survey. *Yale Law & Policy Review, 32*, 149–189.

Bronson, J., & Carson, E. A. (2019). Prisoners in 2017. (April 2019, NCJ 252156). *Bureau of Justice Statistics.* https://www.bjs.gov/content/pub/pdf/p17.pdf

Charles, P., Muentner, L., & Kjellstrand, J. (2019). Parenting and incarceration: Perspectives on father-child involvement during reentry from prison. *Social Service Review, 93*, 218–261.

Charles, P., Frankham, E., Garthe, R., Visher, C., & Kay, A. (2021). Father involvement in the first year after prison: Considerations for social work intervention research. *Research on Social Work Practice.* Advance online publication. https://doi.org/10.1177/10497315211022806

Christian, J. (2005). Riding the bus: Barriers to prison visitation and family management strategies. *Journal of Contemporary Criminal Justice, 21*(1), 31–48.

Christian, J., Mellow, J., & Thomas, S. (2006). Social and economic implications of family connections to prisoners. *Journal of Criminal Justice, 34*(4), 443–452.

Clark, V. A., & Duwe, G. (2017). Distance matters: Examining the factors that impact prisoner visitation in Minnesota. *Criminal Justice and Behavior, 44*(2), 184–204.

Cochran, J. C. (2012). The ties that bind or the ties that break: Examining the relationship between visitation and prisoner misconduct. *Journal of Criminal Justice, 40*(5), 433–440.

Cochran, J. C., Mears, D. P., Bales, W. D., & Stewart, E. A. (2016). Spatial distance, community disadvantage, and racial and ethnic variation in prison inmate access to social ties. *Journal of Research in Crime and Delinquency, 53*(2), 220–254.

De Claire, K., & Dixon, L. (2017). The effects of prison visits from family members on prisoners' Well-being, prison rule breaking, and recidivism: A review of research since 1991. *Trauma, Violence, & Abuse, 18*(2), 185–199.

Duwe, G., & Clark, V. (2013). Blessed be the social tie that binds: The effects of prison visitation on offender recidivism. *Criminal Justice Policy Review, 24*, 271–296.

Dworksky, A., Fedock, G., Schlecht, C., Malcome, M., Murray, C., & Hazel, C. (2020). *Addressing the needs of incarcerated mothers and their children in Illinois.* Chapin Hall at The University of Chicago, The University of Chicago School of Social Services Administration. https://www.chapinhall.org/wp-content/uploads/PDF/Incarcerated-Mothers-FINAL-2020.pdf

Eddy, J. M., & Poehlmann-Tynan. (2019). Interdisciplinary perspectives on research and intervention with children of incarcerated parents. In J. M. Eddy & J. Poehlmann-Tynan (Eds.), *Handbook on children with incarcerated parents: Research, policy, and practice* (pp. 1–10). Springer.

Eddy, J. M., Martinez, C. R., & Burraston, B. (2013). A randomized controlled trial of a parent management training program for incarcerated parents: Proximal impacts. *Monographs of the Society for Research in Child Development, 78*, 75–93.

Eddy, J. M., Kjellstrand, J. M., Martinez, C. R., Jr., Newton, R., Herrera, D., Wheeler, A., Wu Shortt, J., Schumer, J. E., Burraston, B. O., & Lorber, F. (2019). Theory-based multimodal parenting intervention for incarcerated parents and their children. In J. M. Eddy & J. Poehlmann-Tynan (Eds.), *Handbook on children with incarcerated parents: Research, policy, and practice* (pp. 219–235). Springer.

Epperson, M. W., & Pettus-Davis, C. (2015). *Smart decarceration: Guiding concepts for an era of criminal justice transformation* (CSD Working Paper No. 15–53). Washington University, Center for Social Development. https://openscholarship.wustl.edu/cgi/viewcontent.cgi?article=1573&context=csd_research

Epperson, M., & Pettus-Davis, C. (2017). *Smart decarceration: Achieving criminal justice transformation in the 21st century*. Oxford University Press.

Epperson, M. W., Wolff, N., Morgan, R. D., Fisher, W. H., Frueh, B. C., & Huening, J. (2014). Envisioning the next generation of behavioral health and criminal justice interventions. *International Journal of Law and Psychiatry, 37*(5), 427–438.

Folk, J. B., Stuewig, J., Mashek, D., Tangney, J. P., & Grossmann, J. (2019). Behind bars but connected to family: Evidence for the benefits of family contact during incarceration. *Journal of Family Psychology, 33*(4), 453.

Fontaine, J., Cramer, L., & Paddock, E. (2017). *Encouraging responsible parenting among fathers with histories of incarceration: Activities and lessons from six responsible fatherhood programs*. Urban Institute. http://www.urban.org/sites/default/files/publication/89771/responsible_parenting_brief_1.pdf

Fry-Geier, L., & Hellman, C. M. (2017). School aged children of incarcerated parents: The effects of alternative criminal sentencing. *Child Indicators Research, 10*(3), 859–879.

Glaze, L. E., & Maruschak, L. M. (2010). *Parents in prison and their minor children*. Bureau of Justice Statistics. https://www.bjs.gov/index.cfm?ty=pbdetail&iid=823

Goldman, A. W., Andersen, L. H., & Wildeman, C. (2019). Can alternatives to incarceration enhance child Well-being? In J. M. Eddy & J. Poehlmann-Tynan (Eds.), *Handbook on children with incarcerated parents: Research, policy, and practice* (pp. 237–248). Springer. Gottlieb, A. (2016). Household incarceration in early adolescence and risk of premarital first birth. *Children and Youth Services Review*, 61, 126-134

Holmes, T. R., Belmonte, K., Wentworth, M., & Tillman, K. (2010). Parents "in the system": An ecological systems approach to the development of children with incarcerated parents. In Y. R. Harris, J. A. Graham, & G. J. O. Carpenter (Eds.), *Children of incarcerated parents* (pp. 21–43). Springer.

Honegger, L. N. (2015). Does the evidence support the case for mental health courts? A review of the literature. *Law and Human Behavior, 39*(5), 478–488.

Loper, A. B., Carlson, L. W., Levitt, L., & Scheffel, K. (2009). Parenting stress, alliance, child contact, and adjustment of imprisoned mothers and fathers. *Journal of Offender Rehabilitation, 48*(6), 483–503.

Loper, A. B., Clarke, C. N., & Dallaire, D. H. (2019). Parenting programs for incarcerated fathers and mothers: Current research and new directions. In J. M. Eddy & J. Poehlmann-Tynan (Eds.), *Handbook on children with incarcerated parents: Research, policy, and practice* (pp. 183–203). Springer.

McKay, T., Corwin, E., Herman-Stahl, M., Bir, A., Lindquist, C., Smiley-McDonald, H., & Siegel, S. (2010). *Parenting from prison: Innovative programs to support incarcerated and reentering fathers*. Office of the Assistant Secretary for Planning and Evaluation, U.S. DHHS. https://aspe.hhs.gov/system/files/pdf/109006/rb.pdf

McLeod, B. A., & Bonsu, J. (2018). The benefits and challenges of visitation practices in correctional settings: Will video visitation assist incarcerated fathers and their children? *Children and Youth Services Review, 93*, 30–35.

Miller, H. V., & Miller, J. M. (2010). Community in reach through jail reentry: Findings from a quasi-experimental design. *Justice Quarterly, 27*(6), 893–910.

Miller, A. L., Weston, L. E., Perryman, J., Horwitz, T., Franzen, S., & Cochran, S. (2014). Parenting while incarcerated: Tailoring the strengthening families program for use with jailed mothers. *Children and Youth Services Review, 44*, 163–170.

Muentner, L., & Charles, P. (2020). A qualitative exploration of reentry service needs: The case of fathers returning from prison. *Child & Family Social Work, 25*, 63–72.

Murphey, D., & Cooper, P. M. (2015). *Parents behind bars: What happens to their children?* Child Trends. https://www.childtrends.org/wp-content/uploads/2015/10/2015-42ParentsBehindBars.pdf
Oregon Department of Human Services (2019, January 23). *Family sentencing alternative pilot program report to the senate and house committees on judiciary.* https://www.oregon.gov/cjc/SAC/Documents/FSAPPJointReport2019.pdf
Peterson, B. E., Cramer, L., Kurs, E., Fontaine, J., & Center, J. P. (2015). *Toolkit for developing family-focused jail programs.* Urban Institute. https://www.urban.org/sites/default/files/publication/53726/2000255-Toolkit-for-Developing-Family-Focused-Jail-Programs.pdf
Peterson, B. E., Fontaine, J., Cramer, L., Reisman, A., Cuthrell, H., Goff, M., McCoy, E., & Reginal, T. (2019). *Model practices for parents in prisons and jails: Reducing barriers for families while maximizing safety and security.* Bureau of Justice Assistance and the National Institute of Corrections. https://www.urban.org/sites/default/files/publication/100531/model_practices_for_parents_in_prisons_and_jails_0.pdf
Pettus-Davis, C. (2012). Reverse social work's neglect of adults involved in the criminal justice system: The intersection and an agenda. *Social Work Research, 36*(1), 3–8.
Pettus-Davis, C. (2021). Support4Families: A proposed intervention model to support families of individuals returning home from incarceration. *Families in Society: The Journal of Contemporary Social Services, 102*(3), 316-332.
Pierce, M. B., Freiburger, T. L., Chapin, J. R., Epling, B., & Madden, T. J. (2018). Assessing the impact of visitation on inmate misconduct within a county jail. *Security Journal, 31*(1), 1–20.
Poehlmann, J., Dallaire, D., Loper, A. B., & Shear, L. D. (2010). Children's contact with their incarcerated parents: Research findings and recommendations. *American Psychologist, 65*(6), 575–598.
Poehlmann-Tyan, J., & Pritzl, K. (2019). Parent-child visits when parents are incarcerated in prison or jail. In J. M. Eddy & J. Poehlmann-Tynan (Eds.), *Handbook on children with incarcerated parents* (2nd ed., pp. 131–147). Springer.
Poehlmann-Tyan, J., Cuthrell, H., Weymouth, L., Burnson, C., Frerks, L., Muentner, L., Holder, N., Milavetz, Z., Lauter, L., Hindt, L., Davis, L., Schuber, E., & Shlafer, R. (2020). Multisite randomized efficacy trial of educational materials for young children with incarcerated parents. *Development and Psychopathology,* 1–17.
Poehlmann-Tynan, J. (2015). Children's contact with incarcerated parents: Summary and recommendations. In J. Poehlmann-Tynan (Ed.), *Children's contact with incarcerated parents* (pp. 83–92). Springer.
Poehlmann-Tynan, J., & Eddy, J. M. (2019). A research and intervention agenda for children with incarcerated parents and their families. In J. M. Eddy & J. Poehlmann-Tynan (Eds.), *Handbook on children with incarcerated parents: Research, policy, and practice* (pp. 353–371). Springer.
Poehlmann-Tynan, J., Runion, H., Burnson, C., Maleck, S., Weymouth, L., Pettit, K., & Huser, M. (2015). Young children's behavioral and emotional reactions to plexiglas and video visits with jailed parents. In *Children's contact with incarcerated parents* (2nd ed., pp. 39–58). Springer.
Rabuy, B., & Wagner, P. (2015). Screening out family time: The for-profit video visitation industry in prisons and jails. Prison Policy Initiative. http://www.prisonpolicy.org/visitation/report
Raher, S. (2016). You've got mail: *The promise of cyber communication in prisons and the need for regulation.* Prison Policy Initiative. https://www.prisonpolicy.org/messaging/report.html
Rubenstein, B. Y., Toman, E. L., & Cochran, J. C. (2019). Socioeconomic barriers to child contact with incarcerated parents. *Justice Quarterly*, 1–27.
Sawyer, W., & Wagner, P. (2020). *Mass incarceration: The whole pie 2020.* Prison Policy Initiative. https://www.prisonpolicy.org/reports/pie2020.html
Schirmer, S., Nellis, A., & Mauer, M. (2009). Incarcerated parents and their children: Trends 1991–2007. The Sentencing Project: Research and Advocacy for Reform. https://www.sentencingproject.org/wp-content/uploads/2016/01/Incarcerated-Parents-and-Their-Children-Trends-1991-2007.pdf

Schwartz-Soicher, O., Geller, A., & Garfinkel, I. (2011). The effect of paternal incarceration on material hardship. *Social Service Review, 85*(3), 447–473.

Shlafer, R. J., Loper, A. B., & Schillmoeller, L. (2015). Introduction and literature review: Is parent-child contact during parental incarceration beneficial? In J. Poehlmann-Tynan (Ed.), *Children's contact with incarcerated parents* (pp. 1–21). Springer.

Shlafer, R. J., Davis, L., Hindt, L., Weymouth, L., Cuthrell, H., Burnson, C., & Poehlmann-Tynan, J. (2020). Fathers in jail and their minor children: Paternal characteristics and associations with father-child contact. *Journal of Child and Family Studies, 29*(3), 791–801.

Siegel, J. A., & Luther, K. (2019). Qualitative research on children of incarcerate parents: Findings, challenges, and future directions. In J. M. Eddy & J. Poehlmann-Tynan (Eds.), *Handbook on children with incarcerated parents: Research, policy, and practice* (2nd ed., pp. 149–163). Springer.

Skora Horgan, E., & Poehlmann-Tynan, J. (2020). In-home video chat for young children and their incarcerated parents. *Journal of Children and Media, 14*(3), 400–406.

Sugie, N. F. (2012). Punishment and welfare: Paternal incarceration and families' receipt of public assistance. *Social Forces, 90*(4), 1403–1427.

The Pew Charitable Trusts. (2010). *Collateral costs: Incarceration's effect on economic mobility.* https://www.pewtrusts.org/~/media/legacy/uploadedfiles/pcs_assets/2010/collateralcosts1pdf.pdf

The Sentencing Project. (2019). *Private prisons in the United States.* https://www.sentencingproject.org/publications/private-prisons-united-states/

Turney, K. (2018). Adverse childhood experiences among children of incarcerated parents. *Children and Youth Services Review, 89*, 218–225.

Turney, K., & Goodsell, R. (2018). Parental incarceration and children's wellbeing. *The Future of Children, 28*(1), 147–164.

Tyuse, S. W., & Linhorst, D. M. (2005). Drug courts and mental health courts: Implications for social work. *Health & Social Work, 30*(3), 233–240.

Veeh, C. A., Renn, T., & Pettus-Davis, C. (2018). Promoting reentry Well-being: A novel assessment tool for individualized service assignment in prisoner reentry programs. *Social Work, 63*(1), 91–96.

Visher, C. A. (2013). Incarcerated fathers: Pathways from prison to home. *Criminal Justice Policy Review, 24*(1), 9–26.

Visher, C. A., Bakken, N. W., & Gunter, W. D. (2013). Fatherhood, community reintegration, and successful outcomes. *Journal of Offender Rehabilitation, 52*, 451–469.

Wakefield, S., & Uggen, C. (2010). Incarceration and stratification. *Annual Review of Sociology, 36*, 387–406.

Wakefield, S., & Wildeman, C. (2014). *Children of the prison boom: Mass incarceration and the future of American inequality*. Oxford University Press.

Wakefield, S., & Wildeman, C. (2018). *How parental incarceration harms children and what to do about it.* National Council on Family Relations, Policy Brief (Vol. 3, Issue 1).

Ward, T. (2015). Detection of dynamic risk factors and correctional practice. *Criminology & Public Policy, 14*(1), 105–112.

Western, B. (2018). *Homeward: Life in the year after prison*. Russell Sage Foundation.

Wildeman, C. (2009). Parental imprisonment, the prison boom, and the concentration of childhood disadvantage. *Demography, 46*(2), 265–280.

Wildeman, C., & Andersen, S. H. (2017). Paternal incarceration and children's risk of being charged by early adulthood. *Criminology, 55*(1), 32–58.

Zeng, Z. (2019). *Jail inmates in 2017* (NCJ 251774). U.S. Department of Justice, Bureau of Justice Statistics. https://www.bjs.gov/content/pub/pdf/ji17.pdf

Epilogue

I was fortunate to have been asked to deliver the closing keynote address for the Arizona State University Children of Incarcerated Parents (CIP) Annual Conference in Phoenix on April 17, 2019. The following is not a mere duplication of that talk, but instead an attempt to restyle it in a way more suitable for this volume.

I am pleased that I had the opportunity to attend the multiday conference which began in April 14. With the closing address in mind, I paid close attention to the messages presented in plenary sessions, workshops, the informal discussions with attendees at tables and during breaks, as well as with exhibitors at their booths. I was fascinated to have met some extremely talented persons committed to learning more about, and furthering the knowledge of, CIP.

My career in corrections administration began in 1973. Among other posts, it included years of service as prison warden, Deputy Director, and Director of the Ohio Department of Rehabilitation and Correction. I held the director's position for over 15 years until my retirement from state service in 2006. Additionally, I have served as president of two national corrections organizations and vice-chair of an international prisons association—allowing me to stay active with this work on a global scale.

From the outset of my corrections career, I strove to better understand, and in turn educate persons about, CIP. This commitment included developing programs and services intended to "break the cycle" of children of incarcerated persons beating the odds of becoming justice involved. Following my retirement, my drive to advance social justice did not wane.

In choosing the title of my keynote address, "A Call to Action," I considered that despite the ever-emerging data and increased societal awareness around CIP, a long road of advocacy lies ahead. The mass incarceration of persons in the United States has undoubtedly exacerbated concerns regarding the children with a parent behind bars, especially considering the following:

J. Krysik, N. Rodriguez (eds.), *Children of Incarcerated Parents*, Children of Incarcerated Parents: From Understanding to Impact,
https://doi.org/10.1007/978-3-030-84713-5

- The United States has the highest incarceration rate in the world, with over 2.3 million Americans incarcerated.
- The number of African American men incarcerated compete with the number enrolled in institutions of higher education.

Causes for these devastating realities include but are not limited to mandatory minimum sentences, increased sentence lengths, a lack of non-prison sanctions, the so-called war on drugs, "truth in sentencing," and zero-tolerance practices for minor parole/probation violations.

According to The Pew Charitable Trusts (2016), the percentage of US prisoners who are parents with children include more than 120,000 mothers and 1.1 million fathers. Pew further reported that 1 in every 28 children (3.6%) has a parent in prison. The following statistic is particularly disconcerting: one in nine African American children has an incarcerated parent. Among Hispanic youths, it is 1 in 28 and, in white children, 1 in 57. Thus, a black child is more than six times more likely to have a parent who is an inmate than a white child. While the Hispanic CIP rate reflects the national average, the numbers are, nonetheless, disturbingly high.

It is not just the stigma of a child having an incarcerated mother and/or a father that is all too devastating. These are some of the residual consequences: because of collateral sanctions/punishments, once released from incarceration, the struggles to secure employment, licenses, and college enrollment begin. Furthermore, a high percentage of inmates have a diagnosed mental illness which can adversely impact relationships with their children. Those symptoms of depression and anxiety typically do not go away upon release from confinement. Feelings of embarrassment among children of a formally incarcerated parent can induce even more trauma, especially without intervention. While we are still learning about the physical and emotional impacts on these populations, many CIP remain in jeopardy.

This is further evidenced by the State of Pennsylvania (2017) that has collected data on CIP which states, "few communities in the Commonwealth have been spared the crippling effects of fatherless and motherless homes" and provided these figures:

- 81,096—the number children incarcerated with a parent in a PA prison
- 75,747—the number CIP dads
- 5,349—the number of CIP moms

The Pennsylvania Department of Corrections, in turn, identified four initiatives that they deploy to address this predicament:

1. Expansion of nurse-family partnerships
2. Access early childhood learning
3. Promotion of personal mentoring
4. Encourage regular family visits

The Secretary of the PA DOC, John Wetzel, mused: "Spend the money before they get to us. Isn't America about giving people a fair shot? If we can make significant investments in kids to really give them a fair shot, why shouldn't we do that?"

To further underscore the importance of breaking the cycle of incarceration, the Annie E. Casey Foundation summarized a study they commissioned in 2016. The report noted, "Sixteen percent of children in Arkansas had at some point in their lives a parent or guardian locked up in prison or jail. That was the highest percentage of any state. Some nearby states had similar percentages" (Moritz, 2017).

It should be noted that forward-thinking staff at correctional institutions such as the Ohio Reformatory for Women has a praiseworthy history of addressing CIP programming. In addition to a myriad of training and treatment options at ORW, an incarcerated woman can take part in numerous services designed to keep them involved with their children. These programs include but are not limited to:

- Achieving Baby Care Success (A.B.C.S.): Family nursing program, established in 2001.
- Girl Scouts of America: Bond Beyond Bars. Inmates' daughters and granddaughters ages 5–18 can participate.
- Mom and Kids Day. Twice a year children can spend a full day with their incarcerated mother, engaged in a variety of activities.
- Reintegration Units: Dormitories that offer pre-release readiness services.

Unlike most at-risk youth-related topics one might encounter in the media, coverage of issues affecting CIP does not typically reverberate with the average citizen whom it often does not reach. But there are examples of how impactful, if not heartbreaking, the challenge of CIP can be. A letter handwritten by a 10-year-old girl named Darina about the harmful effects her father's incarceration was having on her life is a case in point. She lamented that he will not get to see her grow up and that she has been able to visit him only twice in 4 years because he is far away. She wrote:

> I spent most of my life with a step dad. Special holidays are hard for me (for example Christmas, Fathers Day, my birth-day) because he's not there. When my Dad calls me at my aunt's house I get super excited.

With the stories of children like Darina in mind, I found the workshops at the Annual Conference to be well led, relevant, and often promising. I again extend my gratitude to all the presenters of these sessions. During a workshop entitled "Letters to Children," two faculty members from the University of Arkansas, Kim Strauss and John Gallagher, presented details of their work. The essence of this initiative is to encourage inmates, in this case mothers, to write to their children. All letters are hand-written to strike a more personal tone, and the inmates are instructed to avoid prison-centric subject matter. Instead, the content of the letters should be motivating and upbeat.

Another presentation by staff from the Coffee Creek Correctional Facility, a female prison in Oregon, discussed a program called "Through A Child's Eyes," founded by the Wilsonville Rotary. Children can visit their mothers at CCCF and participate in a series of activities designed to improve relationships by enhancing parenting skills and more. These are just but two examples of workshops I found to be both fascinating and enlightening at the Annual Conference.

Thus, we see that throughout the United States, tremendous strides are being made through top-notch programs and services designed to further improve CIP programming. I was personally pleased, for instance, to become reacquainted with the Children of Incarcerated Parents: A Bill of Rights. In 2003 the San Francisco Partnership for Incarcerated Parents created and published the eight rights. While listed below, I enthusiastically encourage readers to further familiarize themselves with the backgrounds and explanations of each. They are critical to this subject and are as follows:

1. I have the right to be kept safe and informed at the time of my parent's arrest.
2. I have the right to be heard when decisions are made about me.
3. I have the right to be considered when decisions are made about my parent.
4. I have the right to be well cared for in my parent's absence.
5. I have the right to speak with, see, and touch my parent.
6. I have the right to support as I struggle with my parent's incarceration.
7. I have the right not to be judged, blamed, or labeled because of my parent's incarceration.
8. I have the right to a lifelong relationship with my parents.

Recent CIP research indicates that new studies are not solely emerging from the fields of sociology and social work; they are also rooted in medical science. An article entitled "Parents in Prison and the Lasting Health Effects on Children" that appeared in a Harvard University Kennedy School publication (Reichel, 2018) revealed some unsettling findings regarding CIP. Among other findings, the article cites conclusions published in a 2017 edition of *Pediatrics*:

- Adults who as children grew up with incarcerated parents are less likely to get medical care when they need it and more likely to engage in risky behaviors compared with peers whose parents were not incarcerated.
- Parental incarceration is considered an adverse childhood experience (ACE). Adverse childhood experiences are linked with worsened health and well-being outcomes later in life.
- Prior research has established ties between parental incarceration and physical and mental health outcomes, including increased likelihood of depression, asthma, and HIV/AIDS.

This pediatric research analyzed responses recorded during the last period of data collection of the study to determine whether parental incarceration had any long-term associations with various health behaviors. It states, "Compared with respondents whose parents were not incarcerated, those who had grown up with an incarcerated mother or father..."

1. Were less likely to seek medical care when they needed it
2. Were more likely to abuse prescription drugs, smoke cigarettes, and have drinking problems
3. Were more likely to have ten or more sexual partners

Furthermore, some medical behaviors differed depending on which parent was incarcerated:

- Those with incarcerated mothers were more likely to use the emergency room as a usual source of care than those whose parents were not incarcerated. They also were more likely to have had sex in exchange for money.
- Adults with incarcerated fathers were more likely to inject illicit drugs than those whose parents were not incarcerated. They also were more likely to engage in behaviors linked to obesity, such as watching 50 or more hours of television per week and drinking sugary drinks.

As I previously discussed, various prisons (mostly women's institutions) have developed bonding programs allowing children to spend a day with the parent in a controlled environment inside the prison fences. These events are not as common as they could, or should be, however. The main source of parental contact is still via institution-visiting opportunities. While I believe prison visitation can be constructive, it is prudent to consider all potential consequences of this approach. A colleague of mine, Tessa Unwin, and I expressed concern in a corrections textbook a chapter entitled "Bringing families together is a laudable endeavor. Yet one must wonder about the lasting effects on children of seeing a parent in prison" (1999).

Robert Ross and Elizabeth Fabiano (1986) previously remarked:

> The effects of such visits on the mother and child when the visit ends, the feeling of other mothers who do not have contact with their children, the effects on the child of seeing the often frightening physical structure of prisons, and the possible long-term effects on the child of living in a prison for short or long periods of time are all significant issues.

Prison visitation's productivity, however—as we can see through existing and emerging initiatives—is constantly increasing. For instance, not over-restricting personal contact can lead to the better expression of family affection. Some prisons have made the visiting experience more family and child friendly. Examples include adding playrooms and child reading rooms to the visiting area. Painting murals on the wall and making other visual improvements can also induce a more relaxed environment.

There are, of course, other avenues for the inmate parent and their children to maintain contact. Video visitation (tele-visiting) is possible through various forms of electronic technology. Phone calls are the most prevalent source of staying in touch with children and other family members. And, of course, letter writing is still an irreplaceable standard.

In the keynote address, I was not shy about discussing how racism and bias enter into the CIP picture. Given the circumstances that are presently engulfing our nation, confronting the "difficult conversations" about race and social justice is not only important; it is essential. With reminders of the vastly disproportionate number of African American children who have an incarcerated parent versus white children, it does not take much to conclude how the justice process incurred this regrettable history of bias. It must be held to account.

To highlight an example of racial bias in our society and justice system, I presented slides of images from a basic Google search. I simply searched for "three white teens." The screenshot outcomes overwhelmingly portrayed happy-go-lucky, wholesome teens neatly dressed and smiling. The image results generated from my search for "three black teens," on the other hand, were sadly predictable: the slide primarily displayed various mug shots of the teens. Except for a couple of images of teen girls, there were no healthy-looking or smiling black teens depicted in the photographs. Google is not responsible for the search results, but our society is. The implicit and explicit biases that permeate our communities are not minor phenomena. Thus, it is not happenstance that the data generally associated with race and CIP is disparate.

Furthermore, a comprehensive approach to handling trauma-informed education is imperative. Most recently, through my work with the Ohio State Board of Education and from hearing public testimony from teachers, I am dedicated to effecting change on this front. Summarized testimonials from educators were in no uncertain terms; if persons who are well trained in the content areas of this subject do not deliver this curriculum, it can cause additional harm. Thus, we need to guarantee that quality assurance is built into the curricula that address this adverse childhood experiences.

Moreover, all trauma-informed care programming should include "resilience education." My mother used to warn my siblings and me to not "throw the baby out with the bath water." Let's also build on the positive aspects and experiences of those who have an incarcerated parent. Identifying and promoting resilience education and behavior can have a significant impact on those who undergo this programming. The Mayo Clinic (2019) described resilience education as follows:

Resilience is your ability to adapt well and recover quickly after stress, adversity, trauma or tragedy. If you have a resilient disposition, you are better able to maintain poise and a healthy level of physical and psychological wellness in the face of life's challenges.

Like trauma-informed training, resilience education should be taught by competent, if not certified, professionals. This education is not just effective for CIP; it could also be productive for inmate parents. Correctional facilities would be well served to integrate this coursework onto its in-prison treatment programming list.

Still, I am encouraged by the growing multitude of successful organizations dedicated to reversing the misfortunes of CIP. I was happy to highlight a few of these programs at the Annual Conference. Here is very short list of these groups:

- The Osborne Association—New York City
- Prison Fellowship Ministries, Angel Tree—Lansdowne, VA
- Goodwill, Kids of Incarcerated Parents Program (KIPP)—Wyoming
- Save Kids of Incarcerated Program (SKIP, Inc.)—Hope Hull, AL
- Children of Incarcerated Parents Partnership (COIPP)—Frederick, MD
- Project New Start—Wilmington, DE
- International Coalition for Children with Incarcerated Parents (INCCIP)—Scotland, UK

In addition to the above organizations (excepting for INCCIP), there were many more represented at the conference, along with the scores of others making a difference in communities throughout the United States and abroad. They all deserve our ongoing appreciation for their amazing contributions.

As I wrap up this concluding chapter of *Children of Incarcerated Parents: Situating the Lives of Children*, I will make a few additional points I find critical to this subject area. First, the construct of restorative and community justice can be instrumental in addressing challenges associated with CIP. In fact, I considered this matter so important that it was the theme of my doctoral dissertation. While it is impossible to detail every component of restorative justice in this chapter, below is a listing of its more salient aspects which I also spoke about at the CIP convening. I highly recommend conducting additional research on this topic, whether to further your interest or refine your existing knowledge of restorative justice, which promotes:

- Community and neighborhood building
- Families (healthy relationships)
- Victims and survivors of crime
- Faith-based involvement
- Repairing the harm
- Preventing harmful behavior

While serving as head of the Ohio corrections system, my mantra was "If it ain't broke, fix it anyway." That said, I will leave you with a few notions for next steps:

- More scientific studies are warranted. The more advanced data that is collected, the easier it will be to tackle the tough challenges associated with CIP.
- Existing programs should conduct routine evaluations of their services. This means we should not just operate and provide services, but we should assess their effectiveness.
- We should share innovations. Benchmarking and networking with colleagues contribute to building more resource options.
- Educate stakeholders and policymakers about not just the services you provide but also why they are necessary.
- Tell your stories to media. It is important that the wonderful work you do not languish.

In closing, I thank the editors of this volume for asking me to be part of this journey. It was the visions of Drs. Judy Krysik and Nancy Rodriguez for the Children of Incarcerated Parents Annual Conference, this publication, and for keeping the importance of addressing issues for children who have incarcerated parents as a mainstream approach to fairness in the justice system. I express my appreciation, as well, to the authors of the chapters that preceded this one. They each add value to the quest we share: to ensure progress in serving and reducing the number of children who have an incarcerated mother or father.

References

Heard-Garris, N., et al. (2018). Health care use and health behaviors among young adults with history of parental incarceration. *Pediatrics*. https://doi.org/10.1542/peds.2017-4314

Mayo Clinic. (2019). Resilience Training, www.mayoclinic.org

Moritz, J. (2017). *State ranked 1st in count of kids of jailed parents. Arkansas Democrat Gazzette.*

Pennsylvania Department of Corrections. (2017) *Children of Incarcerated Parents*. www.cor.pa.gov.

Reichel, C. (2018). Parents in prison and the lasting health effects on children. *Journalist Resource* (Harvard University).

Ross, R., & Fabiano, E. (1986). *Female Offenders: Correctional Afterthoughts* (p. 58). McFarland and Company.

Wilkinson, R., & Unwin, T. (1999). "The operation of a visitation program is an integral element of any prison system." *Prison and Jail Administration's Practices and Theory.*

Wiltz, T. (2016). "Having a Parent Behind Bars Costs Children, States." *Stateline* (Pew Charitable Trusts).

Index

J. Krysik, N. Rodriguez (eds.), *Children of Incarcerated Parents*, Children of Incarcerated Parents: From Understanding to Impact,
https://doi.org/10.1007/978-3-030-84713-5

The manufacturer's authorised representative in the EU is Springer Nature Customer Service Centre GmbH, Europaplatz 3, 69115 Heidelberg, Germany. If you have any concerns regarding our products, please contact ProductSafety@springernature.com

Printed and bound by CPI Group (UK) Ltd, Croydon, CR0 4YY
06/10/2026
02225252-0009